BRITISH RAILWAY CARRIAGES OF THE 20th CENTURY

DAVID JENKINSON BSc FRSA

Volume 2: The years of consolidation, 1923~53

PSL
PATRICK STEPHENS LIMITED

First published in 1990

British Library Cataloguing in Publication Data

Jenkinson, David
    British railway carriages of the 20th century
    Vol 2: The years of consolidation, 1923-53
    1. Railroads—Great Britain—
    Passenger-cars—History
    I. Title
    625.2′3   TF455

    ISBN 0-85059-912-1

Patrick Stephens Limited, part of Thorsons, a division of the Collins Publishing Group, has published authoritative, quality books for enthusiasts for more than twenty years. During that time the company has established a reputation as one of the world's leading publishers of books on aviation, maritime, military, model-making, motor cycling, motoring, motor racing, railway and railway modelling subjects. Readers or authors with suggestions for books they would like to see published are invited to write to: The Editorial Director, Patrick Stephens Limited, Thorsons Publishing Group, Wellingborough, Northants, NN8 2RQ.

Patrick Stephens Limited is part of the Thorsons Publishing Group, Wellingborough, Northamptonshire NN8 2RQ, England.

Printed in Great Britain at The Bath Press, Avon
Typeset by MJL Limited, Hitchin, Hertfordshire.

10 9 8 7 6 5 4 3 2 1

By the same author

Rails in the Fells: a railway case study
An Illustrated History of LNWR Coaches
The Power of the Duchesses
The Power of the Royal Scots
Profile of the Duchesses
Modelling Historic Railways
Eric Treacy's LMS
The London and Birmingham: a railway of consequence
British Railway Carriages of the 20th Century, Volume 1

With the late F.J. Bellwood
Gresley and Stanier

With N.H. Campling
Historic Carriage Drawings in 4mm scale

With R.J. Essery
Locomotive Liveries of the LMS
The LMS Coach
An Illustrated History of LMS Coaches
An Illustrated History of LMS Locomotives
    (5 volumes)
Midland Carriages: an Illustrated Review
An Illustrated Review of Midland Locomotives
    (4 volumes)

With Gwen Townend
Palaces on Wheels (Royal Saloons at the NRM)

With R.J. Essery and V.R. Anderson
Portrait of the LMS

Front endpaper *The down 'Royal Scot' express of the LMS in 1928, in large part composed of the pioneering but still traditional-looking new standard carriages, including luxury lounge brakes, passes through Rugby behind 4-6-0 No 6134* Atlas *(Author's collection).*

Title page *Gresley's LNER at King's Cross in 1938. On the left the famous 'Coronation' streamliner accelerates up the bank, on the right streamlined No 4468* Mallard *heads a heavier train of teak-bodied corridors; between them, a typical suburban articulated set lurks in the smoke (Herbert Collection, NRM).*

Rear endpaper *The electrically transformed Southern Railway at Guildford at 9.30 am on 11 August 1939. On the left an original LSWR suburban unit heads a stopping train to Waterloo via Cobham; in the centre, two 4COR sets form a Portsmouth-Waterloo direct corridor express; and on the right, a 2BIL cross-country unit makes up a Guildford-Aldershot train (Box Collection, NRM).*

Contents

Author's introduction

By the time this book appears, there will only be some ten years left of the twentieth century, yet in purely time terms, this second part of the story of the British railway carriage scarcely gets us past the half-way point so far, and this merits some amplification.

In my first volume, I reviewed what was almost certainly the most diverse period of carriage development in Great Britain and it took many pages merely to outline the events of little more than 20 years, and much still remained unsaid, if for no other reason than that so many companies had to be included in a finite amount of space. In 1923, these many and very varied companies were amalgamated into but four main-line systems which themselves only lasted for 25 years, so it might well be supposed that to describe their new carriages would take far less space than was needed for the far greater number of companies covered in the first volume. In the strictly literal sense this is partly true, but there are many other points which come into the reckoning so it seemed only sensible, just as with my first volume, for me to try and state the parameters within which this second contribution has been written.

Firstly, although there are now but four main-line companies to consider in the period under review, all of them in their own ways made significantly more progress in the carriage field than most of their individual constituents had done during the previous 20-25 years, so more would need to be said about each of them anyway. Secondly, even the smallest of the 'Big Four' grouped companies had to address a much more comprehensive range of carriage activities than all but the very largest of the pre-group companies had done, so each of them would inevitably merit far more comprehensive treatment than most of the pre-group railways were given in the earlier book. Thirdly, and by no means an unimportant aspect, many thousands of pre-group carriages continued to serve their new masters well for a generation or more and it would be quite wrong to exclude the more vital aspects of their later history from our story. Indeed, the post-1922 fortunes of older-design carriages is one of the more fascinating elements of the 1923-48 tale, and in many cases they actually went on into BR days, so we have not quite heard the last of them, even here!

A second factor influencing my choice of period to be covered in this part of the series is the fact that the story of the vehicles which, in due course, came into the ownership of London Transport was given but short measure in the first volume. For one thing, so much space was needed to tackle the main line companies, not to mention explaining the business

of carriage construction generally, that it was not possible to give fair measure to the purely London-based contribution. A second reason was based on the fact that the amalgamation which created London Transport did not take place until 1933, ten years after the main-line grouping. This clearly puts the whole business well into the period covered by the second volume, so it seemed more logical to treat the major part of the earlier history of London Transport as an integral part of the larger story. In this volume, therefore, there will be a fair amount of coverage of the pre-1923 situation as far as London Transport is concerned. Furthermore, to some extent this retrospective argument also applies to a few other areas of carriage stock which were mentioned but briefly in the first book; this too will be rectified in this volume.

In attempting to assess the development of railway carriages during the last years of the company period, I have, with a few obvious exceptions, tried to resist the obvious temptation to give individual chapters to each separate member of the club, preferring instead to continue the methodology of the first volume by approaching the subject on a thematic basis. This does, of course, mean that within the categories I have chosen, there will rarely be an exactly proportional balance between the individual railways, nor will every carriage type find mention. But in so far as the dominance of, say, the LMS in some aspects of the main-line field is balanced by the superior status of the Southern in the suburban electrification area, I hope this form of approach is acceptable. In almost every category, one or other of the four companies had the principal part to play, while Pullman, of course, continued to perform in its own idiosyncratic way. I hope that this, too, comes over!

During the period covered by this volume, the evolution of self-propelled coaching stock assumed increasing importance as a proportion of the whole and therefore raises the matter of whether this survey should dwell at all upon the technical aspects of the various modes of propulsion. After due consideration, I eventually concluded that my introduction to Volume 1 still held true: railway carriages are, above all, vehicles in which people travel and this aspect of their evolution will still predominate. At the same time, I am aware that the need to house propulsion gear could, to some extent, also influence the interior passenger layouts adopted, so some mention of the differing forms of propulsion must obviously be made. There will not, however, be any deep technical analysis of the various forms of electrification or other traction modes, any more than it was deemed necessary to include explanatory details of steam locomotives in my first Volume. These matters are well recorded elsewhere and the Bibliography gives much follow-up for those who would wish to know more.

As ever, I am deeply indebted to those who have helped me in this project, in particular my former colleagues at the National Railway Museum, Phil Atkins and John Edgington, for their willing collaboration in helping me to find many new pictures. As before, the majority of illustrations have come from the NRM and I am once again happy to acknowledge the continued support of the Museum authorities. Those attributed to BR, I obtained many years ago; they too are mostly now housed at the NRM, but sadly, the GWR official pictures were, at the time of writing, mostly inaccessible either from BR or the NRM and I regret the slightly 'thin' coverage of this system in consequence. Fortunately, many of them have been published in other works — see the Bibliography. Finally, I must renew my especial thanks to my good friends Bob Essery and Barry Lane for once again doing me the courtesy of reading the work before publication and offering their support along with many valuable comments. This is much appreciated as is the fact that my publishers have again allowed me to tackle the subject without any real constraints as to content — I hope their faith is justified.

Despite having made much use of contemporary and other sources, many of them quoted at the end of the book, I must again stress that I have done all my own research and, in consequence, assume responsibility both for the choices of emphasis and for all mistakes; I hope they are few and that readers might advise the publisher should they spot any. But in the last resort, I must offer my especial thanks to my wife and long-suffering family for enduring without complaint the many hours I have spent in preparing this work. I have enjoyed it immensely and for their tolerance and understanding, I am inordinately grateful!

David Jenkinson
Knaresborough, North Yorkshire

There can be little doubt that one of the great features of the grouping period was the considerable effort made to improve the lot of the third class passenger on the long-distance trains. Nowhere was this better exemplified than in the Pullman cars of the 1920s. This is an unidentified third class interior, most probably from a 'K' type car (see page 235) (Author's collection).

1. The Great Amalgamations and their aftermath

Every now and then, an event occurs in world history which, however important in itself, has a 'spin-off' effect even wider than anyone can have foreseen at the time. Such, in terms of British railway history, was the consequence of the assassination of Archduke Franz Ferdinand at Sarajevo on that fateful day in August 1914 which launched the world into the first of its two holocausts during the first half of the twentieth century. It almost seems tasteless to link the evolution of railway history with these two vast human tragedies, yet such was the case; the effect of these two conflagrations cannot be excluded from our story. This volume takes us through that turbulent time when the world went mad, for the course of British railway history would almost certainly have been different had it not been for those greater realities and what happened in their wake. Of course, it was never that simple, but let me at least try to make the linkage by way of background to this book.

In 1914, so as to serve in the strategic national interest, the many private British railways were brought under centralized Government control and operated by a Railway Executive Committee. Although they continued to operate under their old names, they were, for all practical purposes, nationalized. This continued to be the case during the 1914-18 period and it established a sort of feeling that perhaps things should stay this way after the war. It was, in fact, no new idea; Gladstone had, after all, advocated a form of state ownership as early as his celebrated Railways Act of 1844. However, the country did not seem quite ready for this fundamental re-appraisal and, as is its wont when faced with real decisions, Parliament came up with a compromise solution which we now know as the 'Grouping'.

In this, the railways were retained in private ownership but combined into four 'groups' of existing companies to form new and larger organizations. Most of the old companies — and certainly all those with which this survey is concerned — were known as 'constituents' of the new groups, the latter being determined largely on territorial grounds. There was a degree of competition retained 'at the edges', so to speak, but this was no more than the natural consequence of the decision to keep the former company boundaries inviolate with no attempt to tidy them up where the old borders crossed each other. Thus, for example, the London Midland and Scottish (via its inclusion of the former LNWR and MR) found itself with penetrating arms through GWR territory into South Wales, while the London and North Eastern (having taken charge of the former GCR) now possessed a second main line to London from the north, almost completely surrounded by LMS lines, as well as the old GNR line to King's Cross.

No doubt Parliament was happy to maintain a form of spurious competition but, overall, it fooled no one at the fundamental level and, save for some economies of scale, did not really achieve very much which could not equally well have been expected from the old pre-group companies had they gone back to their old boundaries. In the event, the necessarily 'shot-gun' marriages which were forced on the old companies in consequence of the Grouping, often exacerbated rather than reduced their differences. Prior to the Grouping, each company could take pride in its own achievements and pursue commercial rivalry or co-operation with its contemporaries without any serious fear of loss of identity, or indeed, *esprit de corps*; but when amalgamation with a rival loomed ahead, it was inevitable that something would have to give. Put in a nutshell, there had to be winners and losers in the new amalgamations and this was not, psychologically, the best way to launch these new enterprises. It was one thing to collaborate with a rival in the interests of a better commercial return for both, but it was quite another to be swallowed up — and there was a good deal of the latter in 1923, nowhere more than in the realm of preferred designs to be adopted, be they locomotives, wagons or carriages.

Now it is an interesting fact that whereas in the locomotive field some of the old companies' efforts were far more worthy of continuation than others (not

Above left *Though all railways soon began to build new carriages, there were so many old ones in stock that many had a very long innings -- see also Chapter 10. Here at Tunbridge Wells, a sort of frontier town between the SE & CR and the LB & SCR, the symbolic marriage under Southern colours of a former Brighton 0-4-2T No 2221 and one of the well-found SE & CR 'birdcage' sets makes the sort of pleasing and typical combination that could be witnessed for a generation or more* (Ransome-Wallis Collection, NRM).

Left *Pullman retained its connection with the Brighton line long after the grouping and continued to provide most of the catering services, a typical example being seen here in the form of two quite elderly specimens in the centre of a neat set of low elliptical roof ex-LSWR corridors bound for Eastbourne behind 2-6-0 No 1906* (NRM collection).

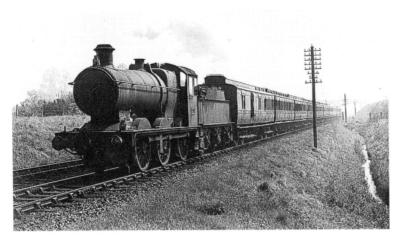

that this always happened, by the way!), the same was not quite so true in the field of the passenger carriage. Much of the background to this state of affairs has been given in the previous volume but it will do no harm briefly to recapitulate the principal trends which dominated as far as the new grouped companies were concerned, starting with the smallest of them and ending with the most awkward.

The Southern Railway (basically LSWR/LB & SCR/SE & CR) did not face too much of a problem. Each of its constituents held a form of territorial monopoly already, give or take a few exceptions, so the greater company was little different in this respect. It also had an edge-on boundary with the GWR, but this was no whit different than had formerly been the case, since this boundary was almost wholly LSWR/GWR. Furthermore, for reasons given in my first volume, the LSWR was the only SR constituent which had needed seriously to address the long-distance problem, so there could be no real objection to the Southern's long-distance philosophy continuing in the LSWR tradition; it made sense.

There can be no doubt that this was rendered more palatable to the LB & SCR and SE & CR sections by the facts that the new Southern CME, R.E.L. Maunsell, was an ex-SE & CR man and that the Brighton line had never built any true long-distance carriages anyway. In any case, Maunsell continued to develop the already ordered SE & CR corridor stock to some extent and fairly soon moved the new SR standard vehicles to a form which, though mostly LSWR-inspired, was far more obviously 'Southern' than pre-grouping. Moreover, as we shall see, the new Southern carriages were built to various structural 'envelopes' so as to fit the varying loading gauges of the SR constituents. Maunsell was clearly something of a diplomat.

Diplomatic, too, if somewhat 'forced', was the solution to the provisioning of shorter-distance coaching stock. The SR had, at an early stage, determined on wholesale suburban electrification and the fact that there was something of an unholy row about which system should be adopted (see Chapter 6) did not seriously affect the carriage design side. For one thing, the SR was not a wealthy company and since all three of its constituents had already re-equipped with quite reasonable bogie non-corridor stock, it made eminent sense to convert many of these carriages to electrical multiple unit (EMU) form for the suburban lines. Thus the Brighton electrics continued to look 'LB & SCR', the South Eastern area 'SE & CR' and the trains from Waterloo very much 'LSWR' — honours more or less even all round. Furthermore, when Maunsell built new EMUs for the further extensions of the electrified system, they were distinctly 'Southern' in concept with little harking back to the old days.

Inspired too, if less than visually exciting, was Maunsell's final choice of SR carriage colour scheme. Had he gone for the most attractive of the constituent companies' liveries (arguably the LSWR salmon-pink and brown), this may have been undiplomatic; had he chosen the SE & CR (crimson) or the LB & SCR (umber and cream), the same diplomatic problems might also have occurred, but he would also have adopted liveries very close to those of the LMS and GWR respectively. This may not have seemed the best choice in view of what was probably felt to be a need to establish a new 'corporate identity' in the post-1922 era. He therefore chose the all-over sage green, originally adopted purely for LSWR EMUs but applied to all LSWR stock after March 1921. Some no doubt saw this as a victory for Waterloo, but the chosen scheme had some positive virtues in its own right.

Firstly, it was different from that of the other three 'Big Four' companies — and likely to remain so; secondly it was already identified with 'electric trains', a point which the SR, from an early date, put high on its list of publicity priorities. It also differentiated the Southern Electric trains from those of the often competing London underground lines, even before the latter were amalgamated in 1933. Lastly, it was a very practical and economic livery to apply. That the SR subsequently found itself not quite sure what the precise shade of green either was or should be is a different story!

Thus, the SR achieved a reasonable carriage compromise — and it did the same with Pullman on the catering front too. The latter company maintained its traditional influence on the former LB & SCR and SE & CR operating areas, while the purely Southern catering contribution was mainly concentrated in erstwhile LSWR territory. At all events, it seems to have worked pretty well for over 20 years and when Bulleid, in the 1940s, finally had to address the whole problem of large-scale carriage replacement, it was only to be expected that he would and did come up with totally new designs.

However, if there were no outright 'winners' and 'losers' on the Southern, the same was not the case with the Great Western. Here, everybody 'lost', save for the title company itself. The original GWR was so much bigger than any of the other constituents of the proposed 'Western' group that the old title was kept and the smaller fry were absorbed, almost literally, into the greater GWR. In carriage terms, this made much sense. None of the smaller constituents had developed its carriages to anything like the extent or variety of those produced at Swindon. The Cambrian had, perhaps, come closest, but it was still a very long way behind. In consequence, the evolution of GWR stock continued, without interruption, from the Churchward 'Toplight' phase (see Volume 1).

In a sense this was slightly unfortunate, for whatever the problems of the three other newly grouped companies — and there were many — there is no doubt that the fusion of ideas between their various

constituents was ultimately to be of benefit to all, even if occasionally it took some time to befall. On the other hand, the newly enlarged GWR found that there was far less stimulus to change, largely because there was no really meaningful 'alternative' input from its constituents; in consequence, GWR carriage design tended to stagnate in the 1920s and 1930s. By the latter period, the two larger groups, particularly the LMS, had well outstripped the GWR in terms of the quality of their general service long-distance stock.

The LNER inherited many fine carriages from its constituents and many of them were to serve their new owners for quite a few more decades — until well into BR days as it turned out. In the event, however, although the GCR, GER, NER and NBR could all offer some excellent vehicles, it was the GNR influence which prevailed. Volume 1 has explained how this came to be — largely, in fact, in consequence of Nigel Gresley's position and the fact that the East Coast Joint Stock (a sort of pre-group unifying influence) had, for the most part, adopted GN-type styling. By 1923, this had become pure 'Gresley' and, save to the cognoscenti, was virtually indistinguishable from the 'proper' GNR carriages.

Technically, too, there were many good reasons why Gresley's precepts should continue. He was, of course, originally a carriage designer and, by 1923, had given his company by far the best bogie design in Britain; furthermore, his old company (and the ECJS) had long since adopted the more efficient Pullman gangway and buckeye coupling as standard, while Gresley's articulation ideas, of great value in reducing train weight without loss of amenity, had progressed well beyond the experimental stage. None of the other LNER constituents — nor much of Britain either for that matter — could match this. Moreover, the great NER carriage works at York (inevitably bound to play a vital role in the new enlarged LNER) was already experienced in build-

ing Gresley-type carriages for the ECJS, so the transition could perhaps be rendered relatively painless.

On the more cosmetic side, teak was still a favoured and durable material — in spite of the increasing use of sheet steel by other companies — so its continuation by Gresley also made some sense and certainly determined the new LNER carriage livery. The company adopted the ECJS variant of the traditional varnished teak as its new standard scheme. The ECJS differed from that of the GNR and the 'GNR/NER Joint' fleets only in respect of the fine lining down the edges of the gold/yellow stripes on the beading and the colour of the shading to the carriage insignia: GNR — blue; GNR/NER — green; ECJS — vermilion. This meant that, fine lining and insignia shading apart, many thousands of carriages were already correctly finished. Additionally, the GCR also employed a varnished wood finish and many GER carriages were also in this style. The only other conceivable choice for an LNER carriage colour would have been the crimson lake of the NER and NBR (also, to some extent, adopted in its later years by the GER), but since it probably seemed fairly certain that the other three grouped companies would all adopt painted finishes, the LNER would be distinctively different if it continued with varnished natural teak. It proved to be a wise choice since the LMS chose a crimson lake colour scheme.

The biggest 'loser' on the LNER, in strictly carriage terms, was the North Eastern Railway, for reasons outlined in Volume 1, but it did not vanish without trace. Its main-line stock was distinctly good — some would even argue that it was more advanced and aesthetically more harmonious than the GNR

product — and it lasted well; but so too did much of that of the other LNER constituents. The LNER was always 'stretching' for capital investment and was forced to maintain many older coaches in service. This, as an almost irreverent aside, put it in the rather curious situation of still operating some 50 per cent of the total surviving *British* four-wheel and six-wheel fleet at the same time as it was proudly advertising its celebrated, ultra-modern, streamlined trains!

The LMS, the fourth and largest of the British main-line companies formed in 1923, was the most comprehensive in terms of its inherited carriage fleet. As Volume 1 has revealed, the LNW and Midland railways dominated, but there were significant contributions of both stock and ideas from the LYR and the Caledonian. As it transpired, Midland domination at Board level determined such relatively insignificant matters as carriage livery and external styling (both of which continued in the MR tradition), but conceptually, the needs of the other LMS constituents, particularly but not exclusively the LNWR, had a very considerable influence on the choice and quantity of carriage types built by the new group.

As things turned out, the LMS standard carriage soon began to look very distinctly 'Midland'. It made use of the MR-derived angle-trussed underframe and bogie and deployed Midland-style detail treatment. There were some quite sound technical reasons why this should be so, not simply because the new LMS carriage chief, R.W. Reid, was ex-MR, but mainly for the fact that he, alone of his contemporaries, had begun to address the whole business of more economic carriage building and had, naturally, started the process at Derby. The LMS was soon to benefit

Left *The LNER's inheritance was very mixed, and because the company was never wealthy it kept a far higher proportion of six-wheel carriages in service than anyone else. This delectable assortment of ex-GCR museum pieces probably dated back to nineteenth-century MSLR days, yet it is seen here near Woodhouse in the late 1920s behind 4-6-0 No 5052 with the engine carrying express head lamps. The reporting number on the engine probably indicates excursion use (Ransome-Wallis Collection, NRM).*

Above right *No amount of tinkering about with new liveries could disguise the Wolverton origins of former West Coast Joint Stock dining car No 10421 dating from 1905; one must also concede that the new livery sat very well on these handsome cars. When this picture was taken in the mid-1920s, the cars had just received a complete refurbishment of the interior — see overleaf (LMS official, NRM).*

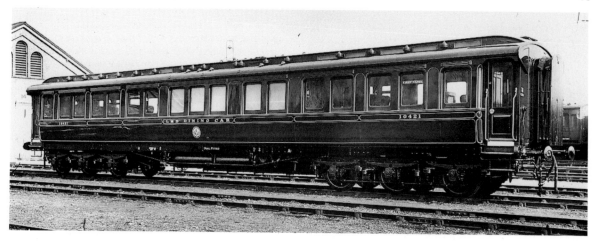

and its carriage building rapidly began to be influenced by Reid's ideas which he fairly smartly soon put into operation at Wolverton (ex-LNWR) and Newton Heath (ex-LYR) as well. By contrast with the contemporary developments in the locomotive department, Reid's changes do not seem to have encountered any real hostility. Like Maunsell on the SR, he seems to have been a bit of a diplomat.

For one thing, although the new LMS carriages looked superficially Midland, Reid really did attempt to come to grips with the realities of the new company. Thus, for example, his first generation LMS twelve-wheel sleeping and dining cars had far more Wolverton (LNWR) thinking in them than Derby (MR). There was, in truth, little to chose in absolute terms between the best of the LNWR and MR coaches at the time, or those of the LYR and CR for that matter, but the LNWR was by far the greatest user of twelve-wheelers at the time; Reid seems to have been aware of the importance of such matters and this particular appreciation of the greater company need was not to be an isolated instance in the LMS carriage building business.

The apparently Midland nature of LMS carriages was, of course, reinforced by the choice of MR livery. But even if the MR influence had not been present at high level, the LMS would probably have had some difficulty in arriving at a universally acceptable standard carriage colour. The MR, GSWR and NSR all used crimson lake (the NSR called its slightly darker shade 'Madder' lake), the LNWR and Caledonian had near-identical carmine lake and off-white liveries, the LYR used a similar carmine lake and 'tan' while the smaller constituents offered blue (Furness) and greens (Highland, and Maryport and Carlisle). One can be fairly certain, however, by virtue of its 'common factor' status amongst most of the constituents, that a dark(ish) red, in some form or

another, was bound to have figured in the LMS carriage scheme, and had the choice been the LNWR/CR style, in all logic the only other real contender apart from a totally new livery, this too would have had its opponents. One could, perhaps, argue that a combination of Midland engine colours with West Coast carriage livery might have been the best of all possible worlds, but this can never be more than a matter of opinion. In purely objective terms, the crimson livery looked good and, like the Southern dark green, was both hard wearing and practical.

All told, therefore, the apparently 'Midland' nature of the first generation LMS coaches was more superficial than real and long before the end of the 1920s the LMS, more than any of the other companies, had begun a significant break-out from the pre-grouping mould. Meantime, like the LNER, it continued to make use of its better pre-grouping stock. The LMS was, however, less constrained in terms of new capital investment than its East Coast rival and, in consequence, was able to do away with a much higher proportion of the older four-wheel and six-wheel carriages. In part, this was made simpler by the high quality of much of the later pre-grouping stock. As new LMS carriages came into service in their hundreds, much of the newer pre-1923 stock was 'cascaded' to replace old bone-shakers in the Highlands and elsewhere. Some of the more fascinating examples of this re-location are offered in Chapter 10.

Having therefore set the background to the dominant influences which were ultimately to prevail after 1922, it only remains necessary at this point to review those carriages which, although appearing after the Grouping, managed to perpetuate pure pre-group (or near enough so) characteristics. This time, however, it seems logical to review them in terms of the speed with which the four new companies settled down after 1922. We thus start with the GWR, since

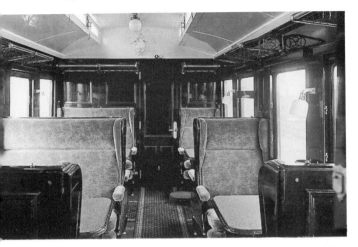

Left *Unlike the GWR (see Chapter 5), the LMS did not rebuild its pre-group dining cars but it did re-work their interiors which allowed them to hold the fort until the massive replacement programme of the 1930s. This is the remodelled interior of No 10421 with cleaned-up surfaces and new 'LMS'-marked luggage racks. The cars were nominally composite and this is the first class end. The third class was identical save for a change in upholstery cloth* (LMS official, NRM).

Middle left *The LMS, like the LNER, kept more than a few six-wheelers in gainful employment for many years. Former North Staffordshire Railway brake third No 27770 still looked smart in its fully lined livery at Waterhouses in 1933* (Author's collection).

this company needed no settling down period at all; it had already decided what to do in 1922 and the grouping made no difference.

We left the GWR in the previous volume at the end of the 'Toplight' era, a period of carriage design started by Churchward in 1907 in the fully beaded wood-panelled form and concluded in 1922 by the final examples with steel sheet outer panelling with little or no raised mouldings. The 'Toplight' designation arose from the presence in most of them of small, shallow depth, fixed lights in the area between the cantrail and the top of the conventionally positioned main windows. Many other railways — the GNR, LNWR, MR and NER to name but four — had done the same from time to time but the feature was particularly associated with Swindon. These carriages, even when built, were no quantum step ahead of the better competition in terms of size, comfort or amenity, save for the sheer length of the earlier 70-foot examples, but from the outset they were quite recognisably twentieth century in outline and in the

context of their use of smoother outer steel panelling, they accurately predicted one of the most obvious evolutionary characteristics which was eventually to take place in all companies of the 'Big Four' era.

Right at the time of the grouping, 1922 to be precise, the GWR moved away from the 'Toplight' form to a rather dull and uninspiring period of carriage design, generally referred to as the 'Bow-ended' era, which lasted until the mid-1930s and will be considered in later chapters. It is only because the first few examples appeared (literally) as pre-Group vehicles that they are mentioned here at all. The 'Bow-ended' carriages were, in effect, the first post-group GWR standard types.

The next quickest group to resolve its carriage policy was the LNER. Here, the Gresley/ECJS influence dominated and by the end of 1923 the new company had determined that its standard policy would be an uninterrupted continuation of Doncaster (GNR) practice. However, there was a slight difference compared with Swindon in that the LNER (as did the LMS and SR) also inherited existing orders for pre-group stock. In most cases, these were merely fulfilled, after which the old works then moved over to LNER designs. Thus Dukinfield (GCR) and Stratford (GER) merely completed existing orders (basically non-corridor types) before moving to LNER group standard practices. In fact, it was not long before Stratford stopped building new coaches altogether, 1927 seeing its last new vehicles emerge. The transformation in Scotland was even more rapid. Cowlairs (NBR) had nothing new on hand at the grouping and Inverurie (GNSR) merely finished a handful of non-corridors; neither place built another new carriage.

The great exception to this post-1922 pattern was to be found at York, ex-NER. Even before the grouping, there had always been great rivalry between the two great carriage building establishments at York and Doncaster which, at times, had taken on almost tribal characteristics — and when two Yorkshiremen disagree, the consequences can be interesting to say the least! Nowhere was this more the case in the LNER carriage context than at these two places and to understand subsequent LNER policies, one must comprehend this fact.

It all stemmed from the fact that although the NER was bigger than the GNR, the latter's design influence, largely through Gresley, had been dominant in the pre-1923 evolution of the East Coast Joint Stock. But York always felt that it made its carriages rather better than they did at Doncaster regardless of design, and in truth this was almost certainly the case in purely objective terms; principal main-line stock excepted (where there was little difference in quality), the NER operated far superior and better-built carriages than did the GNR. Added to this was the undoubted fact that the absolute building capacity at York was greater than at Doncaster so the LNER had to resolve the problem or face some degree of crisis. That it did so was to the credit of both the two rival works themselves and the LNER CME, Nigel Gresley.

The crucial point was in the field of long-distance carriages where the NER had already proved itself capable of designing very good examples for its own services, being, for example, an early railway to abandon individual outside compartment doors as I have previously noted in Volume 1. Even though these stylish vehicles were rather few in number compared with

Left *The post-grouping transition on the GWR was so imperceptible that it is difficult to pin-point a time when things were obviously different. This example dates from the mid-1930s, but apart from the obviously more modern bow-ended carriage at No 3, such was the quality of the original Churchward stock that several fully panelled 'Toplights' and at least one 'Dreadnought' still harmonize well with the train, an up South Wales express near Pilning behind 4-6-0 No 5040* Stokesay Castle *(Soole Collection, NRM).*

Right *After the grouping, Gresley's carriage ideas soon held sway on the non-GNR parts of the system, and remained there for a generation or more. This is a pair of 'Quin-arts' dating from the 1920s at Hackney Downs in 1948 behind 0-6-2T No 9671; and they still had many more years to go* (Ransome-Wallis Collection, NRM).

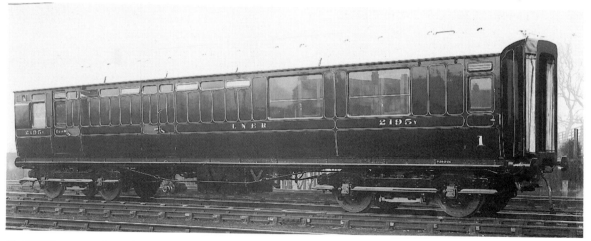

No 2195Y was one of several types of NER-styled coaches built by the LNER for the GE section, though there were only two first brakes of this type. Only the LNER standard gangways, couplings and bogies distinguish it from the pre-1923 version (LNER official, NRM).

the Gresley 'breed', there can be no doubt of their quality or style — better than most. Fortunately, in purely design terms, there was also at York, as well as a fair degree of company pride, a considerable appreciation of Nigel Gresley's talent as a carriage designer and this, in the end, turned out to be the key factor. York had long being building GN-styled vehicles as its share of the ECJS and always felt that it could outdo Doncaster if put to the test, and Gresley probably knew this. It may, therefore, have been a stroke of some genius that led him to order from York some NER-styled carriages for the GER section soon after the grouping!

The GER section, for reasons which even now are not fully understandable — something to do with

platform capacity at Liverpool Street and other problems elsewhere, I believe — was not, after the grouping, immediately able to accept the new LNER standard 61 ft 6 in corridor carriages. In due course the solution turned out to be a 52 ft 6 in version of the LNER standard type, but the interim answer was found in Gresley's decision to give them some pretty well unmodified NER-style 53 ft 6 in corridors, no doubt to the immense satisfaction of the York builders! I have never seen the point put this way before, but this decision may well be a contributory reason for the fact that York never created any real problems during the LNER period and was always the principal LNER carriage building establishment and a considerable exponent of the best of Gresley's LNER practice even though Doncaster continued to build the bulk of the special stock (eg the Stream-

Figure 1 Elevations and plans of the late vintage four-wheelers of Caledonian design built early in 1923.

Scale: 2mm = 1ft

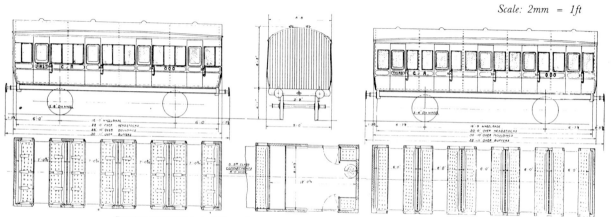

Drawing showing Principal Dimensions of 4-wheeled Coaching Stock built for Suburban Services.

liners — Chapter 10). In more modern BR days, York long outlived Doncaster as a carriage building location and is still active today.

Turning now to the LMS, the ultimate Derby stylistic influence has been mentioned and it is a moot point whether this company or the LNER was the quicker to determine new standards after the grouping. At that time, there was on hand a fair amount of pre-1923 work at all four of the principal LMS works. Wolverton (LNWR) was building some 57-foot non-corridors, Newton Heath (LYR) was turning out both corridor and non-corridor examples of its final standard styles, and up in the north St Rollox was finishing off the final Caledonian designs, including some quite amazingly late examples of the four-wheel genre for suburban services in fashionable Edinburgh, of all places. This actually took place early in 1923 at that curious time when, for six months, the Caledonian was not legally part of the LMS group to which it was assigned but which it only joined, officially, in mid-year (for the record, the North Staffordshire Railway was similar). It need hardly be said that the unsentimental LMS soon put a stop to all this.

Meantime, Derby Works was not only introducing what turned out to be the first of the true LMS standard carriage types but was, under the direction of R.W. Reid, also being reorganized to produce its carriages in a quite new form of mass production which was to revolutionize the LMS (see Chapter 2).

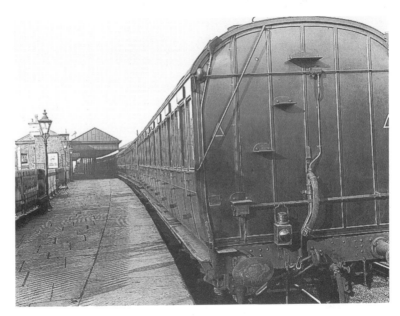

Right *Late period LYR carriages had an almost identical profile to those of the MR, LNWR and CR but were, on the whole, rather smoother sided, a point well illustrated by this steeply angled view of a non-corridor set at Darwen in the early LMS period. Note the inward taper of the sides to the guard's lookout, just visible at the near end of the second vehicle, a typical LYR feature and shared with the LSWR 'Ironclads'. Note too that the nearer coach still carries LYR livery (LMS official, NRM).*

Below *This northbound stopping train at Northchurch tunnel circa 1930 headed by 4-4-0 No 5308* Simoom *not only shows the similarity of size and roof profile between the mainly ex-LNWR coaches and the one and only LMS standard type (fifth vehicle) but also illustrates the increasingly common LMS practice of operating 'cascaded' corridor stock on many semi-fast services (Main Line Collection, NRM).*

Left *The first three carriages in this down boat train at Herne Hill in 1928 behind 4-6-0 No 767* Sir Valence *display the distinctive style of the so-called Southern 'Continental' corridor stock based on the SE & CR designs. The first and third examples are to the post-1923 8 ft 6 in width and the middle one is of the older 8-foot type. Typically, four Pullmans are also present (still in pre-umber and cream livery as far as can be seen) and the train has at least two more 'Continentals' in the rear* (Ransome-Wallis Collection, NRM).

Figure 2 *Elevations and plans of two SR-built 'Ironclad' corridor coaches of the early 1920s.*

Scale: $^1/_{10}$ " = 1ft

These methods were, in due course, to be applied at Wolverton, principally, and also, to a lesser extent, at Newton Heath. However, just as on the LNER, there were to be no more new carriages built at many of the old works; and before the 1930s were scarce started, these new manufacturing methods made it possible for Derby and Wolverton to meet virtually all the LMS requirement for new carriages.

The final pre-group carriages built during LMS days to the designs of its principal constituents were much closer together in concept than those of the LNER or Southern constituents and, apart from fine detail, shared many features in common, not least their overall shape and size. Most were within the 54-57 ft long by 9 ft wide 'envelope', embodying full elliptical roofs and not dissimilar forms of construction. Indeed, when the final pre-group designs were actually turned out in full LMS colours, there could often be seen far more closeness in general style between them all than anyone might have supposed. Save for the exterior panelling, the general shape and characteristics of CR, LNWR, LYR and MR carriages, not to mention some from the Furness and GSWR, were all very similar, so when it finally appeared, the new LMS standard carriage was no real surprise.

It was, in fact, the Southern Railway which displayed the most lengthy and interesting transition from pre-Group to post-group practice. By comparison with the other three companies, the Southern had some catching up to do and it is now necessary to devote some space to its consideration, if only to bring the SR to the same point in the broader national story.

New developments were confined entirely to mainline stock, the reasons being bound up very closely with the rather different nature which the Southern had both revealed from the outset and continued to demonstrate. For instance, the fact that the Southern built no new locomotive-hauled local stock during the whole of its existence is mostly due to its electrification policy. This latter point will be considered in due course but the residual effect on the non-electrified stopping services was to reduce their need for new stock to nothing that could not be and usually was provided by 'cascaded' older vehicles. For one thing, there was a fair chance that within a few years these lines too would be electrified, so why build new coaches? Such need as did arise for something more 'modern' during the later 1930s could still be met, for the most part, by that time-honoured Southern trick, first revealed in quantity during the suburban electrification phase, of rebuilding serviceable older carriage bodies on to new frames. A fair number of robust ex-LSWR non-corridors received a new lease of life in the mid-1930s in consequence.

There was, however, a real need for something better on both the long and medium distance routes; in particular there was a growing demand for gangwayed stock both to bring the Southern up to the standard of the rest of the country and to avoid losing business. With a few noteworthy exceptions, the Southern showed up badly in 1923, compared with the other new companies, largely because its constituents had no real tradition of building long-distance gangwayed stock in any quantity. The Southern was thus able to develop its own style more or less free from too many preconceived prejudices. The fact that it took only some three or four years to evolve a unified style was, in the circumstances, no mean achievement when set against the 20 years or more of corridor coach evolution which had already taken effect on other lines. It was an interesting time in consequence.

I have already opined that the Southern CME,

Maunsell, seems to have been something of a diplomat, a view reinforced by the events of the 1923-26 period. He inherited but two lines of corridor coach development: the relatively recent proposals of his old company, the SE & CR, and the much longer-standing experience, though not in fact translated into too many vehicles, of the LSWR. Like his LMS and LNER counterparts, Maunsell also inherited existing pre-Group orders but, unlike the engineers of the two northern companies, he allowed them to develop, rather than switch abruptly to new styles. He clearly used these pre-Group ideas as a sort of intermediate

stage in the evolution of his own, recognisably 'Southern' carriages of the mid-1920s onwards.

Least changed from their pre-Group forebears, and the first actually to be authorized by the new SR, were further examples of the SE & CR type, side-corridor coaches for the Kent Coast boat trains, the pioneer example of which, a train of eight vehicles, had appeared in 1921. Their flat-sided appearance, with its vertical 'matchboard' panelling below the waist line, was rather attractive in a European sort of way and they were fitted with 'state of the art' Pullman gangways, save at the outer brake ends. Hardly sur-

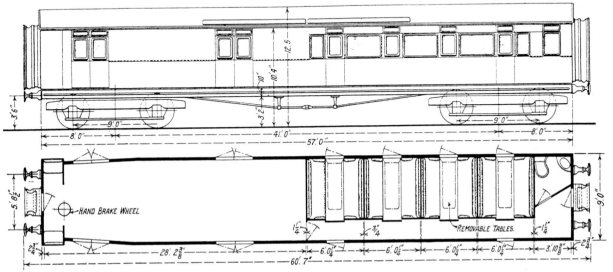

Brake Third-Class Carriage.

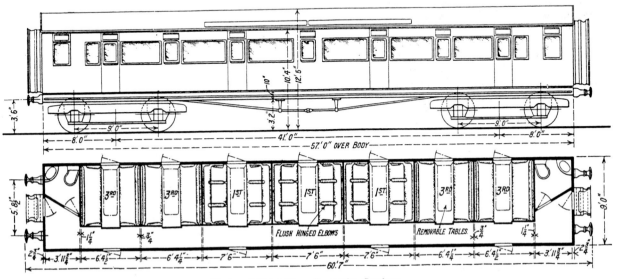

First and Third-Class Composite Carriage.

prisingly, they were often referred to as 'Continental' stock and were usually operated with a Pullman or two somewhere in the middle of the formation. Because of lineside loading gauge restrictions they were kept to a nominal width of 8 ft (actually 8 ft 0¾ in) but they displayed a generous 62-foot length over the body, a dimension not exceeded on the Southern until Bulleid's time.

Some of the extra carriages were actually on order before 1923 and the SR added to this order, the carriages appearing in 1923 and 1924. Those built by the SR itself in 1923 retained the 8-ft nominal width, but those which appeared in 1924 were to a new 8 ft 6 in wide dimension. There was also one final and suprisingly late series of carriages built to this style in 1927 at Eastleigh (LSWR) of all places; previous examples had either come from Ashford (SE & CR) or outside contractors. An interesting minor point about them was that because of their well nigh exclusive boat train usage, they were predominantly first and second class when built, with only one third class type (a third brake) appearing, and that not until the contractor-built batch of 1924. In due course, the seconds were downgraded to third and the Southern adopted its own peculiar solution to the residual second class customers by making use of what it called 'nondescript' carriages — see page 68).

Simultaneously with the continuation of SE & CR designs, Maunsell also went on with the construction

of LSWR-type 'Ironclad' corridor coaches. These were of much more traditionally British outline and their nickname derived simply from their steel sheet outer panelling. In this, they were somewhat akin to the more or less contemporary later period GWR 'Toplights' and they shared very similar dimensions (57 ft long, 9 ft wide). Like the SE & CR designs, some had been ordered before the grouping and these came out with the cumbersome and massive looking LSWR outside framed bogies. When Maunsell ordered further 'Ironclads', the later-built examples from this series were fitted with SE & CR type bogies, the type which by then (late 1923) had been adopted as the SR standard.

Further orders followed, including those which provided the first proper corridor stock on the former LB & SCR main line. Its introduction as the 'City Limited' late in 1925, along with some further 'Ironclads' a few months later for services to Bognor and Worthing, marked the end of this particular line of development. By contrast with the SE & CR types, these LSWR-inspired carriages were all fitted with conventional gangways and couplings, the SR not yet having made up its mind which to adopt. It eventually, and sensibly, went for Pullman type gangways plus buckeye couplings for long-distance stock.

The drafting of 'Ironclads' into areas other than ex-LSWR territory gave them a sort of 'standard' status, unlike the SE & CR-styled 'Continental' stock, but they did not, in the event, turn out to be the precursors of the true SR standard types. The more probable contenders for this distinction were some carriages to a new design which Maunsell introduced

The form of the Southern 'Ironclads' is well-revealed in this circa *1936 view of a Brighton-Cardiff train at Patchway behind GWR 2-6-0 No 8323. The first two and last vehicles have the LSWR outside-framed bogies and may even be of LSWR origin, but the third has SR bogies. The smoother appearance of the fourth carriage reveals it to be of post-'Ironclad' vintage (Soole Collection, NRM).*

Close up detail of an early 'Ironclad' at Havant in 1937. Note the inward taper of the guard's lookout and the very heavy outside frame of the bogie (Box Collection, NRM).

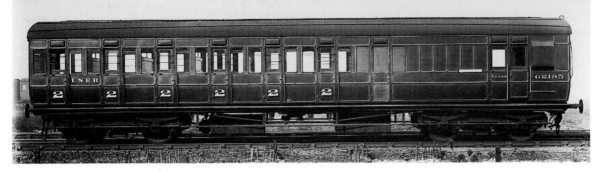

simultaneously with his continuance of the SE & CR and LSWR ideas. Yet again, they arose because of the unsatisfactory nature of existing pre-group provisioning to an important area of the Southern's hinterland, the Kent Coast.

The old SE & CR had provided, for its longer-distance services, some very agreeable bogie noncorridor stock, often with lavatories, during Wainwright's time and later (see Volume 1), but apart from the above-mentioned boat trains, the corridor carriage was almost unknown. By 1923, this was not considered adequate, hence Maunsell's new Kent Coast stock of 1924-25. They looked rather like mini-'Ironclads' and were to the same length and general cross-profile. But, again for structure gauge reasons, their width was kept down to 8 ft 6½ in. They also displayed predominantly SE & CR-type detail fittings, but in their use of British Standard gangways they followed LSWR precedent. They were also given angle-trussed underframes — unlike the 'Ironclads' which had the turnbuckle type — so in every significant way, Maunsell was now beginning to arrive at some form of synthesis for his new railway.

These Kent Coast corridors were built in some quantity and were a familiar enough sight for more than 30 years until the eventual BR electrification. If not the most inspiring of designs, they were no worse in absolute terms than much which was to be seen throughout Britain on many of the longer-established 'corridor' lines, and they certainly provided an adequate basis from which the Southern CME could develop his eventual standard types in 1926 and later.

Thus it was that by the mid-1920s, all four new companies had arrived at their new 'group standards' for carriage construction. To be honest, save for a few noteworthy exceptions — and those mostly attributable to their pre-group constituents — none of them had anything either markedly superior to those of their rivals or, for that matter, anything which would have suprised their forebears either; many Edwardian carriages were just as good as anything which had succeeded them. But it may be helpful briefly to summarize the overall situation in outline before continuing the story.

In the short-distance and medium-distance field, the non-corridor compartment coach reigned

This former Great Eastern brake second No 62185 in LNER colours was, in spite of its quite modern roof shape and general proportions, far too typical of many coaches in the 1920s and 1930s. The very spartan seats — particularly in view of its class designation — can be seen through the windows, but were not unusual. Second class survived for some time in the London area, largely because, at the time, third class season tickets were not available (LNER official, NRM).

supreme, regardless of company. Some had lavatories but far too many did not and there was an altogether too high proportion of four-wheel and six-wheel stock still in regular use. Even the newly electrified Southern lines made use of non-corridor compartment stock. Similarly, in the long-distance field, side corridors were by far the most dominant gangwayed type with very little use being made of the centre aisle open saloon alternative. Virtually all side corridor stock had a full complement of outside compartment doors, in spite of valiant attempts by some companies to wean the public on to something more modern, and there were still far too many so-called expresses making use of non-gangwayed carriages anyway.

Technologically, there was still massive inconsistency between systems in such things as brakes, gangways and couplings. Steam heating was fairly well universal in the locomotive-hauled field, but in the realm of carriage lighting far too many vehicles remained obstinately gas lit in spite of the fact that a satisfactory electrical alternative had existed for a generation. Structurally, the wood-framed body on a steel underframe was all but universal but only the two smaller companies, the GWR and SR, had moved, definitively, away from wood panelled exteriors for new construction.

Neither was there too much evidence of a fundamental change in attitude as the railways embarked on what was to prove their most critical phase so far. They entered the troubled years of the inter-war period in a stolidly traditional way and remained thus for far too long. In the next few chapters, we shall consider in more detail how the situation gradually changed. For all that it seems, in retrospect, to have been frustratingly slow, it was not really seen to be so at the time; it was by no means lacking in interest and, as always, some surprisingly beautiful and enterprising things did eventually emerge.

2. Post-grouping changes in carriage technology

The advent of mass production

The carriage builders of the grouped railways were heirs to almost a century of tradition, and although such matters can be valuable in the right context, one cannot help feel that there was too much slavish adherence to this tradition in the 1920s and 1930s. This was particularly so in the field of carriage design, especially in the long-distance sector where new competition threatened. There were, however, some general moves forward across the board in the specific area of carriage assembly and technology and it is thought helpful to consider these aspects first, leaving the design developments until later chapters. For clarity, this and the next few chapters will concern hauled stock only, leaving the more specialized vehicles, mostly of a self-propelled type, to be covered separately.

Although it is a pity that better assembly and technology were not married to more enterprising basic design, save in a modest number of cases, in pure economic terms it was undoubtedly significant. Like many things, its origins can be discerned in the Great War and, of course, some railways went further down the new route than others. Put at its simplest, the carriage builders began to adopt some of the techniques of mass-production.

Before the 1914-18 war, there were few machine tools available to industry which were capable of mass-production with any great precision, but the demands of the war caused great strides to be made in this field and by the end of the conflict the dream of mass-production in the transport arena had become a reality. This concept was and is, of course, much more familiar in the road vehicle industry, but the very nature of a railway carriage made it extremely unlikely that it could be put on the conveyor belt in the manner of a Model T Ford. However, the commercial advantages of mass-production were such as to make railways look at the idea. In essence, it showed a considerable reduction in labour costs, provided that the capital cost of the machinery could be met and that it was capable of making items to a high standard of dimensional accuracy, thus avoiding much labour-intensive hand finishing.

Left *R. W. Reid's mass production methods at the three principal LMS carriage works showing: carriage roof assembly at Derby; carriage side panels under construction at Wolverton; and non-corridor carriage ends being fabricated at Newton Heath* (all LMS official, NRM).

Applied to the traditional and still favourite method of coachbuilding — the timber frame covered with sheets of wood or metal panelling — the techniques lent themselves best to the prefabrication of carriage component parts with the minimum of subsequent 'cleaning up'. To some extent this fought against the traditional idea of roughly machining the joints and components over-size and then allowing the carpenters to finish and fit them by hand. Many felt that this was still the best way — and in the hands of the best coachbuilders it probably was — but its success did rather depend on the individual skills of the carpenters and they were not all uniformly talented.

The leader in the field was undoubtedly the LMS and, in fact, the origins were Midland in the person of R.W.Reid. Before 1923 he had already begun to set up a new method of carriage building at Derby and it was first put to use in building what were to become the first LMS standard carriages. The secret, if such it may be called, was the use of precision jigs in the sawmill. In place of the individual marking out of each component, a single accurate template was used and the machines then cut as many repeats as were required. Each part was, of course, carefully gauged before leaving the sawmill, but once the machined parts had left the mill any one example of a particular component was interchangeable with any other. It did, of course, demand seasoned timber but this was not the problem it is in the 1980s, since railway carriage timber had usually been naturally seasoned for several years before use. There was none of the modern kiln drying and its attendant problems so, as far as can be judged, the amount of defective timber was kept acceptably low.

An obvious disadvantage to mass-production in the modern sense is that, because of the high cost of obtaining and setting up the machines, one has to envisage a good long 'production run' to make the system pay for itself. This can, of course, limit to some extent the variation of or improvement to design, save after a reasonable period of time. Reid was no doubt aware of this but by concentrating his efforts on producing individual components, he could permutate them in a variety of ways to produce the many different carriage types needed. Thus, a typical LMS carriage, of whatever type, would always have identical doors, ventilators, fixed and drop lights, carriage seat ends or any other item which could usefully be made in bulk — and most of them could. This

Above *The finished product: LMS standard open third No 8506 photographed in 1939. The view is of additional interest in that it was taken just as the vehicle was about to be converted for war-time ambulance use (see also page 258)* (R.J. Essery Collection).

Figure 3 *Reid's 'Progressive Assembly' layout as adopted at Wolverton (ex-LNWR) for new carriages. Note that where appropriate it was also integrated with wagon-building operations.*

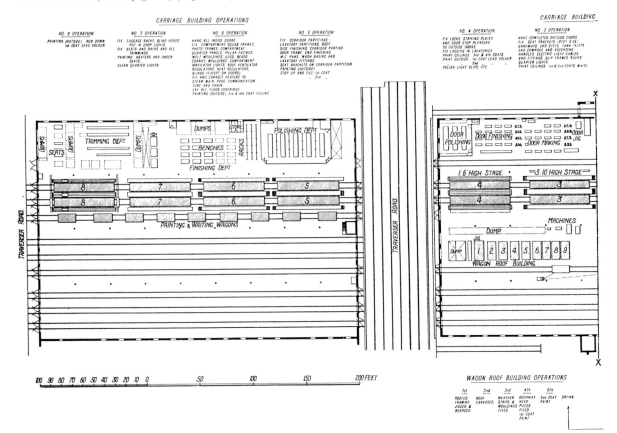

in turn caused a new method of carriage assembly to develop which reduced the building time of a single vehicle from six weeks to six days and the erection time of the basic carcass from floorboard to roof to only one hour!

What it amounted to was the prefabrication from the above-mentioned standard components of all the basic sub-assemblies needed for a particular carriage. These sub-assemblies were known as 'units' and the production of several types of units could be carried out simultaneously, whether it be ends, doors, side panel sections or a complete roof. The latter was, by the way, built on a jig at floor level, again from prefabricated accurately cut components. At the due time, all the necessary 'unit assemblies' would be positioned in the erecting shop, and a complete carriage underframe was then wheeled in on to which was already attached the floor framing and floorboards. Using compressed air power tools, the two completed ends would be pulled down on to the floor tenons, followed by the two side assemblies in rather similar manner and then the completed roof. It was in every sense analogous to using a kit of parts with

the certain knowledge that because of the precision in manufacture, all the pieces would fit together accurately. At this point, the interior fitting out could then commence, again using prefabricated finished components.

To make the best use of this new method of assembly, it was also found desirable to reorganize the layout of the carriage works themselves to a sort of 'flow-line' arrangement and by mid-1925 Reid's methods were also in full operation at Wolverton (ex-LNWR). It was called 'Progressive Construction' and the appended contemporary drawing should be self-explanatory. In effect, the finished components were taken to the appropriate part of the production line in sufficient quantity to be available on demand without delay.

So successful was this progressive approach to carriage building that it was also adopted for carriage repairs at the LMS main shops and it was not long (1927) before Newton Heath (ex-LYR) followed Derby and Wolverton in benefiting from this modernization. While no two works were identical — their structural forms would have precluded exact dupli-

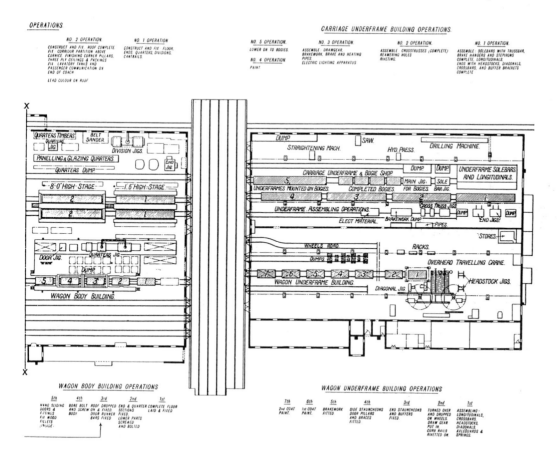

cation — the principles were identical and designed to fulfil several criteria:

a) Elimination of manhandling
b) Allocating a definite type of work to a definite location
c) Allocation of men to specific type of operations
d) Moving work to the men, not men to the work
e) Movements of vehicles between sections of the line at defined times
f) Ensuring all component parts were properly pre-positioned both in terms of type and quantity
g) Making sure (in the case of repairs) that the supply of carriages for attention was kept constant
h) Paying attention to good heating, lighting and working conditions

Students of these matters will detect considerable similarities with the 'belt' system of locomotive repairs introduced by the LMS at Crewe at much the same time and, just as in the case of locomotives, so too with carriages, it enabled the company to make huge works economies by contemporary standards. Railway works rationalization is no modern phenomenon and by 1931 the LMS had dispensed with all but its two biggest carriage works (Derby and Wolver-

ton) as far as new construction was concerned. In fact, Newton Heath was the only other LMS carriage works to build standard design carriages for the new company — and even then, only humble non-corridors — yet even though it had been similarly modernized, there was no call for new carriages from this works after 1931, so efficient had the other two become. And it was not a question of smaller quantities of carriages either. The LMS built massively throughout the pre-war period and it need hardly be stated that its new construction and repair methods stood the test of transition to new materials as the grouping period evolved.

Figure 4 *Southern Railway 'Progressive Repair' layout at Lancing (ex-LB & SCR). On completion of repairs, carriages were moved to the separate paintshop for finishing. The numbered repair roads were used as follows, marked 'stages' on each road being reserved for defined operations within the overall category of that road:*
1-3: Intermediate repairs: bodies, underframes and bogies respectively
4-6: General repairs: bogies, underframes and windows respectively
7-8: General repairs: interior stripping and burning off paintwork
9-12: General repairs: interior refitting, completion of exterior filling and staining
13: General repairs: exterior filling, first stage
14-15: General repairs: bodywork

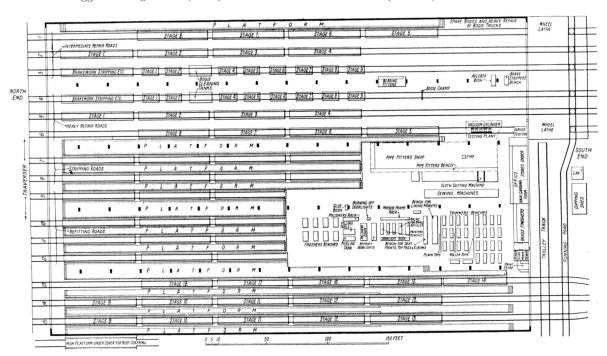

Layout of Carriage Shop for Progressive Repairs, Lancing, Southern Railway.

The LMS experience was not confined to that company, though it was the leader in the field. On the Southern, for example, Maunsell began to rationalize methods along similar if not identical lines. By 1928, he had resolved to reorganize rolling-stock building and repair using his three principal pre-group workshops. Eastleigh (ex-LSWR) and Ashford (ex-SE & CR) became responsible for the building of carriage bodies and the building and repair of wagons, while Lancing (ex-LB & SCR) became a dedicated carriage repair works on a rather similar 'progressive' system to that introduced by the LMS. However, the Southern never adopted the true mass-production techniques of the LMS for new construction and at the height of its electrification in the late 1920s and 1930s it made extensive use of outside contractors for much new EMU stock.

The LNER experience was a little more complex. It had, of course, rather more carriage works than the Southern yet, though smaller than the LMS, it kept more of them actively building new carriages than did its principal rival — at least for a time. But it rarely worked them to capacity as did the LMS and often placed substantial outside orders with 'the trade' even when it might have been supposed that the company works could have tackled more themselves. The LMS did place orders with outside contractors but, with few exceptions — mainly the 'all steel' vehicles (see below) — only when its own works had no spare capacity.

The LNER, like its rivals, reorganized its carriage works in the 1920s along the fashionable 'progressive repair' lines, and this included, as well as York and Doncaster, both Stratford (ex-GER) and Dukinfield (ex-GCR). There was even some modernization at Cowlairs (ex-NBR) but it never took on the wholesale re-shaping that happened on the LMS. As stated in the previous chapter, Stratford built no new carriages after 1927 (it had, in point of fact, plenty of workload in keeping the GE section fleet repaired), but until 1939 York, Doncaster and Dukinfield were all kept busy on new construction. In the LNER case, unlike the LMS, there was also a much greater degree of sub-specialization between works. Thus Doncaster built most of the special stock, including the sleeping and dining cars and the streamliners, the ex-GCR establishment concentrated on non-corridor and much of the non-passenger coaching stock, while York tackled the general service long-distance fleet. After 1939, all new work was concentrated on York and Doncaster.

Even so, the LNER system of carriage building was never as efficient *per se* as that of the LMS. There was little in it for quality, but whereas the LMS had reduced its typical building time per carriage from six weeks to one week by the mid-1920s, the best the LNER could do was to reduce it from about the same original figure to a value still more than twice that of the LMS. Most of this reduction was achieved by a similar 'unit assembly' method as Reid had initiated at Derby but it did not, at first, go hand in glove with the 'progressive' idea, which approach had been mainly confined to repair work only on the LNER. It was not until well into the 1930s, under A.H. Peppercorn, that a similar type of flowline production, allied with mass-produced components, was introduced for new construction and even then, although several new carriages could be built simultaneously, the LNER never matched the sheer output rate of the LMS works.

The GWR remained stolidly traditional in its constructional methods and, of course, had the indubitable advantage of being able to concentrate activity at Swindon. It actually built a formidable number of new coaches during the grouping period as will be seen but it was distinctly unadventurous both in design and carriage building technology. One wonders just what might have been possible had Swindon been reorganized along similar lines to those of Derby or Wolverton from the outset. It was not, in the event, until after the Second World War that Hawksworth's direct building system began to make Swindon look more like a modern carriage works.

To be fair to GWR carriage building technique, however, it was probably in a better state of health than most of the rest at the time of grouping, and with none of the concomitant problems of the latter event to overcome. Needless to say, much of this was attributable to Churchward who, long before 1923, had re-equipped the carriage works with modern machinery and initiated repair and overhaul procedures which were, for the most part, far superior to the rest of the country. Yet again, there was probably little in it in terms of the absolute quality of carriages built compared with other systems, but the GWR's relatively unchanged status after 1922 once again led to a sort of conceptual complacency both in design and technique. This resulted in little real change in carriage building methods at Swindon for more than 20 years, save for a bit of extra machinery, and by the end of the pre-BR period, GWR carriage building methods were lagging behind more than somewhat. This is not to say, of course, that the GWR made no contribution to the evolution of carriage construction; and it is to this aspect that we must now return.

Timber versus steel construction

At this point, however, it is more important to define a few terms of reference to avoid ambiguity. So far, I have considered only changes in the methods of

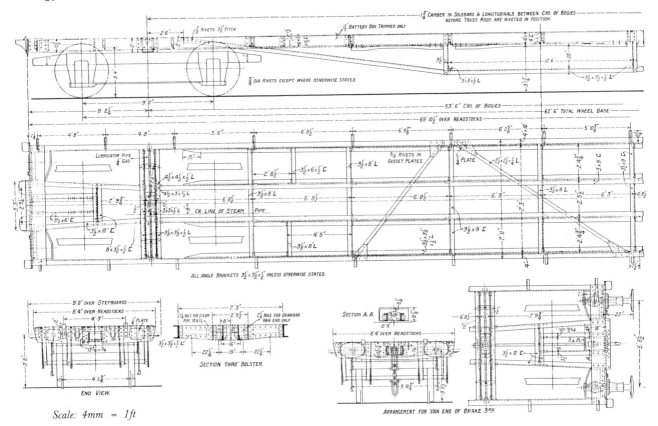

Scale: 4mm = 1ft

Figure 5 *Half elevation and plan of GWR angle-trussed 70-foot underframe for the 1923 bow-ended stock.*

assembling new carriages rather than their fundamental design and construction. In these two latter respects, though the methods of building them may have been changed to some extent, the basic nature of the British locomotive-hauled coach was slow to alter during the grouping period. In the rest of this chapter, hopefully in the interests of greater clarity, attention will be concentrated solely on the forms of construction adopted during this time, and the changing nature of materials used, both within and without the carriage, leaving the matter of general design concept and amenity to be tackled later.

For almost the whole of the 'Big Four' period, the British carriage remained very traditional, at least in terms of its basic construction. Save for a few exceptions, to be considered shortly, it retained the separate body and chassis form described in some detail in the first volume and almost always displayed the familiar timber-framed body, covered with panelling of either timber or steel sheet. Its chassis was by now wholly made from steel and all railways very soon adopted the angle-trussed form, the LNER being the last to abandon the older round bar and turnbuckle style.

As already stated, couplings and gangways retained their Byzantine inconsistency and braking was slow to harmonize, eventually going the wrong way — save on electrified lines — by standardizing on the automatic vacuum rather than the more efficient air brake.

The first railways to break out of this mould — and both did it before 1923 — were the GWR and LSWR when they began to use sheet steel outer panelling. It was, to be sure, but a small step forward, but it eventually became universal. The GWR was the more enterprising since it took the process further and its motivation seems largely to have been so as to overcome the problem of leaking, splitting or rotting panelling and leaky roofs.

Taking panelling first, the GWR used mahogany — an excellent timber in many ways (see Volume 1, Chapter 3) — but no matter how carefully made, panels were prone to split and the moulded beading could demonstrate a tendency to lift off the panels. These characteristics, in turn, let in water and thus caused rotting. Repairs involved not only replacement panelling but often replacement beading as well and even, occasionally, some repairs to the carriage framework. All of this cost money and the GWR began to experiment with steel and iron panel renewal to see whether savings could be made. For a while this worked, but there then arose the matter of corrosion of the steel, usually from the inside of the panel. On investigation, this turned out to be due to the tannic acid in the oak framing which, in association with the inevitable moisture, began to attack the metal plates. It was eventually overcome by the use of galvanized steel panels. Interestingly, other railways which adopted sheet steel were often slow to

Angle-trussed underframes from the other members of the 'Big Four' showing their remarkable similarity of form both to each other and also to the GWR pattern. They are, in order: LMS 57 ft, SR 59 ft, LNER 60 ft (Company official views, NRM).

appreciate the virtues of galvanized panelling (it was, unsurprisingly, more expensive) and it became an unfortunate characteristic of many steel-panelled coaches, well into BR Mk 1 days, to gain an unsavoury reputation as 'rot boxes', usually revealed to the eye by much external patchwork. Even so, it was cheaper than the all-wood option.

The GWR also addressed the roof problem. The traditional tongue and groove roof boards with their impregnated roofing canvas covering were in time subject to the depredations of both perished paintwork and canvas becoming porous. This also caused leaks unless remedied by repainting and/or re-treating the canvas — or even *in extremis* replacing the latter. The GWR therefore began to use galvanized steel for roof sheeting as well. There was also some reduction of fire risk as a result of these moves and the GWR developed matters further by making its carriage floors, not of traditional wooden floorboards, but of

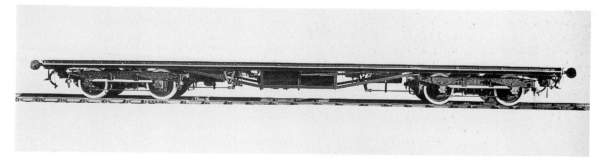

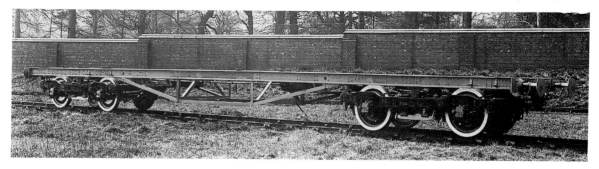

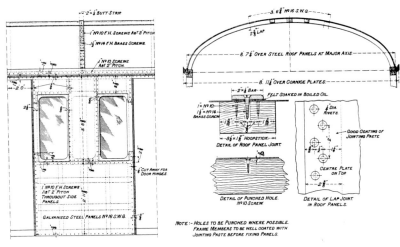

Panelling Methods on Carriage Stock, Great Western Railway.

Figure 6 *Diagram to show the fixing methods adopted by the GWR for steel panels on a timber frame.*

Below left *Close-up of the elaborately executed full lining used on GWR flush-panelled carriages until 1927. The example illustrated is a two-coach 'B' set with a semi-permanent centre coupling (see page 48). Note too the distinctive bowed ends (GWR official, Author's collection).*

Figure 7 *Arrangement of structural framing for the 'all-steel' LMS open stock of 1926-7.*

corrugated steel plates covered with a fireproof material. Steel sheet was also applied to panel replacement on repaired stock on an 'as required' basis. It was no doubt effective but led to a certain degree of external untidiness when a carriage displayed a mixture of original wooden and replacement steel panelling.

For a few years, this was effectively disguised from all but the closest examination by the GWR retaining its elaborate and attractive fully lined chocolate and cream livery. This colour scheme was, wisely, reinstated after the grouping in replacement of the erstwhile 'all lake' version, and the painters went to extraordinary lengths to re-create the impression of the fully beaded panelling, with its raised bolection mouldings, even on flush steel stock. It looked very attractive, but one does rather wonder how much of the savings achieved by steel panelling were lost by the retention of expensive painting.

The GWR was not alone in this particular practice — in fact, all four main-line railways did it with their first flush steel coaches — and it was in the end the GWR which was the first to dispense with an elaborate livery when, in 1927, it introduced a new simplified form of carriage decoration. This change was accompanied by a fair degree of self-satisfied justification in publicity terms, based on its apparent 'modernity' compared with the older form of painting. So it was, but it was also a good deal cheaper to put on the carriage and this was the *real* reason for its adoption!

The LSWR 'Ironclads' were the other principal vehicles to display the new steel-panelled technique and the Southern carried on with the idea for all its new carriages. Like the GWR, it too saw the virtues of galvanized sheet as opposed to plain steel and also retained a pseudo-'panelled' livery for many years. In the Southern case, however, the simplification of lining was slow to develop and came about gradually during the 1930s rather than abruptly at one point in time. It was, in fact, left to Oliver Bulleid to take the Southern into a fully simplified painting style in the late 1930s, when he simply suppressed all lining entirely. In one fundamental respect, how-

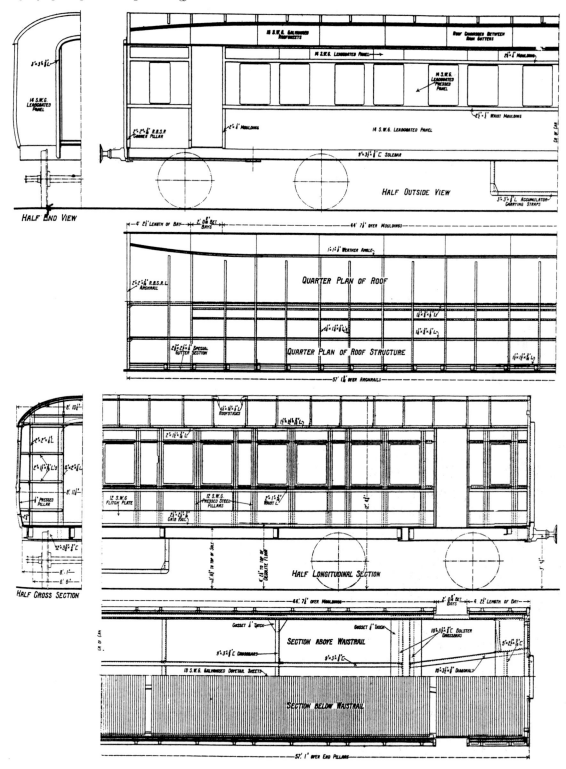

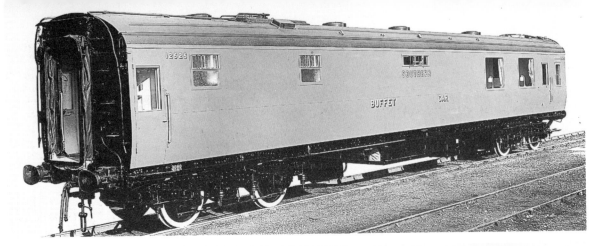

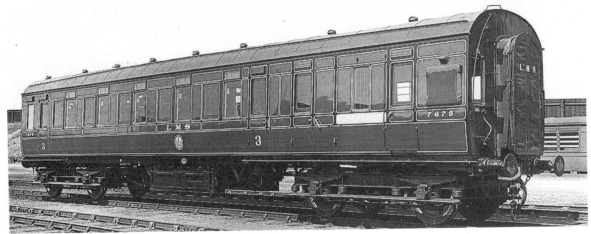

Top *Plain but honest: Bulleid's unlined malachite green was first applied to coaching stock in 1938; this is 'Bognor Buffet' No 12525 from one of the 4BUF sets (SR official, NRM).*

Middle *Fully panelled livery treatment applied to 'all-steel' LMS open brake third No 7675 in 1927 (BR LMR).*

Bottom *For a year or two after his new carriages appeared, Stanier's flush-sided stock was given a fully lined livery which, though suggestive of traditional panelling, also suited the modern lines of the coaches. This is open first class dining car No 7495 in 1934 (BR LMR).*

ever, the Southern did not take matters as far as did, eventually, all the other companies. The company remained faithful to wood and canvas roof construction right into the totally flush-sided period, after the second war.

The next railway to espouse steel panelling in a major way was the LMS and it did so in two ways, the first of which, in 1926, was of more than usual significance. In that year the company introduced the 'all-steel' carriage, rather than the intermediate version adopted by the GWR and Southern. If truth be told, the LMS made rather more of a fuss about it than was perhaps justified, but it was innovatory in constructional terms if for no other reason than that it had no separate underframe.

The superstructure of the vehicle, which was carried on standard LMS bogies, was in the form of a steel box-girder (it was called a tubular girder at the time) whose bottom member was, in effect, the two solebars connected by the corrugated steel floor and whose upper component was formed from the cantrails, roof sticks and roof sheets. Also made of steel were the pressed channel pillars which connected roof and solebar and to which were riveted the body side plates, the whole forming a rigid structure which could withstand considerable compression stress. They were probably the strongest carriage bodies built for general service main-line use in Britain until the early 1950s.

To allow the solebars to take the complete buffing and drawgear stresses without the need for the trussing of a conventional separate underframe, the new LMS carriages had a box girder at each end of the frame which consisted of the customary rolled steel channel headstock and crossbar (which formed the buffing girder) connected at top and bottom by web plates and further reinforced by longitudinal angle members. Further crossbars between the solebars were calculated to carry all the floor loading and at the bogie centres a double channel bolster girder took care of vertical loading and brake stresses. It was claimed for them that the whole formed '...a reasonably light and very rigid body to resist all the stress occasioned by travelling at high speeds, and should be very much stronger than a composite wood body and steel underframe under collision conditions'.

The latter claim was tested, under rather dramatic live conditions, in an accident to the 'Royal Highlander' at Dinwoodie in 1928 when the leading 'All Steel' full brake was found to have absorbed much of the collision impact. This led to the LMS trying to adopt a blanket policy that these all-steel brakes should always be run at the head of principal trains. It was, needless to say, very much a forlorn hope — there were simply not enough of them to go round —

but there were many instances where these vehicles could indeed be marshalled at the head of the train.

The principal building of all-steel carriages took place in 1926-7 and all were built by outside contractors, the general consensus being that one reason for their introduction was so as to give tangible assistance to outside industry at a difficult time. Other than the full brakes already mentioned, the only other carriages were of the centre-aisle open type and were exclusively third class. Most were full thirds but some had brake ends and their overall style copied the by now quite typical LMS open carriages (see Chapter 4). The interiors generally followed conventional practice, being finished in wood, but a few were given steel interior seat frames and other details. And there the experiment more or less began and ended! A few years later, a handful of side-corridor brake firsts and brake thirds were built on the same principles, but the LMS clearly seems to have taken a somewhat ambivalent view of these vehicles. Though at the time of their introduction, the Chairman of Cammell Laird (one of the contracting firms), who was also an LMS director, is on record as having stated that the steel coach was here to stay, the LMS clearly thought otherwise and more or less abandoned the idea for more than 20 years.

It is tempting to speculate why this should have been the case, for as far as the types built were concerned, they were in no way inferior to the more conventional vehicles — they weighed no more and their far greater strength was, presumably, a plus factor. However, the railways were not in the habit of wrecking trains with gay abandon, and in any case the conventional separate steel underframe could stand quite a degree of strain. It therefore seems likely that the rarely encountered 'accident factor' would not count too highly when set against the undoubted fact that the LMS carriage workshops were by now geared up to manufacture conventional carriages on mass-production lines and the company always preferred to build its own stock wherever possible.

Thus the LMS eventually decided to follow the GWR and Southern and confine the use of steel to underframes, outer panelling and, of course, the traditional reinforcement of the carriage framing, especially the roof. This it began to do in 1929-30, and within three years the familiar Stanier-pattern flush-sided stock had begun to appear after a short interregnum of more conventionally styled steel-panelled carriages. Needless to say, both the 'All Steel' and the early steel-panelled carriages were all arrayed in the full panoply of the lined crimson livery, only slightly simplified in the earlier 1930s. Interestingly, it was not long after Stanier had assumed responsibility for LMS matters that he introduced a much simpler livery for carriages in 1934. One can perhaps read some of Stanier's old company influence in this move, for the LMS switched immediately to the new style just as had the GWR some seven years earlier and for much the same reasons. We are, however, by mentioning Stanier, moving a little ahead in the chronology for the moment.

Meantime, the LNER continued to produce the handsomely styled Gresley carriages for almost 20 years after the grouping, little changed in superficial outer appearance from those of the GNR. For reasons already stated, they were in fact rather stronger than their wooden bodies might have suggested, partly because teak itself is tough material but also by virtue of their buckeye couplers. The only really surprising fact is the long retention of the turnbuckle underframe, and it was not until 1930-31, largely as a consequence of the introduction of a longer 65-foot chassis, that the angle-trussed underframe became the LNER standard.

Like the LMS, the LNER also toyed with the idea of 'All Steel' carriages but, also like the LMS, their works were geared to the production of wooden-framed vehicles so the idea was not pursued to any significant extent. A few open thirds and full brakes were obtained from 'the trade' in 1927 which, like the LMS equivalent, were devoid of conventional underframes, but whereas the LMS bought hundreds, the LNER settled for but a few dozen all told. It seems that they were more expensive to pro-

cure than conventional carriages and, in the LNER case, there was also a slight weight penalty compared with the teak-bodied version. Their livery was a quite extraordinarily complex business for not only did they have full lining (as in the case of the LMS examples), but they were also given an elaborately 'grain-painted' finish to match the normal stock. This was amazingly convincing, but at what cost one wonders.

There can be little doubt that the lack of real enthusiasm for all-steel carriages by the two largest British companies was the prime reason why the idea did not take hold for fully a generation, even though when it did finally re-appear in BR days, slightly modified, the methods adopted for body construction were not dissimilar to those pioneered in the 1920s; but this development must wait its time for the moment. What is, perhaps, more surprising is that Gresley did not, in the 1930s, move in any significant degree to the by now customary British practice of steel panelling on wood frames. By the mid-1930s, economics were causing him to question the cost of teak panelling and some carriages were in fact built with steel panelling (fully 'grain-painted' of course), but teak panelling remained the norm until Thompson swept it into limbo for new building in and after 1944. Before this, however, and perhaps even more unusual, was the use by the LNER of plywood outer panelling on the distinctive green and cream 'Tourist' stock of the 1930s. This

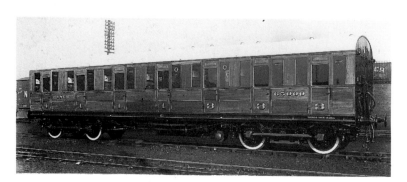

Left *An astonishingly realistic impression of grained teak was always achieved by the LNER painters on the small amount of conventional steel-clad stock which was built between the wars. This example is non-corridor composite No 65000, outshopped from Dukinfield in 1933. Though this is not an 'all-steel' carriage, the latter were treated in like manner* (LNER official, NRM).

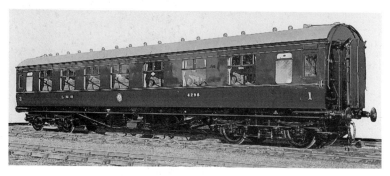

Left *Stanier-pattern corridor composite No 4298, built in 1939, clearly shows the extent to which the LMS had moved styling onwards during the 1930s. Note the suspended-pattern gangway and the welded bogie. The underframe is still, however, riveted* (BR LMR).

Figure 8 *This sectional drawing shows the essential differences between the traditional wooden framing and panelling of an early LMS sleeping car (upper elevation) and the later form of part welded steel and part wood framing of the Stanier sleeping cars (centre and below).*

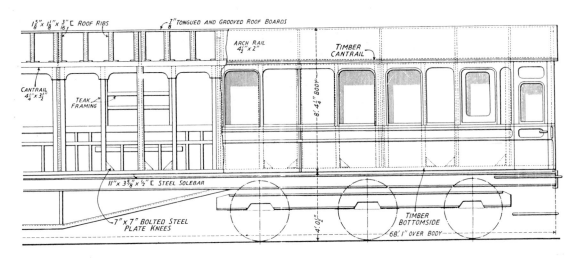

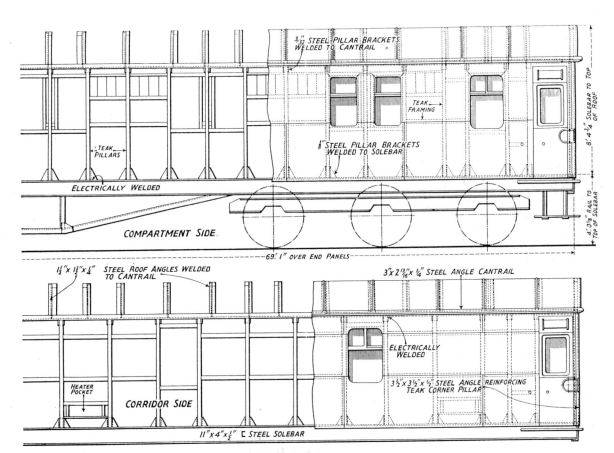

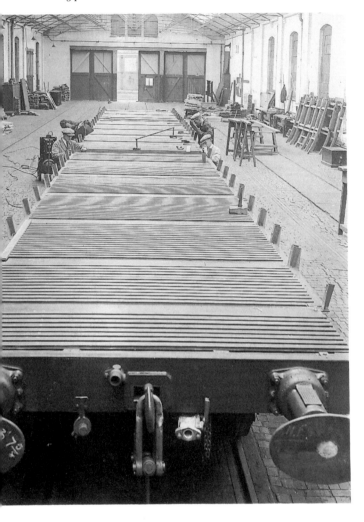

and these changes, when allied to the increasing elimination of capping strips between panel sections and the new simpler liveries, gave carriages far smoother exteriors and, in consequence, a more modern appearance. The modernity was, however, rarely more than skin deep and these slightly newer constructional ideas were rarely made the opportunity for innovative new design concepts for many years, as we shall see.

It was the LMS in the person of William Stanier which first began to marry new constructional methods with changed design ideas and here it is very tempting to draw parallels with his locomotive work on the LMS. He clearly brought the 'flush-clad' method with him from the GWR (which had started the business) and as with locomotives, took it further on his new company than did his old system. The GWR did not really take the design possibilities of flush-clad, steel-panelled carriages to a logical conclusion until late in the 1930s and it was not until after the war, with the new Hawksworth types, that GWR design caught up with that of its famous, but now LMS-employed son! In like manner, the Southern and LNER did not really adopt the flush-clad style in any major way until Bulleid and Thompson took over, well after the Second World War. The more detailed design implications of these changes will be considered later.

As for basic carriage technology itself, little else of consequence really changed in the constructional field and most things which did occur were merely in the form of slight adaptations of existing practice. Thus, for example, the GWR introduced a modified form for the British standard gangway housing in which the familiar lazy tongs (which allowed the moving part to extend from the fixed housing) gave way to a 'suspended' form of attachment at the top of the moving frame. Needless to say, Stanier took this idea to the LMS with him. Likewise, the main change in underframe construction, once all railways had moved to the angle-trussed form, was the gradual introduction of welded rather than riveted fixing from the mid-1930s. It never became exclusive, however, until BR days, even though the underframe was rendered far more rigid if the components were welded together.

An interesting use of welding, particularly on the LMS, was that which allowed the elimination of the bottom horizontal timber frame members for the carriage side. In this revised arrangement, steel 'pockets' were welded to the top of the underframe into which were directly fixed the vertical timber frame pieces, the underframe itself acting as the lower horizontal component. It saved a bit of weight and, possibly, a degree of rotting in the timber frame (the lower member was always the most vulnerable with steel panel-

was an undoubted economy move but was not entirely successful (see Chapter 4).

Perhaps the most visibly obvious changes, consequential upon the gradual supersession of wood by steel panelling over the years, were those of least importance in terms of fundamental carriage construction. Starting with the GWR *circa* 1930 and closely followed by the LMS in 1932-3, the now customary 'flush-clad' carriage made its first widespread appearance. In these vehicles, the only real change was the elimination of the familiar bolection mouldings round the fixed windows. In their place, the glazing was set in a concealed frame immediately behind the outer steel sheets and thus the glass was only the thickness of the outer sheeting behind the panel itself. The fixed lights were often given markedly rounded corners in association with this new form of treatment

Left and right *These three views show different aspects of the later LMS method of carriage body construction. In order: twelve-wheel underframe and floor with steel pockets welded to accept the timber framing uprights; part assembled frame showing composite wood and welded steel framing; and finally, the interior panel fixing. Note particularly the concealed wooden window frame behind the outer steel panelling in the latter view (LMS official, NRM; centre, BR LMR).*

Right *LMS six-wheel bogie of totally welded construction save for the components which need to be periodically replaced. Note, however, the retention of Mansell-pattern wood-centred wheels, probably one of the last examples of the use of this type on new stock (BR LMR).*

ling if for no other reason than that water gravitated downwards and tended to rest behind the panels above the lower frame itself) but the idea never became universal.

Bogies too remained largely unaltered in basic principle from that described in the previous volume. Welded frames sometimes replaced a riveted assembly, as with underframes, but the 'swing link plus bolster' allied to leaf spring primary suspension was always the norm in the company period. There were, it is true, various categories of bogie available, and the choice of which to use was largely determined by the size and weight of the vehicle carried on them, but this mostly affected such matters as spring strength or wheel journal and axlebox sizes. No one attempted to make any progressive step forward and, in strictly technological terms, the best of the bunch was still the Gresley 'double bolster' bogie adopted as standard by the LNER throughout its lifetime for all its best stock; but even the LNER had a single bolster version for the lesser fry — Gresley's more sophisticated type was somewhat more expensive to build! As an aside, in early BR days the more expensive Gresley bogie was still preferred to the newer BR type for some EMU stock.

In a sense, the latter statement gives a sort of clue as to why basic carriage technology did not change too much in the post-grouping period. For all that I have sometimes remarked on the generally conservative nature of *design* developments during this time,

Traditional upholstery with slightly brighter walls and ceilings in an 'all-steel' LMS open brake third of 1927. The overall effect is still fairly solidly pre-group in flavour (BR LMR).

these comments must be set against the fact that viewed *purely as a vehicle*, the British carriage was by no means backward in the pre-grouping era. If post-group technology seemed conservative at times, it was in part because earlier carriage builders had moved matters forward so much, especially when compared with most contemporary practice in other countries, save for the very best examples. In consequence, many of the technical ideas which developed in Britain during the first quarter of the century stood the test of time, not because the railways were unable or unwilling to change but more because there was no need to change. In a very real sense, this statement held true for maybe the first 10-15 years of the BR period too and there, for the moment, we must leave the technicalities of the vehicle itself. There will, of course, be need to come back to the matter from time to time.

Vehicle interiors

Turning now to the vehicle interior, yet again traditional methods remained the norm for by far the bulk of carriages as far as construction was concerned, the biggest changes to be observed being, as indeed they had always been, in response to the changing fashions of the day. Thus — and this had actually started well before the grouping — there was increasing use of simpler and much plainer wood finishes than in earlier days. The florid Victorian excesses had long gone, but even the more restrained and delicate Edwardian styles were in due course to give way to still less elaborate treatments. Much of this will be covered in later chapters, but in general terms the carriages of the 'twenties and 'thirties strove, not always successfully it must be admitted, to give a brighter and more airy appearance than hitherto and painted surfaces often replaced the heavier treatments such as Lincrusta and wood panelling.

This topic is, of course, at the interface between construction and design and it is a moot point whether it should be considered here rather than later. However, since new-style finishes were regularly applied to carriages whose layout was in every other respect thoroughly old-fashioned, it seems better to consider the subject at this point. In fact, though most railways seemed to attempt to move with the times only as far as was possible without seriously incommoding their traditional ways of doing things, their compromises often turned out rather better than might have been expected.

One factor which always militated against a truly avant-garde approach to railway carriage interior design (it still does by the way) is the sheer longevity of the vehicle itself. Forty years was a by no means abnormal life for a carriage and some lasted very much longer, during which time fashions may well

The restrained use of simple, if dark, wood surfaces with only modest detail in combination with plain upholstery material offers a relaxed if not especially avant-garde *environment in this GWR first class compartment of 1935 (GWR official, NRM).*

panelled style — became quite popular and increasing use was made of plywood which could carry many more varieties of decorative timber (applied in the form of veneer) as its visible layer than were afforded by the traditional solid oak, teak and mahogany of the older carriages. Thus, timber varieties increased rapidly and the LMS in particular made great play of its use of 'Selected Empire Timbers' in its new carriages. Veneered plywood could be worked just as easily, if not more so, than the traditional solid wood, but gave rather more scope for variety and quite a number of new-style surface patterns could be developed by butting together contrasting colours or grain patterns, relying on the texture of the timber surface itself rather than using elaborate mouldings or beading. This became particularly widespread during the 'Art Deco' period of the 1930s and, while not always successful, its better manifestations were of a very high order.

Upholstery, too, underwent changes but here recognition had to be made of the fact that patterned designs and darker colours were less likely to show dirt than plain cloth and lighter shades. The trouble with many of the newer patterns was that while the cloth itself was every bit as good as hitherto, the pattern repeats were often larger than before and since the railways liked to 'centre' the designs on seats and backs. there could be quite a lot of cutting to waste compared with a smaller pattern. Furthermore, a

This rather modish experimental Stanier interior from the mid-1930s shows a not entirely unsuccessful use of Art Deco-style materials. Note the care taken to position the large pattern repeats in exactly the same place on every seat unit (BR LMR).

have changed more than once. It was therefore customary for railways to play safe and adopt somewhat conservatively styled interiors which would not date too quickly nor cause undue offence to their many less fashion conscious customers. As has already been outlined in the previous volume, it was normal railway custom to use the very best materials anyway and these too would have a long life. Interior woodwork might well be expected to last the lifetime of a carriage while upholstery should be good for 15 or more years of even the most vigorous usage. But re-trimming with a newer-fashioned upholstery cloth could not really disguise an older style of basic interior treatment so there was a natural tendency for many otherwise perfectly serviceable and comfortable carriages to look old-fashioned in terms of decor.

It was really only in the realm of new vehicles that any more adventurous ideas began to appear and these mostly tended to be found in wall finishes and, to some extent, light fittings and upholstery cloth. The flush-finished wall — as opposed to the older large pattern size tends to make a carriage interior seem smaller, so those attempts to use the most popular 'jazz' patterns of the age were not always particularly successful. In general, the better solutions always seemed to be achieved with less strident designs and it became quite common to see small pattern repeats but devoid of the Victorian and Edwardian fussiness of actual design. Thus interiors gradually became simpler and less fussy, often augmented by much simpler picture or mirror frames or even, quite commonly, frameless mirrors.

In the realm of carriage lighting, electricity was, of course, the norm for new construction, and while many railways continued to use bare bulbs in plain holders (particularly in corridors and lavatories), there was increasing and widespread use of more modern lampshade designs, the geometric type being very popular during the 1930s and later. The better examples were often in the open carriages and some railways even went in for concealed cornice lighting in their open saloons giving them a rather 'Odeon'-style character in consequence, but by no means unpleasing in the better examples.

Much more use was made of painted surfaces inside the carriages than hitherto and this gave a much lighter appearance, while a particularly popular innovation from the 1920s onwards was the use of Rexine leathercloth as a finish. The SR actually tried this as an exterior carriage covering on one experimental vehicle, but apart from this and the rather special case of the LNER 'Silver Jubilee' train (see Chapter 11), Rexine was pre-eminently a useful interior material. The advantages were considerable. It cost little to maintain and could be kept clean by washing with soap and water. It was cheaper and quicker to apply to the surface (by glueing in position) and had good scratch-resistant quality. It was available in a considerable variety of patterns and,

not least because it could be applied quickly and by unskilled labour, was also cheaper to replace should a panel become either worn or damaged. Though the GWR and LMS used it to some extent, the Southern and the LNER were probably the major users, standardizing the material for window blinds and, in the case of the Southern, for the lining of door panels. The LNER used it in some of its sleeping cars and it became particularly widespread in buffet cars and other catering vehicles where its 'wipe-down' property was of considerable practical benefit.

Other areas where some slight moves forward were made were in floor coverings and window curtains (where present). Linoleum and carpet were the traditional floor materials and continued to be widespread — indeed, the carpet never lost favour in the better carriages — but rubber composition flooring was increasingly used, laid direct on to wood or steel, often applied in layers up to 1 inch thick and sometimes taken a few inches up the carriage side in the form of a coved skirting to facilitate cleaning. As with upholstery, the patterns used for carpets and curtains were gradually simplified and the better results were achieved with the less 'loud' designs.

In most other respects, little really changed. Carriage ventilation and heating still followed traditional custom and the openable window remained a British favourite throughout the 'Big Four' period. Quite a bit was said in the contemporary technical press about the virtues of full air-conditioning, but it did not happen for the ordinary passenger. The nearest approach was a sort of pressure heating and ventila-

Traditional LNER, and none the worse for that: only the angle-trussed underframe reveals that LNER corridor third brake No 52221 was built in the 1930s (1934 to be exact). Its handsome Gresley-styled body form goes back to the pre-1914 GNR (LNER official, NRM).

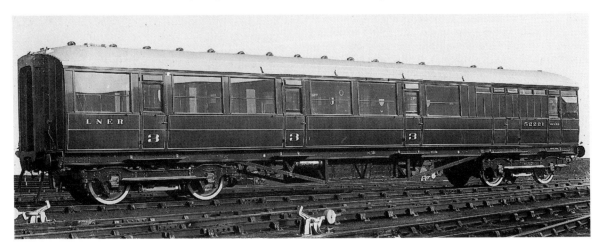

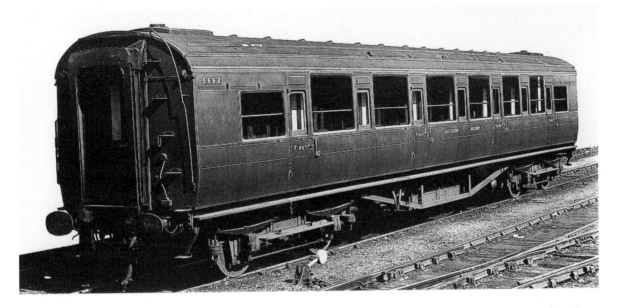

Neat but conservative: a characteristic Maunsell SR exterior of the 1930s, in this case a corridor composite No 5662 from the 1932 series with 'tall' corridor-side windows (SR official, NRM).

tion system adopted in some sleeping cars. Those carriages which did display larger windows — regrettably rather fewer than perhaps should have been the case — eventually mostly settled down to having the top quarter or so fitted with one or two of the familiar sliding elements, but far too many long-distance carriages retained a full array of outside doors to the compartments which prevented more widespread use of larger 'picture' windows; and these doors, of course, always carried the obligatory drop light.

It was mostly these latter features which caused many British carriages to seem obstinately conservative; but conservative or no, the end result was almost always a high-quality product. The 'soft third class' was still very much a British speciality compared with overseas, and as the years progressed the already high standard of accommodation for the average traveller continued to improve. If it had a weakness, it was the lack of much design innovation, most noticeably in the field of interior layout. Some, of course, would argue that this was no bad thing anyway on the basis that if traditional layouts were popular, why change them? The next two chapters take a much closer look at this particular aspect, but by way of concluding this technical overview, a few words on building costs and carriage maintenance will not come amiss.

Building and maintenance costs

Carriages were a major part of railway capital expenditure and, as the next few chapters will reveal, some 27,000 locomotive-hauled coaches were built to company designs over a period of some 30 years. If to these are added the various self-propelled and other vehicles, something like 1,000 new vehicles per year were added to stock between 1923 and 1953, even discounting non-passenger-carrying vehicles. This was probably three times the number of locomotives built during the same time and undoubtedly totalled more actual cash expenditure than did the locomotives which hauled them. Yet it is one of the more surprising features of recorded railway history that little mention is made of the actual costs incurred. Furthermore, not too much detailed contemporary evidence seems to have survived. However, enough does exist to allow a few points to be made.

At this point in time, the ravages of half a century of inflation make the actual number of pounds sterling seem trivial indeed, but, even allowing for this fact, the railway carriage was by no means an expensive item to procure. Some of the detailed figures for the LNER and the SR have survived to reach the NRM records and these show the following actual values:

a) Southern Railway eight-compartment corridor third, 1924-5:

Material:	£1,568 12s 10d (£1,568.64)
Wages etc:	£630 16s 2d (£630.81)
Oncost and Supervision:	£301 19s 2d (£301.96)
Total	£2,501 8s 2d (£2,501.41)

b) LNER five compartment corridor brake third, 1929-30:

Material:	£1,606 13s 8d (£1,606.68)
Wages:	£539 17s 9d (£539.89)
Workshop expenses:	£153 17s 4d (£153.87)
Total	£2,299 18s 9d (£2,299.94)

Though the basis of comparison is not quite the same, there was negligible inflation during the 1920s and 1930s (amazingly, there was actually deflation during some years!) so the figures are broadly the same. However, low though these values are by present-day standards, I still cannot resist making the point that the cost of applying the full varnished teak LNER livery (including all materials and lining out) came to no more than £101 13s 4d (£101.67); which has to be a bargain compared with current NRM restoration costs!

Exact equivalences are not known for the LMS save that when the 1937 'Coronation Scot' sets were built (see Chapter 11), the company reckoned that the average cost for a new corridor vehicle was some £2-2,500. So the LMS may have been reaping benefit from its more modern mass-production methods. Comparable GWR figures do not seem to have survived. However, such figures as have been published for the pre-1914-18 war period suggest that a turn of the century non-corridor came in at about £1,000 and that a 'Dreadnought' sleeping car of 1907 cost over £3,000. The latter type of vehicles were always more expensive on all railways, and there was some quite considerable inflation during the First World War, but since it is known that LNER sleeping and dining cars were only costing about £4,000 in the inter-war years, maybe the GWR vehicles remained a little above the rest.

But in all conscience there can have been little in it between all the companies, and an average figure of some £2,500 per carriage (less for non-corridors, more for special stock) would seem about right. The overall carriage investment in new stock by the 'Big Four' must therefore have been in the order of £75,000,000 over the period — a not inconsiderable sum which probably needs multiplying fortyfold to give a comparable modern figure (BR MkIII stock was quoted at some £100,000 per unit in the early 1980s). To put this into further relevant perspective, brand new LMS Stanier Class '5' 4-6-0s were costing about £6,000 each before the war.

Even allowing for the imprecision of these figures,

their size relative to other aspects of railway expenditure meant that maintenance costs loomed high, and here the SR and LMS seem to have benefited from their 'progressive' system of carriage repairs. Full data is not available, but Table 1 has been compiled from the official Railway Clearing House returns for the last ten years of the company period and the SR performance during the war years can be seen to be quite outstanding, all the more so since it probably bore the brunt of air raid damage. The LMS only got into difficulties towards the end of the period but the poor old GWR had almost a quarter of its stock awaiting repair in 1947[1] and the LNER was little better. Yet all had started from broadly comparable situations in 1938. Though I cannot prove it, this situation may even have had some bearing on the fact that the subsequent BR standard carriages drew more heavily on SR and LMS practice than the rest.

It can therefore be appreciated that however the figures be interpreted, the provisioning and maintenance of carriage stock was a vital and at times costly element in the last years of the private railways of Great Britain as they strove to keep pace with the ever-increasing volume of competition from alternative modes of transport. It is to their credit that the companies did not stint in their efforts, even though at times they may have seemed a little old-fashioned. So, having set the background, we can now take a longer look at what they actually built.

Table 1   Coaches under/awaiting repair 1938-1947 (% of operating stock)

Company	1938	1941	1944	1947
GWR	5.8	7.1	12.8	23.5[1]
LNER	6.4	6.4	9.0	18.5
LMS	6.5	5.0	7.7	9.2
SR	5.3	6.4	5.8	6.4
Great Britain (total)	6.2	5.9	8.5	13.4

Worst Years (%)	Best Years (%)
GWR (23.5%) 1947	GWR (5.8%) 1938
LNER (20.1%) 1946	LNER (5.4%) 1939
LMS (9.2%) 1947	LMS (5.0%) 1941
SR (7.4%) 1946	SR (4.4%) 1940

[1] This figure was probably inflated by the aftermath of a long strike at Swindon Carriage Works in 1946.

3. Design tradition dies hard

In this and the next chapter we turn to the design of the many general service carriages built during the 'Big Four' company period. However, since developments did not take place simultaneously on all four lines, there is some degree of chronological overlap between the two chapters. In general, this chapter tackles the traditional approaches, and the next the more modern ideas. In this context, 'modern' should not be taken to mean the flush-sided form of construction. Many of the latter vehicles were thoroughly old-fashioned in concept and it is with conceptual ideas that we are principally concerned here.

Before analysing the carriages, however, it is useful to know the scale against which the carriage building efforts of the old companies should be measured, and Table 2 attempts to show this. From this it can be seen that the 48,000 or more pre-group carriages inherited by the 'Big Four' were reduced in total by well over 8,000 during the 25 years in question, yet the number of seats actually provided was maintained at broadly the same level until the war years and only slightly reduced thereafter. Some of this may even have been due to war damage or have arisen in consequence of the 'Is your journey really necessary?' campaign. This changeover was entirely the consequence of much new building and although it is not possible to give absolutely precise figures (statistical sources do not always quite correspond), by the time that purely company designs stopped building (*circa* 1953-4), over 27,000 new locomotive-hauled coaches had been built and well over 70 per cent of the inherited pre-group fleet had been replaced. Of the new vehicles, some two thirds were gangwayed, the rest being of the non-corridor variety, and it is with these that we start the review.

Non-gangwayed carriages

Throughout the 'Big Four' period, the non-gang-wayed carriage continued to be built in quantity, though it eventually yielded its numerical superiority over all others. Most of them were of the traditional compartment style with individual side doors and although many new examples were built, their totals were swelled considerably by the many thousands of similar vehicles which had been inherited from the pre-group companies. The latter were often of high quality and a fair proportion served right through to BR days. The new construction is tabulated, as far as available statistics make possible, in Table 3. It came, of course, from only three of the four companies, the Southern, for reasons already given, finding it unnecessary to build new non-gangwayed stock for locomotive-hauled shorter-distance services. To get a fully balanced picture, one should not forget the 'New Build' EMU stock (Chapter 6) which, on the Southern, took the place of the new locomotive-hauled non-corridors of the other lines.

Meantime, the other three carried on much as their constituents had done before and it is a moot point which of them deserves the 'booby prize' for being the least enterprising! In truth, of course, the old-fashioned non-lavatory compartment coach was slowly going out of fashion for most purposes; but it was still one of the best means of moving large numbers of people and getting them on and off the train quickly, so it tended to have no real competition in the suburban and/or short-distance mode. In consequence, the railways tended to go on churning them out much as before but they were increasingly confined to the short-haul mode as years went by. Most of them were like-for-like replacements (in kind if not in size) of earlier four-wheel and six-wheel carriages, usually on the basis of *seats provided* rather than numbers of vehicles. Thus a typical 9-foot wide eight- or nine-compartment third, seating 96 or 108, would probably replace two former five-compartment six-wheelers of narrower width, each seating 50 people.

Table 2 Passenger carriage totals 1923-1947 (including both hauled and multiple-unit stock)

Note These figures are abstracted from official returns to the Board of Trade.

Company	1923			1930			1937			1947		
	Total carriages	Seats (1000s)	Seats per carriage	Total carriages	Seats (1000s)	Seats per carriage	Total carriages	Seats (1000s)	Seats per carriage	Total carriages	Seats (1000s)	Seats per carriage
LMS	19663	1018	51.8	19536	1121	57.4	17409	1057	60.7	16354	1002	61.3
LNER	14314	721	50.3	13620	732	53.7	12430	681	54.8	11567	648	56.0
SR	7469	401	53.7	7089	411	58.0	6682	404	60.5	6318	408	64.6
GWR	6768	350	51.7	6768	371	54.8	6248	362	57.9	5791	340	58.7
Totals	48214	2490	51.6	47013	2635	56.0	42769	2504	58.5	40030	2398	59.9

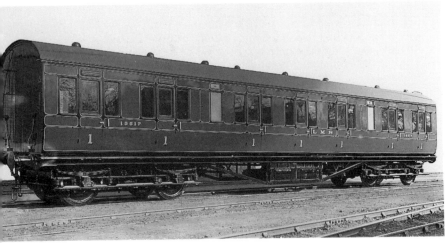

This rather good-looking non-corridor lavatory first, No 15517 of 1927, not only represents the first LMS standard style of wood-panelled and beaded body but was almost certainly the best designed non-corridor carriage type ever built by that company. Even so, three out of seven compartments were denied access to the toilet (BR LMR).

The 57-foot nine-compartment composite No 3096 was the LMS norm in the non-corridor, non-lavatory field from 1923 until the early 1950s. This is a 1931-built example from the initial steel-panelled period, ie with retained window bolection mouldings rather than flush-fitting quarterlights (LMS official, NRM).

Stanier-pattern LMS 57-foot non-corridor third brake No 20609 was one of the very first flush-panelled examples, dating from 1933, and still carried the fully lined livery abandoned a year or so later (BR LMR).

Right *Third class compartment interior of LMS pattern composite No 16751 built by BR in 1949 was in all essentials indistinguishable from its predecessors of a generation earlier (BR LMR).*

Table 3 Non-corridor locomotive stock — new build: 1923-54

Note: These values have been extracted from various published works and may contain occasional discrepancies from other sources in the units column. Overall, they represent within 1 per cent of the precise totals and serve adequately for comparative purposes.

Company	Carriage type[1]									
	FL	CL	TL	BTL	F	C	T	BC	BT	Total
LMS	30	200	—	273	132	936	1616	—	1356	4543
LNER	—	310	81	—	132	347	1156	85	898	3009
GWR	—	—	—	—	10	313[2]	542	330[3]	495	1690
Totals	30	510	81	273	274	1596	3314	415	2749	9242

1 Carriage types are identified by standard BR codes (see page 288). Those built as second class are considered 'third' for the purpose of this summary. Each unit of an articulated set counts as one carriage.
2 Of which 80 were built in 1953 for the LMR and numbered in the ex-LMS series.
3 Of which, all but circa 60 vehicles were built as two-coach 'B-sets'.

In strictly design terms — and in marked contrast to its long-distance achievements — the LMS probably held the palm for sheer stagnation of thought. It established its 57-foot standard non-corridor carriage designs in 1923 and proceeded to produce them in vast quantities for the rest of its life. By far the majority consisted of but three types: nine-compartment thirds and composites (6T + 3F) and six-compartment brake thirds. There were a few eight-compartment full firsts for good measure, plus a few non-standard layouts for the North London line which incorporated second class as well, most of which latter types appeared within the first ten years after grouping. All these carriages were handsome enough from the outside, especially when fully lined, but internally nothing of significance changed for almost 30 years until the last of them appeared in the early 1950s under BR auspices. From 1923 to 1930 they were wooden-bodied with full beading and full lining; 1931-2 saw a change to outer steel panelling (still fully lined out) and from 1933 onwards came the flush-sided 'Stanier' versions, mostly with the simplified 1934 livery. However, throughout the whole period the interior layout or amenities scarce altered; in part, no doubt, this was the inevitable economic consequence of mass-production.

Amongst the vast horde of non-lavatory stock, the LMS also had one last fling at the now largely outmoded non-corridor lavatory style, most of whose sundry ramifications were well covered in the last volume. There were some full firsts, by far and away the best non-corridors ever built by the LMS, but most were brake thirds or composites and these too were quite agreeable withal. They were mostly formed into 'Inter-District lavatory sets' — at least in theory — but if truth be told, none of them were anything like as generous in their lavatory provisioning as the best of the pre-group offerings of the same type. One still had to be something of a detective to be sure of getting access to a lavatory. None was built after 1930.

Added to this 57-foot proliferation, there was a somewhat smaller number of 54-foot equivalents, differing mainly in their slightly more cramped compartment sizes which, even so, were rather better than those of the LNER. Although some went into general service, the majority were set to work on the Tilbury line in set formations where their marginally shorter length allowed, or so it is said, one extra coach per train to be provided for this busy route. Included amongst them was a quite absurd lavatory composite which, in an otherwise toilet-less eleven-coach formation, allowed but one first and one third class compartment a modicum of creature comfort! When somewhat similar five-coach sets of 'short' stock were built with steel panelling for the Cathcart Circle route

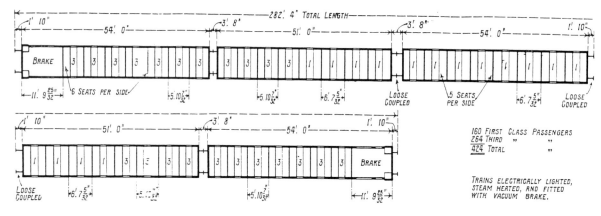

in Glasgow in 1926, the lavatories were left out, the composites in consequence being reduced to a 51-foot length. The LMS claimed great things for these Glasgow area carriages but they had five-per-side firsts without armrests and a contemporary account unconsciously revealed something closer to the real truth:

> 'The interior furnishing of the compartments has been designed with a view to providing the greatest possible comfort for the passengers, and to facilitate cleaning by the eliminating of carved and decorated surfaces, which collect dust. The ceiling is formed of three-ply, finished in glossy white enamel, which surface acts as a reflector for the lights.'

In other words, they were utilitarian...and you can bet that the lights were reduced in number in consequence of the glossy ceilings!

This apart, just about the only other development of interest in the LMS non-corridor field was a half-

Figure 9 Simplified floor plans of the spartan LMS Cathcart Circle non-corridor stock of 1926.

hearted attempt at articulation in 1937. Eleven triplet sets were made, none of the operating divisions were wildly enthusiastic about them and they were never repeated; but mention of articulated carriages brings us naturally to their prime exponent, Gresley's LNER.

The LNER was simultaneously better and worse than the LMS in the short-distance field. While many quite reasonable conventional carriages were made (see below), much of the purely suburban effort was concentrated on the celebrated articulated stock designed by Gresley, and in this particular arena the LNER was disgracefully parsimonious with space. The origins and weight-saving advantages of this method of construction were discussed in Volume 1

LMS Stanier non-corridor articulated triplet of 1937, Nos 60003/4/5 in simplified LMS livery (BR LMR).

and for quite some time prior to 1923 articulation was also regularly seen as a convenient means of re-using serviceable bodies which had hitherto been carried on four or six wheels. As such it undoubtedly succeeded in giving a better ride quality and no doubt saved money too. New articulated stock, both long-distance and suburban, had also been made before the grouping, but it was only after 1922 that the LNER began to introduce new four-unit and five-unit sets (known as 'Quad-Arts' and 'Quin-Arts') in any real quantity.

From the outside they looked suitably '20th Century' (full elliptical roofs, etc) and the Gresley bogies no doubt improved the ride; they were also given the full works as far as the teak livery was concerned, but the compartment sizes were every bit as mean and cramped as their Howlden predecessors with far less good reason, and the firsts were actually smaller between partitions than most LMS non-corridor *thirds*. In fact, for all their uninspiring nature, LMS non-corridors (including even the parsimonious Cathcart Circle stock) gave a far more comfortable seat to both classes of passenger than ever did their LNER articulated suburban contemporaries. One really would have thought that having saved so much weight on bogies, the LNER could have offered a bit more space between partitions without serious penalty. Maybe platform length had something to do with it, but for nigh on 40 years they trundled commuters to and from King's Cross and Liverpool Street and many other places too. When they finally departed (well into BR days), they were mourned by very few

LNER (GE section) brake tri-composite 'Quad-art' unit No 159, built in 1929, dates from the period when three-class accommodation was still provided by the LNER, mainly for the benefit of season ticket holders at a time when third class season tickets were not issued (LNER official, NRM).

save for those who put nostalgia above creature comfort! One 'Quad-Art' set is privately preserved.

By contrast with these spartan-like offerings to the harassed commuters, the LNER's other non-corridors were considerably better and, in one case, of genuine quality. Unlike the LMS, which put its non-corridors on the same length chassis as most of its gangwayed stock, the LNER, for some reason, adopted a much shorter 51-foot length for most of its single unit non-gangwayed stock and also retained conventional side buffers and screw couplings for these vehicles. It also built a fair number of articulated 'twins' with much more generously proportioned compartments than the 'quads' and 'quins', and in this guise the articulated style continued in construction, to a limited extent, well into the steel-panelled era, the last examples appearing during the early 1940s.

In the single unit category, five out of the six theoretically possible types were built, the omitted style being a brake first; in fact, no post-group non-corridor brake firsts appeared from any company. LNER brake composites were also quite rare and confined to Scotland, but brake thirds came in considerable numbers and assorted compartment configurations between three and six. All had quite spacious compartments, generally *circa* 7 ft 3 in first and 6 ft 2 in third, with the composites even more generously dimensioned in both classes; there were also a few second class examples and odd batches of brake thirds and full thirds were built to slightly longer dimensions (54 ft and 56 ft respectively).

In addition to these non-lavatory types, the LNER also introduced some far more agreeable intermediate-distance non-gangwayed lavatory stock than almost anywhere else in Britain. To be more accurate it continued an existing idea, for several LNER constituents had done something similar (the GNR,

NER and NBR to note but three). The carriages mostly took the form of lavatory composites with half-length side corridors leading to a pair of centrally located lavatories, one for each class. All passengers could thus gain access to the toilet rather than 'second guess' the state of affairs as was usually the case on the LMS (if it provided lavatories at all). The basic idea was carried on during Thompson's time in office and after, many being built during the early BR era. There were also a few lavatory thirds, some of which had a sort of open-plan interior.

There seem to have been no hard and fast rules as to which services these better non-corridors should operate, but I have strong personal memories of an odd composite or two scattered amongst the mostly ex-NER non-lavatory stock which was the common carriage choice on many of the West Riding local trains of my youth. Some of them even had folding armrests in the thirds, if I recall aright, and they gave off a characteristic and not entirely disagreeable smell!

Turning now to the GWR, it too offered little of

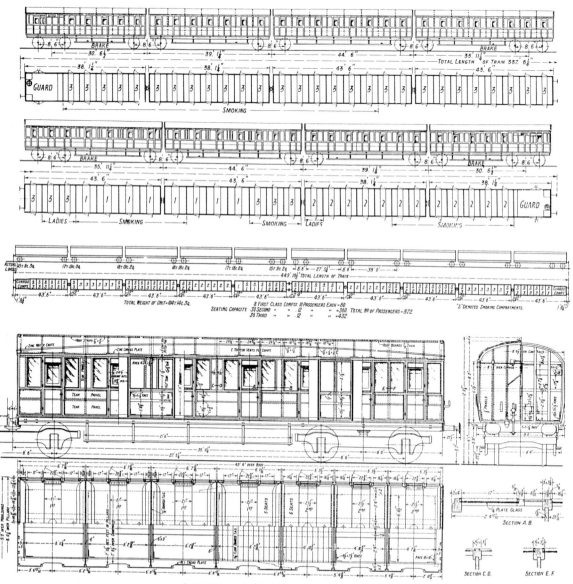

General Arrangement of First and Second Class Composite Coach.

Figure 10 *These drawings and plans of Gresley suburban articulated stock show, from top to bottom:*
a) *Simplified elevations and plans of a typical eight-coach train of 'Quad-arts' with short brake vans.*
b) *Sketch plans of a ten-coach 'Quin-art' train.*
c) *Detailed drawings of the outer (first/ second class composite) end of a 'Quin-art' set.*

Scale: $^1/_{10}''$ = 1ft

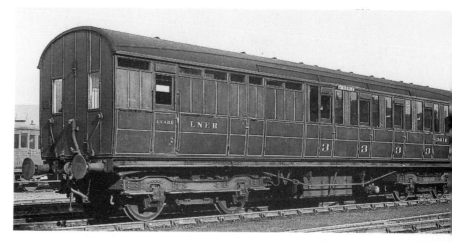

Top *Typical 51-foot five-compartment LNER non-corridor brake third No 3616 of 1925, seen operating in Scotland (Scot/ C Collection, NRM).*

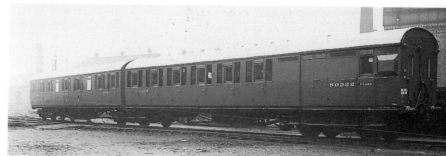

Right *Late period LNER articulated non-corridor twin brake third/lavatory composite No 80322/3 built in 1940 for King's Cross outer suburban use and carrying wartime utility brown livery. This set was steel-panelled, not teak, and anticipated many features of the post-war Thompson stock, but the rectangular-shaped lavatory windows reveal its Gresley origin (LNER official, NRM).*

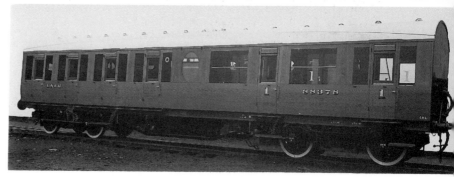

Above right and right *Typical LNER centre-lavatory non-corridor composites: Gresley pattern No 32454 of 1927 and a steel-panelled Thompson version, No 88378 from 1947. They were internally all but identical save for their opposite-handed layout, but the post-war example lasted little more than ten years, swept away by the DMU tide (LNER official, NRM).*

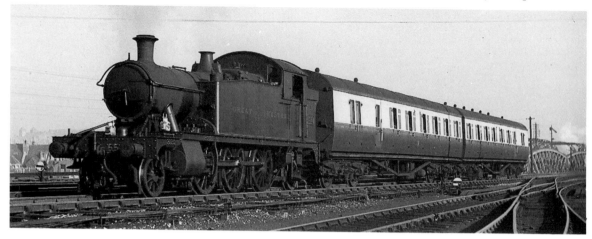

any truly innovatory nature in the non-corridor field, and in terms of conceptual dullness was worse than either of the two companies so far mentioned: it never offered lavatories in non-corridor stock. In part this was because many of its country districts were served by short branch lines where transit time hardly merited lavatories, and in those cases where distances were longer, 'hand-me-down' older corridor stock often sufficed. Furthermore, the GWR's country districts were increasingly to become the home of that characteristic feature, the auto-train (see Chapter 13).

To a considerable extent, the GWR had addressed the more purely suburban problem during the Dean and 'Toplight' eras, culminating in a number of quite substantially sized and up-to-date full elliptical roof vehicles, some of which were illustrated in the first volume. These older carriages had a long innings, many lasting well into BR days, and the bow-ended and subsequent eras saw little if anything better offered to the GWR commuters. In this respect it was no whit different from either the LMS or the LNER. Uninspiring examples came out during the whole of the inter-war period and their external styling merely followed the current contemporary fashion. But there, apart from two quite well-known exceptions, the matter started and finished.

If the GWR can be said to have made any form of distinctively unique non-corridor contribution in the 1923-39 period, it was its espousal of the two-coach 'B Set'. This was a pair of permanently close-coupled brake composites, utilizing a centre coupling, set brake ends outwards, usually with small van portions and each coach containing but *one* first class compartment. There were no lavatories, of course, and there was also some degree of indecision over the years as to where the solitary 'state apartment' should go. As new batches were built, it gradually migrated from the inner ends of the carriages (ie the centre of

GWR 'B Set' in operation behind 2-6-2T No 5540 circa 1936. This was one of the later sets with the first class compartment of each coach next but one to the luggage van. For a close-up of the centre coupling of a similar set, see page 28 (Soole Collection, NRM).

the formation) via an intermediate location to a final resting place next but one to the van. They were neat sets, much used on those routes, including many branch lines, where traffic exceeded the capacity of a single auto-coach, and since they did not require a specially adapted locomotive the latter could be gainfully occupied on other duties as well if opportunity allowed — which it regularly did in the more bucolic parts of the GWR empire!

Like the LMS, the GWR also dabbled with articulation in the non-corridor field and, like the LNER, it managed to produce some diabolical compartments in consequence. The carriages concerned were rather mean six-unit formations of which three sets were built in 1925, originally for through working on to the Metropolitan widened lines but which left the London area at the outbreak of the Second World War when through services between the GWR and London Transport were suspended. They were inelegant carriages and, again like the LMS examples of the genre, they led to nothing significant. In fact, only the LNER really made extensive use of this form of construction and even that line found, as years went by, that the articulated principle was only advantageous for universal use on inner suburban work where fixed sets could be virtually guaranteed not to need much alteration. Elsewhere, the need for operational flexibility made single unit stock far more useful as a general rule, albeit often in association with the articulated 'twins' already mentioned.

But if truth be told, when compared with their various efforts in the self-propelled field (see Chapters

8 and 9), none of the three companies which went on building locomotive-hauled non-corridor stock produced any conceptual 'leap forward' beyond those established in the pre-group period. There was, without doubt, no perceived need. The carriages did, however, carry prodigious numbers of customers in the heavily populated areas and should not be despised for their lack of enterprise. Most of them probably earned their keep several times over.

Corridor carriages

I have deliberately used the word 'corridor' rather than 'gangway' for this part of the story in order to concentrate attention on this specific type of carriage, leaving the 'open' and specialized stock for the time being, in the former case largely because it was part of the move to modernity (see Chapter 4). In this context, it is rather more helpful to summarize the building of new stock in a different way than for non-corridors, and in Table 4 I have isolated the 1923-43 'build' which forms the basis of the next part of the discussion. To get a truer balance of the long-distance carriage output of each company, the open stock built for general service during the same period

(mostly LMS and LNER) should be added to the totals (see Table 5, page 60). But regardless of this latter fact, the output of side-corridor stock during the inter-war years was formidable, some twice that achieved in the non-corridor field.

The reason for this rapid expansion seems clear: the side-corridor coach had only become the accepted long-distance norm during the generation or so preceding the grouping. In consequence, many services still remained in the hands of non-gangwayed stock; the companies were anxious to change this state of affairs and they did indeed do so. Perhaps it was because of this need for rapid change in fundamental carriage type and the fact that side-corridors were still (relatively) new, compared with railway carriages in general, that early post-grouping corridor coach developments seemed to move forward but little in pure design terms. In any case, many of the larger railways had entered the amalgamations with a fair number of more than reasonable and quite recently built 'state of the art' offerings, and the concept of the side-corridor carriage was, in the British context, a very sound one for reasons explained in the previous volume; so they may have felt little need to experiment further.

Table 4 Side-corridor stock — new build: 1923-43

Notes: 1. These values have been extracted from various published works and may contain occasional discrepancies from other sources in the units column. Overall, they represent within 1 per cent of the precise totals and serve adequately for comparative purposes.
2. Although built until 1943 in some cases, all carriages listed are to unmodified pre-war design. For post-war continuation, see Table 9, page 272.

Company Style	Carriage type[1]						
	FK	CK	TK	BFK	BCK	BTK	Totals
LMS/Non-standard (LNW type)[2]	—	—	5	—	—	8	13 ⎫
LMS/1923-32 standard	23	329	295	47	184[5]	239	1117 ⎬ 3182
LMS/1933-40 (Stanier)	41	501	611	12	93	794	2052 ⎭
LNER/Non-standard (NER type)	—	22	8	2	15	13	60 ⎫
LNER/Gresley (1923-33)[3]	41	110	291	6	58	235	741 ⎬ 2515
LNER/Gresley (1934-43)[3]	37	361	766	16	103	431	1714 ⎭
GWR/'Toplight'[2]	—	—	25	—	—	22	47 ⎫
GWR/'Bow-ended' period	6	297	648	6	94	269	1320 ⎬ 2402
GWR/1934-40 standard	30	178	493	—	137	197	1035 ⎭
SR/Non-standard[4]	67	46	76	13	5	67	274 ⎫ 1316
SR/1926-36 standard	68	173	405	2	120	274	1042 ⎭
Totals	313	2017	3623	104	809	2549	9415

1 Carriage types are identified by standard BR codes (see page 288). Those built as second class are considered 'third' for this summary. Each unit of an articulated set counts as one carriage.
2 Ex-First World War Ambulance coaches, not strictly 'new'.
3 Listed separately mainly to give quantitative comparisons with LMS and GWR figures during similar building period.
4 Includes SE&CR, LSWR and 'Kent Coast' designs — see Chapter 1.
5 Including 100 later (*circa* 1939) rebuilt with 'Stanier' outer panelling.

What is certain is that there was no contemporary feeling that any really fundamental change was necessary. Indeed, the first generation of post-group corridor stock, regardless of company, was often greeted in semi-eulogistic fashion by contemporary writers as though it was something radically new. The reality was somewhat different and, if truth be told, some of the descriptions do rather reveal this when read between the lines with the benefit of hindsight. Take, for example, the new 'Flying Scotsman' sets built for the LNER in 1924. The vehicles were handsome enough from the outside, of course, and the 'triplet' articulated diners (see Chapter 5) were mildly innovatory, but the *Railway Gazette* seems to have had some difficulty in finding evidence of any real improvement in the ordinary coaches (author's comments in [brackets]):

> 'The ordinary vehicles. . .correspond substantially with standard East Coast designs [hardly surprising], except that many detail improvements [all unspecified] are included, and advantage has been taken of all good features [again unspecified] . . . of the companies now included in the LNER . . . It is claimed [by whom?] that these new trains are the most comfortable and luxurious in the world for passengers paying ordinary fares.'

This last statement was palpable nonsense. Both the first class and third class compartments were *smaller* than the equivalent Midland offerings of more than a decade earlier and all compartments still had a full

The LNER was still building much 'all-door' corridor stock in the late 1930s. This is composite No 24359, ex-works from York in 1937. The thirds were now three per side, but note the retained first class half compartment in the centre (LNER official, NRM).

Figure 11 *Floor plans and carriage formations of the LNER 'Flying Scotsman' set of 1924 and the Leeds–Glasgow set of 1931.*

set of outside doors on the compartment side. The LNWR (as early as 1907-8) had suppressed these features on its celebrated '2pm' twelve wheelers with larger compartments to boot; the GWR had done it even earlier with its 'Dreadnoughts' and the NER had even produced 'doorless' compartments in the thoroughly modern idiom, ie with large picture windows. The fact was, of course, that individual outside doors were mostly still considered necessary, though whether this desire was felt by the passengers or the railway administrators is hard to determine at this point in time. Either way, it served little useful purpose, but tradition died hard. True, the LNER only claimed six seats per compartment in the third class parts of the 'Scotsman' set, but the carriages lacked the necessary armrests to ensure that this principle held good; one doubts not that eight per compartment (the pre-group norm in a 9-foot wide carriage) were often carried.

A year or so later, the 'Hook Continental' was similarly re-equipped, this time first and second class only (it was a boat train), but the second class seems to have been scarce distinguishable from the thirds of the 'Scotsman' set, at least in terms of seat density or compartment size. And when, as late as 1931, a new Leeds-Glasgow set was proudly announced as embodying the latest LNER practice, all was revealed when the third class was quoted officially as having eight seats per compartment, still with outside doors!

All of which may seem rather unfair to the LNER, but the LMS was no better in the early 1920s. It too put a full set of outside doors on all its corridor coach compartments, though the latter were usually a frac-

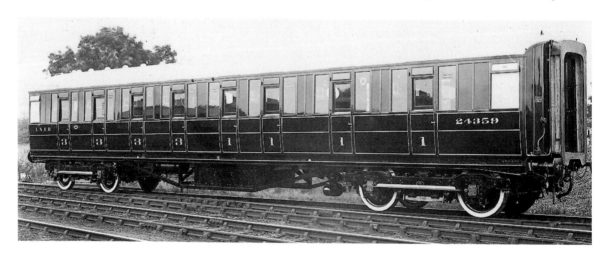

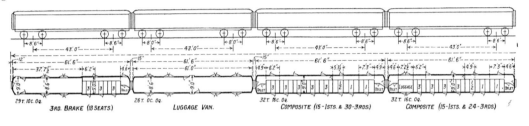

3RD. BRAKE (18 SEATS.)   LUGGAGE VAN.   COMPOSITE (15-1STS. & 30-3RDS.)   COMPOSITE (15-1STS. & 24-3RDS.)

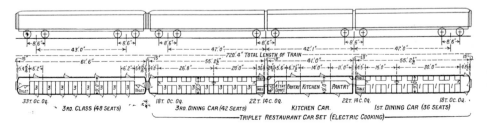

3RD. CLASS (48 SEATS)   3RD. DINING CAR (42 SEATS)   KITCHEN CAR.   1ST. DINING CAR (36 SEATS)

TRIPLET RESTAURANT CAR SET (ELECTRIC COOKING)

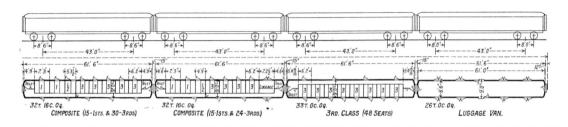

COMPOSITE (15-1STS. & 30-3RDS.)   COMPOSITE (15-1STS. & 24-3RDS.)   3RD. CLASS (48 SEATS)   LUGGAGE VAN.

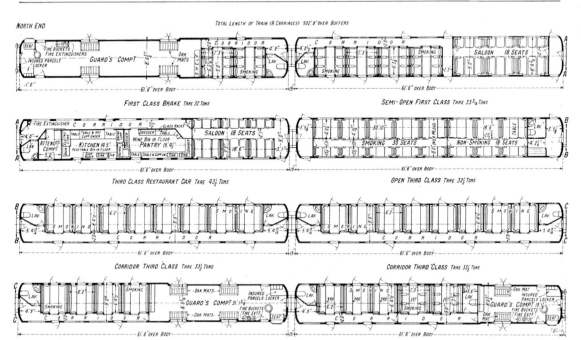

NORTH END   Total Length of Train (8 Carriages) 502'9" over Buffers

FIRST CLASS BRAKE TARE 32 TONS   SEMI-OPEN FIRST CLASS TARE 33¾ TONS

THIRD CLASS RESTAURANT CAR TARE 43½ TONS   OPEN THIRD CLASS TARE 32½ TONS

CORRIDOR THIRD CLASS TARE 33½ TONS   CORRIDOR THIRD CLASS TARE 33½ TONS

THIRD CLASS BRAKE TARE 32 TONS   COMPOSITE BRAKE TARE 33½ TONS   SOUTH END

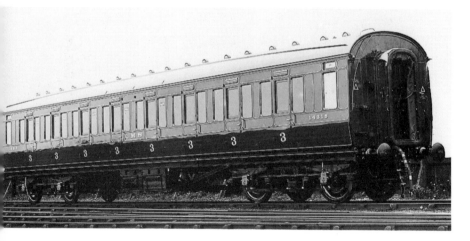

Neat but unimaginative: 'all-door' corridor third No 14318 of 1928 was to be one of the last batch of such vehicles to be turned out by the LMS. A year later, no new corridor coaches from this company had individual outer doors (BR LMR).

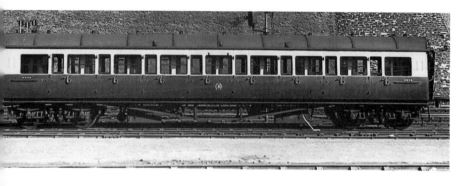

Left and below left *Not much change was seen in GWR main-line stock for many years after the grouping as may be seen by comparing the corridor side of bow-ended corridor third No 4840 of 1926 and brake composite No 6909 of 1934. There is some simplification in the later example but both had a full set of outer doors on the other side (Soole Collection and GWR official, NRM).*

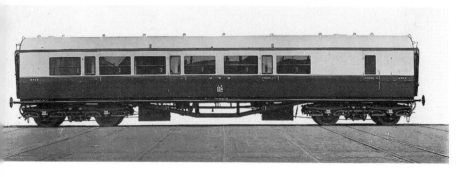

Figure 12 *Detailed drawings and full train plan of the GWR 70-foot bow-ended set of 1923.*

Scale: 3mm = 1 ft (main drawing)

tion larger between partitions than those of the LNER; but its vehicles were shorter and did not have the more up-to-date buckeye couplers and Pullman gangways of the LNER equivalent. Neither, in fact, could claim seriously that they had made any great improvement over their pre-group antecedents in the early days. Perhaps they were taking stock after the great amalgamations, who knows?

No such excuse could, however, be offered for the GWR. Having established a degree of pre-group modernity by introducing steel panelling, it ground

to a conceptual halt for a decade or more. The actual beginning was in 1922 when the 'Toplight' era was succeeded by the so-called 'Bow-ended' period, whose self-descriptive nomenclature needs no real amplification: some of them had curved carriage ends on plan which, with their reversion to the famous GWR 'chocolate and cream' livery after a decade or more of all-over crimson lake, just about says all! A definitive account of this period states: '...the first new post-war coaches to be painted in the reintroduced brown and cream livery... preceded a period of con-

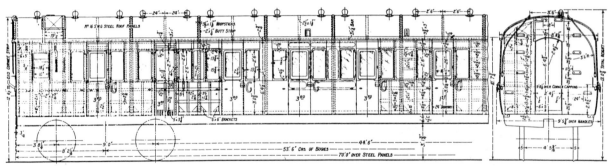

Compartment Side, 70-ft. Composite Carriage.

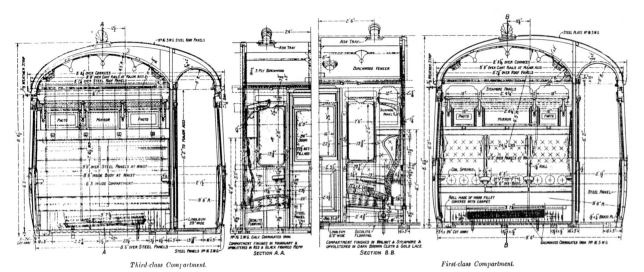

Third-class Compartment.   First-class Compartment.

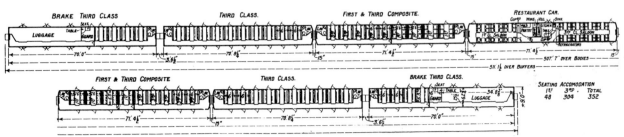

servative design with little inspiration'.*

Now, not unnaturally, contemporary accounts were somewhat less scathing, but let us examine the facts. The first examples marked the last GWR essay at the 70-foot length and some of them even had buckeye couplers. So far so good, but they did not copy the LNER pattern, having hinged 'drop-down' buffers rather than the quasi-standard pull-out type (see

* *Great Western Coaches, 1890-1954*: M.Harris, David and Charles, 1966/72

Volume 1 page 28); their Pullman pattern gangways were not compatible with the LNER type and not all coaches were so fitted anyway, the outer ends having conventional screw couplings, British Standard gangways and *flat* ends! All told it was a curious mishmash of indecision, and to claim, as did the contemporary *Railway Engineer*, that: '. . .it would, we think, be difficult to plan, within the available loading gauge dimensions, a more roomy and well-appointed set of coaches of the corridor compartment type', was arrant rubbish; others had already done it, years earlier!

Typical GWR four-per-side third class seating and sombre wood finish in brake composite No 6909 (see previous view) (GWR official, NRM).

To be fair, the first class was generously dimensioned at 7 ft 6 in between partitions and the carriages looked handsomely distinguished in the reintroduced and fully lined two-tone livery, but the thirds were a bit parsimonious at 6 ft and four-per-side seating, while there was still the matter of outside doors to all compartments. They were put into service on the South Wales and Birmingham/Birkenhead routes, after which time the GWR reverted to a standard 57-foot length from 1923-29. They were simply shortened versions of the 70-foot bow-enders and back came the screw couplings and British Standard gangways, many earlier ones with flat ends to boot. In fact, in all essentials they were indistinguishable in amenity from the earlier 'Toplights', but like most things GW, they were built to last and survived well into BR days.

Much the same continued to be true during the whole of the bow-ended era, and even the much vaunted 'Cornish Riviera' stock of 1929 was no quantum improvement, save for a welcome increase in third class compartment size to some 6 ft 4½ in (6 ft

8 in in the composites); but they still had a full array of outside doors and no armrests. Indeed, I still recall the surprise when, in 1950 (my first venture down the former GWR main line to South Wales), I found myself in a four-per-side third with compartment door and no armrests; the old LMS and LNER lines had long abandoned this sort of thing by then — at least on their longer distance services!

During this at best rather debilitating period, the GWR (inevitably?) had to have a go at articulation (during 1925), making quite a fuss about it in the process. However, the various individual components rarely exceeded a 50 ft 6 in length — the GWR never really showed the flair of Gresley's LNER in this respect — and as far as the passenger was concerned, compartment size and amenity showed no real improvement over the 70-foot and 57-foot standard single unit carriages. The idea never really caught on and they were subsequently rebuilt (being lengthened in the process) to conventional single unit carriages. As such, two of the open third class dining carriages survive in the National Railway Museum collection.

It was all rather sad for such a distinguished company — and the new, so-called 'Modern' livery of 1927 fooled no one at the fundamental level. However, by 1929 the GWR showed that it could do better if wanted when it introduced a slight modification in the form of a modest increase in length to 60 ft, a rather wider carriage profile which gave a bit more space in the thirds (still four-per-side and 'all-door', however) and a more flush-sided form of panelling. Moreover, in the form of its quite magnificent Special and Super Saloons of 1929-31, the GWR also revealed a hitherto unsuspected ability to really 'go to town' if it so desired. We shall have cause to come back to these vehicles later in the book (Chapter 11) and the real tragedy is that the genuinely advanced ideas which they embodied were not transferred across to the more orthodox side-corridor field. Even the later and generally far better 1935-40 stock (page 80) was uninspiring by comparison.

The Southern Railway, meanwhile, gradually moved itself into a position of more or less full compatability with its more traditionally 'corridor'-orientated contemporaries. Chapter 1 has outlined how Maunsell fairly speedily developed a new 'Southern' approach to the business from very limited beginnings, and by 1926 the first of the true SR 'standard' corridors had appeared. They were actually ordered in 1925 and at 59 ft long by 9 ft wide were, in contemporary terms, usually exceeded in size only by Gresley's LNER offerings. Like the LNER, the SR eventually opted for buckeye couplings and Pullman-type gangways, and, like the GWR, it went for steel panelling from the outset. Some were built

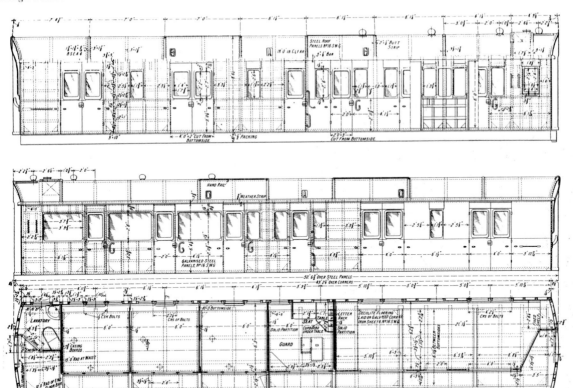

Corridor Brake Third-Class Carriage, G.W.R. Articulated Train.

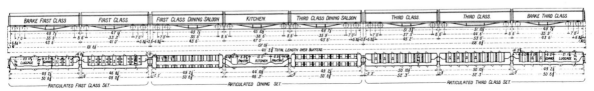

Formation and Leading Dimensions of G.W.R. Articulated Express Train.

Figure 13 *Typical carriage arrangement and full train plan of the 1925 GWR articulated trains.*

Scale: 3mm = 1 ft (main drawing)

The first SR standard corridor style: Maunsell brake third No 3226 of 1925 vintage, built as part of three-coach sets with two brake thirds and a full composite (SR official, NRM).

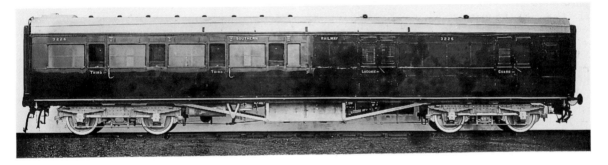

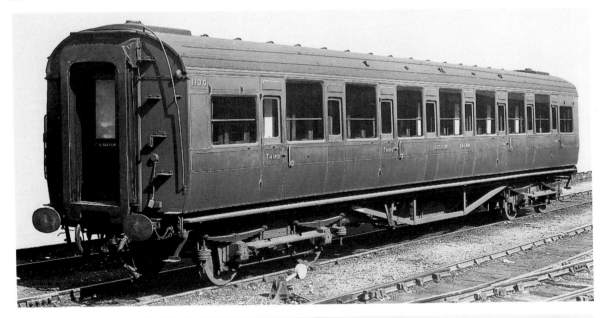

Top *The later Maunsell corridor style with 'tall' corridor windows is exemplified by full third No 1130 of 1930. Note the Pullman gangway and buckeye coupling of this very neatly conceived design (SR official, NRM).*

Above *The Southern's last pre-Bulleid corridors came out in 1935-6. This is brake composite No 6695, almost flush-sided but with a fair amount of visible riveting and still deploying a full set of compartment-side outer doors (SR official, NRM).*

to a narrower and more straight-sided 8 ft 6 in width in 1928 for the Kent Coast.

Loading gauge restrictions always bedevilled the Southern more than any of the other companies and this inevitably fought against true standardization on the LMS pattern; but regardless of width, Maunsell's first stock was every bit as good as most of the opposition, and when he slightly modernized the designs in 1929-30 by introducing full height corridor side windows, a quite distinctly handsome ensemble resulted. By now, there were also 8-foot wide vehi-

cles for the Hastings line to add to the two earlier width dimensions, and in the mid-1930s the Southern moved to a slightly more modern style with almost fully flush-clad carriages. There were not, however, too many in this latter category and the Southern built no more corridor stock after these 1935 orders (built in 1936) until the post-war Bulleid years. During not much more than ten years, however, the Southern had added over 1,000 new corridor coaches to its fleet and had completely revolutionized its longer-distance services in consequence.

The Southern's corridor carriages were mostly very orthodox and all of them had the seemingly inevitable outside doors to all compartments. But in this respect the company was little different from most of the rest. Yet there was an alternative, and by the mid-1930s one of the 'Big Four', the LMS, had already begun to go well down the road in the direction of more modern ideas in the long-distance carriage field.

If one looks in detail at Table 4, it is immediately obvious that some two-thirds of the LMS build of corridor stock in the pre-war period was to the so-called Stanier style, first introduced in 1932. These were the first carriages to be built in quantity which incorporated the sort of design ideas which we would now consider to be 'modern' in the sense that they can be seen as leading to the vehicles of our own time; but it is important to remember that for some years prior to their introduction, the LMS had also been the first company to break out of the interior design mould even while its carriages were otherwise still very much in the traditional exterior form.

The most numerous examples of this were, at first, in the 'open' carriage category, and the large-scale building of this type of vehicle was undoubtedly the reason why the number of new LMS side-corridor coaches were rather smaller than might otherwise have been expected during the pre-Stanier era. However, before analysing the reasons for and the consequences of these changes, it will be useful to conclude this part of the discussion by a further examination of the figures quoted in Table 4, in which I have deliberately isolated the corridor coach construction of the inter-war period, mainly to reveal the extent to which the LMS differed from its rivals.

If one counts only orthodox 'all-door' carriages, then the LMS total in the 1923-32 period is still further reduced, for only some two-thirds of the total listed (752 out of 1,117 to be precise) were in this configuration. The LMS move to new standards began, in fact, during 1927, and after 1930 it built no more side-corridor stock with outside compartment doors, in which respect it was almost alone for many years. As far as the GWR and SR were concerned, their corridor coaches were mostly or wholly of the 'all-door' kind until the late 1940s, and by far the bulk of those built by the LNER also followed the traditional style until the post-war years, though in fairness it must be pointed out that by the late 1930s the LNER and GWR had begun to make something of a move towards change.

None of which, of course, should be taken to imply criticism of the quality of vehicles built by those companies which remained faithful to the older design ideas. The overall quality of the British general service coach, regardless of company, was always high and there was little or nothing to choose between them when it came to quality of workmanship or robustness of construction. But some of them were more old-fashioned than others, and if one discounts the relatively small number of Gresley LNER corridor carriages built without compartment doors, along with the few examples of rather more specialized carriages built by all companies from time to time, then the fact remains that the LMS largely led the way for almost 20 years in terms of interior design as far as the long-distance general traveller was concerned. The next chapter takes a closer look at the causes, nature and implications of this situation.

4. New ideas emerge — but slowly

During the early part of 1925, accompanied by a suitable fanfare from modestly sized trumpets, the LMS announced the introduction of a 'New Type of Set Train' for an accelerated service between London and Bradford via the Midland line. It even went so far as to distribute external views of the train which at first glance seemed no different from many of its predecessors. It was headed by a Midland Compound 4-4-0 (LMS-built, of course!) and the front and rear carriages were seen to be former Midland clerestories, the like of which had not been built for a least half a generation. In fact, the chosen carriages dated from 1909; so what, precisely, was new?

Well, in the literal sense, nothing really, apart from the engine itself and the rest of the carriages. The LYR had built much the same sort of train well before the First World War, but for some reason, this LMS revival of the old LYR venture did catch on. Its so-called newness stemmed solely from the fact that it was wholly composed of open, centre-aisle stock, most of which was of the latest LMS standard pattern . . . and the Midland brakes? They were simply included because at this time the LMS had not yet introduced its own design of brake-ended open carriage and the Midland happened to have a few, which it regarded as 'Excursion' stock, by the way. In the event it turned out to be the forerunner of almost every InterCity express of our present day so it behoves us to look at it in a little detail.

The train plan is appended herewith (Figure 14) and is self-explanatory. Its stated aim was: '. . .to meet the needs of the considerable business travel between Bradford and Sheffield and London'. It was later

The so-called 'new' LMS train of 1925, though only the really clever could tell it apart from its Midland forbears, did in fact represent some genuinely fresh thinking (LMS official, NRM).

known as the 'Yorkshireman', but its schedule would rather surprise the modern-day business traveller on the same route, even if its interior layout might well seem rather familiar. It left Bradford at 9.10 am, arrived in London at 1.25 pm, '. . .thus allowing for a full afternoon's business in London. . .', and departed St Pancras at 4.55 pm. One can only conclude that in the 1920s, business must have been concluded rather more rapidly if 3½ hours represented a 'full' afternoon! Joking apart, however, it was the start of a new concept in long-distance travel and the LMS was the prime instigator; indeed, it was almost the sole protagonist in the main-line sense until late in the 1930s, when the LNER began to copy.

Open stock, as such, was nothing new — see Volume 1, Chapter 10, for a more detailed analysis of its origins — but apart from a few specifically dedicated cases, like that of the LYR above mentioned and, of course, dining purposes, most railways tended to regard the open saloon carriage as best suited for excursion and similar duties, perhaps on the basis that its internal layout was more friendly and sociable than the conventional corridor carriage. But even that was only partly true, for the railways also continued to make widespread use of compartment stock, both corridor and non-corridor, for much of their widespread excursion and holiday traffic. To find a more long-lasting reason for the LMS attempt to change emphasis, we need to look a little below the surface, and contemporary accounts of the pioneering Bradford train give a few clues.

The *Railway Gazette* of 1925 records, *inter alia*:

'. . .the new Bradford train includes six passenger coaches, arranged three each side of the kitchen car. . .All vehicles are of the central gangway type. . .and every seat in the train has table equipment. . .Obviously, in the ordinary way,

Plan of New Vestibuled Train with Kitchen Car for London-Bradford Services, L.M.S.R.
Seating Capacity: 234 Third-Class; 36 First-Class; Total 270. Total Weight of Train, 189 tons. Steam Heated and Electrically Lighted.

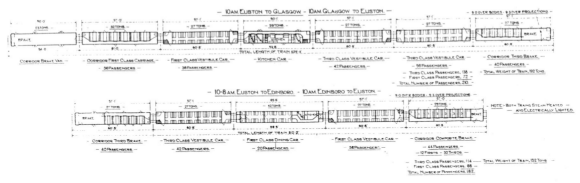

Figure 14 *Sketch plans of the LMS 'Bradford' set (above) and the morning Euston to Scotland train (below) of 1925.*

passengers taking lunch or dinner will be concentrated, as far as possible, in the vehicles immediately adjacent to the kitchen car, but if there is sufficient demand the kitchen car staff will be prepared to serve meals in any part of the train... Even if not required for meal purposes the tables will no doubt be appreciated very greatly by passengers, in that business men will be able to attend to correspondence, &c, while travelling...

'Another point of interest is that some, if not all, of the third class cars have practically the same seating and other dimensions as the first class cars, so that no inconvenience arises when two passengers (particularly if substantially built) are seated on the same side of a table, as it does in some third class dining cars, which may at times be somewhat uncomfortably crowded for this reason... notwithstanding the comfort of the seating accommodation and the high quality of the appointment and fittings of the train, no charge is incurred beyond the payment of ordinary fares.'

No doubt the magazine's correspondent was well looked after by his hosts, but even allowing some reservation for literary licence, there is a clear hint that the LMS was making a conscious attempt to produce an improved travelling environment for the long-distance ordinary traveller. The train was very heavily biased in favour of third class seats and would that the modern BR was prepared to serve meals 'in

any part of the train'! As a second (sorry, *standard*!) class passenger these days, it is almost impossible to find a full dining car service; such is the price of progress.

There were also some very practical issues. Open stock was rather cheaper to build, having less outer doors and inner partitions, and well-suited to Reid's new mass-production techniques. It also weighed slightly less, seat for seat, than corridor stock and thus, no doubt, suited the rapidly developing cost-conscious management approach of the new LMS; it is therefore no surprise that the very first carriages to be constructed on the mass-production principle were these new generation open saloons. They also, by way of bonus, gave marginally more comfortable seats in the 'two plus two' configuration than was offered by a four-per-side third class corridor compartment. Given these facts, it must have seemed sensible to the LMS to try and sell its new conceptual ideas in a positive way and this it proceeded to do.

On the same day as it introduced its Bradford service, the LMS did much the same sort of thing with its well-known 10.00 am train from Euston to Glasgow and Edinburgh. Once again it seems to have been anxious to get its new ideas into the public domain as soon as possible, for perusal of the train plan (Figure 14) reveals that the dining car of the Edinburgh section was of turn of the century LNWR vintage. This time, however, there was a mix of corridor and open stock, all of new LMS standard style, and it is interesting to speculate whether this was because of an absence of open saloon brakes or whether the company was deliberately offering a comparison to its patrons as part of the 'educational' process. At this time, the corridor coaches had doors to all compartments, of course, but it is also interesting to note the pair of 'two plus one' third class opens as opposed to only one 'two plus two' version. This was ostensibly to allow more seat space for dining but the LMS did encourage 'all the way' travel in this kind of vehicle and was by no means parsimonious in its provisioning as the years went by.

There was, however, undoubtedly a psychological barrier to overcome on the issue of compartment versus open stock as far as the passenger was concerned. The British like their privacy, the compartment provided it and events were to show that the LMS eventually built more corridor stock than open coaches. But the fact remains that during the early and mid-1920s, the company produced far more open carriages than side-corridors and one cannot help but feel that their weight-saving quality was paramount — this was the era of the Midland-inspired 'small engine and train' policy on the LMS, be it remembered, and much remained subservient to this basic philosophy for a few years. Be that as it may, within five years of the grouping, by far the bulk of the early standard open stock listed in Table 5 was in service and they were not all for excursion use, though many were employed in that mode.

The carriages themselves were rather traditional and very much in the Midland mode; in fact, the very

Figure 15 Elevations, plans and sections of the characteristic LMS-pattern open thirds and third brakes of the 1920s. These are in fact the 'all-steel' versions (see page 31) but the wooden-bodied stock was identically laid out. The upper set show the brake thirds from the Leeds Forge Co and the lower drawings are of a full third from the Metropolitan C & W series.

Scale: 4mm = 1ft

first of all the hundreds of open thirds was to a Midland design and the LMS standard version only differed significantly in the matter of outer door handles! Their most distinctive outer feature was the 'twin window per seating bay' which derived mostly from MR practice but was not, if truth be told, unknown on the LNWR lines. There was, needless to say, much use of dark polished walnut and blue cloth in the first class while mahogany with velvet or moquette served for the thirds. They were very well made and I can vouch for the high quality and durability of their interior finish, having been much involved in the restoration of those in the NRM collection. Only a few were first class or composite, the main thrust to a new style of accommodation being directed towards the third class traveller, and in 1926 the LMS-built wooden-bodied third class versions were supplemented by the several hundred 'all-steel'

Table 5 Open gangwayed stock — new build: 1923-39

Notes: 1. These values have been extracted from various published works and may contain occasional discrepancies from other sources in the units column. Overall, they represent within 1 per cent of precise totals and serve adequately for comparative purposes.
2. The tables include all non-kitchen vehicles built for dining purposes.

Company/Style	Carriage type[1]						
	FO	CO	TO	BFO	BCO	BTO	Totals
LMS/1923-32 standard	106[2]	20	1305	5[4]	—	90	1526 } 2515
LMS/1933-39 (Stanier)	86	50	664	—	—	189	989
LNER/Non-standard (NER type)	5	—	5	—	—	—	10
LNER/Gresley (1923-33)[3]	20[2]	—	142	—	—	12	174 } 1029
LNER/Gresley (1934-43)[3]	34[2]	—	675	—	—	136	845
GWR/'Bow-ended'	6	6	32	—	—	—	44 } 131
GWR/1934-40 standard	—	—	75	—	—	12	87
SR Maunsell standard	—	63[5]	159	—	20[5]	—	242
Totals	257	139	3057	5	20	439	3917

1 Carriage types are identified by standard BR codes (see page 288). Those built as second class are considered 'third' for this summary. Each unit of an articulated set counts as one carriage.
2 Includes some semi-FO types.
3 Listed separately mainly to give quantitative comparisons with LMS and GWR figures during similar building period.
4 Lounge brakes.
5 Classed as 'Nondescript' but effectively for either class.

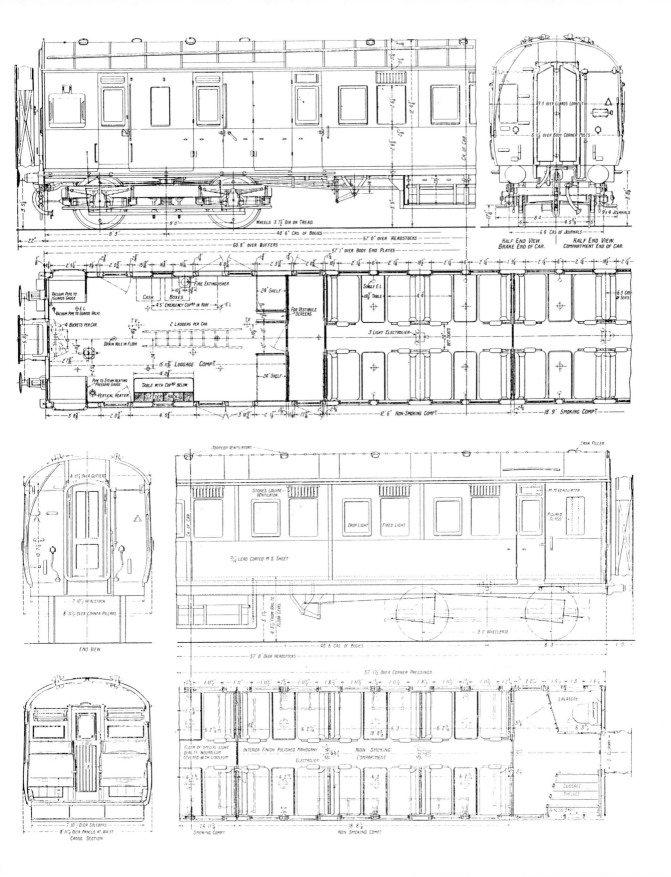

equivalents purchased from trade sources and already mentioned in Chapter 2. Taken as a group, these thousand or more third class carriages marked a significant milestone in British carriage history, if only by virtue of their sheer numbers. It is fortunate that we still have a few to be examined.

Meantime, the other companies seem either to have ignored this major LMS innovation or were not convinced of its relevance. In any case, one of them, the Southern, was probably far too busy with its attempts to catch up in the basic corridor mode to be overly concerned about yet another conceptual idea; but the attitude of the GWR and LNER does merit a few words.

If, indeed, the matter of weight-saving was the key factor in the LMS decision to build so many of these carriages in the 1920s, then the GWR and LNER could reasonably claim that such matters were not applicable to them; in the early days they both had express locomotives which, however pro-LMS one might be, were a quantum leap better than anything running out of Euston or St Pancras. Things were, of course, eventually to change, but Table 5 reveals the extent to which both companies largely set their faces against open stock for at least ten years after the grouping. In the case of the GWR, this attitude applied throughout the whole of the inter-war period as well and it built none at all after the war. The fact is that the GWR always took the view that open stock was not for general service use and in consequence made no long-term or lasting contribution in this arena, which was a pity, for its later excursion stock was more than agreeably founded.

The LNER was not very different in the first decade after 1922 and much of its teak-bodied open stock was for dedicated dining use, including some agreeable semi-open firsts. However, it did issue one design of 'two plus two' open third designated for excursion or 'Tourist' use and thereby hangs one of those delightfully inconsequential little tales which bring such joy to the student of railway carriages. The current and long-accepted descriptive BR coach coding (see page 285) was based on the old LNER system and an open third was classified as TO (Third Open) and assumed to have 2 + 1 seating, since most were originally used for dining. If the seat arrangement was 2 + 2, it was therefore regarded as Tourist stock by the LNER, being described, in consequence, as a Tourist Third Open (TTO). When third became second class in 1956, this then translated to TSO, the now universal description for general service _standard_ class open carriages, simply because their seats are arranged 2 + 2. How many, I wonder, realise, when they ride in these parts of the HST 125s or other BR stock of similar ilk, that they are officially classified as Tourists...?

However, the LNER did not multiply this high-density type to any extent and it was only the outside purchase of a few all-steel coaches in 1927 that made even the 1923-32 total of open thirds reach even the modest 142 vehicles which Table 5 reveals. These carriages were the LNER equivalent of the much larger LMS purchase — see page 31 — but did not have anything like the same degree of significance to the parent company at the time. However, unlike the GWR, the LNER did eventually espouse the open carriage to a somewhat greater extent during the 1930s and we shall have cause to come back to them.

Meantime, the LMS continued almost alone with its 'great experiment' in open stock, if thus it may be called, so it must have been slightly surprising in contemporary circles when it, of all companies, chose also to tackle, head on, the almost total conceptual stagnation in the side-corridor field. This must have been most unexpected. It may be a tenable hypothesis that the motive power crisis on the LMS was instrumental in its choosing the 'open' solution to the carriage problem, thus advancing the long-term cause of carriage development in quite a noteworthy way, but weight-saving can hardly have been the prime consideration when, in 1926-7, the LMS decided to make very radical changes in its design of conventional side-corridor carriages by getting rid, once and for all, of the individual side doors to the compartments.

As already indicated, this was no new idea. The GWR, LNWR and NER had all tried it in earlier days to various degrees and without universal acclaim, so it is by no means clear why the LMS, in 1927, chose finally to abandon the use of traditional outside doors on the compartment side of its corridor stock, but the coincidence of date suggests that it had more than a little to do with the growth of commercial rivalry between the LMS and LNER for the Anglo-Scottish trade. This was first revealed in the post-1922 era by the introduction of the 'Royal Scot' locomotives in 1927 and a new train of the same name between London and Scotland — or more correctly, the naming, for quite overt publicity purposes, of the long-established 10.00 am service (see above) as a counterblast to the 'Flying Scotsman' train of the LNER. Hitherto the latter company, with its Gresley 4-6-2 'Pacific' locomotives, had made most of the running, the LMS cause not being in any way helped by the total confusion of purpose in the locomotive department which, for five years, denied it a suitable large locomotive for long-distance work. The 'Royal Scot' 4-6-0s changed all that with their ability to pull heavier trains, and this may have been the key to the new carriage designs.

In strictly carriage terms, if one abandons outside doors in the interest of offering much greater pas-

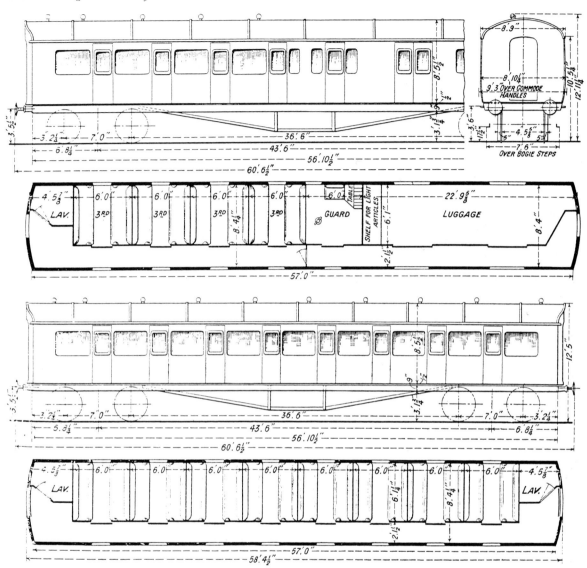

Figure 16 *Even for excursion purposes, the GWR was slow to adopt open stock; these 57-foot bow-ended thirds were its preferred alternative in 1929.*

Scale: $^1/_{10}"$ = *1ft*

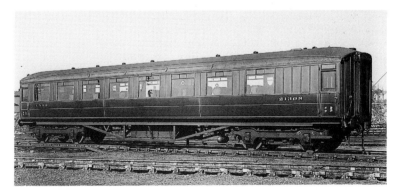

Right *This stylish 48-seat open third No 21308 of 1934 typified most of the earlier traditional teak-bodied LNER open stock in being classed as TO-ie having 2 + 1 seating (see text). It was also a very early LNER example with a welded underframe (LNER official, NRM).*

senger amenity, then some form of entrance lobby (or vestibule) has to be provided from which to gain access to the compartments via the corridor. This takes space and, customarily, reduces by one the number of compartments which can be provided in a given carriage length. The carriage weight per seat must therefore increase and this inevitably means a heavier train for the same number of people, whether by virtue of more carriages of a given size or the same number of larger vehicles. Given that the Anglo-Scottish schedules were, by agreement, pegged to something like eight hours, thus preventing the LNER striking back by speeding up its services on a somewhat less adversely graded route, the LMS

clearly felt it could gain a worthwhile edge by offering a much better passenger environment than its rival, using its new engines to overcome the inevitable weight penalty.

At first, given the improvements to the third class environment in the form of the open stock already mentioned, the enhancements were confined to the first class passenger in the form of some palatial side-corridors with, rather curiously, 4½ compartments in the brakes but only 5½ in the full firsts; note, by the way, the happy revival of the much loved half-compartment, not that it ever did quite go out of fashion (see Volume 1). In exterior styling, the carriages themselves were still rather old-fashioned and

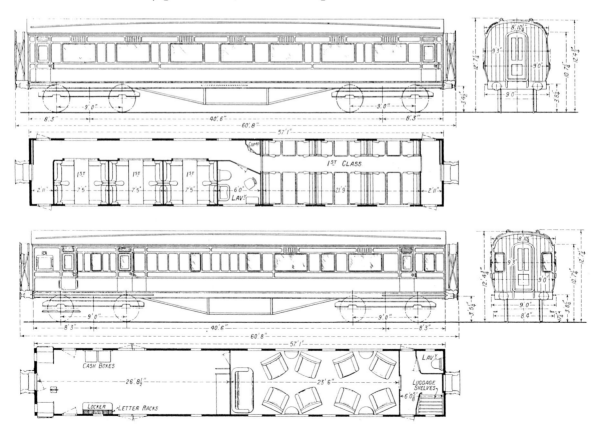

had 'twinned' windows in the compartments, rather in the manner of the now familiar open carriages, but they were soon followed in 1928 by something rather better: a first class semi-open carriage (or 'corridor-vestibule car' as the LMS preferred to style it) with large single picture windows in both the compartments and the dining bays. There were three of the latter, all given the conventional 2 + 1 seating, and they were separated from the three first class compartments by a quite splendid toilet compartment of almost 'powder room' size. But it was the compartments themselves which took the prize, for there were only four seats in each of them; every passenger thus had a corner position and all three compartments were differently trimmed and furnished. When to this is added the fact that the LMS also threw in for good measure a first-class lounge brake with armchairs and settees, picture windows and occasional tables, it will be appreciated that something distinctly new was in the wind.

To this was then added a very agreeable design of 2 + 1 open third class carriage, dedicated to dining purposes and also given large picture windows, and the whole lot rapidly became referred to as the '1928 Royal Scot Stock'. Even though the third class ordi-

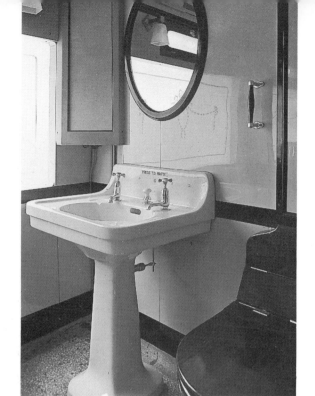

Above left *The new LMS carriage ideas were wrapped in very traditional exterior form at first. Here are seen part of corridor first No 3499 (left) and open first No 15913 (right), both of 1927 vintage; but the left-hand carriage had 'twin' windows (rather in the manner of the open first) on its compartment side, and there were only 5½ compartments in its whole length (LMS official, NRM).*

Figure 17 *Elevations and plans of the 1928 LMS semi-open and lounge brake firsts used on the 'Royal Scot' service.*

Scale: 2mm = 1ft

Right *Characteristic interiors from the LMS 1928 luxury first class stock featured in Figure 17 (BR LMR).*

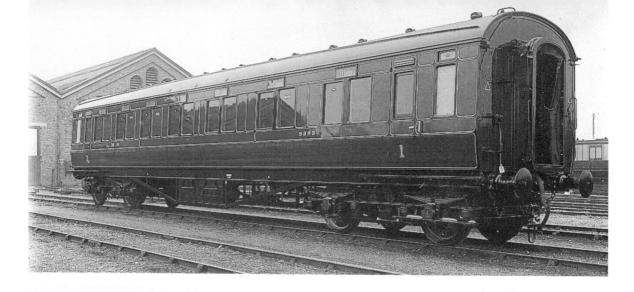

Top *This stylish LMS twin-window corridor composite design No 9383 of 1929 was still rather traditional in body form and construction but much improved in passenger amenity* (BR LMR).

Above and left *Further LMS third class improvements in 1930: corridor third No 3031 showing the new low waist and large picture windows (now fitted to both sides of the carriage), and an interior view of a contemporary open third class dining carriage* (BR LMR).

Figure 18 *'All-steel' corridor brake third to the new 1930 LMS style.*

Scale: $^1/_{10}$" = 1ft

nary was still partly confined to four per side compartments with outside doors, the signs of change were there, and within two years the LMS went several stages further.

As early as 1929, the third class passenger gained advantage from the new thinking as a result of the introduction of some splendid corridor composite carriages (both brake-ended and orthodox) which combined twin windows in the compartments (and no outside doors) with large picture windows on the corridor side, and these introduced a new 60-foot carriage length to LMS design. In the previous volume, I indicated how the demands of differentially sized first and third class compartments could fight against total standardization of carriage length, and the LMS in 1929-30 seems finally to have accepted that the best solution was to add an extra 3 ft of length to its composites. The net result was to the benefit of everybody.

Only a year later, the LMS made a further stylistic change to its long-distance carriages, this time by lowering the waist level by a few inches and suppressing the separate exterior waist panelling, thus giving the passenger a much improved outlook from the large picture windows and also imparting an altogether more 'svelte' look to its offerings from the outside. The semi-open firsts and the corridor composites and brakes were repeated in this style, as were the open diners — the latter were also enhanced to a 60-foot length; but the lounge brakes gave way to well-appointed brake firsts of conventional compartment style, but still four per compartment, however. These were altogether some of the most stylish carriages ever offered to the non-supplementary passenger at the time and the whole re-appraisal was culminated by giving to the *third* class passenger a 60 ft long side-corridor coach with similar lavish facilities — large

windows, low waist, only seven compartments (each 6 ft 6 in long and designated for six passengers only) and no outside doors. Only two years after it had put the 1928 stock into service, the LMS again re-equipped the 'Royal Scot' train with these new offerings.

To be fair, the LMS did not build too many of these new vehicles at the time, but their speed of conception and introduction puts our own age to shame. When to this is added the fact that, simultaneously, the company was finally moving to a new policy of steel-panelled exteriors — best exemplified by the quite magnificent twelve-wheel sleeping and dining cars of 1930-31 (see Chapter 5) — then it may be appreciated how significant, in retrospect, were these changes. The final flowering of this highly creative period of design evolution was to be witnessed during 1930-2 when the LMS added to its laurels by building some 300 orthodox 2 + 2 open thirds to the new style, this time to the conventional 57-foot length, along with some further outside procurement of all-steel brake firsts and thirds from 'the trade'. In all this rapid development, the credit may justly be given to Reid for first establishing the wherewithal by which it could be achieved, but tribute must also be awarded to his successor, Ernest Lemon, for seeing it through to such a splendid conclusion.

Thus it was that by the time William Stanier arrived on the scene in 1932, and in quite stark contrast to the semi-chaos which existed on the locomotive front, the LMS was exceptionally well placed to take advantage of any 'Wiltshire Wisdom' which the new man might wish to impose in the carriage building field. In the event, all that Stanier seems to have done is to introduce the mostly GWR-inspired 'suspended' gangway and encourage the quick move to

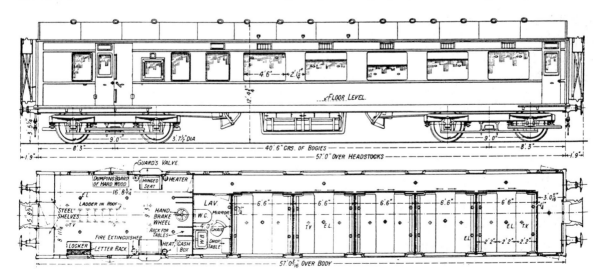

Left *Picture window and superb light-toned woodwork in one of the 1930 LMS brake thirds. Courtesy lights over the seats have also appeared, and the individual armrests soon followed* (BR LMR).

Below *This luxury LMS 4½-compartment brake No 2554 was the contemporary 'all-steel' first class equipment of the third class type shown in Figure 18, and appeared in 1931* (LMS official, NRM).

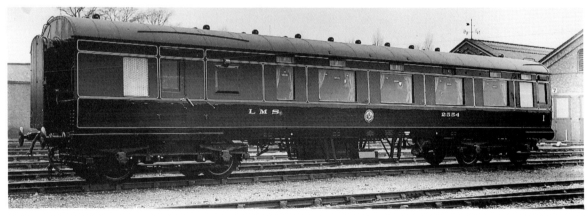

totally flush-clad carriage exteriors, including some of their smaller detail points, already well-established at Swindon (see below). The first exemplar of this fusion of ideas was quick to emerge: the quite magnificent Stanier corridor brake composites of 1932, the pioneer carriages built by the LMS in the Stanier era, in which stood revealed all the essential ingredients of the modern long-distance railway carriage. However, before coming on to discuss these carriages, we must first take stock of what was happening elsewhere.

The year 1930 seems to have marked something of a watershed for all the British companies, for if the LMS was the most active, the others were at least beginning to re-assess matters. By now the Southern was well into its stride with its corridor building activities, and its 1930 programme included its own first essay into the open third field which took the form of some rather well thought out carriages with large single windows. Each of the latter was in effect

a frameless droplight and could be lowered in its frame, somewhat in the manner of those fitted to the new generation LMS carriages. The Southern thirds were initially intended to run with first class dining cars — the Southern in pre-Bulleid days never offering a third class kitchen/diner (see Chapter 5) — but they were of 'general service' configuration and over the next few years the SR built rather more of them and their successors than could ever have been needed in the dining mode. Two worthwhile features of their design would do well to have been copied by other railways: the spacious 'L'-shaped entrance vestibules and the very useful luggage 'baskets' which were fixed above all seats. The final pre-war examples, to a new design in 1934, were the first SR coaches to exhibit flush-sided body construction and rounded window corners.

It was the Southern too which made use of that lovely word 'Nondescript' in describing some of its open stock. Two varieties were built, the first, also

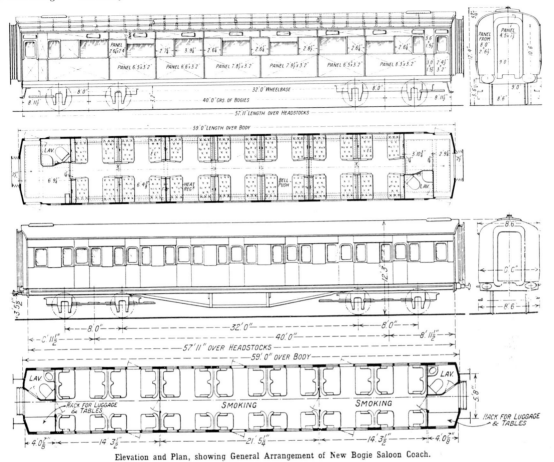

Elevation and Plan, showing General Arrangement of New Bogie Saloon Coach.
NEW BOGIE SALOON COACHES, SOUTHERN RAILWAY.

Figure 19 *Elevations and plans of the first Southern Railway essay in the third class open stock field, the 56-seaters of 1930, and the nondescript saloons of 1931.*

Scale 2mm: 1ft

Right *The well-finished interior of an earlier SR saloon, No 7988 of 1928, seems hardly to justify the description 'nondescript'; it was clearly of first class quality (SR official, NRM).*

termed 'General Saloons', dating from 1928, while a brake-ended version of rather more modern exterior styling appeared in 1933. Both were built to the 8 ft 6 in width for greater availability and embodied a 2 + 1 seating configuration. They were anything but 'nondescript' in quality, being in all vital respects first class in standard, but they had detachable 'class'

boards and were used as second class for the continental boat trains (which retained three class travel) and the brakes were almost exclusively confined to this purpose. The full saloons were even regarded as third class for school use; but then the SR had some very plushy schools in its bailiwick! Both versions had intermediate side doors to some of the seating bays,

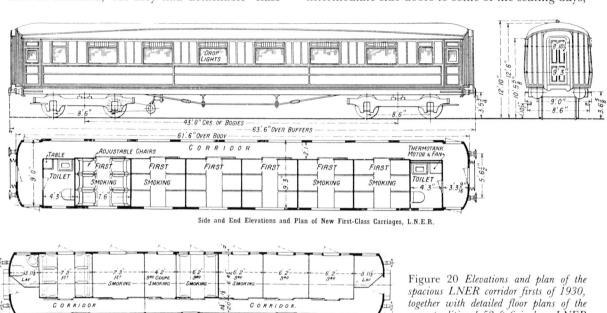

Side and End Elevations and Plan of New First-Class Carriages, L.N.E.R.

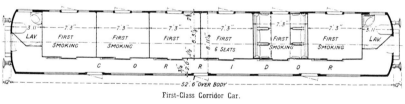

Composite Corridor Car.

Figure 20 *Elevations and plan of the spacious LNER corridor firsts of 1930, together with detailed floor plans of the more traditional 52 ft 6 in long LNER corridor coaches for use on the GE section of the system.*

Scale: 2mm = 1ft

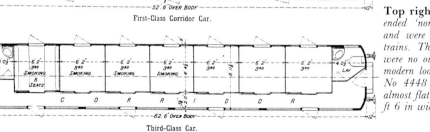

First-Class Corridor Car.

Top right *The one batch of SR brake-ended 'non-descripts' dated from 1933 and were almost wholly used for boat trains. Their large windows where there were no outside doors gave them a more modern look. This crisp official view of No 4448 when new clearly shows the almost flat sides in consequence of their 8 ft 6 in width (SR official, NRM).*

Third-Class Car.

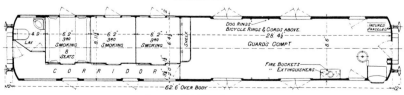

Composite Third-Class Brake Car.

Above right *The much improved look which the suppression of compartment doors gave to LNER stock is well shown in this view of corridor composite No 32386 when new in 1937 (LNER official, NRM).*

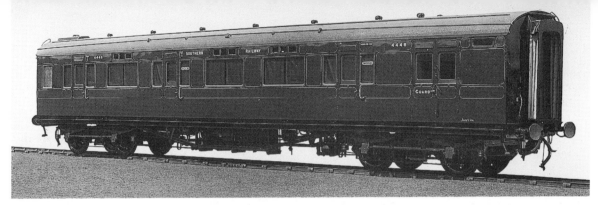

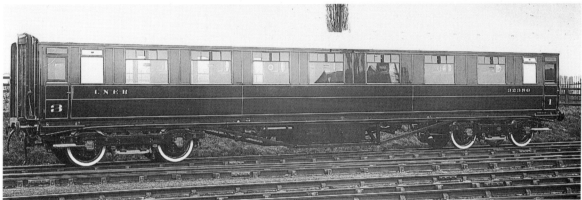

and though only one batch of brakes was ever built, the earlier design was repeated at intervals.

The Southern Railway was not really in serious competition with any other railway save the GWR, and its main-line carriages could now certainly stand favourable comparison with all but the best of those from Swindon, but the same was not true of the LNER in relation to its chief rival, the LMS. Many of its trains connected the same terminal points, and by 1930, though the standard Gresley corridor was still without peer as far as its vehicular quality was concerned, in all other respects it showed the same uninspired standards throughout the 1920s as did all but the latest LMS offerings.

Contemporary sources do not give precise reasons for the subsequent LNER changes which began to emerge from 1930 onwards, but it is hard not to see the competition from the LMS as being partly responsible. What is certain is that in 1930 (first class) and 1932 (third class), the LNER too abandoned side doors on at least some of its new main-line stock in favour of large side windows and entrance lobbies — and some exceedingly handsome vehicles resulted, both inside and out. They were, of course, still fully teak-bodied in the traditional East Coast style, but the new carriages, devoid of the interruptions to the styling consequential upon many outer doors, revealed an exterior elegance which, in the view of this writer, made already good-looking carriages even bet-

ter, and whose visual harmony was rarely bettered.

Nor was it a case, as so often transpired in these matters, of flattering to deceive; the interiors were every bit as good and the first class version, in particular, was just as comfortable as its LMS contemporary. It was also quite definitely more modern in its styling and only suffered in comparison because six people were still seated therein. However, the LMS four-seaters were very thin on the ground and six per compartment was its usual standard, so honours were just about even. This applied to the third class too which, like the latest LMS offerings, also gave a 6 ft 6 in compartment to its patrons with a single large outer window. In due course, brake-ended and composite versions followed in all categories save that of brake composite, and all were built to the new standard 9 ft 3 in width, this having largely superseded the slightly narrower 9 ft dimension which, hitherto, the LNER had built turn and turn about with its slightly wider stock.

There was only one adverse aspect to this welcome change on the LNER; it also chose to retain the 'all-door' alternative and, indeed, it was to be 1936 before any brake thirds to the new style appeared. Furthermore, none of the more modern corridors were ever built to the shorter standard 52 ft 6 in length which the LNER employed very widely in its former GER territory. These remained entirely conventional, being mostly one compartment less in length than their

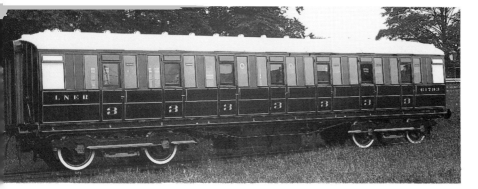

Left *Undoubtedly very smart but equally rather dated: LNER (GE section) 'short' corridor third No 61793 of 1934 (LNER official, NRM).*

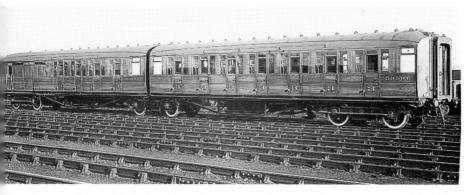

Left and below left *Though dated in concept with their retained outside doors, these two examples of flush-sided steel-panelled LNER stock leave one lost in admiration for the brilliant representation of teak livery achieved by the painters, all the more so since they were finished in August and November 1939 respectively, right on the outbreak of war. They are articulated twin third brake No 53500/1 and composite No 58107, both seen ex-works at York (LNER official, NRM).*

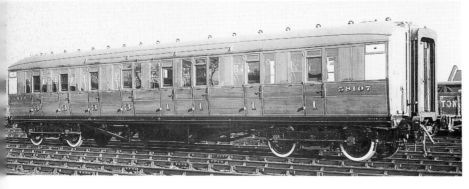

Left *Green and cream LNER 'Tourist' open brake third No 43500, ex-works at Doncaster in 1933 (LNER official, NRM).*

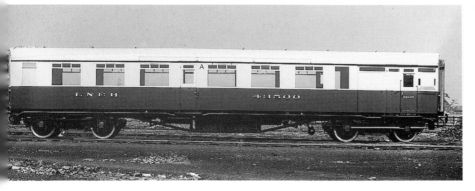

Right *LNER 'Tourist' stock interior, complete with the innovatory but not much loved 'bucket' seats (LNER official, NRM).*

61 ft 6 in contemporaries. Thus there never was as much consistency in the accommodation offered in its main long-distance trains as the LMS achieved during the 1930s. Even so, the LNER did build more than a token number of corridor carriages to this new standard, and personal recollection of riding in them brings back happy memories of the relaxed environment they offered, and especially their superb riding quality.

The later 1930s period also marked a somewhat half-hearted LNER attempt to produce steel-panelled main-line stock, teak having increased in cost. All that happened was that steel sheet replaced teak on the outer surfaces of otherwise unaltered designs. This went on intermittently until the war years, but no real attempt was made to re-style the vehicles to suit the new material, and the steel-panelled versions were by no means the most distinguished of the genre, being generally employed on more secondary workings, leaving the main lines almost exclusively in the hands of the orthodox teak carriages. And there such matters rested (save for the celebrated special stock — see Chapter 11) until the end of the teak-bodied era.

At the same time as it began to improve at least some of its side-corridor stock, the LNER also began to adopt the open configuration in the third class to a much greater extent than in its first ten years. As with the LMS, one cannot be certain of the precise thinking which went behind them, but it does seem that their Tourist and excursion potential came high on the list of considerations and, indeed, they came in two forms.

First on to the stage were some dedicated 'Tourist' trains in 1933 which made a serious if not always successful attempt to offer new design thinking in an important new market area, that of competition with the growing road coach excursion business. Their most striking external feature was their bright and cheerful green and cream livery, hitherto associated only with steam railcars (see Chapter 9) and their most innovatory constructional detail was the use of plywood outer panelling. In fact, they were built to something of a budget and lacked the form and comeliness of traditional teak-bodied stock, being devoid of domed roof ends, for example. A full set of them did, however, look rather good, and their external lines gave more than a hint of the soon to emerge special streamlined trains of the later 1930s. The brake ends and buffet cars were single units, but the bulk were built as articulated third class 'twins'. They became popular with the public and further sets, some of the later ones with slight modifications, emerged at intervals until 1939.

Within the vehicles, the interiors were somewhat brightly spartan with much glossy paint and pale-coloured Rexine replacing former wood finishes, and naked lamp bulbs were considered sufficient to illuminate the interiors. There was much use of fashionable chrome-plated fittings, rather in the manner of the best contemporary cinema interior practice, especially in the buffet cars (see Chapter 5) which also had chrome-plated tubular steel chairs of fairly atrocious aspect and comfort! The main seats, however, were distinctly new and clearly reckoned to be of pioneering importance. They were of a semi-bucket type with Alpax legs, and were designed to allow each passenger a seat to himself with, and I quote, '. . .the maximum of room and the greatest comfort'. Would that this had been so. Having got over their novelty value — which did not take long — they were amongst the most diabolically uncomfortable seats which I have ever experienced in a railway carriage, and many were subsequently replaced by more conventional straight-backed versions.

Very similar general service carriages with conventional teak-panelled bodies also emerged during the same time and were given an all but identical interior arrangement, including the dreaded bucket seats which were eventually all replaced. In this case, there were quite a number built to the GE section 52 ft 6 in length. Like the pure 'Tourist' sets, the teak-bodied coaches were mostly used for excursion work and the LNER never used its considerable fleet of

open thirds for pure main-line use to anything like the extent as did the LMS. The teak-bodied examples lasted rather better than the painted carriages, whose plywood panelling gave considerable trouble in later years.

Turning now to the GWR, this company has not received too many plaudits so far in its post-1922 carriage building activities, but it finally began to make forward progress again at almost exactly the same time as the great LMS changes in the side-corridor field already mentioned. Though still regarded as part of the 'Bow-ended' era and not married to any radical re-design of carriage interiors, the new GWR main-line coaches of 1929 and later are noteworthy as being the first British vehicles to embody flush-sided exteriors in recognisably modern form. Even the door handles were recessed, and on its 'Cornish Riviera' stock of 1929-30 the GWR also permitted

itself, for almost the first time since Churchward's huge 'Dreadnoughts' (see Volume 1) to take advantage of its more generous structure gauge and build carriages to a near 9 ft 7 in width. It also extended them to a 60-foot length and this, even allowing for some sterility in terms of interior amenity, gave them a far more spacious look.

The non-kitchen dining cars of this series also embodied large windows with sliding top sections to afford ventilation, and this produced a very pleasing if simple outline. When the GWR then proceeded to put further 9 ft and 9 ft 3 in wide coaches of broadly similar style on to its other services, it did seem for

Figure 21 *Floor plans showing the spacious interior dimensions of the 1929 GWR 'Cornish Riviera' stock.*

Scale: $^1/_{10}'' = 1ft$

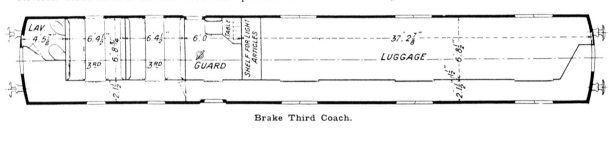

Brake Third Coach.

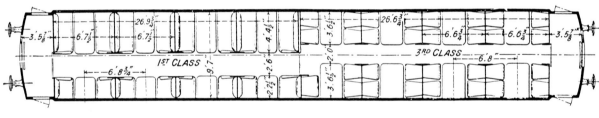

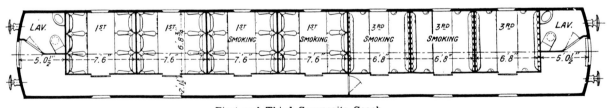

First and Third Composite Coach.

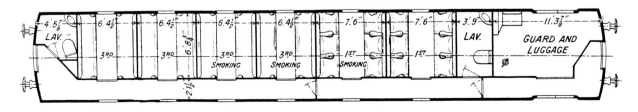

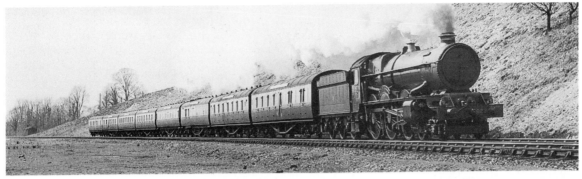

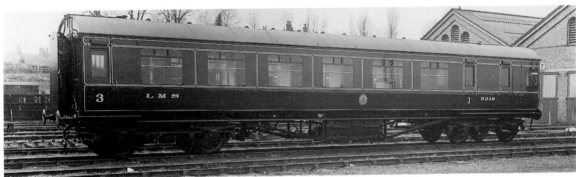

Top *This splendid view of the up 'Cornish Riviera' at Somerton circa 1935, headed by 4-6-0 No 6023* King Edward II *and almost wholly composed of 1929 stock, clearly shows the smooth exterior of this first British flush-sided carriage style and the pronounced widening at the waist which the GWR loading gauge permitted. The particularly clean lines of the dining cars (vehicles three and four) in consequence of their large windows and few doors is especially noticeable. It was, however, rather rare for a GWR train to be visually so neat and tidy at this point in time! (Soole Collection, NRM).*

Above *Stanier's first carriage essay: No 9318, one of the excellent and trend-setting brake composites, ex-works at Wolverton in 1932, in the short-lived but very attractive fully lined livery which was only to survive until 1934 on new stock (LMS official, NRM).*

a while as if things had changed. But apart from the dining saloons, a full set of doors on the compartment side was still considered essential, so some of the apparent modernity was lost. Furthermore, from 1933-6 the company then went back to the 57-foot length, reinstated flat ends and stubbornly persisted with 'high-waisted' carriages when other lines, particularly the LMS, were giving the passenger the benefit of a lower window-sill for a better view out. One writer has described them as '. . . probably the most undistinguished of GWR coaches'.*

In several respects, however, the GWR influence was greater than may have been supposed. For one thing, it was simultaneously building some very fine special stock (see Chapter 11) and, perhaps even more important, a considerable infusion of its constructional practices seem to have gone to the LMS in 1932

Great Western Coaches: M.Harris (*ibid*)

in the person of William Stanier. Just as in the case of locomotives, so too in the realm of carriages, it was left to the LMS to develop Swindon's ideas to a far greater extent than on the parent company, and it was not until the late 1930s and 1940s that any degree of re-importation took place. So it is to the LMS that we once again must turn to continue the story.

When William Stanier arrived on the LMS, its newest long-distance stock displayed considerable interior design innovation but was associated with somewhat traditional constructional practices. Stanier seems to have almost instantaneously grafted the best of the new GWR constructional techniques on to the carriages of his new company, and before his first year with the LMS was out, there had emerged the first of what were to become possibly the most familiar outline main-line carriages in the pre-BR MkI era, the pioneering essay being a quite splendid brake composite on a 60-foot chassis.

It set new standards in two quite specific ways. First and most obviously, it established a totally new body construction style of quite definitely modern aspect. The GWR-inspired flush-sided form of bodyside

Figure 22 Elevations and plans, plus typical detail features, of characteristic Stanier corridor stock from 1934 onwards. Note that the contemporary draughtsman put a non-existent rain strip on the carriage roof!

Scale of whole elevations: $^1/_{16}$" = 1ft

panelling was married to the already existing LMS espousal of large windows in all its main-line stock to produce a very distinguished-looking ensemble. Even the fact that it was given a fully lined livery suggestive of panelling did not impart a pseudo feeling, and there were many who later wished that Stanier had not moved to the pretty uninspired exterior decoration which became so boringly familiar after 1934! Stanier main-line stock in the more fully lined form always looked good.

Constructionally, apart from the changes consequential upon the use of flush-sided outer panelling, one could also note such 'GWR' touches as 'shell'-pattern roof ventilators, upper window 'sliders', steel sheet roof covering in place of roofboards and canvas, 'suspended'-pattern British Standard gangways and the very practical water-filling pipes which, doubling as end handrails, allowed the water tanks to be filled from platform level by means of a hosepipe, rather than scaling the roof to open the top hatches. The underframe retained all its essential LMS characteristics and Stanier clearly saw no need to change the excellent LMS bogie or the 'Wolverton' lighting system. If there was one fault it was that the LMS chose not to go the 'whole hog' and adopt buckeye couplings and Pullman gangways. Given the sheer weight of numbers of Stanier carriages eventually to be built, it would have been a worthwhile change.

Within the vehicle, the already existing LMS improvements were further refined. The LMS was very much wedded to timber finishes so its compartment interiors remained rather more sombre than some of the newer LNER offerings in this respect,

but this apart, it led the field. First class compartments were variously two or three per side, depending on whether classed as 'luxury' stock, and the thirds were now consistently three per side only and were given the luxury of folding armrests and additional courtesy lights above the seat position; these modifications were also made retrospectively to much of the better older stock. A particularly practical touch was the use of double sliding doors to the corridor which opened wide enough to give more than sufficient space for passengers to manoeuvre their luggage. This idea actually stemmed from the immediate pre-Stanier corridor stock but remained an exclusively LMS feature. Other lines would have done well to copy it and it is a surprising if not very happy thought to recall that the BR standard stock did not copy it either.

With regard to seat and other interior design features, Stanier LMS stock continued the simplification of styles which had first appeared in the 1930-32 era and, at long last, the LMS moved permanently away from the somewhat stodgy upholstery patterns which had hitherto found favour. To be candid, some of the new styles of trimming did not work — especially if they tried to ape too closely the various currently fashionable 'jazz' patterns and the like — but on the whole such a good standard was achieved as to stand the test of time for almost 20 years. The very last Stanier-type corridors did not emerge until the early 1950s — they were hardly changed from those of the early 1930s and they still looked as modern as anything which the other companies had designed later.

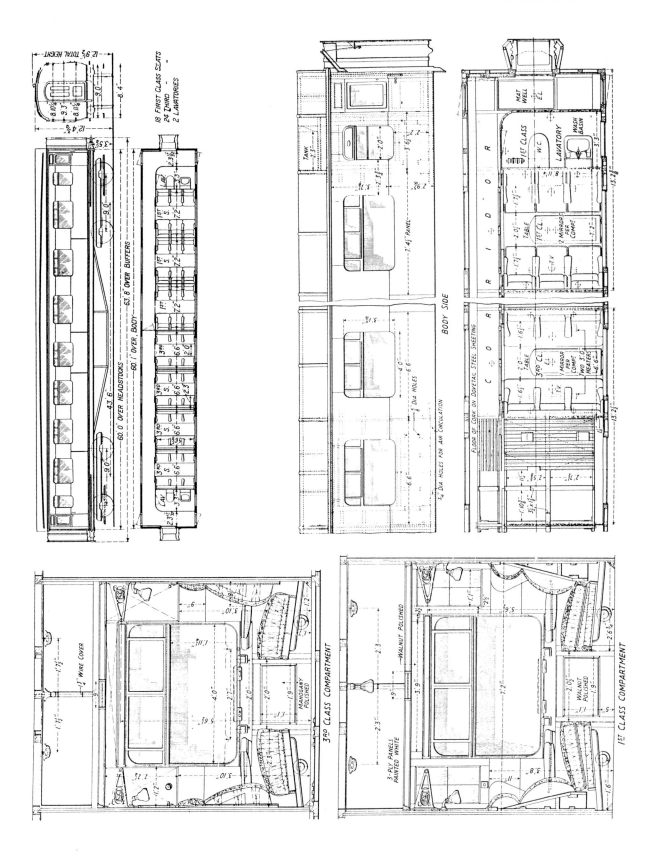

BODY SIDE

FLOOR OF CORK ON DOVETAIL STEEL SHEETING

18 FIRST CLASS SEATS
24 THIRD
2 LAVATORIES

3RD CLASS COMPARTMENT

1ST CLASS COMPARTMENT

Left *The more typical pattern of sliding window ventilator and the new simplified carriage livery are both seen in this 1936 high-capacity (60-seat) LMS open third No 9178. Note the half bay of seats at the far end of the coach.* (BR LMR).

Below left *The favoured 'Empire timber' is well seen in the veneers used in this LMS open third brake interior of 1938. The neat door label (always a feature of LMS coaches of this era) states it to be Indian Laurel in this particular example* (BR LMR).

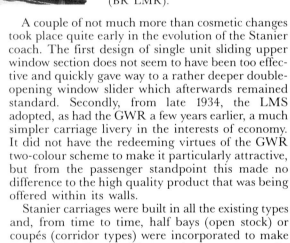

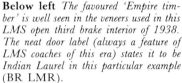

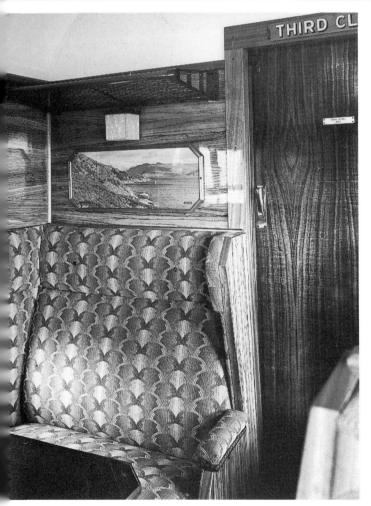

A couple of not much more than cosmetic changes took place quite early in the evolution of the Stanier coach. The first design of single unit sliding upper window section does not seem to have been too effective and quickly gave way to a rather deeper double-opening window slider which afterwards remained standard. Secondly, from late 1934, the LMS adopted, as had the GWR a few years earlier, a much simpler carriage livery in the interests of economy. It did not have the redeeming virtues of the GWR two-colour scheme to make it particularly attractive, but from the passenger standpoint this made no difference to the high quality product that was being offered within its walls.

Stanier carriages were built in all the existing types and, from time to time, half bays (open stock) or coupés (corridor types) were incorporated to make up the vehicle length. The coupés were most usually found in the brake composites, including the first ever examples (see above), but in the pre-war full firsts only 5½ compartments were offered on a 57-foot chassis which, like its pre-1932 predecessor, was wildly extravagant of space. After 1945, a small reduction in compartment size was adopted to give a full six compartment form — a much more logical solution to the problem. This apart and taken overall, the Stanier revolution — and this is not an over-extravagant use of language — was almost completely successful. Having said this, however, it would not be correct to infer that all was sweetness and light after Stanier arrived on the LMS, and one aspect of the Stanier coaching stock era is worthy of further mention; it forms a sort of curious interlude in the generally self-confident evolution of LMS carriage design during the 1932-47 period.

Earlier in the chapter I tried to explain, as best I could, how the LMS made a quite deliberate attempt

Close-up detail of flush-sided Stanier articulated third class open stock of 1937, again with a welded bogie (BR LMR).

Close-up detail of flush-sided Stanier articulated third class open stock of 1937, again with a welded bogie (BR LMR).

to move long-distance travel — especially in the third class — away from the conventional side-corridor style in favour of the open configuration. The Stanier era continued this principle to some extent, but perusal of Table 4 (page 49) in comparison with Table 5 (page 60) will reveal that it was only partly successful. During the 1932-9 period, in spite of the huge building of open stock prior to Stanier's arrival, the fact remains that the company still felt it expedient to build more than twice as many side-corridors during his first seven years than were offered in the open style. Yet one senses that the LMS still remained to be totally convinced, for amongst all this it decided to have yet another radical 'go' at open stock and it took the form of a more than experimental flirtation with articulated construction.

In 1936-7, the LMS was still, in spite of its more puissant Stanier locomotives, clearly concerned with weight-saving in terms of carriage building, and even built an experimental brake third with a new type of centrally trussed, lightweight underframe so as to evaluate its new ideas. In the event, the full realization of these thoughts was to achieve fruition in the form of a series of articulated open 'twins' which, collectively, numbered over 100 individual carriage units. Why the open configuration was preferred to the side-corridor form is not at all certain — it probably had something to do with reducing the cost of excursion stock, eg the LNER 'Tourist' experience (see above) — but, by using a 2 + 2 layout the LMS managed to accommodate 112 passengers in a less than 50 ton 'twin pair' of open thirds, compared with the approximately 60 tons which two single unit vehicles with the same capacity would have tared. It is interesting to note, *en passant,* that the design of the BR Mk 1 underframe followed, quite closely, that of these 1937 LMS designs.

Although these new LMS carriages may have originally been mostly intended for excursion use, in due course they found their way into normal workings, an event of far more significance than the somewhat half-hearted effort at non-corridor articulation mentioned in the previous chapter. It also had more than a degree of design spin-off into the radically conceived articulated sets of carriages for the re-vamped 'Coronation Scot' of 1939 (see Chapter 11). It is more than sad that the Second World War intervened at this interesting point in carriage evolution and we can but speculate what the eventual LMS solution might have been. What can be said — and this without any caveat whatsoever — is that the LMS, before the war, does seem to have been addressing the carriage business with a far greater degree of thoroughness than any of its rivals.

Given this virtual revolution in carriage design by the LMS, it remains a source of some surprise that the other companies did not copy it until very much later, but the LNER, as has been noted, made some move in the direction of the LMS approach to matters. This was by no means whole-hearted, but did copy the LMS to the extent of putting armrests and courtesy lights in the third class (whether with outer doors or no) and again, like the LMS, made some modifications of like kind to older stock. The Southern, however, never offered side-corridor stock with picture windows in the compartments, nor did it offer three per side in the thirds (save in restricted dimension stock) and never with armrests. Its final pre-war offerings were in the fashionable flush-clad idiom, superficially quite modern looking, but most certainly not revolutionary in quality. In fact, the Southern's move to flush-sided carriages was hesitant, interrupted by a curious short-lived period wherein all the screw heads fixing the outer steel sheets were

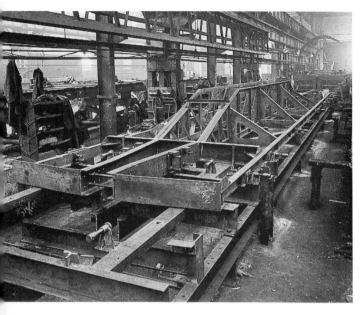

there was a modest reinstatement of corridor-side doors, and in some of the later examples one compartment reverted to the outer door style, presumably to speed up the boarding and leaving of vehicles at intermediate points. These styles became, in effect, the design basis for the post-war GWR carriages.

Slightly before this modest move forward, the GWR had introduced its first recognizably 'modern' carriages in the form of its final series of open stock, again classified for excursion use, though they were undoubtedly also used for summer relief workings as well. Designed for use with intermediate kitchen cars with an implicit promise of 'meals at all seats' (did it actually happen, one wonders?), the early examples had nice big drop windows while later examples were given double sliding top sections much in the fashion of Stanier's LMS or the GWR's own 'Sunshine' stock, but the ledges of the windows were retained at an old-fashioned higher level, thus impeding the view to some extent. They were roughly contemporary with the LNER Tourist sets but rather better furnished. Lamps had shades, for example, and the interiors, though still light and airy, did not entirely eschew the use of wood finishes. Very much in the Art Deco idiom, a particularly nice touch was the low-backed seating which would undoubtedly permit passengers a better view across the aisle, but there were insufficient of them to make an appreciable impact on general GWR philosophy.

Thus, but for these well-recorded exceptions, the LMS gradually moved itself well ahead of the competition in the long distance carriage field and Table 6 attempts to show how dominant it became. Bearing in mind that of its more than 5,000 side-corridors, only some 750 had outside doors to the compartments and well over 4,000 were to the Stanier pattern, then its leading role is quite clear. Even allowing that it would always hold the primacy in absolute numbers simply by virtue of its larger size, it is still worth noting that its new gangwayed coaches represented some

left rather prominently visible. The Southern built no new corridor stock after 1936 until the post-war Bulleid era when it did eventually move to the more modern style, more or less coincidentally with the similar adoption of more modern carriage designs by the LNER and GWR as well.

Meantime, what of the latter company? Its best pre-war contributions were, without doubt, the 'Centenary' and 'Special' stock (see Chapter 11), but in the later 1930s it finally recognized some of the new thinking in its so-called 'Sunshine' corridor stock of 1936 which finally suppressed the outside doors in favour of end entrances only and low-waisted configuration. Stylistically, and stripped of GWR livery and bogies, they might well have been cloned from Stanier via Derby or Wolverton, save that they never had three-per-side thirds. A few years later, however,

Table 6 Gangwayed coaches: new build, all types 1923-53

Note: This table summarises the data in Tables 4, 5 and 9 (Chapter 14).
The latter gives a full analysis of the post-war continuation.

Company	Corridor stock			Open stock			Grand total
	Pre-war	Post-war	Sub total	Pre-war	Post-war	Sub total	
LMS	3182	2067	5249	2515	370	2885	8134
LNER	2515	830	3345	1029	42	1071	4416
GWR	2402	495	2897	131	—	131	3028
SR	1316	494	1810	242	350	592	2402
Totals	9415	3886	13301	3917	762	4679	17980

45 per cent or more of all new British main-line stock built during the final 30 years or so of pure company designs as opposed to its only some 40 per cent share of the total British carriage fleet in 1923. Table 6 includes for completeness the post-war carriages built by all four companies and again the LMS dominates. However, to maintain some element of chronology to the story, these will not be covered until the final chapter.

But if the LMS was absolutely dominant in the general service 'ordinary' field, there was a rather greater parity of achievement in the realm of the more specialized carriage stock during the 'Big Four' period, and to some of these vehicles we must now turn our attention.

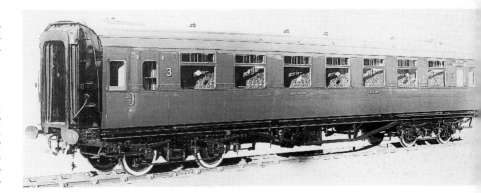

Left *A new type of 'lightweight', centrally-trussed mostly welded underframe under construction at Derby in 1936 for the LMS articulated sets. Note the far lighter solebar sections (BR LMR).*

Right and below right *These two views of Southern open thirds Nos 1311 and 1450 of 1935 and 1936 respectively show how a somewhat half-hearted attempt at flush-sided treatment quickly gave way to a rather more conventional form with visible window frames. Honesty compels one to admit that in this case, the older concept was of rather more handsome aspect (SF official, NRM).*

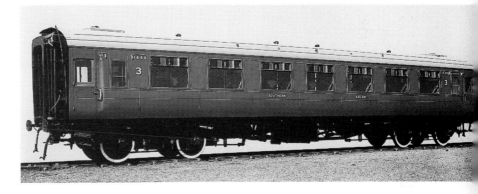

Below *This fine view of the up GWR 'Bristolian' somewhere between Bristol and Filton Junction circa 1936-7, headed by 4-6-0 No 6014 King Henry VII, is of especial interest in showing how very stylish an almost complete train of the newly introduced 'Sunshine' coaches could look, compared with the previous high-waisted form, here represented solely by the 'quick lunch' buffet car (see page 105), halfway down the formation. The engine still carries some of the absurd streamline fairings fitted in 1935 (see page 218) (Soole Collection, NRM).*

5. Sleeping and dining car development

The fundamental characteristics of railway sleeping and dining cars had been well established during the pre-group period and they changed but little afterwards; there was no real need in most cases since the ideas were soundly based in the first place. The post-grouping period was therefore mostly one of consolidation and improvement rather than outright innovation. Having said that, however, the period in question was also full of great interest, not least in the sheer number of such vehicles built after 1922. This latter point is even more surprising when one considers both the large number of generally quite modern overnight and catering vehicles which the 'Big Four' had inherited and, in many cases, their long revenue life thereafter. It was, for instance, not at all unusual for pre-group examples to outlast the company period itself, albeit by then somewhat relegated in terms of service status.

Table 7 attempts to summarize the situation for the post-1922 'new' build of 'mobile hotel' vehicles, and two basic points should be made. Firstly, the grand total was high in absolute terms and secondly, expressed as a fraction of all new carriages, it represented some 3.5 per cent of the total. This may not

Table 7 Sleeping and dining cars: new build, 1923-52

Notes: 1. These values have been extracted from various published works and may show odd discrepancies from other sources. This should not affect their value for comparative purposes.
2. It should be appreciated that much of the post-war build in these categories took place after the nationalisation of the British railway system in 1948.
3. Individual elements of articulated 'sets' are counted as one unit.

Company/Style	Sleeping cars				Dining/Kitchen cars						Grand Total
	SLF	SLC	SLT	Total	RF	RC	RT	RK	RB	Total	
LMS/1923-32 standard	52	12	85	149	24	18	—	73	1	116	265
LMS/Stanier, 1933-1939	26	13	15	54	20	13	44	35	4	116	170
LMS/Stanier, 1945 on	25	—	25	50	1[1]	—	—	—	—[2]	1[1]	50
Sub totals	103	25	125	253	44	31	44	108	5	232	485
LNER/Gresley (to 1933)	33	11	46	90	27	—	4	10	12[3]	53	143
LNER/Gresley (from 1934)	16	3	—	19	22	16	7	4	37	86	105
LNER/Thompson	5	—	17	22	13	—	—	11	2	26	48
Sub totals	54	14	63	131	62	16	11	25	51	165	296
GWR/1930-34	9	1	15[4]	25	10	15	—	13	9	47	72
GWR/1934-40	—	—	—	—	4	5	—	10	9	28	28
GWR/Hawksworth	4	—	—	4	—	—	—	—	—	—	4
Sub totals	13	1	15	29	14	20	—	23	18	75	104
SR/Non standard	—	—	—	—	—	—	8	—	—	8	8
SR/Maunsell	—	—	—	—	46	—	—	—	—	46	46
SR/Bulleid	1[5]	—	—	1	—	—	11	—	8[6]	19	20
Sub totals	1	—	—	1	46	—	19	—	8	73	74
Grand totals	171	40	203	414	166	67	74	156	82	545	959

[1] Rebuilt former pre-war carriage.
[2] Many old sleeping/kitchen/dining cars in old LMS series were rebuilt to this form in early BR days.
[3] Including 'Tourist' stock.
[4] Two were later converted to corridor third, one to SLC.
[5] Not for general service, classified Inspection Saloon (see Chapter 13).
[6] Tavern Cars, later converted to RKB (ie. Kitchen and Buffet).

Table 8 Comparative analysis of ordinary and special stock

Company	All stock[1]		Specialized stock[2]					
			Sleeping		Dining		All special stock	
	Total	per cent	Total	per cent	Total	per cent	Total	per cent
LMS	16354	40.8	253	61.1	232	42.55	485	50.6
LNER	11567	28.9	131	31.65	165	30.3	296	30.9
GWR	6318	15.8	29	7.0	75	13.75	104	10.8
SR	5791	14.5	1	0.25	73	13.4	74	7.7
Totals	40030	100	414	100	545	100	959	100

[1] 1947 values used for comparison (see Table 2).
[2] Post-1922 builds as a proportion of all stock owned. If pre-group vehicles are added, LMS/LNER dominance is increased.

at first glance seem very high, but when one considers the thousands of non-corridor carriages included in those totals which could never run with sleeping or catering carriages anyway, the matter takes on a somewhat different perspective. When expressed as a proportion of new *gangwayed* stock — perhaps a more reasonable comparator — the figure rises to over 5 per cent and even this is still probably misleading since, like non-corridor carriages, much gangwayed ordinary stock was used for services devoid of 'hotel' facilities.

A more realistic assessment of the figures might therefore be that up to 10 per cent of the principal main-line stock was of the specialized kind, and this would certainly be true if one added to the tabulated totals the hundreds of non-kitchen open coaches used for dining purposes. In fact, it is this latter aspect alone which explains why the sleeping car total is almost as big as the catering fleet; the latter only includes carriages which had cooking facilities as part of their make-up.

It is thus readily apparent that the railways, in spite of the higher unit cost of specialized vehicles, felt obliged to provide them in some abundance, and the rationale for their construction can only be explained in terms of meeting the increased competition from other modes of transport combined with a greater public expectation of what ought to be provided. One doubts not that the four railways of the final company years were just as aware of the deadweight and potential non-revenue earning characteristics of these vehicles as is their BR successor! This, perhaps, merits a little more explanation.

Sleeping and dining vehicles are heavier, passenger for passenger, than ordinary stock and their capacity for revenue generation is therefore not as high per ton weight as a conventional day carriage. A typical twelve-wheel sleeping car of the inter-war period, for example, would weigh 40 tons or more yet only accommodate maybe 12 berths. These would, addi-

tional to the fares paid, only earn the equivalent in supplementary berth charges of a few more passengers in normal seats at standard fare; and the carriages stood idle for over half the day anyway! One orthodox corridor carriage (of whatever class) could earn as much revenue as at least two sleeping cars. Much the same is true of dining vehicles. In this case, the traditional car was 100 per cent deadweight, save for the profit from meal service, since the passengers were most usually accommodated elsewhere in the train. Small wonder that the LMS (probably the most cost-conscious of them all) felt it expedient to offer meals at seats with a kitchen-only car somewhere in the train (see page 59).

All things considered, therefore, it is remarkable how lavish were the provisions made for what can, at best, have been only a marginally profitable operation, and at worst a heavy loss-maker. But the railways were clearly convinced (as indeed to a lesser extent is the BR management of the present time) that travellers will pay due regard to 'on train' facilities in making the fundamental decision whether to travel by rail at all. For this reason, the railways continued to build their mostly magnificent dining and sleeping cars — and glad we should be that they did. In fact, it is not too far off the mark to state that it was in this field that most of the more interesting developments, both in terms of interior amenity and vehicle technology, first began to appear.

Hardly surprisingly, the two bigger long-distance companies led the field both in quantity and quality and, as with gangwayed stock in general, the LMS led the way with over 50 per cent of the total, a rather higher proportion than was true for its coaching stock taken overall (see Table 8). The LNER too had a higher than expected quota of these vehicles; but perhaps the most revealing is the low proportion represented in the GWR and SR fleets. In the latter case, the absence of sleeping cars — save for Mr Bulleid's one-off 'maverick' (see page 268) — and the

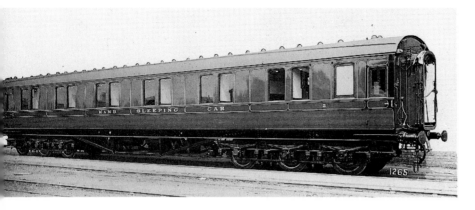

Left *The first generation LMS sleeping cars are well exemplified by this 1927 example, M & NB No 2. Ownership markings apart (see text), it was to the pure LMS pattern and painted in LMS colours (BR LMR).*

Figure 23 *Comparative floor plan diagrams of LNER single unit and articulated twin sleeping cars.*

presence of Pullman on the catering side are, no doubt, much of the explanation, but what of the GWR? Overall, though owning more than half as many coaches as the LNER and approaching 40 per cent of the LMS total, it possessed but 35 and 21 per cent respectively of their specialized fleets.

One should not make too much of statistics — they can only reveal facts and not causes — but the variation in the figures quoted does seem to reveal something about the different characteristics of the four post-grouping railways. On the whole, it seems likely that the high LMS/LNER values were in part caused by their mutual competition for much of the traffic to the Midlands, North of England and Scotland, whereas the GWR had more of a monopoly in its hinterland, save 'at the edges', so to speak. There was therefore probably some element of over-provisioning on the LMS and LNER (for competitive reasons?) which was not felt to be needed by the GWR. The latter company also had more holiday traffic (as, indeed, did the SR) which clearly would not warrant very much catering provision in the traditional form.

But whatever the precise reasons, there was less difference in carriage quality between the coaches which were built than might be supposed from the unevenness of the totals quoted. Sleeping and dining cars were always the type of vehicles which gave railways publicity and status, especially on their more celebrated trains and all four companies made significant forward steps during the period in question. Some ideas were more far-reaching than others, and a few bordered on the ridiculous, but they were rarely without interest.

Sleeping cars

In all seriousness, there were really only two significant sleeping car companies during the 'Big Four' period, the LMS and the LNER, and both were rather good at it, though in very different ways at first. Towards the end of their independent existence —

and indeed the design and construction spilled over into early BR days — there was a great deal of coming together of ideas, and this proved to be both influential and fortuitous when it came to designing the first generation BR standard sleeping cars of the 1950s. In effect, the LMS and LNER had done most of the hard work!

The traditional British sleeping car layout (side-corridor giving access to a series of compartments with berths set transversely to the longitudinal axis) never varied during the whole of the grouping period, but the individual LMS and LNER solutions to it were often quite different in fundamental structural terms, especially in the first class arena. This, of course, was the only type existing in 1923 and it was not until 1928 that the overnight third class patron got his shout. Interestingly, it was the need to meet this eventuality which caused the first convergence of ideas between the two main companies. . .but back to 1923.

In this year, the inherited LMS sleeping car tradition was dominated by the two English giants, the LNWR and Midland, for reasons given in Volume 1. But it was really no contest, for the LNWR had far more experience of the business than had the MR and, unlike most things during early LMS days, the LNWR's ideas were to prevail. This resulted in a quick standardization of the 68-foot twelve-wheel car, based on final Wolverton LNWR practice; in fact, Wolverton Works built every single first class twelve-wheel sleeping car constructed to LMS design. The first ones even looked mostly like LNWR carriages and a few even had LNWR rather than the new LMS standard bogies, though they all made use of the new angle-trussed underframe. They had handsome, conventionally timber-built bodies and their panelling, save for a modest bit of deepening at the waist to more Midland-like proportions, was pure 'Wolverton'. Dozens were made down to 1930 and the later examples saw some important internal changes.

Within the cars, 12 single first class berths was normal, some having interconnecting (lockable) doors to make double berths if needed. The lavatories and attendant's compartment completed the assemblage and the first series had ponderously heavy interior treatment, mostly in the form of seemingly endless acres of traditional mahogany panelling from floor to cornice. They were, needless to say, magnificently appointed, their ride quality was without peer and they were wonderfully well finished, but they were rather old-fashioned.

In the later series, the LMS improved the interiors by painting the walls above the dado in white enamel and, in the final batches, began to fit the now-familiar corner washbasins in place of the older fold-away type. The company also coved the floor angles (see page 38) to facilitate cleaning. All of them were given more than adequate heating, and individual electric fans supplemented the conventional ventilation. One interesting small point was the fitting of frameless droplights to the compartment and the provision of vertical 'rolling' shutters rather than conventional window blinds to give, as it was said, '. . .a general appearance of warmth and cosiness. . .' One rather interesting aspect of this long-lived series of cars (most lasted well into the early 1960s) was that a pair of them were built in 1927 for the M & NB joint stock for service between St Pancras and Edinburgh. This stock was not formally divided between the LMS and LNER until 1928, and the LNER got one of them in its share of spoils. It was fairly swiftly transferred back to LMS stock!

Almost at the end of the building period of this style of car, in 1929, the LMS equipped one of them with a new type of ventilation system known as the 'Thermotank' apparatus. This was a fan-driven air circulation system, driven by a 250 watt electric motor fed from the 24-32 volt carriage lighting circuit. This served each compartment through a 'Punkah' louvre from a roof level air duct installed below the corridor ceiling. It could be arranged either to deliver fresh air or extract stale air from the compartment, and the compartment louvre — which was under passenger control — could also be swivelled to direct the air over a wide area. Its capacity was 40 cubic feet per minute per berth and the passenger could, if desired, close it off completely. It proved a remarkably successful idea and became the basis of the method which was designed into the later LMS and BR standard sleeping cars right until the Mk III era.

No less comfortable than these opulent but somewhat dated sleeping cars — and arguably more technically innovative — were some of the contemporary LNER offerings wherein, of course, the hand of Nigel Gresley was to be seen at work. In 1923, the LNER — no doubt influenced by cost and weight consider-

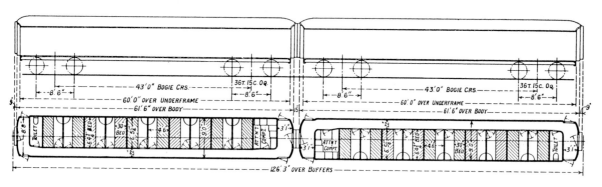

Diagram giving proportions of Two Single Unit Sleeping Carriages.

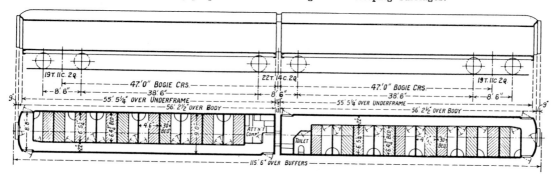

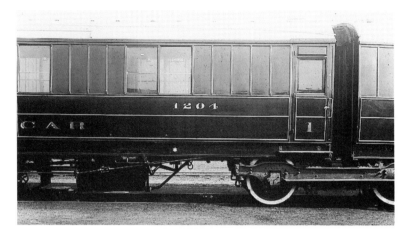

Close-up detail of LNER twin sleeper first No 1204/5 of 1926, taken in 1930 when the set was fitted with the shower compartment (whose door is just visible through the window) in place of one berth, so as to match the later single unit series — see text (LNER official, NRM).

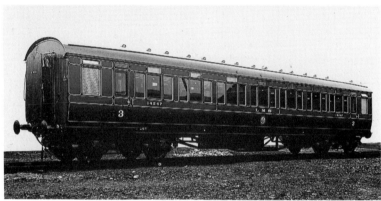

Compartment-side elevation of LMS third class sleeping car No 14247. Along with the LNER equivalents (see Figure 24), these were the first of any post-grouping third class side-corridor carriages to dispense with outer compartment-side doors (BR LMR).

Figure 24 *Elevation and plan of LNER third class sleeping car of 1928; the LMS version was identically arranged.*

Scale: $^1/_{10}"$ = *1 ft*

ations — set in motion an interesting comparison between single unit and articulated sleeping car pairs. The individual vehicles were ten-berth carriages on a standard eight-wheel underframe and conceptually no different from the LMS examples, save that their shorter length was reflected in their smaller carrying capacity. The twins, however did make quite a weight saving. Each half still had ten births, but length and weight were saved both by articulation and by only offering one toilet and one attendant's compartment, each now serving 20 berths. The basic arrangement is given in the appended drawings and it gave a nearly 8 per cent length reduction and an almost 16 per cent weight advantage compared with two single cars. The problem was that they could not be operated unless a destination required at least 20 berths to be offered. Many did not, so there was still a need for the single unit type; but the twin sleepers remained a characteristic feature on the East Coast route for many a long year.

Outwardly, the new LNER sleeping cars showed even less change from pre-group days than did those of the LMS, being solidly in the GNR tradition as

would be expected, but in purely interior terms they were marginally better in that they had corner washbasins and white enamel paint above the dado from the outset. There seems little doubt that in this respect the LMS may have copied the LNER. But this 'anything you can do' attitude was quite characteristic of these two great companies during this period and the traffic in ideas was by no means one way. Thus the LNER, in 1929, copied the idea long used by the LMS when it substituted sliding window shutters for blinds and curtains, but the LNER shutters slid horizontally, were each panelled to match the compartment interiors and had auxiliary louvres opposite those in the windows themselves.

Likewise, the LNER began to experiment with 'forced' ventilation of its sleeping cars in 1929. It called it 'Pressure Ventilation' and according to *The Railway Engineer*, the system was developed by J Stone & Co rather than by Thermotank Ltd as on the LMS. However, another source states the system to have been of 'Thermotank pattern'[*] and the mode of oper-

---

[*] *Gresley's Coaches*, M.Harris, David and Charles, 1973

ation was identical; no doubt each company made full publicity value out of its 'different' system!

In one respect, however, the LNER was more adventurous than its LMS rival: water heating. Here, after experiments involving keeping pre-heated water warm by using the train lighting circuits, Gresley managed to install what amounted to a totally self-contained water heating system in sleeping cars by fitting a supplementary belt-driven generator and storage cells, fully independent of the lighting system. This added weight but eliminated the need for the use of oil gas water heating. The LNER was more keen than the LMS in ridding itself of oil gas for heating and conducted considerable experiments in both the sleeping and dining car field in pursuance of this aim (see below). Meantime, large gas tanks for heating were always to be found below the floors of LMS twelve-wheelers.

Honours were, therefore, just about even between the LMS and LNER during the 1920s and remained so during the 1930s, but before resuming the story of first class developments on the two principal railways, we must first turn to the introduction of third class sleeping cars and also catch up with the GWR contribution to the story, such as it was!

On 24 September 1928 — and in a spirit of harmony between the railway companies — the GWR, LMS and LNER simultaneously introduced the final phase in the emancipation of the ordinary traveller (which had begun so long ago with the nineteenth century Midland Railway) when they offered proper sleeping cars to third class passengers. As usual, the two northern companies led the way both in terms of concept and quantity and each offered what amounted to an identical vehicle, an eight-wheeler on a 60-foot underframe, the LNER examples being

61 ft 6 in over body because of their bow ends, of course. Within these new carriages, layouts were identical: seven compartments to which access was gained from end entrance lobbies, each of which also had access to lavatory and toilet.

In both cases compartments were 6 ft 4 in between partitions, neither type had outside compartment doors and both of them featured two quarterlights flanking a central frameless droplight on the compartment side, combined with large picture windows on the corridor side. Within the compartments, a convertible arrangement was offered with four berths at night, the upper ones folding against the partition by day to produce a fairly orthodox side-corridor third with eight seats per compartment. Pillows and rugs were provided for night use at a modest supplement, 6s (30p) or 7s (35p) per passenger depending on the distance travelled.

They were uncommonly handsome vehicles and proved deservedly popular, so much so that repeat orders were soon forthcoming by both companies, the LMS, as usual, building about twice as many as the LNER. It seems likely, in view of their striking similarity, that there must have been some sort of collaboration between the two companies in terms of their design. Happily, a fully restored LMS example from the very first batch is preserved at the NRM.

Meantime, the first GWR offering was rather different and consisted of but three carriages which did not display much imagination compared with the new LMS and LNER carriages. They followed the customary 'bow-ended' stylistic practice, having eight compartments without entrance vestibules; but only three had the convertible berth arrangement with no outside compartment doors, pretty well identical to the LMS and LNER versions. The remaining five

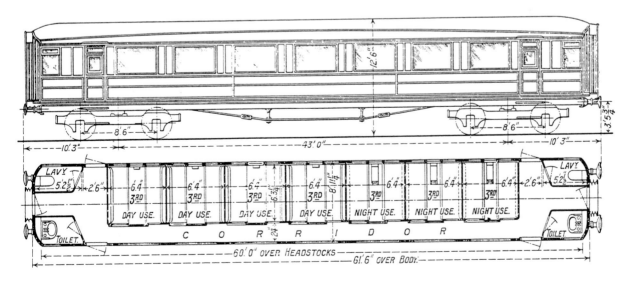

This view of an up GWR express at Somerton circa *1935 behind 4-6-0 No 4097* Kenilworth Castle *shows a very characteristic mixture of GWR carriage styling, dominant amongst which is the bulging profile of the leading first class sleeping car and the similar profile of the third class version at vehicle No 3. For the record, other identifiable types are the three 'Sunshine' corridor coaches in the middle of the train and a 'Dreadnought' diner, third from the rear. Unfortunately the train itself is not identified* (Soole Collection, NRM).

compartments were arranged very conventionally with day seats only and outside doors. On the corridor side, long lights alternated with outside doors save at the sleeping end, where there were simply droplights in place of doors. In 1935, the GWR brought this experiment to an end when it converted two of them to orthodox corridor thirds, the odd man out becoming a composite sleeping car.

Clearly, the GWR had been over-cautious and only a few months later, in 1929, its own genuine third class sleeping cars on the LMS/LNER pattern began to emerge. There were only nine of them but they were much better than the original trio. For one thing, they made full use of the generous GWR structure gauge and were given bulging sides in order to lengthen the berths slightly. They also had recessed end entrance doors, and in these two respects they also set the pattern for the few first class sleeping cars

which the GWR built during the grouping period. Three further third class sleepers with rather more restricted dimensions for cross-country working were built in 1934.

In 1930 and 1931, coincidental with the bulging-side third class cars, the GWR introduced the only first class sleeping cars built by the company proper between 1923 and 1947. Again nine only in total, their appearance almost exactly matched that of the third class carriages, save that they had six-wheel bogies to carry the extra weight, and they were by no means ill-looking vehicles in a ponderous sort of way. But their ten-berth interiors were stodgy in the extreme and not as good as even the most conservative of the first post-1923 LMS offerings, leave alone the better ideas which both it and the LNER were actively pursuing by this time.

In fact, despite William Dean's fine pioneering work in late Victorian times (see Volume 1), the subsequent GWR contribution to twentieth century British sleeping car development was minimal to

Until purpose-built composite sleeping cars were introduced, the two-class form was usually first class sleeping plus third class ordinary. This LNER example No 10207J, built in 1925, was typical. The 'J' suffix denoted East Coast main line allocation (LNER official, NRM).

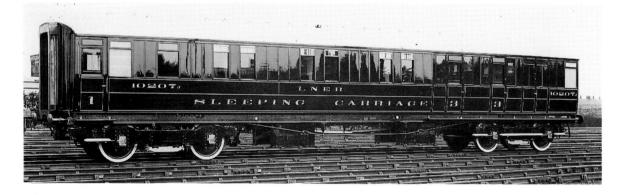

Figure 25 *Elevations and plan of the LMS composite sleeping carriages of 1930 and 1931. In later years, part of the compartment immediately to the left of the first class section was converted into a third lavatory (for the first class section only) by inserting a partition where a pecked line is marked and moving the corridor door into line with it. At the same time, the remaining 14 convertible third class berths were altered to a fixed arrangement.*

Scale: ¹/₁₀″ = 1 ft

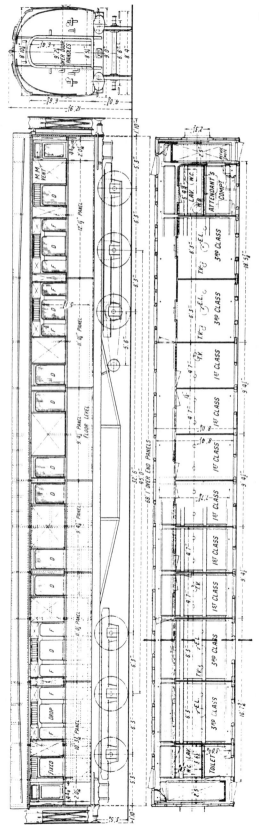

non-existent. Apart from a couple of equally unexciting composites (the above-mentioned conversion and one further example to the bulging-side style), the only other sleeping cars built to GWR design after its final trio of third class carriages in 1934 were four first class examples to the Hawksworth pattern in 1951, after nationalisation. These were ten-berth twelve-wheelers, like their predecessors, but it is a sad measure of the generally uninspired situation at Swindon in this particular field that these were the first and only GWR-design sleeping cars to have air conditioning in any form — and even this was only pressure ventilation of the kind introduced by the LMS and LNER more than 20 years previously! So it is to these two companies that we must turn again to round out the British sleeping car story.

It is not too surprising that after the introduction of proper third class sleeping cars, there should also develop a demand for a composite pattern which would offer both classes of sleeping accommodation to many of the destinations served by the railways which did not warrant more than one through carriage. In this respect, the LMS took the lead in 1930 — probably because it had rather more of such destinations — in the form of some quite splendid twelve-wheelers in which one could also discern the last fling of pure 'Wolverton'(LNWR) as opposed to LMS standard styling. It was by now the start of the LMS steel-panelled era so these new cars were devoid of external beading, but their window style and general configuration harked back to LNWR days and their layout was both logical and well-balanced: six conventional first class berths in the centre (between the bogies), flanked by two convertible third class compartments on each side. Fully lined out, they were a considerable credit to the company. They were later modified to fixed berth arrangement in the third class and lasted until the 1960s.

Meantime, the contemporary LNER composite contribution was rather muted, taking the form of a single vehicle (for the former M & NB service) plus, perhaps inevitably, a pair of articulated twins, each half first and half third class, (one of the compartments from a third class portion is beautifully preserved at the NRM). But if the LNER was slow to follow the LMS lead in terms of numbers (it built very few composites even in later years), it most certainly set the pace in terms of better amenity inside

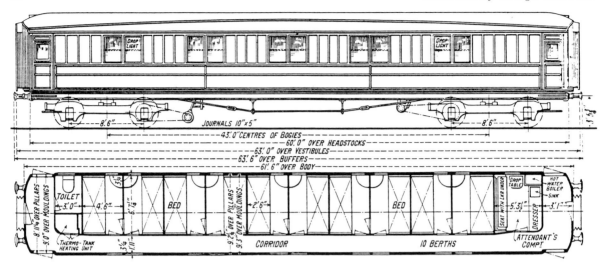

the cars themselves. As early as 1931, a clutch of dedicated thirds (ie non-convertible with fixed berths) was built on a new 65-foot design of underframe. This permitted eight compartments, all of which were given much more lavish facilities including mirrors, individual bedhead lights and coathooks, while a supply of filtered drinking water was a very welcome addition.

Even before this, however, in 1930, the LNER had taken further important steps forward in terms of compartment comfort in the first class. These were to banish forever the somewhat dated and at times gloomy interiors of most British sleeping cars to date. It would seem that Messrs Waring and Gillow were called in to decorate the berths in two of these cars

and decided upon a totally new-style painted finish of light colour (blue was chosen). This had the effect of making the berths seem more spacious and henceforth became the standard LNER treatment. In spite of their internal modernity, these 1930 carriages were still mounted on the standard 60-foot underframe with turnbuckle trussing, and it was not until 1932 that the newly introduced 65-foot chassis was used beneath first class sleeping cars; it was this new length of underframe which caused the LNER to adopt the more modern angle-trussed form for all stock.

Within these new 65-foot first class cars, the LNER did not, as might other railways, add an extra berth to the layout; instead it fitted a shower cubicle, the

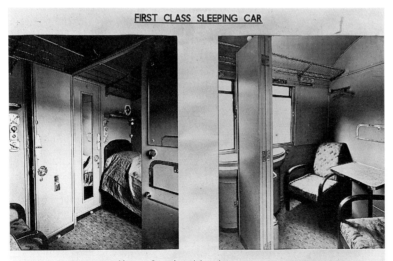

Views of combined berth-sitting room.

Figure 26 *Elevation and plan of a typical LNER first class sleeping car of 1930.*

Scale: $^1/_{10}"$ = 1 ft

Left *The new and lighter-toned interior decor of LNER sleeping cars based on Rexine finishes is seen to good advantage in this posed publicity view of a combined berth and sitting room in twin sleeping car No 1156/7 of 1932 (LNER official, NRM).*

Above right *Compartment-side view of LMS fixed berth third class sleeping car No 585 of 1933. This was the prototype which toured in North America with* Royal Scot *(see text) (BR LMR).*

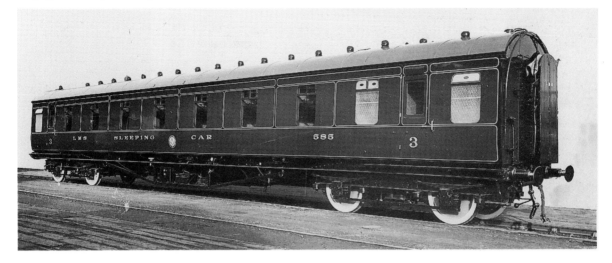

first such example in a British sleeping car. The 1934 examples in the same idiom were even better and a fine model of one of them may be seen at the NRM. However, despite the changes wrought by the LNER in terms of interior design and amenity, the cars themselves somewhat belied their modern nature by still maintaining a traditional panelled teak finish, handsome though it was, and it was left to the LMS (as in the general service arena) to put a properly modern interior into a vehicle whose exterior also indicated an up-to-date approach to the subject. The instigator was, of course, William Stanier.

Interestingly, the first beneficiaries were the third class travellers when in 1933 the LMS introduced what were undeniably some of the most handsomely styled carriages ever to emerge in the modern flush-sided idiom. They, like those of the LNER, also used a new 65-foot underframe and their fixed berths and other internal accoutrements undoubtedly imitated those of the 1931 Gresley vehicles, but there were still only seven compartments since, for the first time ever in a third class-car, an attendant's compartment was provided. Moreover, by means of outside air-scoops on the corridor side of the body, fresh air (passed through oil filters) could enter the carriage and be admitted to compartments by floor-level grills in the compartment doors. The first of these fine carriages was sent with *Royal Scot* on its tour of North America in 1933 where, largely in consequence of the overall quality offered to 'ordinary' passengers, it caused something of a mild sensation by contrast with American 'coach' class travel.

Finally, in 1935, the Stanier approach was applied to first class sleeping cars. The twelve-wheel, twelve-berth style was retained but, for no readily apparent reason, the body length was increased by another foot to 69 ft; the attendant was the sole beneficiary of this

expensive largesse! The cars also displayed a slightly bulging profile (ex-GWR via Stanier again?) and this added some 3 ins to the berth length. By some margin, these were the largest passenger carrying vehicles ever built by the LMS but, for all that, were commendably light in weight at 42 tons, only 5 tons more than the above-mentioned 65-foot third class cars.

This was undoubtedly achieved largely by means of a whole host of new constructional features which Stanier incorporated into their design and which were given considerable publicity in the contemporary press. Most of the change was in the extensive use made of electric arc welding in the bogies, underframe and carriage roof frames. The elimination of most rivets not only saved weight in itself but also enabled lighter steel sections to be used in some parts of the carriage, simply because there were no rivet holes to weaken the structure, This was augmented by the elimination of the heavy bottom bodyside timber members (see page 34), the simplification and lightening of the basic timber body frame and the use of a steel cantrail. Many of these new ideas were also embodied in contemporary corridor stock, yet the rigidity of the structure was, if anything, better than the traditional form. It is, in fact, rather surprising that the LMS did not wholly standardize this form of construction from then on.

Inside the cars, the decor largely copied that which had been LNER practice for some four or five years and represented one of the few occasions in which the LMS made use of Rexine in any great quantity. A slightly new touch was the use of four different interior colours within each car (three compartments each in yellow, green, blue and beige) with sanitary ware to match in an unconscious and early anticipation of 1970s 'Habitat' styling! However, the corridors

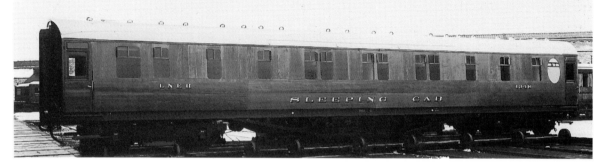

Top *The final LMS twelve-wheel sleeping car form was 69 ft long. This is Derby-built composite No 713 of 1936. Note the recessed handles to allow a little more width at the waist and the late use of Mansell wood-centred wheels, probably for a quieter ride (BR LMR).*

Above and left *Exterior and interior views of experimental Thompson LNER third class sleeping car No 1348 of 1947. The compartment shown is one of the twin berth types with high-level beds — see the sections and plans in Figure 27 (both LNER official, NRM).*

Below *Quite apart from its flush-sided form, the post-war LNER pattern first class sleeping cars differed from tradition in having single rather than 'twinned' compartment side windows. No E1257 was the first of five in 1950 (BR ER official, NRM).*

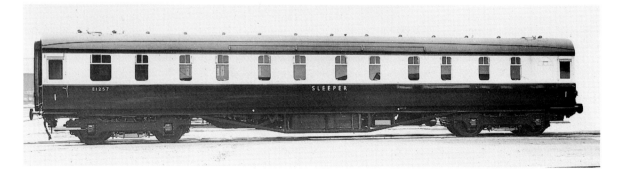

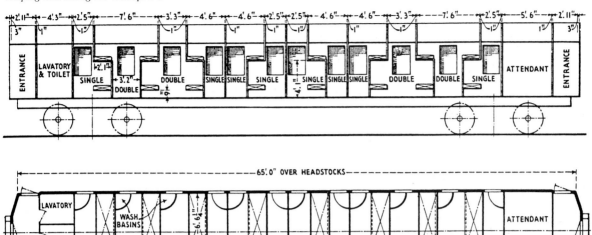

Figure 27 *Longitudinal section and plan of Thompson's experimental third class 'interlocking berth' sleeping car for the LNER.*

faithfully maintained the LMS traditions; walnut and sycamore. All the internal passenger facilities which had evolved after the grouping were installed and one of them, slightly modified, also went to the USA, this time in 1939 accompanying the new 'Coronation Scot' set (see page 229). A model of the standard type is also at the NRM.

Very soon afterwards, the LMS produced some composite sleeping cars to the new Stanier pattern. These too were 69-foot vehicles and the only twelve-wheel LMS pattern sleeping cars to be built at Derby. The latter works had been the source of supply of all the LMS third class sleeping cars and rather more than half the LMS twelve-wheel diners (see below), but the old LNWR tradition seems to have more or less ensured that *first* class sleeping cars were a Wolverton speciality; maybe composites were different! In them, the fixed berth compartments of the 1933 third class type were combined with the single berths of the 1935 first class cars to produce a predictable end product. Unlike the earlier composites, they were arranged with first class at one end, third at the other.

Thus it was that by the outbreak of war, there was little to choose in terms of quality between the best of the LMS and LNER fleet, and the final coming together of design after the war was probably inevitable. By then, the LNER had gone to the flush-sided style and only built one further sleeping car in its own name. This was a mildly experimental Thompson third class car in 1947 which, by means of an interlocking berth layout, enabled both single and double

compartments to be contrived. But in its anticipation of providing fewer than four berths in a third class compartment, it probably had some influence on the final designs which were to post-date the onset of BR. Outwardly, this first Thompson sleeping car was (ersatz teak livery excepted) much more akin to the LMS styling than any of its Gresley forbears.

Apart from this one car, the final LMS and LNER sleeping car designs all post-dated BR in terms of entry to service. This was quite characteristic of many of the final company designs of carriage (see Chapter 14). The LMS ordered up another batch of Stanier-style first class twelve-wheelers (built 1950-51), which were almost identical to the pre-war series, and Thompson on the LNER produced what amounted to a ten-berth equivalent on an eight-wheel chassis. Length apart, and the fact that there were far more of the LMS pattern, there was little significant difference; and Gresley's shower cubicle did not return in the LNER type, more's the pity.

It was finally in the third class (soon to become second class) field that the ultimate fusion of ideas took place. Here, in 1951-2, both Doncaster (ex-LNER) and Derby (ex-LMS), came up with a new concept for overnight third class travel. Unsurprisingly, both places used a 65-foot chassis and the layout was conventionally side-corridor, but all compartments in both series were twin berth only and given first class type pressure heating and ventilation. Their origins may have had something of Thompson's influence in them, but a further factor may have been the not uncommon practice during the war of adding upper berths to some first class compartments. Be that as it may, they, along with their first class con-

temporaries, were so nearly identical as to be the inevitable influence on future development — and there we must leave it until we take a closer look at them as a prelude to the BR designs in Volume 3.

Catering vehicles

The dedicated catering vehicle — and in this chapter the discussion will be confined solely to carriages with some form of on-board cooking facility — came in but one of the three basic types during the final years of the company period: the Dining Car 'proper' (ie a vehicle with kitchen, pantry and seats at which passengers could take their meals), its 'poor' relation the Buffet Car, and the Kitchen Only Car, usually called simply a Kitchen Car — ie a carriage which is completely full of kitchen and pantry equipment without seats for patrons. To some extent, the type of vehicle favoured reflected the differing approaches of the companies themselves. Thus, for example, the LMS was by far the largest user of kitchen cars just as the LNER was well ahead of the field in its early espousal of the buffet car; but this was by no means a clear-cut distinction. It therefore seems helpful to start this section with a general look at the nature of on-train catering in the 1920s and 1930s.

The desirability of having catering facilities on a train went way back into Victorian times, so by the

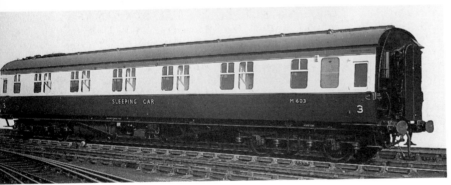

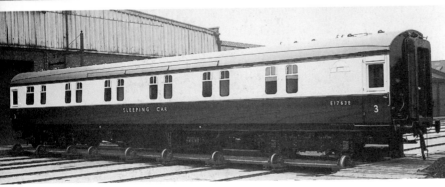

Above left *This wartime conversion to twin berth of an LMS first class sleeping car not only typifies final LMS pattern sleeping car interior styling but undoubtedly set the style for the post-BR twin-berth third class form adopted by the successors to both the LMS and LNER (BR LMR).*

Left *The considerable similarity between final LMS and LNER third class design practice is well shown in these ex-works views of LMS type twin-berth car No M603 of 1951 and LNER pattern No E1763E of 1952. Both were built new carrying BR standard red and cream livery, a style which suited the 'LNER' cars far better than painted 'teak'! (BR LMR; BR ER Collection, NRM).*

Figure 28 *The twin-berth third class sleeping car arrangement adopted by the London Midland Region. The final 'LNER' version was similar.*

Right *The classic kitchen/dining car: LNER third class No 10215J, built in 1925 for East Coast main line service (LNER official, NRM).*

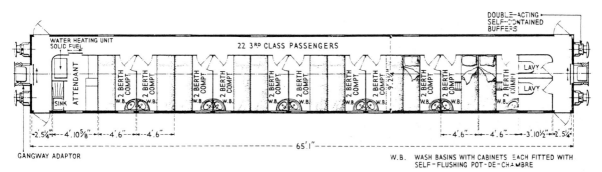

time of the grouping the general idea was well established. At the time it mostly took the form of a full dining car, but there had already been some mild experiments with kitchen and buffet cars and the grouping was to see further changes. Even though the modern proliferation of mini- and micro-buffet cars, griddle cars or what have you was still to come, one can detect its seeds in the activities of the inter-war period.

Starting with the full dining car, its earliest form was designed to serve the first class passenger exclusively and this was to remain the most common form of conventional car right through the grouping period (see Table 7). But the growing demands of the third class passenger did not have to wait long. Even by the grouping, such famous companies as the LNWR had long been building both composite and third class dining cars in the traditional mode — often inserting one of each type into the more important trains — while such as the Midland had long realized that the kitchen of the dining car proper was well able to produce far more meals than the typically 18-24 seat capacity of the car itself could consume, and had therefore settled on an almost semi-standardized arrangement of first class diner plus open third class diner for its main trains. The composite type, characteristically with about 30 seats (12 first plus 18 third) was often sufficient for the smaller trains and this had an interesting alternative: the so-called 'common' or 'unclassed' dining car. This was an all-comers vehicles and the nearest approach the British companies ever came to the typical Wagons-Lits approach which was so popular in mainland Europe. In fact, the preserved ex-MR dining car at the National Railway Museum, though built to a third class design, was mostly used in this mode.

Several alternatives also began to find favour. One of these reversed the normal pattern and operated a third class dining car with an open first. Though this happened before 1923, it became much more common thereafter, often with the first class dining seats occupying only half of the adjacent non-kitchen carriage which could, therefore, be of either semi-open configuration or even composite in its layout, thus giving more flexibility. This became particularly favoured on the LMS. But such was the growing demand for meals that the bigger trains could not always be served in this fashion and a very typical 1920s and 1930s solution was to place a full kitchen car between at least two fully open carriages (one first, one third). In some cases, three or even four open carriages could be thus served. The LMS was a great protagonist of this method but the LNER and GWR also found it advantageous, the former often in the form of an articulated 'triplet' set. The GWR also tried articulation, but fairly swiftly rebuilt its offerings into single unit carriages (see page 54).

The buffet car solution was very much a child of

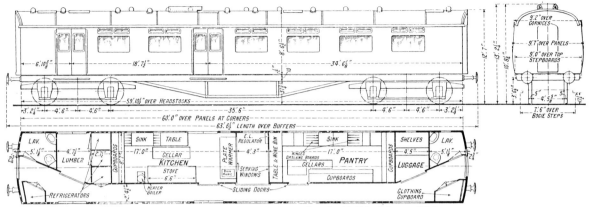

Side and End Elevations and Plan of New Kitchen Car, "Cornish Riviera" Express, G.W.R. 1929

Figure 29 *Elevations and floor plan of the GWR 1929 'Cornish Riviera' stock kitchen cars, very typical of the facilities to be found in most examples of the genre.*

Scale: 2mm = 1 ft

Left *Equally classic LMS dining car interiors: twin window open first class No 3716 of 1925 (which would normally be served from a full kitchen car), and kitchen/first No 3129 of 1930 (BR LMR).*

Above right *LNER Buffet car No 61496 was converted from a former GER coach and was one of several such in the early 1930s which led to the building of many new examples of the type (LNER official, NRM).*

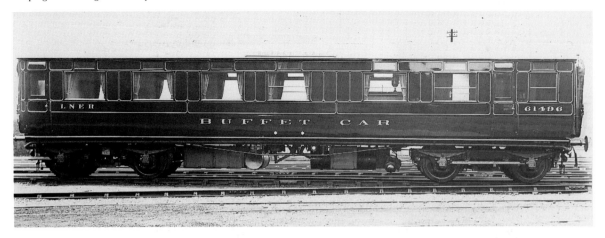

the LNER and met with considerable success as the numbers in Table 7 reveal. What is perhaps most surprising is that the other companies did not seem to see it the same way. The GWR had a few but the LMS merely tinkered with the idea and the SR did not bother at all until Bulleid's time, and even this post-dated the formation of BR except for EMU stock. To the modern traveller, even discounting the cost advantage compared with the full dining car, the buffet car is so well established as the normal form of train catering that it is rarely possible to get the full meal service unless travelling first class — full circle indeed. We are told that there is no longer a demand for such things — and this may be true — but one cannot help but think that the intrinsic cost disadvantages of a full catering service, adumbrated on page 83, have at last been allowed to govern the overall policy.

We have perhaps strayed a little forward of the grouping period in this regard, so these issues will mostly have to await the next volume to discuss more fully. Meantime, what it meant in practical terms was that the proper dining car, with a few exceptions, probably reached its apogee during the final company period and nothing built since nationalization displayed any conceptual improvement. In fact, looking back to early BR days, it is noteworthy how often the catering facilities were regularly provided by company-designed vehicles in an otherwise BR standard carriage formation; few of the LMS standard dining cars, for example, were withdrawn before the late 1950s and most served into the early 1960s.

As with sleeping cars, the two major Anglo-Scottish companies were also dominant in the catering field (see Tables 7 and 8) and if buffet cars are excluded, the LMS again occupied an even more leading role (almost 50 per cent) in terms of its more conventional catering stock. To some extent, this degree of imbalance is to be expected, given the nature of the

services operated by both it and the LNER; and undoubtedly the latter company redressed the balance more than somewhat by using buffet cars where the LMS would offer a more conventional alternative. But what it is perhaps most surprising is that unlike sleeping cars, where the northern lines would naturally take precedence, train catering is a daytime activity so one would have expected the GWR in particular to have been rather better represented. It did, of course, have a fine inheritance of catering vehicles in 1923 so perhaps the need was less, but whereas the LMS and LNER went on building newer and better vehicles to supplement their own, usually quite excellent, pre-1923 fleets, the GWR yet again seems to have taken a rather complacent line.

In the first volume I stated that the grouping probably did the GWR no favours in terms of carriage design compared with its rivals and this does seem to be reflected in much of its inter-war activities. Supporters of this company may well feel that this is a somewhat harsh judgement, but it is hard not to make it — and catering vehicles were no exception. Even one of its most noted apologists has written that GWR dining cars after the grouping were often 'unremarkable' and 'without any special distinctions' * and this seems to have extended to the numbers built as well.

The Southern's situation was rather different and in many respects its approach to the train catering problem was the most praiseworthy of the four companies. It started from a low point compared with the others (a handful of ex-LSWR dining cars and little else) while two of its three constituents had put all their catering into the hands of the Pullman Company. Although this latter situation was to be maintained (and even increased — see Chapter 12), the SR, never the richest of companies, managed to build

* *Great Western Coaches*: M.Harris *(ibid)*

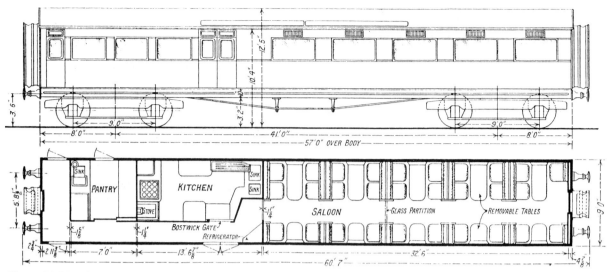

Figure 30 *Elevation and plan of Maunsell's first SR dining car, the 29-seat third class carriages built in 1925 as part of the final 'Ironclad' series (see page 18).*

Scale: $^1/_{10}"$ = 1ft

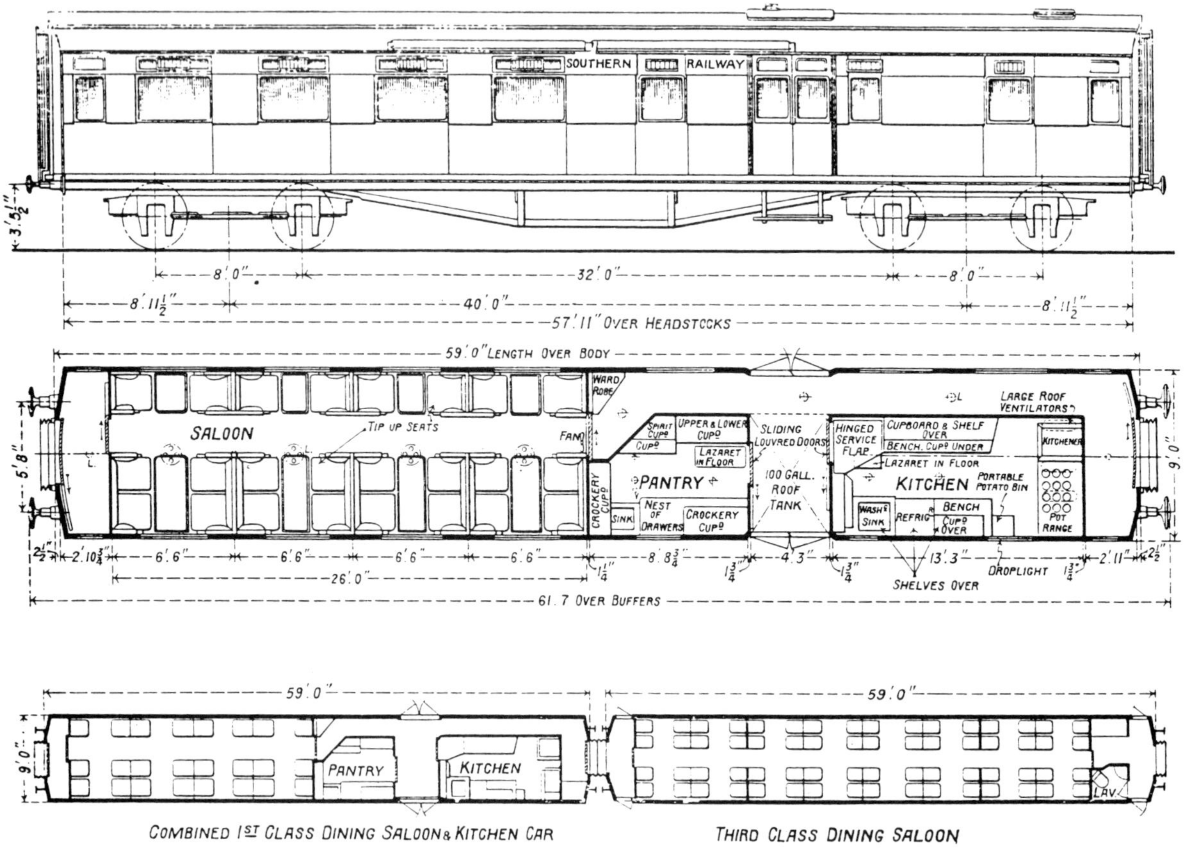

Figure 31 *Elevation and plan of the initial Maunsell SR standard first class dining cars of 1927, along with schematic floor plans of the normal Southern Railway dining car pairing.*

Scale: $^1/_{10}"$ = 1ft

COMBINED 1ST CLASS DINING SALOON & KITCHEN CAR

THIRD CLASS DINING SALOON

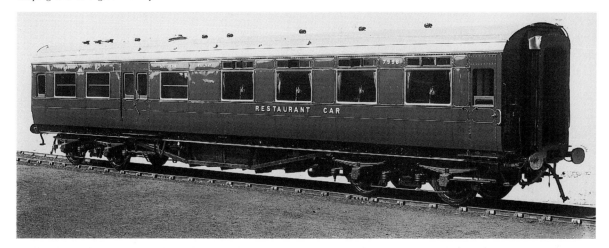

The final Maunsell diners appeared in 1934 and No 7998 was one of them. It differed very little from the 1927 type in Figure 31, save for the outer end passenger doors (SR official, NRM).

more first class dining cars than did the LMS and only marginally fewer than did the LNER. The LMS position was, of course, influenced by its large number of third class dining cars and kitchen cars, but offsetting this was the fact that the Southern's fleet was almost exclusively devoted to the former LSWR lines where it probably deployed almost as many dining cars as did the GWR on the whole of its larger system.

The Southern Railway, of course, though perhaps better known for its great electrification programmes, was pre-eminently a passenger railway throughout its whole territory for reasons given in the previous volume, and this fact alone clearly influenced all its activities. Indeed, one writer has stated, *inter alia*: 'The coaches of Richard Maunsell were the last to be designed for the Southern with the absolute right of passenger preference in mind.'[*] Given the lack of cash resources in absolute terms which it often suffered (hence its major reconstruction of old steam stock for electric services), the Southern made a quite remarkable effort to woo its customers, and the fleet of dining cars can clearly be seen as part of this endeavour.

So much, then, by way of overview; what of the vehicles themselves?

In terms of vehicle design, and in spite of my strictures about the GWR, there was probably little to choose between any of them in terms of fundamental quality and constructional excellence. By now this was an expected attribute of British carriage builders and was almost always present. The major interest, therefore, lies more in the slight variations of concept between the companies combined with those few design innovations and technical improvements which some of them began to make. And having arrived on

[*] *Maunsell's SR Steam Passenger Stock*: David Gould, Oakwood Press, 1978

the Southern Railway, we might as well remain there for the moment.

In 1923, in association with those determined efforts to improve the long-distance image of the company mentioned in previous chapters, Maunsell seems to have resolved that all the principal West of England services should have proper catering facilities. At the time, such few as were available were provided by centre-kitchen composite dining cars running in the centre of fixed, usually five-coach, corridor sets. At first, Maunsell took these as his role model, and in 1923 and 1925, as part of the last 'Ironclad' series — see Chapter 1 — a further eight diners were built, this time end-kitchen, officially third class and seating 29, though it appears likely that they may often have operated as 'common' cars.

Very soon thereafter, the capacity of these LSWR-inspired carriages was considered inadequate, and by 1927 the first of the Maunsell standard dining cars appeared. They were end-kitchen first class only, seating 24, but were designed from the outset to run with a full open third dining car, and this became the standard Southern arrangement until Bulleid's time. The open thirds were 64-seaters and the SR never adopted the more generous 2 + 1 seating arrangement in its third class open diners. This, in fact, was probably the only slightly parsimonious feature of Southern catering and compared less than favourably with the LMS and LNER which, as already indicated, generally favoured the more spacious arrangement in their third class dining vehicles. From the Southern standpoint, however, it doubtless made economic sense since its GWR rival also favoured 2 + 2 seating in

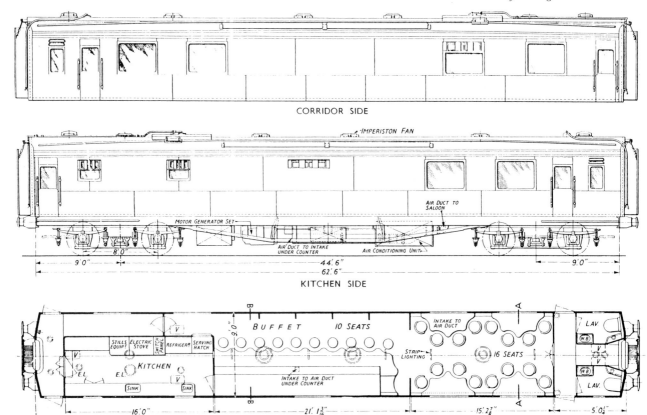

CORRIDOR SIDE

KITCHEN SIDE

SECTION A.A.   SECTION B.B.

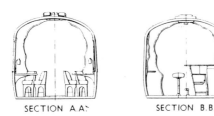

Figure 32 *Elevations and plans of the 'Bognor' buffet cars incorporated in the 4BUF EMU sets of 1938 (see page 138).*

Scale: $^1/_{10}$" = 1ft

Below right *The 'Bognor' buffet car interior was certainly different, but the lack of side windows at the counter end was not well liked. The later 'Tavern' cars repeated this mistake (SR official, NRM).*

the third class, and if all 64 seats could be filled with happily eating customers, so much the better!

The dining cars themselves were to the standard 59-foot length, eight wheeled and of characteristically solid Maunsell style. The design scarcely altered until the last of them was built in 1934, save that the earlier examples were built without the outside passenger entrance doors which later versions sported. They were handsomely proportioned vehicles, with more than a hint of Pullman in their decor— including individual table lamps — and a fairly mandatory quota of wood panelling and moquette. The more avant-garde interior decor ideas, much favoured by Gresley on the LNER, never penetrated the Southern until Bulleid's time, and then in much different form.

Their lack of external doors and very soundly conceived window ventilation gave them quite a modern look compared with most Maunsell corridor stock, but the fact that they were identical in size and shape to the general service carriages meant that they did not stand out in the train compared with their pre-group clerestory ancestors; but then the best Southern expresses of the 1920s and 1930s were mostly very neat and tidy.

Maunsell had achieved so much by the mid-1930s that there was no need for Bulleid to do very much at all for more than ten years afterwards in terms of new catering vehicles, and of course, the war intervened to slow things down even further. But needless to say, when this extraordinary man began to address the problem it would have been surprising indeed had there been no changes — and so there were. Bulleid was a fine carriage designer and, as will be seen in Chapter 14, most of his stylistic ideas were probably more in tune with modern ideas than any of his contemporaries. In terms of conventional dining provision, this was also made evident when he reversed the Maunsell policy of adding a first class dining car plus open third to almost any express formation by adopting a fully integrated dining facility in the main set of carriages.

Bulleid employed a third class dining car plus open first arrangement. In fact, it was a semi-open first, still offering 24 dining seats, but this then made it possible to put another open third at the opposite end of the dining car and all 11 of the new-style dining cars were thus employed in fixed formation sets for the Waterloo-Bournemouth services. Clearly, the existing first class accommodation was considered adequate and it was the third class which was given augmented provisioning. The only mean thing about it was the retention of 2 + 2 seating in the third class dining areas, and history does not tell us how capable Bulleid's kitchens were of serving meals to 24 first class and no fewer than 96 third class passengers on a two-hour trip. One wonders if they ever tried — the LMS would undoubtedly have used a full kitchen car and double-strength catering crew for this level of patronage! But at the very least it indicated a willingness to think about the problem.

It was Bulleid too who first addressed the 'buffet car' concept on the SR with any degree of conviction. In this, it is hard not to see his experience of LNER buffet cars at work; he was, after all, Gresley's chief assistant until 1937. At its most successful, the buffet car was first seen on the newly electrified medium-distance services to the south coast from 1937 onwards in the form of the well-known '4BUF' units which are also considered in context in the next chapter. At this juncture, therefore, it is perhaps sufficient to say that in them he first displayed his old master Gresley's characteristic of 'daring to be different' in the context of interior carriage decor. The 'Bognor' buffets, as they were fairly quickly christened, were most certainly that, and by no means to everybody's taste, unlike the often 'French-inspired' interiors adopted by his old LNER chief which almost always got a good press. But they did fill a conceptual gap in SR catering and were regularly well patronized; so maybe it is best left there!

But in his final years, after nationalization, the very final fling in the railway carriage field of this highly idiosyncratic man was to cause even more than the normal controversy which usually surrounded him. I have repeatedly said or inferred, in both this and the previous volume, that railway carriages are as much about people as about technology, and nowhere can this have been more true than in the case of Bulleid's celebrated 'Tavern' cars of 1949. They were, of course, officially 'BR'; and even though they will return in the next volume in the context of BR's own developments in catering vehicles, no one can reasonably doubt that they were also a final manifestation of company individuality and, as such, should equally be considered here.

In essence, the Tavern cars were buffet cars with kitchen and pantry plus the usual passenger seating facilities; but there all resemblance to any other catering vehicle for British service before or since, or even overseas for that matter, ended. It is a moot point whether they were so awful as to break through the taste barrier and come out the other side unscathed or whether they were simply vulgar in the extreme; for what Bulleid had done was to try and put an English (not British, be it noted!) 'pub' into a roughly 64 ft long by 9 ft wide 'envelope' and put it on to railway wheels. Even the new BR red and cream livery helped him, for he could paint the exteriors in imitation half-timbering above the waist and 'English Bond' brickwork on the lower portions — and he even had the temerity to put 'traditional' pub signs on the outside! As if to compound this presumption, it was applied to the 'Tavern' end of the carriage only, the other bit having conventional BR red/cream livery, while within the carriages, dark oak settles and 'ye olde'-type tables, not to mention pseudo half-timbering, were employed in profusion, the latter wall treatment being mostly at the expense of any outside

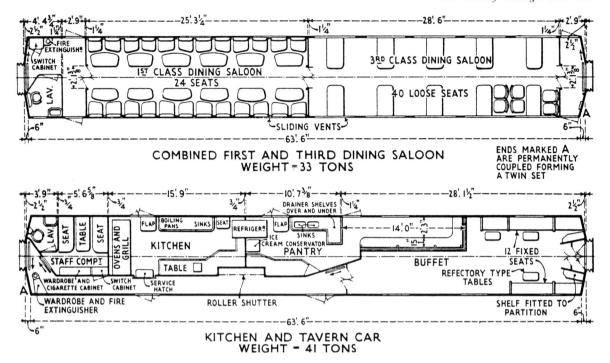

COMBINED FIRST AND THIRD DINING SALOON
WEIGHT = 33 TONS

ENDS MARKED A
ARE PERMANENTLY
COUPLED FORMING
A TWIN SET

KITCHEN AND TAVERN CAR
WEIGHT - 41 TONS

Figure 33 *Floor plans of Bulleid's controversial 'Tavern' cars and the equally unorthodox composite open dining saloons which ran with them. Neither the 'back to the wall' seating in the first class or the almost windowless refectory end of the Taverns met with much approval.*

windows through which the passenger could see out! The whole pastiche was completed (or betrayed, according to opinion) by the bar area then being given a superabundance of 'state of the art' stainless steel, chrome plate and plastic. In general, passengers were less than well pleased and were not long in complaining.

It was all most curious, and those who never saw them — they were not to remain long in their original form — may, even now, doubt their very existence; but was it any worse in principle that the currently fashionable vogue for the spurious and inappropriate 'Edwardianization' of many licensed premises, the re-using of grounded ex-Pullman Car bodies as 'Yuppie' annexes to fashionable restaurants, or pretending that by renovating old Pullman and Wagons-Lits carriages and whirling them at £600 per throw to Venice and elsewhere we are somehow re-creating the days of the great trains? Frankly I don't know, but I think I would rather have liked to have experienced one of Mr Bulleid's 'Taverns' for all that. They most certainly brought some life to the scene in those rather grey austerity post-war years and, who

knows, their less outrageous features may even have made some small contribution to later developments in the BR rail catering field — and there we must leave them for the time being.

If the Southern was most remarkable for its speedy meeting of customer demand in the 1920s and 1930s, and for its adventurous innovations in the 1940s, then the GWR must surely have been one of the last bastions of tradition in the railway scene — and none the worse for that, if truth be told. So maybe this is the right moment at which to redress some of the balance concerning this great railway which has, so far, received little praise in these pages in terms of its post-1922 contribution to carriage building developments.

In purely catering terms, the GWR was well established at the grouping and its pre-1923 dining cars could stand comparison with the very best — see, for example, Volume 1, pages 204-5 — and maybe this was the problem. For, as has been suggested already, there was probably a degree of complacency about the post-1922 GWR which all but its most bigoted supporters must concede. It had good cause, for a variety of reasons, and it is a measure of the absolute quality of its pre-1923 contribution, whether in the realm of locomotives or carriages, that there was no perceived need to make too many changes. After all, even the GWR had to pay dividends and, no matter what one's personal views may be, the hard-nosed

Above *Detail of a Bulleid Tavern car in service on the 'Atlantic Coast Express', showing the painted fake brickwork and half timbering, the 'pub sign' and the very small high-level windows* (NRM Collection).

Above right *The 'Olde Englishe' interior of a Bulleid Tavern* (NRM Collection).

railway management of the 1920s and 1930s, even that of the highly image-conscious GWR, would be indisposed to make too many changes unless they were needed. If proof be needed of this fact, one has merely to consider the GWR's highly significant pioneering work in the field of cross-country diesel traction (see Chapter 9), where its contribution to future development was probably as important as its conventional carriage building was not!

The fact is that the GWR probably did not need to improve its main-line services with quite the sense of urgency as did its rivals. For one thing, its principal competitor to the West of England — and even then not all parts — was the LSWR, and there was no real threat there until after the grouping when Maunsell had turned the Southern Railway round, so to speak (see above). On its other flank, the GWR mostly had the LMS to contend with, but not to any great extent save for the Birmingham traffic and, to a much lesser extent, some degree of more penetrating competition into Wales and the Welsh Marchlands, plus an element of *frisson* in the Wirral region

north of Chester. It may, therefore, reasonably be assumed that Paddington took the view that a relatively modest and economically acceptable injection of new ideas would suffice for most purposes — and so it was to prove. In effect, the GWR had a fair degree of territorial monopoly and while it would not deliberately 'short change' its patrons, it probably did not see the need to try as hard as did the LMS and LNER in their mutual rivalry nor even the Southern in its commendable attempts to match its larger rivals.

Given this assessment, which does not seem too unreasonable, the GWR carriage building activities of the 1920s and 1930s make rather more sense. At all events, the GWR catering contribution was characteristically one of quite cautious change rather than staggering innovation. Symptomatic of this approach — and by no means the least of the reasons why there were less new dining cars than might otherwise have been expected — was the extensive rebuilding of many of the Churchward era dining cars during the 1930s at a time when the LMS and LNER were scrapping their more or less contemporary vehicles. Such was the high quality of the Edwardian GWR diners that a dozen or so were thus treated when they were between 20 and 30 years old; with new flush-style exteriors replacing their former beaded configuration, they were scarce distinguishable from the new vehicles with which they ran. Some

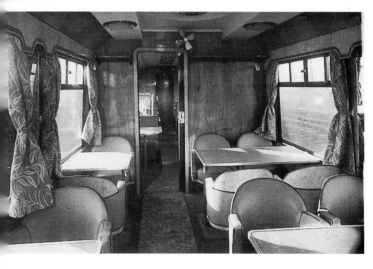

Left *GWR composite restaurant car No 9607 was built in 1930 and typifies the bow-ended, bulging-side style. These cars were the subject of two separate rebuildings — see the next views (GWR official, NRM).*

Middle left *This view shows the first class saloon of No 9602 after some changes to the windows — but there has been no real change in style. It is still very traditional (GWR official, NRM).*

Bottom left *Post-war Hampton-style conversion of an unidentified GWR composite restaurant car. This is the same first class area of the car as shown in the previous view but now looking in the opposite direction. The transformation was complete; note particularly the new-style roof treatment and the third class saloon with its glass-screened seating bays, just visible through the door (GWR official, NRM).*

Right *Exterior and interior views of the GWR 'quick lunch' buffet car No 9631 when new in 1934 (GWR official, NRM).*

were, additionally, mounted on heavier duty six-wheel bogies and most remained active until the late 1950s and early 1960s. In fact, the rebuilding of older dining cars — or at very least a comprehensive internal refurbishment — was a characteristic GWR policy and was to be repeated after the Second World War in 1947 with the well-known 'Hampton' conversions, some of which were in fact 'second time round' rebuilds of later pre-group stock of 1922 vintage which had already had one major pre-war face-lift.

Turning now to new carriages, the bow-ended era saw the introduction of further dining cars of no great pioneering significance, though they were, of course, very well built. But there were no signs that the company wished to make any striking changes. Thus, even the celebrated articulated triplets of 1923 seem, in retrospect, to have been more of a gesture than anything else. The open first plus kitchen car plus open third made eminently good sense, and was a common GWR arrangement, but one senses that the articulated versions were introduced with no great conviction and their subsequent rebuilding as single unit vehicles was to prove this point.

Approximately equal in emphasis to the use of a kitchen car flanked by open stock was the familiar pairing of first class dining car plus open third but, and proportionally rather more so than on other lines, the single unit composite diner devoid of supplementary open carriages was almost as common a solution on the GWR as the other two ideas added together.

In terms of styling, the new GWR carriages followed contemporary company practice, including the bulging-side profile of the later bow-ended period, but internally there were no great innovations and, like the Southern, the GWR also favoured 2 + 2 seating in the third class. Even the above-mentioned

rebuilds often retained much of their original interior and it was not until the post-war era that anything distinctively different began to appear. As far as can be judged, this was probably inspired by the final series of pre-war buffet and dining cars wherein the GWR made a rather attractive attempt at combining the then fashionable Art Deco styling with the favoured traditional interior layout. The best of them were undoubtedly the 'Centenary' diners of 1935, but these have their own place in a later chapter. Of the others, the 1938 twelve-wheel buffet cars and composite dining cars were probably the most significant.

One of them was singled out for renovation as a post-war prototype and in fairly short order many more were so treated. Most of the inspiration came from the firm of Hamptons and took the form of installing a somewhat 'Odeon'-style interior into older vehicles, along with better and more modern windows. Typically, the first class areas were given individual revolving 'bucket' seats in grey leather while the thirds, retaining the 2 + 2 arrangement, were offered low-backed green leather bench-type seating, often with decorative glass screens above the seat backs bearing Art Deco pictorial motifs. False ceilings with flat centre sections and concealed lighting, along with modern flush-veneered wood panelling, completed the ensemble. It was certainly different, but such was the strength of tradition that not all approved. While many of the older vehicles undoubtedly needed some form of brightening up, it was perhaps unfortunate that this treatment was also given to the aforementioned Centenary diners; they most certainly did not need it and the preserved example would undoubtedly have said more about the best Swindon practice had it retained its original interior.

Although not as lavish as the LNER in its provi-

sioning, the GWR was a very good runner-up in the buffet car arena, being far better than either the LMS or SR in this respect. Like the LNER, its first efforts were conversions from older pre-group stock, but with its new vehicles of the middle and later 1930s it may even be said to have been the leader of the pack in conceptual terms when it pioneered two particularly interesting new ideas. One of them was the by now well-known 'quick lunch' buffet car of 1934, preserved in the National Collection and currently on loan to the Severn Valley Railway. This vehicle consists simply of a long bar counter running the length of the carriage at which passengers can either stand or sit on fixed stools. A small kitchen is at one end but otherwise the essential facilities are all neatly stowed either under the bar or at the back, all within easy reach of the staff.

Even better than this type (of which only two were

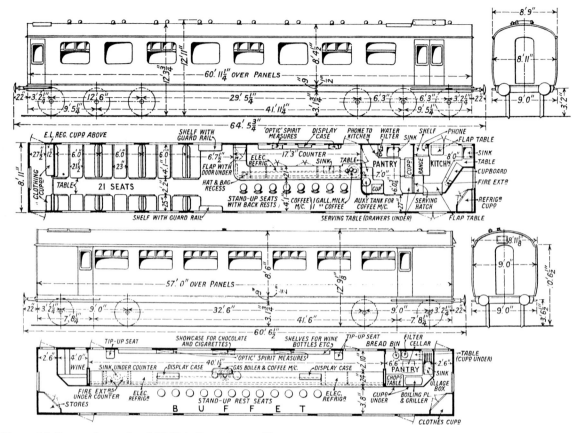

Figure 34 *Two good examples of GWR buffet car layout. The upper was the most favoured type, while the lower shows the 'quick lunch' buffet car.*

Scale: 2mm = 1ft

built) were the twelve-wheel buffet cars of 1938. These combined a somewhat similar bar arrangement with fixed stools (occupying the middle third of the carriage) with, at one end, 21 fixed low-backed leather seats of a type similar to the post-war Hampton conversions and at the opposite end a very adequate kitchen and pantry. As all-purpose catering vehicles they were hard to better and were amongst the very last GWR examples to be withdrawn in the mid-1960s.

Thus, in its final years, the GWR was by no means without enterprise in the catering field, after a somewhat stodgy middle period, and it too dared to innovate. It even put a small and well-designed buffet bar across the end of some of its diesel railcars (see Chapter 9), which was far more comprehensive in its offerings than many a larger more modern BR train!

Turning now to the two big companies, it is easier,

as with their sleeping car designs, to deal with them together, for in a very real sense their catering vehicles were as much a manifestation of their mutual competition as anything else. Each of them built more new dining cars during the company period proper than the GWR and SR between them, and if the LMS built twice as many kitchen cars as all three of its rivals added together, then the LNER buffet car fleet was equally dominant in this particular genre, also representing some two-thirds of the British total.

Quite apart from the purely cosmetic variations caused by their differing liveries and forms of carriage construction, the LMS and LNER tended to adopt rather different approaches to the whole business of train catering. In part, this may have been deliberate in the interests of promoting their individual images, but it was also a consequence of their pre-group inheritance.

Take, for instance, that very characteristic LMS feature, the twelve-wheel diner. It was not that the LNER did not have any, for it inherited a fair number of superb examples from its constituents, but it never built any more after 1922, preferring instead to concentrate its efforts either on the articulated option or the standard length eight-wheel vehicle. By contrast, the LMS never built a full dining car which did not have twelve wheels, and even though the GWR occasionally assayed the type, the LMS was without doubt the last convinced adherent to the form.

In this it seems reasonable to presume that the inherited experience of the LNWR and the MR, particularly the former, were the decisive factors, and it could be significant that the very first of the post-group LMS twelve-wheel dining cars of 1925 (a 30-seat composite) was, like the contemporary sleeping cars, almost undilutedly LNWR in its styling and was fitted with LNWR bogies. However, apart from these few cars it did seem that the LMS had abandoned the full dining car as it proceeded to put into service a quite colossal tranche of more than 70 dedicated kitchen cars between 1924 and 1928. This sudden move to an idea which, though not unheard of, had never been practised to this extent before and was never matched in such quantity by any other company, was almost certainly tied in with the building of large quantities of open stock explained in Chapter 4.

It is not known whether the LMS seriously contemplated an almost total standardization on the kitchen car plus open carriage format. Demand was, of course, rising, but although the full kitchen car could offer a greater number of meals than a conventional dining car, and soon became a feature of most of the bigger trains, there were still many services which would be over-provisioned if this idea was universally adopted. Here, the fact that the LMS had acquired a very good fleet of conventional dining cars from both the LNWR and MR, many of which were of no great age, became relevant; for these were most certainly not put out to grass. However, when they were reaching about 30 years of age, the LMS chose not to rebuild them as had the GWR in similar circumstances, but to replace them almost like-for-like. Thus, the 1930s saw a great resurgence of the twelve-wheel catering vehicle. In the event, this was to prove the final flowering of the twelve-wheel idea in terms of British catering vehicles, and a fine climax it made.

Meantime, the LNER took rather a different line and tended to follow GNR practice, which was also the dominant influence on the East Coast Joint Stock. Here, Gresley had begun to move away from the bigger, all-purpose dining car and fairly soon two principle alternatives began to be the preferred LNER

Figure 35 *Probably the most favoured LNER catering arrangements: articulated triplet set and the first class dining car plus open third pairing.*

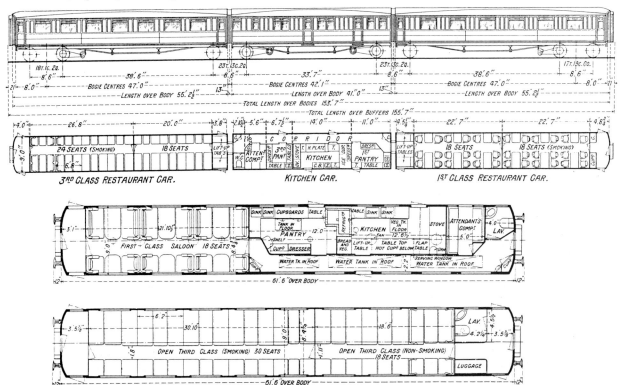

forms. Most celebrated were the articulated triplets in which a central kitchen unit was flanked by open first and third class elements. These were used on the busier services, while simultaneously the alternative preferred form settled down to a conventional non-articulated first class diner plus open third pairing, the thirds being quite often of the type which contained a small pantry (with cupboards and hotplate only) at one end. Like the LMS, the LNER also made full use of its inherited fleet for many years, so the variety to be seen on both lines was rather greater than the above-described standard procedures might suggest. Also, like the LMS, the LNER chose not to rebuild its older cars and let them run on to the end of their useful life — in the event, often quite long.

Technically, there was little remarkable about the vehicles built by either company which was not shared with other general service carriages, and the only serious experiments were connected with a wish to dispense with compressed oil gas as a cooking medium in the kitchens, whether they be in kitchen cars or proper dining cars. This was tied in with a general desire to eliminate gas lighting as well, this time in all carriage stock. The fear, of course, was the greater fire risk, a hazard which had been instrumental in consuming some gas-lit carriages earlier in the century.

Gresley favoured all-electric cooking and had first demonstrated his ideas with the celebrated quintuplet dining car set for the GNR Leeds services in 1921. The method relied on a multiplicity of ground points and battery charging facilities throughout the system, not to mention a far greater battery storage capability on the carriage itself. But the sheer economics of eliminating gas (it was still needed for carriage lighting in many older vehicles) meant that the full economy of completely closing the gas plants could not be achieved. Another disadvantage was the fact that

since they relied on ground facilities, the all-electric dining cars were not self-sufficient and this militated against their use on cross-country services. During 1937, therefore, in conjunction with J.Stone and Co, the LNER conducted experiments with solid fuel cooking which would reduce the call-off on the carriage electrical supply. Anthracite was used to heat the water and main ovens while electricity did the rest. These anthracite-electric cars soon became familiar, and all new construction was to employ this form from 1938 onwards.

The LMS was not quite as concerned about the problems of gas cooking as the LNER, even though its own constituents had been just as prone to having gas fire accidents in their history as had those of the LNER. It thus continued to remain faithful to oil gas until 1933 when, as part of Stanier's re-assessment of the situation, an experimental new all-electric kitchen car was built. In this vehicle, the electricity was provided by two on-board diesel generators, one at each end, and these took up some 11 ft 6 in of the vehicle length, thus causing an enlargement of the whole vehicle from the customary 50 ft of the gas-fitted kitchen cars to a 60-foot length. Again, a handsome modern-looking vehicle resulted, and it too went to North America with *Royal Scot* in 1933. A second car of the same type was finished in 1934, but thereafter the experiment ended with little in the way of published evidence to indicate its success or failure. One does rather suppose that the noise of the generators may well have been an irritant to the catering crews if no one else. Suffice to say that all subsequent Stanier kitchen cars, of which there were a fair number, reverted to the traditional 50-foot length with gas cooking to which the LMS thereafter remained faithful, save for one experiment with solid fuel cooking in the kitchen car of the ill-fated 1939 'Coronation Scot' set (see Chapter 11).

Left *Prototype LMS diesel-electric kitchen car No 30073 showing, at the near end with the doors open, one of the two generator sets. This car went to North America with* Royal Scot *(BR LMR).*

Above right *Though not perhaps quite as celebrated as the 'French'-style interiors of ten years earlier, the LNER 'Flying Scotsman' first class dining ends of the 1938 articulated triplets had a very light and airy interior in a restrained Art Deco style, and were perhaps more typical of British practice generally* (LNER official, NRM).

An interesting conclusion to the LNER and LMS experiments with electric cooking finally arrived in the early 1960s. The two LMS kitchen cars had long been scrapped and the LNER electric cars (of both types) were still proving either expensive to maintain or, in the case of the all-electric versions, were often incapable of operating all their equipment while on the move. BR therefore decided to dispense with electric cooking and standardized all catering vehicles with gas, this time of the bottled propane variety. It was not until our modern Mk III era that electricity returned in the form of microwaves and the like.

Turning now to the general design of dining cars on the LMS and LNER as it affected the passenger, it seems fair to say that they were both, in their way, rather more forward looking than either the GWR or SR. While they were both capable of producing uninspired carriages, they were equally capable of offering vehicles whose internal decor and ambience was the equal of anything which had gone before. Naturally enough, the first class passenger was at the head of the list of clients to be satisfied, and in sheer panache the LNER probably took the prize. In 1928, as part of some new triplet dining sets for the re-equipped and soon to be non-stop 'Flying Scotsman' train, Gresley adopted a new 'French' style of decor. It was a deliberate attempt to produce a sort of eighteenth-century feel to the coaches and the design was put in the hands of White, Allom and Co. This company had also been involved with the experimental re-decoration of the LNER sleeping cars (see above) where its ideas took second place to those of Waring and Gillow and were not adopted; not so in the dining cars.

All natural timber finishes were suppressed, the first class areas being finished in either soft blue and stone (fawn) or red and stone, and individual armchairs were provided instead of fixed seating. Decorative pelmets surmounted the curtained windows and the whole impression was one of relaxed elegance. And it was carried through into the third class as well. Here, fixed seating was adopted with a green and stone colour scheme, but again a most gracious effect resulted, which was rather unusual for the LNER whose third class interiors were not usually as good as those of its rival.

Of course, not all LNER dining cars were given such special treatment and Harris records that public reaction was not particularly favourable*. I must confess that I find this rather suprising, having enjoyed travelling in some later LNER examples of the 'French' style, but the fact remains that the 1929 build of new carriages for the East Anglian services reverted to a somewhat uninspired and very traditional form. However, in 1935 a first class variant of

*Gresley's Coaches: M.Harris (*ibid*)

the 'French' style was again offered on the Anglo-Scottish services and this too seems in retrospect to have been rather good. The LNER's prime achievement in this area was, of course, in its special streamlined stock; but this will have to wait its turn (Chapter 11).

The LMS took no risks with any form of avantgarde interior decor in the pre-Stanier period, but its own development of the traditional forms was very well done. It first appeared in the dining ends of its first class semi-open stock of 1928-30 for the 'Royal Scot' train (see page 65), but was then used in splendidly opulent form in a magnificent series of first class twelve-wheelers built between 1930 and 1932 in the new steel-panelled style. Rarely had a traditional dining car been so agreeably finished, and if it lacked the flair of Gresley's best efforts, it more than compensated in terms of sumptuous comfort.

There were two conceptual aspects which usually diffentiated LMS and LNER first class dining cars. In general, the LNER examples were smaller, being mounted on standard 60-foot underframes and having but 18 seats, while the LMS equivalent always offered 24 (hence the need for 12 wheels); secondly, the LNER had rather more of them in spite of it being a smaller company. Whether the 18-seat capacity was always adequate is not known, but presumably it must have sufficed. In any case, both companies retained the option of operating a full open diner in conjunction with a kitchen car for the busier trains, whether articulated or in the form of individual vehicles.

Another difference in principle was that the LMS, even after Stanier's arrival, was still very disposed to

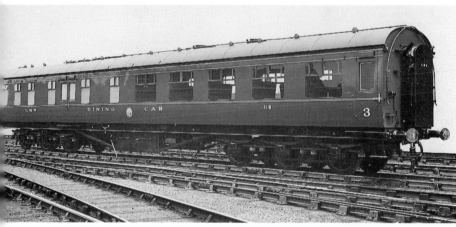

LMS Stanier-pattern third class dining car No 118 of early 1934, just after the change to simplified exterior livery (BR LMR).

Figure 36 *Elevation, plan and interior seating detail of Stanier's initial first class LMS dining cars of 1933.*

Scale: *¹/₁₂"* = *1ft (main elevation)*

adopt traditional finishes, whereas the LNER continued to experiment, particularly in the first class. But if the LNER was more enterprising in this respect, it was in the third class arena that the LMS seems to have redressed the balance. For the most part this is explained by the fact that the LMS built composite and third class dining cars to a much greater extent than did the LNER, and here it showed its strength.

In 1932, coincidental with the above-mentioned first class cars, the LMS also built a clutch of equally splended 30-seat composites for cross-country working. They were, in fact, generally regarded as 'common' diners and had detachable class designation boards in the windows. Apart from slightly smaller seating bay dimensions, they were every bit as well founded as the first class version, and this was to be the prelude to a period when it became harder and harder to differentiate between the first and third class parts of an LMS dining car set. The instigator, once again, was probably William Stanier.

Within his first year or so, the new modern flush-sided exterior styling was applied to the twelve-wheel dining car and no fewer than 77 new diners emerged from both Derby and Wolverton between 1933 and 1937 in all three types. This was the most concentrated building of dedicated dining cars in Britain since Wolverton's LNWR/WCJS efforts early in the century, and was not unconnected with the fact that these new Stanier cars were designed mostly to take their place. From 1936 onwards, most were given pressure heating and ventilation of the type newly developed for the sleeping car fleet. The firsts had the customary 24 seats, the composites and thirds had 30 and it was the third class version which was numerically dominant. Within the cars, though the traditional timber finishes were retained, much variation in timber type and upholstery material was to be found and the seat design was altered to a suitably modern look. The main difference between the first and third class was the provision of window curtains and generally softer upholstery and more heavily padded armrests in the firsts, but in all conscience there was little to choose between them and all, of course, had 2 + 1 seating, this being customary LMS and LNER practice in dining vehicles.

These twelve-wheelers were to be the last of a famous breed and they, together with a few more kitchen cars and, of course, associated open stock, were to see the LMS through to nationalization and, for the most part, for another 10 to 15 years afterwards.

But if the LMS had the edge in third class dining cars, the LNER was undoubtedly the trend-setter when it came to the buffet car alternative. This idea could trace itself back, as far as the LNER was concerned, to pioneering turn of the century efforts by the GCR, and in 1932 the LNER began to experiment with the conversion of some pre-group GER and NER stock, though contemporary accounts rather tried to give the impression that they were new. It quite soon settled down in 1933 to a more or less

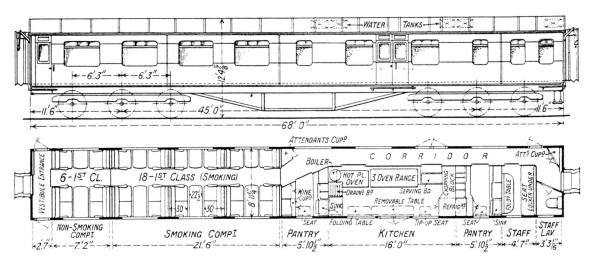

General arrangement of first class dining and kitchen car, L.M.S.R.

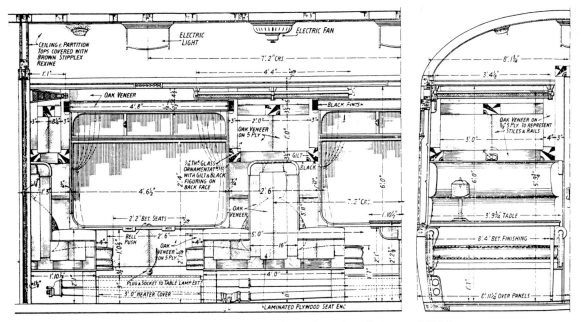

Longitudinal and cross sections of new first class dining car, L.M.S.R.

Left and below left *First and third class ends of LMS composite open dining car No 9755 of 1939; one almost needs the label over the doors to tell them apart. This type of carriage usually operated with the third class diners shown in the previous picture (both BR LMR).*

Below *LNER buffet car No 648 when new in 1935. These were the most common LNER buffets and were to prove the very last Gresley-type vehicles to remain in passenger service on BR. Several are preserved, including one at the NRM (LNER official, NRM).*

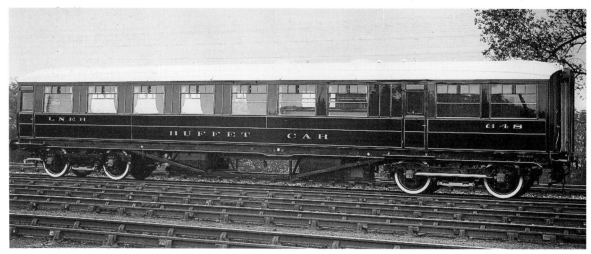

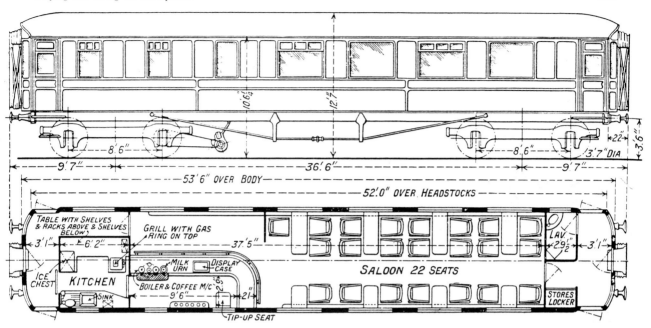

standard arrangement of a kitchen and serving bar at one end with 24 seats at the other, all mounted on the standard 60-foot underframe. It was not, perhaps, quite as well thought out as the later GWR type (see above), nor was the interior decoration anything like as attractive, but in terms of sheer numbers it was undoubtedly more significant, and in them can easily be seen the start of the modern most favoured train catering provision.

The vast majority were trimmed in Rexine with stark chromium-plated seats of dubious aesthetic merit and no comfort whatsoever. They also had painted ceilings and bare light bulbs and were certainly no place to linger, but maybe that was deliberate. Moreover, the value for money in terms of the bill of fare was of a high order. They were destined to become the last Gresley carriages in regular BR service, by now re-equipped and re-trimmed with almost equally awful 1950s-style laminated plastic. Several are preserved, including one at the National Railway Museum.

Paradoxically, though it never really developed the idea, the LMS actually introduced its first buffet car slightly ahead of the LNER. This took the form of a one-off vehicle in 1932, just a few months ahead of the LNER experiment, and it was launched with

Figure 37 Elevation and plan of the prototype LNER buffet car converted from an ex-NER vehicle. This basic layout became the LNER standard.

Scale: 3mm = 1ft

Right *Interior of Gresley LNER buffet car No 24082, showing tables laid up with the favourite 'Keswick'-pattern crockery. The seats were very uncomfortable!* (LNER official, NRM).

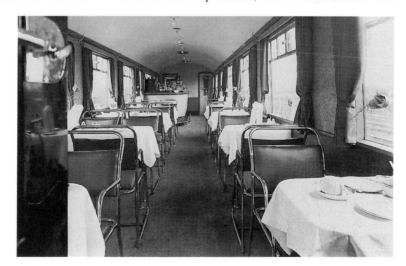

a great deal of fuss and palaver, most of it probably unjustified. The LMS called it a 'Cafeteria' car, though it said 'Buffet' on the outside, and it certainly embodied an interesting layout. The LMS stated 'If the innovation proves as popular as it is anticipated, an order will be placed for a large number of these cars...' So much for fond hopes! Its interior fittings — chrome-plated, naturally, to suit the fashion of the day — were as awesomely bad as those in the later LNER cars and nothing much else happened until 1936 when four more were built to the Stanier pattern but copying the by now normal LNER internal layout. A fair attempt was made to improve the interior decor, and with some success, but the LMS never seemed to know just what to do with the type; although all five lasted until the early 1960s they were

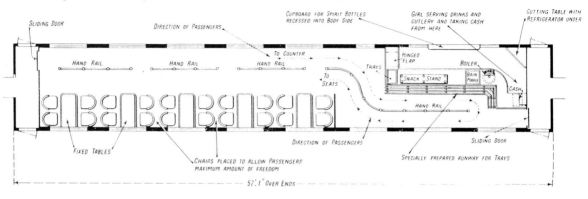

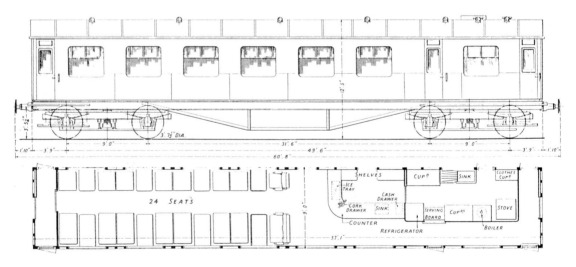

Scale: $^1/_{10}$" = 1ft

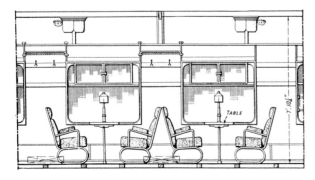

Figure 38 *The two LMS buffet car designs. The upper plan shows the 'Cafeteria' layout first adopted in the prototype car. Its layout was fairly soon altered to something like that of the Stanier-pattern cars shown in the rest of the drawings.*

Right and below right *Contrasting LMS buffet car interiors, separated by only four years in time. The older car shows the rearranged interior of the prototype car whose original floor plan is shown in Figure 38* (BR LMR).

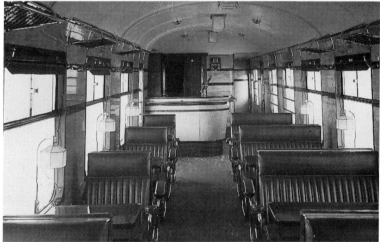

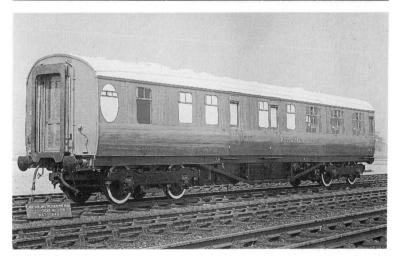

Right *The few post-war LNER-style first class dining cars of 1949, though stylish enough from the outside, were very dreary by comparison with the Gresley breed. This is the first of them, No E1657, outshopped in ersatz teak livery when new* (BR ER official, NRM).

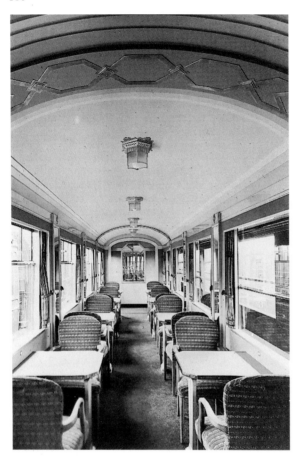

never repeated. A rather clever re-creation of one of them has been built by the Severn Valley Railway in the shell of an orthodox LMS carriage.

Summing up the story, the final verdict between these two great companies is probably 'honours easy', to use the phrase first coined by an earlier writer in reference to their locomotive achievements; and maybe that is as it should be. The great achievements were all made before 1940, and after the war the only new catering vehicles were some not wildly memorable Thompson coaches of very dated and dreary character, most of which actually came out after BR was formed. The LMS contribution was even less, taking the form of two rebuilt carriages in 1947, one open first and one proper diner. They were given loose individual chairs plus a few fixed seats, both of very utilitarian appearance, and although the LMS made its usual publicity meal out of them, it somehow seemed hollow compared with pre-war days. Sadly, and for some unaccountable reason, these really quite awful interiors, particularly the loose chairs, took root in the BR mind and resulted in some of the worst dining car designs ever to be seen emerging as a later BR standard.

Meantime, let no one doubt the real quality of the specialized vehicles which were built by the old private companies. They may not have been perfect, but it is a measure of their quality that, with few exceptions, BR was unable to produce anything better until the days of the Mk III sleeping and dining cars, wherein at last could be seen some real improvements. However, the story of the slow build-up to these events must wait its time for the moment.

Above left *The stylish buffet lounge in the 1938 LNER 'Flying Scotsman' set allowed eating passengers some considerable privacy by means of the by-pass corridor on the right (LNER official, NRM).*

Left *The dated and not very elegant interior of refurbished LMS open first class dining car No 7555 in 1947. It started life with an interior such as that shown on page 112! (BR LMR).*

6. Southern Electric

Regardless of their individual favourites, few would seriously deny that the most far-reaching change in the conceptual development of British carriages during the company period was that wrought by the Southern Railway in its rapid and widespread adoption of electric traction during the 1920s and 1930s. It was not so much that the vehicles themselves were particularly different (they were in fact mostly rather old-fashioned and ordinary for reasons which will be explained), but in the context of a totally changed approach to the business of operating passenger traffic, the Southern stood supreme. One says this, notwithstanding the role of London Transport (see Chapter 7), largely because, unlike the services run by the LPTB, the Southern, within 15 years of the grouping, had transformed a few rather modest suburban ideas in South London into what amounted to a totally integrated electrification policy, embracing almost all categories of passenger transport from inner suburban to main-line operations.

The achievement was all the more remarkable because of the straitened financial circumstances against which it was carried out, and here the major share of the credit must surely go to the Southern's wily General Manager, Sir Herbert Walker KCB. Walker was a dedicated proponent of electrification as the means whereby to counter ever growing road competition. Unfortunately, Southern financial resources were insufficient to meet this threat in the manner which Sir Herbert might well have preferred — brand new rolling-stock to suit a brand new system — but this was not going to stop him. Thus there began that quite astonishing element of carriage rebuilding, often best described as 'make do and mend', which both typified the first 25 years of 'Southern Electric' and also gave it much of its undoubted character. And in this regard, Sir Herbert Walker was more than ably abetted by his CME, Richard Maunsell, whose many other fine achievements have more than once received acclamation in these pages.

The background goes back well before the grouping and was briefly touched upon in the final chapter of the previous volume, but it will be helpful in understanding the fuller development of the whole Southern system if the basic outlines are briefly recapitulated here so that they can be followed through without break into the post-1922 era.

The historical background

The first electrification was that of the Brighton's South London line in 1909 between Victoria and London Bridge via Denmark Hill, closely followed by the Crystal Palace lines well before the First World War. These were electrified on what was, at the time, an advanced 6.7kV AC system: the 'Elevated Electrics', as they were called by virtue of their overhead catenary. Before the grouping, plans were well advanced for further extensions to Coulsdon and Sutton, to the extent that the Brighton overhead system was indeed extended to these two places in 1925 under the auspices of the new Southern Railway. Meantime, from 1915, the LSWR had tackled its own inner suburban services over the Kingston 'roundabout' and from Waterloo to Wimbledon via Putney (plus a few other associated bits and pieces), by means of a radically different 600V DC third rail system. Finally, the SE & CR was planning to go into the electrification business by means of a yet different 1500V DC system, though its ideas had not yet taken tangible form.

There was thus the making of an unholy muddle for the newly amalgamated Southern Railway, and although Walker allowed the Brighton line extensions to go ahead, even by the time they were opened he had realized that the SR must have a unified system of electrification. The final decision was by no means as clear cut as is sometimes supposed, and followed several years of debate, which at times took on quite acrimonious character, between the several protagonists of the various conflicting ideas. The eventual outcome was that the former LSWR three-rail system, later in the field than that of the LB & SCR though arguably less technically advanced, became the new Southern standard. In its favour, however, it did extend over more route mileage than the Brighton overhead in 1923 and was probably more economical to install.*

Added to the economic advantages of the LSWR system was the fact that it made use of rebuilt ex-steam stock, whereas the Brighton overhead had employed new vehicles. The LSWR philosophy in this respect was also adopted, for the most part, by the new Southern Railway and this left a legacy which even today (1990) is by no mean wholly eradicated and which also, curiously enough, represents not the least reason why, in terms of modernity, the Southern Region electrics of the BR period often lingered behind those of other regions until the late 1980s. The

---

* For a far more detailed technical account of the debate surrounding the final adoption of the LSWR 600V system, see *Triumph of the Third Rail* by J.N.Faulkner: 'Railways South East', Vol.1 No.2, Summer 1988.

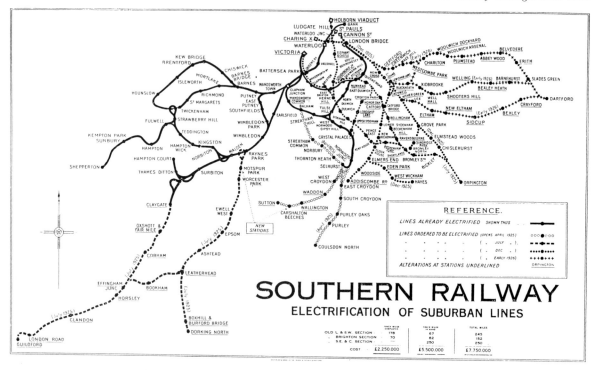

SOUTHERN RAILWAY
ELECTRIFICATION OF SUBURBAN LINES

full story thus embraces both the grouping period and the BR continuation and will figure both here and in the next volume. At this point, therefore, we shall concentrate on the period from the First World War to the end of the Bulleid era, starting with the very disparate inherited offerings.

In 1918, the LB & SCR had two sorts of new stock in operation on its overhead lines, the original South London stock, quite wide bodied and to a new

square-panelled exterior style, and the later Crystal Palace units, more traditionally 'Brighton' and much narrower in body profile. These were pretty conventional EMUs, ie with passenger-carrying power cars and non-powered trailers, but the extensions to Coulsdon and Sutton added a third approach, though still very much in the Brighton visual idiom, with round-cornered panelling and arc roofs. For these services the SR adopted a quite new (and never

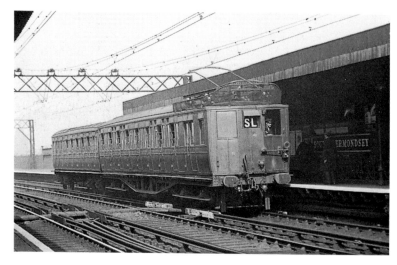

Figure 39 Map showing the early stages of the Southern Railway electrification proposals down to 1926.

Left *Ex-LB & SCR South London two-car unit at South Bermondsey in March 1928, 'wide-bodied' driving motor leading* (H.C. Casserley).

Five-car train of 'Crystal Palace' stock at Victoria early in the SR period. These sets had carriages of much more traditional 'Brighton' outline (Author's collection).

Newly-built third class driving trailer No 9171 for the Coulsdon and Sutton 1925 extensions of the 'elevated electrics'. The lineaments are still very firmly LB & SCR (Metro-Cammell, NRM).

Southern Railway power car No 10101 when new in 1925. Note the guard and luggage space in the centre (Metro-Cammell, NRM).

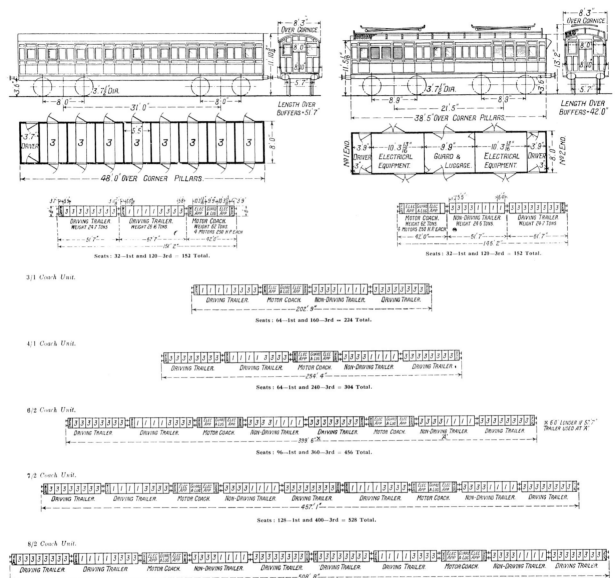

repeated) system of twin-bogie dedicated power cars. They were never called locomotives, presumably because they also incorporated the guard and luggage space, though that is what in effect they were. Commonly nicknamed 'milk vans', they were designed to run with non-powered passenger-carrying trailers in a whole variety of formations, dependent upon traffic demand — see Figure 40 — though the most common was probably one power unit in the centre of a four-car formation. Most of the trailers also had driving cabs to facilitate maximum flexibility of operation.

At the same time, the LSWR had gone for a basic three-car conventional EMU (motor/trailer/motor) with a driving cab at each end and passenger seats in all three carriages. Here, the desired operational flexibility was achieved by means of a single unit for off-peak services, two in multiple being used for busier operations. The vehicles themselves were converted from former suburban steam stock and retained the full LSWR-style panelling and other features. Their new driving cabs, however, displayed distinctively styled 'torpedo'-shaped ends which gave them a very jaunty and highly distinctive appearance.

In only one respect were the Brighton and LSWR carriages remotely similar: their use of conventional compartments. True, some of the LB & SCR first class trailers had a sort of internal 'open' side corridor, but each bay of seats had its own side door and this feature was to remain the norm on SR suburban units, whether the word stood for 'Railway' or 'Region', well into the 1960s. Both of the pre-group companies had offered first and third class accommodation, so the SR continued in this mode. However, the LSWR had used the introduction of its electrics as an excuse to abandon *three*-class provisioning and this too was to prove prophetic when, in logical continuation, first class accommodation was also abandoned on the inner suburban routes throughout the London area in October 1941.

From the outset, the Southern Railway had to reconcile these operational parameters if it was to achieve some sort of uniformity. Fortunately, at this time its immediate thoughts were solely concerned with suburban operations so it is with these that the analysis will start.

Suburban developments, 1925 onwards

'When the present programme is completed, expected before the end of 1926, the Southern Railway will have what is believed to be the most extensive system of Suburban Electrification to be found in this or any other country.'

Thus proclaimed *The Railway Gazette* in March 1925 in the first of what were to prove to be a whole series of highly detailed accounts of Southern electrification for the next 15 years which I am more than happy to acknowledge as a prime source of information for much of the account which follows. In fact, the Southern Electric has attracted to itself a very fine

and detailed literature which makes this writer's task abundantly simpler in terms of trying to distil its essence into a more general overview, and readers who would know more of this fascinating subject are well advised to consult the Bibliography.

The prime reason for Sir Herbert Walker's dedication to electrification seems to have been the substantial success achieved by both the LSWR and the LB & SCR in meeting the challenge of the urban street tramway and reviving their flagging fortunes to a level almost equal to that which pertained before the onset of the electric tramcar. Thus it was not surprising that very soon after the grouping, the various strands of development, independently determined by the three constituents of the SR, were brought together in a comprehensive plan for the wholesale conversion of the South London suburban services to electric operation. Having determined the system to be used (low voltage three-rail DC), the main issue, after meeting the actual cost of the necessary civil and electrical engineering work to effect the change-over, was to determine the most effective and economic way of solving the rolling-stock problem.

In this respect, the LSWR's pre-grouping *modus operandi* seemed, overall, to offer the best way forward. The first intention was, apart from the already agreed 'Brighton' expansion (see above), to extend the existing LSWR system out to Dorking and Guildford and simultaneously inaugurate the former SE & CR proposals from London Bridge as far as Dartford (by all routes) and to Orpington, from Victoria and Holborn Viaduct (via Bromley) and London Bridge (via Chiselhurst), not to mention the considerable 'cat's cradle' of interconnecting lines which, then as now, so characterizes the railways of this part of the country. The SR could only do this within its budget by an extensive rebuilding of steam stock to EMU pat-

Figure 40 *Simplified elevations and plans of the 1925 'elevated' stock together with sketch plans of the many possible train formations which could be made up from this stock.*

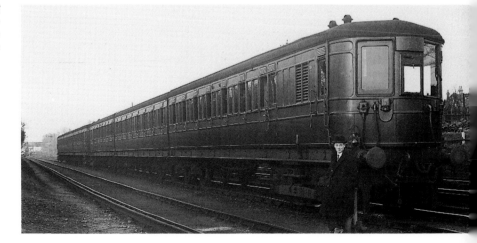

Right *The very first LSWR three-rail EMU, No E1, seen at the head of a six-car train at Strawberry Hill only two months after the grouping. Note the characteristic 'torpedo' front* (H.C. Casserley).

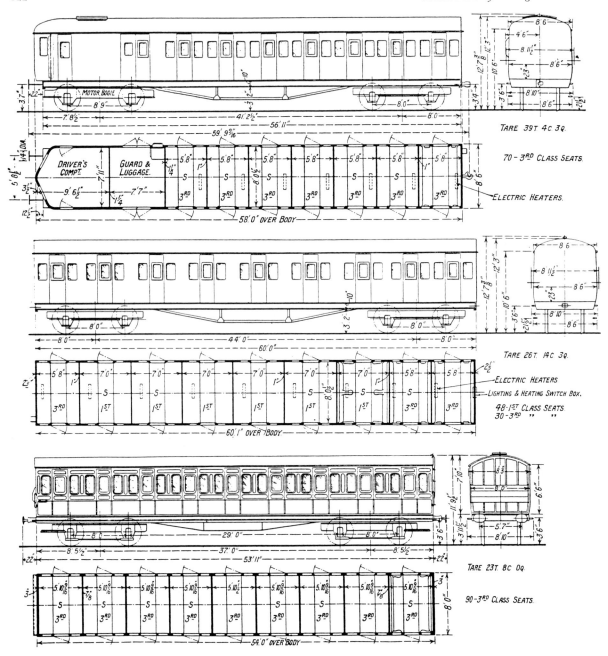

tern, but even this could not wholly solve the problem. Thus began the seemingly unending business of combining newly built with re-worked older stock, the interplay between which constituting much of the fascination of the whole story. Apart from the 'overhead' stock already discussed, the basic LSWR three-car principle was adopted for the rest of the expansion

Figure 41 *Elevations and plans of the 'Western' section new-build EMUs of 1925, together with the converted ex-LB & SCR 'augmentation' trailers.*

Scale: 2mm = 1ft

(motor/trailer/motor), but even so this took three quite distinctive forms.

On the former LSWR lines, now known as the 'Western' section, a tranche of new EMUs was built to supplement the existing converted ex-LSWR steam stock. These consisted of 'torpedo'-fronted 58 ft long third class motor cars and 60-foot composite trailers. Stylistically, they were very much in the newly established, albeit conventional 'Maunsell' SR style with steel outer panelling on timber framing. But their distinctive 'torpedo'-shaped front-end treatment, along with their fully lined 'pseudo-panelled' livery (albeit square-cornered) gave them a strong family resemblance to their LSWR ancestors. In later years they sported round-cornered painted panelling of more orthodox Southern style, and as such one motor car survives in the National Railway Museum at York.

By contrast, the former SE & CR lines, now regarded as the 'Eastern' section, were offered a slight variant of this type, though still retaining the basic 'two motor third plus composite trailer' formation. These too had a mixture of new-build and rebuilt ex-

steam stock, but in this case the former SE & CR carriage length dominated. Thus, the ex-steam stock rebuilds displayed SE & CR lengths and panelling and the corresponding new-built units were to slightly greater (SE & CR) length than their 'Western' section contemporaries. Whether new or rebuilt, motor thirds therefore had eight compartments (rather than seven) and the composites were 7F + 2T rather than the 6F + 3T of the ex-LSWR area. Thus, all Eastern section units were 62 ft long over frames. They also had a very different front-end treatment, much less pointed and conceivably more modern than the shape of the ex-LSWR and new-built 'Western' section units. This revised front-end styling was given to both the ex-SECR steam stock rebuilds and to the new build Eastern section carriages and was, with some slight variations, to become the Southern 'standard' for all EMU stock until the Bulleid era, as indeed was their greater length. Like the new Western section units, the new build Eastern section cars also came into service with square-cornered 'panelling', but before long, round-cornered styling became the Southern norm.

Figure 42 Elevations and plans of the new 'Eastern' section EMUs of 1925 which ran with similar trailers to those shown in Figure 41.

Scale: 2mm = 1ft

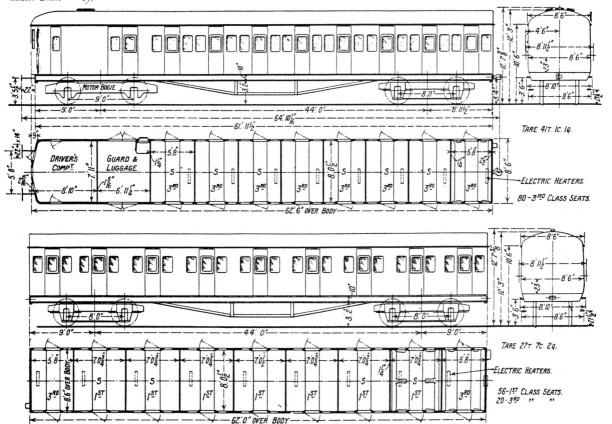

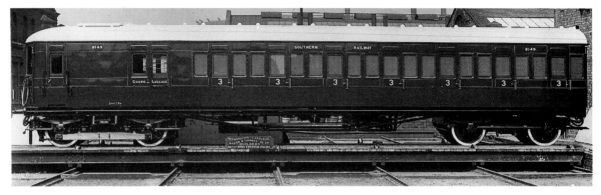

Above *Brand new Western section motor third No 8149 outside Saltley works in the 'square-panelled' version of the Southern livery. The Eastern section units were similarly finished* (Metro-Cammell, NRM).

Left *Third class (formerly composite) trailer coach No 9575 in Eastern section set No 1495, one of many which were converted from former steam stock, in this case two four-wheelers. Note the characteristic form of SE & CR carriage beading, devoid of continuous waist and eaves panels* (Hughes Collection, NRM).

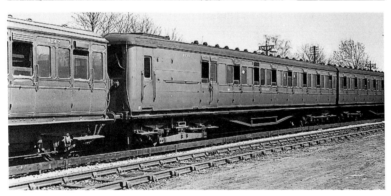

The view shows former LB & SCR augmentation trailer No 9042 coupled to the cab end of motor third No 8833 (set No 1698) which was one of the Southern conversions from LSWR stock embodying the post-grouping standard cab style (Hughes Collection, NRM).

4SUB unit No 4105 was one of the first ten new Bulleid suburban sets, most of which emerged right at the end of the war. It is seen here new, ex-works at Eastleigh (SR official, NRM).

Not surprisingly, given the publicity approach of the day, the Southern Railway tried its level best to kid the public that all these EMU sets were genuinely new vehicles, but since by far the majority (regardless of operating section) were rebuilds, no-one can seriously have been fooled for long! What is more, the pre-group origin of most of the Eastern section fleet was even more obvious than the Western section rebuilds, simply by the lack of genuine waist panelling, ex-SE & CR stock mostly having displayed the 'Wolverton' style of body treatment (see Volume 1, Chapter 7). Perhaps the most beneficial aspect of the whole business all round was the genuinely high quality of both the ex-LSWR and ex-SE & CR steam stock which even allowed such subterfuges to be contemplated!

But that was not all; there was a further 'Joker' in the Southern pack at this fascinating time. The basic three-car (off-peak) and six-car (rush-hour) formation had already been called into question at really busy periods, even at the time of introducing these new Western and Eastern section developments, so the SR, strapped for cash as always, hastily came up with a swift panacea: the insertion of a two-car non-powered third class trailer unit between two of the conventional three-car EMUs. This idea dated back to the LSWR in 1919, but the dead give-away was that these new SR augmentation trailers were neither LSWR, SE & CR nor even new build, but were in fact rebuilds of surplus *Brighton* line steam stock whose length (54 ft) and arc roof profile matched up with neither that of the LSWR nor SE & CR! It was all most democratic, and students of carriage evolution must have been quite fascinated. The appended drawings of the various alternatives will, hopefully, make matters more clear.

The amazing thing was that it all seemed to work and attract still more traffic, so when it was finally determined that the erstwhile 6.7kV Brighton line overhead system should be converted to the now standard three-rail system, it can have occasioned no surprise whatsoever that the basis of many 'new' DC EMUs for the suburban workings on the 'Central' section of the Southern Railway (as the ex-LB & SCR operating area was now called) should now become a fairly catholic mixture of converted ex-steam and overhead stock. They too were mostly rebuilt into the standard three-car Southern EMU form (motor third/composite/motor third), though the wide-bodied 'South London' motors were rebuilt as twin units (now motor plus driving trailer) and went back to their old haunts because of loading gauge restrictions. With their combination of 'Brighton' arc roof carriage styling and quasi-standard Southern front-end treatment (based on that first applied to the ex-SE & CR rebuilds mentioned above), not to mention the

augmentation two-car trailer units, the Central section units became yet another variant to be added to the vast proliferation of styles to be seen on what is even now regarded as having been a very boring railway at the time!

For the Central section suburban services, in addition to the conversion of former Brighton stock, further ex-SE & CR steam stock was also turned into the now standard EMU form in 1928. This gave breathing space for the conversion to DC of the final overhead carriages, and the last overhead electrics ran in 1929.

These first stages of what was a quite remarkable transformation had, therefore, all taken place before 1930 and at an amazingly low cost, all things considered. Certainly nothing like it was happening on any of the other three main-line systems; yet hardly had the SR sorted out this first phase of its suburban affairs than it also started to address the medium and long-distance possibilities of electrification. These developments, even though they were soon to be happening simultaneously, will be left until after the end of the suburban story in the interests of clarity.

When the Central section conversion to DC was approaching completion in 1928, there began a further period of very large-scale ex-LSWR steam stock conversions. These were mostly from the old 'bogie block' sets, but the 1931 examples came from two six-wheelers mounted on a single new underframe. This 'second helping' of ex-LSWR EMUs differed from the original 1915 stock by having the new 'Southern' front-end instead of the old 'torpedo' shape and by being mounted on the now standard SR 62-foot EMU chassis. This was then followed by a lengthening of the original LSWR electric stock to the new standard SR 62-foot dimension by adding two compartments per coach and putting these too on to new frames; but their retained 'torpedo' cabs always identified them as the pioneer three-rail carriages.

Steam stock conversion to the purely inner suburban style went on until 1937, again involving ex-LSWR stock, by which time by far the bulk of the suburban fleet was of one of three styles, each readily identifying its former company of origin, though now all on new SR 62-foot chassis. However, such was the standardization achieved in running equipment, that the three styles were by no means confined to their original pre-group routes. Moreover, the new EMUs built in 1925 were now in a distinct minority. Regardless of exact origin, virtually all the stock was running in three-car units (now known as 3SUB). It remained thus throughout most of the Southern Railway period.

Throughout this time, the strengthening two-car trailer units continued to be used at peak periods. The twin trailer idea, though it originated on the

LSWR in 1919, had by the late 1930s been extended to all lines, while the trailers themselves, also converted from pre-group steam-hauled carriages, were by now a thoroughly heterogeneous mixture of stock from all three companies, by no means always marshalled with 3SUBs of the same architectural parentage. Furthermore, because of their lack of driving cabs, the trailers could occasionally cause operational problems when operating in support of a single 3SUB, it being not unknown for the motor set, *in extremis*, to have to run round its trailers for the reverse working. Oliver Bulleid fairly soon put a stop to this nonsense by taking the obvious step (or at least it seems obvious enough in retrospect) of separating the two trailers and inserting one each into a 3SUB unit, thereby creating the 4SUB, the familiar formation in more modern days.

The idea came from Bulleid's first venture into new stock building for the Southern Electric when, in 1941, he introduced the prototype 4SUB unit No 4101 as the first brand new stock for the purely suburban section of the Southern Railway since the 1925 cars. In them he revealed for the first time the new 'Bulleid' body profile, eventually (in the late 1940s/early 1950s) to become very familiar throughout the system. Its continuously curving side contour enabled six per side, while the compartments were of almost Gresley LNER-like meanness in their inter-partition dimensions. There were ten compartments in the motors and 11 in the third class trailer; maybe there was some inherited influence from Bulleid's old company, who knows? Only one set was built in 1941 and its second trailer was a ten-compartment composite, but at much the same time the railways abolished first class on London's suburban lines and the composite was immediately downgraded. The remaining nine sets of this type appeared in 1944 and 1945 and had two trailer thirds from the start.

In spite of their cramped interiors, the prototype 4SUBs were rather handsome looking sets in which were combined the cab style of the 1939 2HAL units (see page 138) with Bulleid's distinctively new body profile. They certainly looked far more modern than most of their predecessors. But the passengers did not like the cramped compartments and said so; accordingly, the next new 4SUBs in 1946 had one less compartment in each of the two types of carriage. More to the point, however, these new units also had quite different non-domed front-end which thereafter increasingly came to symbolize the Southern Electric in almost all its forms as stock was replaced. Even more significantly — unlike the prototype 4SUBs which retained traditional wood/canvas roofs — they were also all-steel in construction, being built by assembling prefabricated cab and compartment 'modules' on to the standard Southern chassis.

During the next five years until well into BR days (1951), the new Bulleid 4SUBs came into service seemingly by the bucketful. There were subtle

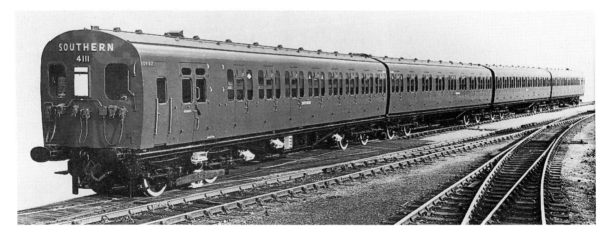

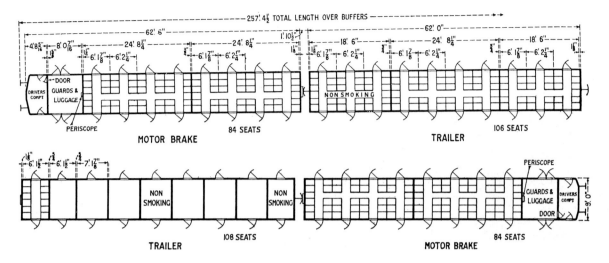

MOTOR BRAKE   84 SEATS   TRAILER   106 SEATS

TRAILER   108 SEATS   MOTOR BRAKE   84 SEATS

Above left *This close-up view of the new-style cab on motor third No 10950 of 4SUB No 4105 also gives clear detail of Bulleid's new curved-side carriage profile* (SR official, NRM).

Below left *The familiar face of the post-war Southern: prototype vertical front 4SUB No 4111 when new in 1946* (BR SR).

Figure 43 *Floor plans of the later centre-aisle 4SUBs together with elevations, plans and perspectives of the experimental 4DD unit. Note the larger centre compartments of the non-open 4SUB trailer, a legacy of the fact that they were designed before the abolition of first class on London surburban workings.*

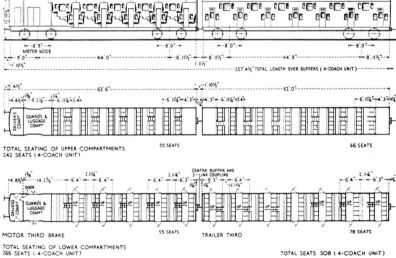

changes between batches, well covered by the more specialized literature, but the only really important innovation in most of the later series was to substitute an 'open'-style interior layout in many of the cars. They still retained a full set of outside doors, but the absence of compartment partitions, combined with a centre aisle, enabled passengers to distribute themselves more evenly through the carriages. Seats were arranged 2 + 3.

Meanwhile, the older units were gradually phased out, but before this happened almost all of them had been, as stated above, converted to 4SUB form by the insertion of an extra trailer. It so transpired that there were not enough pre-group-style trailers to allow all former 3SUBs to be thus enhanced, so a fair number of new augmentation trailers were also built.

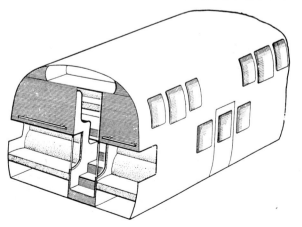

These, naturally, followed the new Bulleid profile so there were ultimately some very odd-looking hybrid units indeed whose constant formation and re-formation no doubt brought great delight to percep-tive observers. Almost any theoretical combination of styles could be and probably was seen. However, large-scale withdrawal of the early pre-war-style units was also being carried out simultaneously with the introduction of new Bulleid 4SUBs, and this led to the final phase in the story.

When the old units were withdrawn, their rebuilt pre-group bodies were by now, of course, mostly run-ning on new SR standard chassis. It will therefore occasion no surprise that when the final new-style 4SUBs were built, all but a few of them utilized the salvaged frames. They were mostly also given the still quite new Bulleid-style augmentation trailers (see above) which, naturally, were not withdrawn when the old 3SUB units went to the scrapyards. Thus, the final 4SUBs were not quite as new as they might have seemed — Southern tradition died hard and was still by no means over, as the next volume will reveal. But at least with the massive re-equipment of the 1945-51 period, Southern suburban services were operated by a far more homogeneous fleet than ever before. It was made even more so when the first genuinely 'BR' continuation came into service in the form of the 4EPB units in 1951 — visual 'clones' of Bulleid stock but with very different traction equipment. But they too must wait their time until Volume 3.

The final purely 'Southern' contribution to the suburban story actually dated from 1949 and was yet another example of Bulleid's rather idiosyncratic approach. This time, however, though the intention was sound, the end product was a bit of a disaster; it was, of course, the celebrated eight-car train, made from two units each type-classified 4DD (Double-Deck). It should, more properly, have been described as a split level design, and came about as a valiant attempt to increase train capacity without adding to train length.

Even though the by now standard 4SUB unit with six-per-side seating, and working in multiple to give an eight-car train at busy times, gave more seats than the old '3SUB plus augmentation trailers' approach, there was still much overcrowding. The 4DD units were a brave attempt to cope but were conceptually flawed on several counts. For one thing, they were, of necessity, built to the maximum possible structure gauge and were thus confined to only a few of the overcrowded routes (Charing Cross and Cannon Street to Dartford and Gravesend) and there were only half as many outside doors as compartments, so loading and unloading took longer. Passengers also complained about the lack of room, lack of comfort and poor ventilation. After about a years's trial, it was decided not to repeat the idea but instead to lengthen station platforms to allow ten-car sets of con-ventional stock to be used. The experimental set did, however, go on serving the Dartford line for 20 years, so maybe it earned its keep. When finally withdrawn in 1971, it probably departed the scene unloved by any save the enthusiast fraternity who could not understand why no one would preserve it! Later, two motors and a trailer were preserved at Ashford and though the trailer was subsequently scrapped, a motor coach still survives, now at the Northampton Steam Railway, Pitsford.

Main-line electrification, 1932 onwards

During the earlier stages of the Southern's electrification, there was a degree of uncertainty as to the wisdom of extending the new system much beyond the 20 to 30 mile distance which the above-mentioned suburban routes mostly represented, partly because the distances involved were considered to be rather

more 'main line' in their characteristics and not wholly appropriate to being served by multiple unit sets of the then 'state of the art' technology. In retrospect, this seems rather absurd considering the non-corridor nature of most long-distance trains on the constituents of the Southern Railway (save for a few LSWR exceptions), but be that as it may, there was a fairly strong feeling that any medium to long-distance services ought to have locomotive haulage, and there was a sound technical reason why this would be difficult to achieve with the now standard three-rail system.

The large number of complicated junctions on the Southern decreed that there had to be numerous gaps in the conductor rails. This posed no problem with multiple unit stock with current collectors at each end, but third rail locomotives might not be able to

Top left 'Hybrid' 4SUB (believed to be set No 4479) consisting of a new Bulleid post-war trailer inserted into a pre-war 3SUB whose carriages are of SE & CR origin (Author's collection).

Above left 4DD unit No 4001 in service, clearly showing the full extent made of the structure gauge in achieving the extra seats (BR SR).

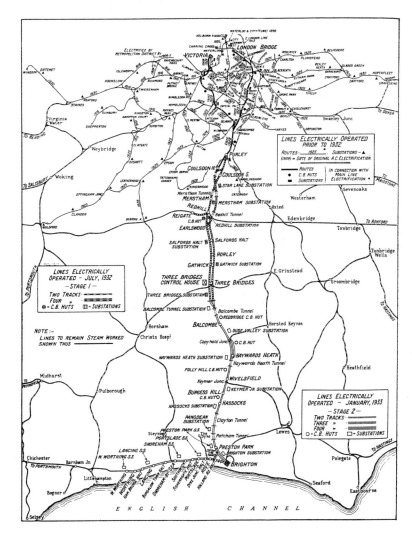

Figure 44 Map showing the scope of the Brighton line electrifications. Though through services to Brighton did not commence until 1933, the Purley-Three Bridges section was in use by mid-1932.

bridge such gaps and in consequence there would probably be the need for expensive overhead wiring at junctions, combined with dual standard collecting equipment. In the event, the company resolved on the EMU solution for the most pressing of the longer-distance routes (that of the former LB & SCR to Brighton) and took advantage of a Government remission of passenger duty in 1929 to help finance not only the extension of the third rail, but also the building of a completely new range of EMU stock.

The full service commenced on 1 January 1933, and the design of the new stock was intended to reflect its main-line nature, but the implementation was, in reality, more in the nature of a long-distance suburban operation than that of a genuine main line. In the context of the Brighton route this was not, perhaps, too unreasonable, but in the event it proved so successful that in due time the EMU concept was extended to most Southern lines and eventually took over routes extending to well over 100 miles from London in the BR period.

The original intention was to alternate express and semi-fast services, and to this end two basic types of unit were introduced. The semi-fast sets were of four cars and not much more than glorified suburban units. They were given the classification 4LAV in the then semi-descriptive form of coding used by the Southern, but there was but a single lavatory-equipped composite to mark them out from their purely suburban brethren. This composite had a side corridor (but no gangway to adjacent vehicles) and a lavatory at each end. Stylistically, they were pure Maunsell, with perhaps a hint of LSWR in their general shape, and they featured the new and rather handsome 'Southern' standard driving cabs with domed roof-end first seen on the Eastern section suburban units of 1925.

For the so-called 'express' services, something distinctly superior was both felt to be desirable and was actually achieved. These were the celebrated six-car sets, the first genuinely long-distance EMUs built in Britain and a quantum leap forward from most stock which had ever served the Brighton line, save for the few decent lavatory and/or Pullman sets in LB & SCR days (see Volume 1) or the early post-group steam-hauled corridor coaches (see page 18). They mostly came in standard formation, but there were two noteworthy groups of 'special' sets and it is worth remarking that Pullman insisted on having its shout in all of them, this being a residue from the pre-group arrangement with the Brighton company.

In all cases, the motor cars were all-steel in construction and came from outside contractors, the order being equally split between Metro-Cammell and the Birmingham RCW Co, following a prototype

from each of these two firms. One of these, that from the Birmingham RCW Co, was a slab-sided unit, whose external lines were rather reminiscent of the SE & CR 'Continental' boat stock (see page 18), but the other prototype followed the more traditional Southern appearance and was to set the style adopted for the production series from both firms. These driving motor thirds were very heavy at 57 tons, they had open-style interiors and were arguably by far the most handsome-looking of the new coaches with their large picture windows and well-schemed front-ends. They were by no means inferior within the walls either.

The standard formation was a 6PUL 'express' unit, gangwayed throughout its length with a mixture of corridor and open accommodation in the third class, side corridor only for the first class ordinary and a Pullman composite kitchen car for the dining provision — hence the 'PUL' in the type designation. The Pullman cars were of a new interior style, there never having been composite kitchen cars (or EMU Pullmans for that matter) before. They made no exterior visual concessions in either style or livery to the new order and added an incongruous look to the sets, in spite of their self-evident appeal. This visual nonconformity between 'inserted' Pullmans and ordinary stock was to last well into BR days on the Southern lines. The side-corridor stock was built by the SR to the now standard Maunsell style (steel body panelling on timber framing with wood/canvas roof) and had the new-style 'tall' corridor windows, but inside a very useful improvement was the double sliding doors to the compartments from the corridors. Regrettably, this very practical idea — also characteristic of most LMS side-corridor stock from this same time onwards — did not long remain a standard Southern offering.

The two special groups were the three 6CIT units for the 'City Limited' service and the celebrated five-car all-Pullman sets for the 'Brighton Belle', type designated 5BEL. The latter will be considered in the Pullman chapter, but it is convenient to mention the 6CIT units here. They were very similar to the 6PULs save that the three side-corridor coaches were all first class and the only third class seats were in the driving motors. The Pullman diner was exactly the same as in the 6PUL sets. The prototype motor thirds (see above) were both used in 6CIT units, but after the war, when first class accommodation was less sought after, some of the cars were downgraded and the units became 6PULs. Plans of the three main types of units (express and semi-fast) are appended, along with more detailed drawings of some of the individual types.

In the event, the designed division between the express services and the slow/semi-fast operations, which justified the different forms of sets, did not

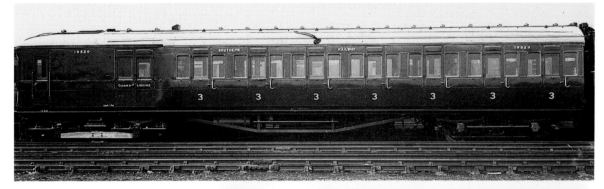

Above *Motor third No 10520 from 4LAV set No 1930, showing its basically suburban nature. By now (see page 123) the Southern EMU livery had settled down to a 'round-panelled' form* (BR SR).

Right *4LAV unit No 1934 in service near Oxshott in 1932, motor third brake No 10527 leading. Note the recessed outer ends, typical of Maunsell's company-built brake-ended 9 ft wide carriages of all types, also the destination boards, typical of much pre-war Southern working, by the guard's door. The high-windowed corridor-side configuration of the lavatory composite can also clearly be seen* (Author's collection).

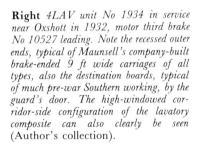

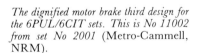

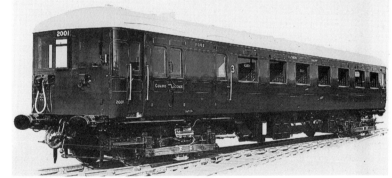

The dignified motor brake third design for the 6PUL/6CIT sets. This is No 11002 from set No 2001 (Metro-Cammell, NRM).

6PUL set No 3002 in service on a down Eastbourne express on the Quarry Line, taken at some time after the set was renumbered from 2002 in 1937 (Author's collection).

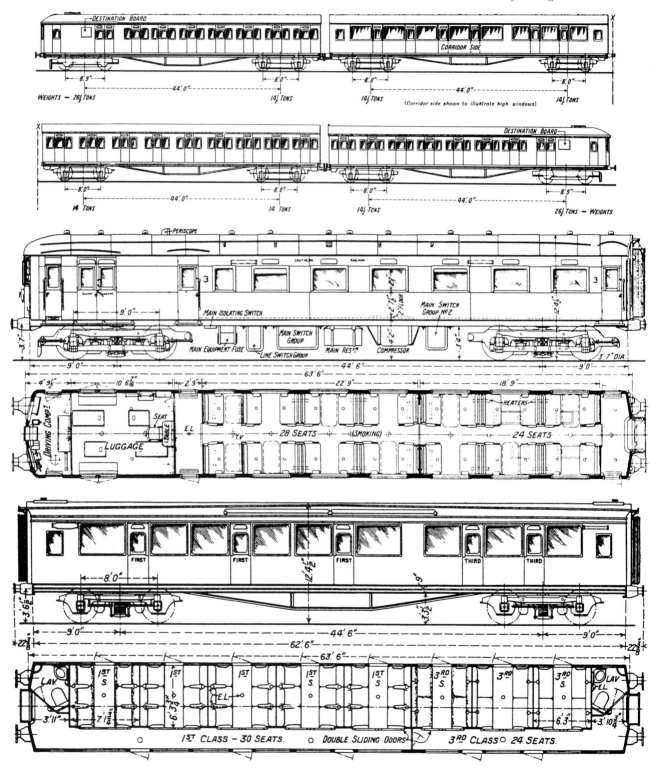

MOTOR 3ᴿᴰ BRAKE. WEIGHT 41 TONS
70 SEATS

1ˢᵀ & 3ᴿᴰ LAV. COMPOSITE. WEIGHT 29 TONS
30 FIRST - 24 THIRD SEATS

1ˢᵀ & 3ᴿᴰ COMPOSITE. WEIGHT 28 TONS
40 FIRST - 40 THIRD SEATS

MOTOR 3ᴿᴰ BRAKE. WEIGHT 41 TONS
70 SEATS

MOTOR 3ᴿᴰ BRAKE WEIGHT 59 TONS
52 SEATS

CORRIDOR THIRD WEIGHT 35 TONS
68 SEATS

1ˢᵀ & 3ᴿᴰ CORRIDOR COMPO WEIGHT 35 T.
30 FIRST-24 THIRD SEATS

PULLMAN CAR-KITCHEN WT 43 T.
12 FIRST - 16 THIRD SEATS

1ˢᵀ & 3ᴿᴰ CORRIDOR COMPO WEIGHT 35 T.
30 FIRST-24 THIRD SEATS

MOTOR 3ᴿᴰ BRAKE. WEIGHT 59 TONS.
52 SEATS

MOTOR 3ᴿᴰ BRAKE WEIGHT 59 TONS
52 SEATS

CORRIDOR 1ˢᵀ WEIGHT 34 TONS
42 SEATS

CORRIDOR 1ˢᵀ WEIGHT 34 TONS
42 SEATS

PULLMAN CAR-KITCHEN. WEIGHT 43 TONS
12 FIRST- 16 THIRD SEATS

CORRIDOR 1ˢᵀ WEIGHT 34 TONS
42 SEATS

MOTOR 3ᴿᴰ BRAKE. WEIGHT 59 TONS
52 SEATS

work out quite as perfectly as might have been expected, and it was by no means rare to see a twelve-car train consisting of three 4LAV units pressed into use on the faster workings — and vice-versa with the express sets, one supposes. BR tried again when it replaced them in the 1960s with two differently conceived units, but met with not much greater success. Some of this nonsense still persists as Volume 3 will reveal.

That apart, the Brighton scheme was a huge success, and before long it was the turn of Eastbourne, Hastings and most points adjacent, to which locations the third rail had penetrated by mid-1935. Once again, new stock was provided, and though the basic Brighton line philosophy was followed, it was not slavishly copied. In this instance the six-car express sets were wholly SR, Pullman only providing the catering crews, not being able to afford further new cars. In consequence, the new trains were altogether neater-looking than the 6PUL sets and were known as 6PANs because their catering was provided from a PANtry in one of the first class vehicles. This car also had its first class side-corridor accommodation arranged without exterior compartment doors, a well nigh revolutionary concept for the Southern but all the more welcome for that. But the single door to the corridor returned, and outside compartment doors were found on all other carriages.

Other than the pantry first, the basic formation employed similarly styled coaches to the Brighton sets, but instead of two composites a full first and full third were offered (see appended plans). The motor thirds were also slightly different in that they featured sliding ventilators above their big picture windows. All told, the 6PANs were a considerable aesthetic improvement on the 6PULs and a fine advertisement for the Southern system. In due course, the 6PANs and 6PULs worked turn and turn about on both the Brighton and the Hastings lines and a sort of standardized 6PUL-6PAN formation became the common twelve-car train for some 30 years.

For the semi-fast and slow services on this latest section of the Southern Electric, including its 'out of town' branches and the shorter purely coastal runs, the 4LAV idea was not repeated; instead, two-car units were provided, one of which was a completely new design — the 2BIL (BI-Lavatory). Though of basic side-corridor form, there was no inter-connecting gangway and each half had its own toilet. One element was a motor third, the other a composite trailer with driving cab, and the idea was that they could be made up into four, six or even eight cars as needed. It was a nice thought — and successful when practical — but there were none too many of

Figure 45 Typical first generation Brighton line EMUs are featured in this set of drawings. They are, from the top:
a) Simplified elevations of the 4LAV sets.
b) Detailed elevations and plans of the motor third brakes and the corridor composite trailers from the 6PUL sets. NB The Pullman drawings to match these cars will be found on page 242).

Scale: ¹/₁₀" = 1ft

c) (above) Sketch plans of the 4LAV, 6PUL and 6CIT units of which 33, 20 and 3 sets respectively were introduced.

Right *The clean lines of the 6PAN units — and the different arrangement of the window ventilators on the motor brakes — are seen in this view of set No 2036 circa 1936 (Author's collection).*

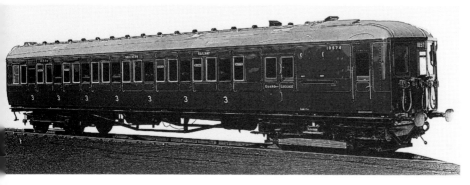

Left *Compartment side of motor third brake No 10574 from 2BIL unit No 1897, one of the ten new 1935 sets. This time, the brake ends were not recessed (SR official, NRM).*

Figure 46 *These drawings show the new stock introduced for the Hastings and Eastbourne extensions and show, from the top:*
a) Sketch plans of a 6PAN set together with semi-detailed elevations and plans of the four carriage types involved.
b) Elevations and plans of the new 2BIL units.
c) Elevations and plans of the 2NOL units, but omitting all evidence of their former LSWR panelling!

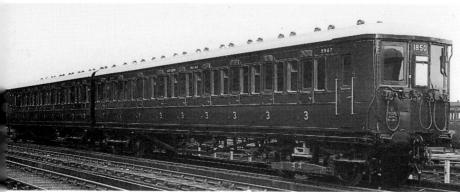

Left *2NOL unit No 1850, one of 78 such sets built from former LSWR steam stock in 1935-6 (BR SR).*

them at first (only ten sets) and to complete the re-equipment the SR, possibly financially exhausted by its unaccustomed building of so much new EMU stock for the new express services, resorted to its familiar 'make do and mend' approach by offering the rest of the 'new' two-car fleet in the form of rebuilt pre-group LSWR steam stock.

So, out again from sundry highways and byways came the old warriors, this time to re-emerge as two-car non-corridor units (motor brake third plus driving trailer composite). They were in effect 2SUBs, but for some reason which is by no means clear, the SR this time preferred to indicate their comfort status (or lack of it!) by classifying them 2NOL (NOn-Lavatory).

The next phase of the main-line electrification was soon destined to reveal itself as the most ambitious to be tackled yet: the direct line of the old LSWR to Portsmouth from Waterloo. By now, some of the limitations of the six-car main-line units were beginning to be clear, not least the lack of gangways between sets. Furthermore, the all-steel motor cars were very heavy and not kind to the track. They were also expensive and the Southern was, yet again, watching its pockets. The consequence of all this was that the new Portsmouth main-line express stock was to a possibly less pleasing exterior design and built

more to a budget. For the first time for main-line EMU stock, the motor cars were built with timber frames and wood/canvas roofs (to save weight), and by the SR not outside contractors. Yet they were also probably the most familiar of all the Southern express EMU types.

Other than the constructional form of the motor thirds, the most obvious change from the earlier main-line express sets was the reduction in number of carriages per set from six to four, combined with through gangway connections at the driving ends. This gave the stock a sort of untidy look compared with the earlier six-car sets, and the slightly asymmetrical one-eyed look of the driving ends caused the units instantly to be nicknamed 'Nelsons', no doubt augmented by the Portsmouth connection. But they were vastly more practical, and the through-gangwayed form set the style for all subsequent main-line EMU stock on the Southern lines right down to the Class 442 'Wessex Electrics' of 1988.

Two types of standard four-car set were offered (see Figure 47), a non-dining 4COR (CORridor) and a dining 4RES (REStaurant) unit. Normally they operated as eight or twelve-car formations with one 4RES per train, but over the years formations tended to change and some of the dining cars were converted to buffets after the war. A rather retrograde step was

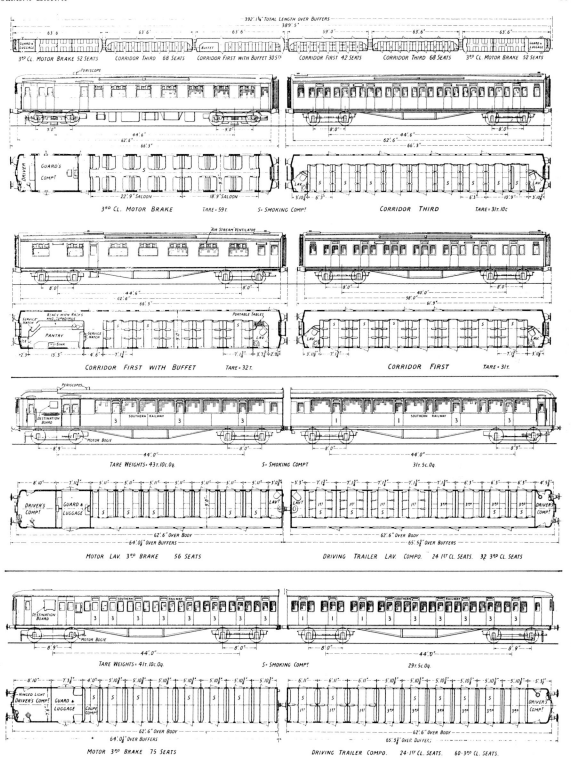

the fitting of screw couplings and non-Pullman gangways to the outer ends, all the more odd since the SR had virtually adopted the more modern alternative by then.

Augmenting the main-line express stock was a modest infusion of additional 3SUBs, augmentation trailer pairs and 2NOLs for inner suburban use (ex-steam stock rebuilds, of course) and a very considerable provisioning of 38 brand new 2BIL sets for semi-

fast working. The latter were obviously proving a boon to the Southern and their ability to be operated in a variety of combinations from two cars upwards no doubt made them very acceptable throughout the system.

The Portsmouth line went all-electric in 1937, and when it was completed there remained only the mid-Sussex area from Dorking to Bognor, Littlehampton and Worthing (via Angmering) to be infilled in order

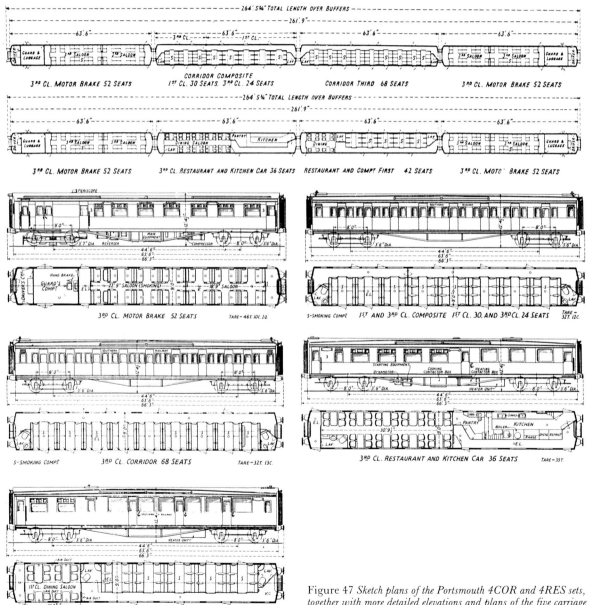

Figure 47 *Sketch plans of the Portsmouth 4COR and 4RES sets, together with more detailed elevations and plans of the five carriage varieties built for the 1937 services.*

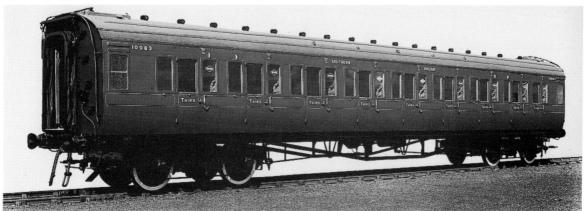

Top *Motor brake third No 11159 from 4RES unit No 3064, showing the first version of the simplified Southern livery which began to emerge at this time — waist 'panelling' only (SR official, NRM).*

Above *Compartment side of corridor third No 10083 from 4COR unit No 3129. Note the half compartment at the far end and the fact that only two compartments were non-smoking! (SR official, NRM).*

Above right *Two 4COR units working in multiple in 1937 headed by set No 3056, which is interesting because No 3056 was actually listed as a 4RES. There are, however, no diners in this train. From this angle, the wood and canvas roof structure of all cars is very clear (BR SR).*

Right *The first class restaurant car interiors of the Portsmouth 4RES units were a little old-fashioned but by no means undignified (BR SR).*

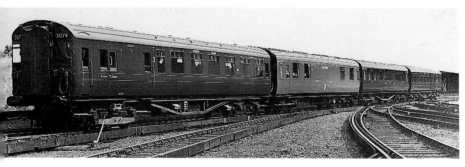

The 4BUF sets came out in 1938 in even more simplified livery — two yellow lines only — and the buffets carried the new unlined Malachite green scheme. Both these features are clearly seen here on set No 3074, the second of the series; for further details of the buffet cars, see page 100 (BR SR).

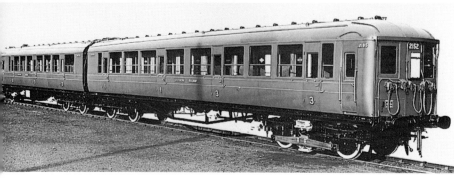

Corridor-side elevation of 2BIL unit No 2152, the last of the 1937-8 batch built in consequence of the Portsmouth and mid-Sussex extensions. Note again the much simplified lining, possibly even malachite green livery too, judging by the light tone (SR official, NRM).

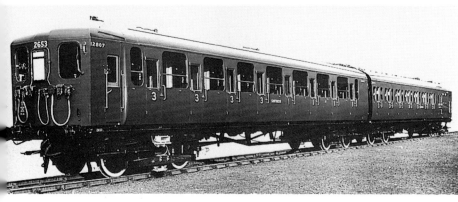

The 2HALs, exemplified here by unit No 2653 built in 1939, were the first SR vehicles to reveal some of Bulleid's new carriage styling ideas: flush sides and round-cornered fixed lights, for example. They also displayed a new-style EMU cab treatment and were finished in unlined malachite green (SR official, NRM).

Right *The comfortless interior of a Bulleid 2HAL (BR SR).*

to virtually complete the electrification of the former LSWR and LB & SCR lines to the south coast. This was in turn completed in 1938 and further 4COR units were built for it along with a new type, the 4BUF (BUFfet), in place of the Portsmouth 4RES units. The new buffet cars in these units were amongst the first SR carriages to display Oliver Bulleid's new Malachite green livery and looked slightly incongruous in the middle of an otherwise olive green train. They also revealed in their interiors some of Mr Bulleid's more *outré* design fancies!

As with the Portsmouth line, the mid-Sussex extensions also received yet another large flotilla of brand new and by now almost ubiquitous 2BIL sets, this time no fewer than 68 twin units being provided. It

is very fitting that the NRM has preserved one of these highly characteristic sets in full working order and left it in the south of England where it makes occasional forays on some of its old stamping ground for the benefit of enthusiasts, often in aid of charity. A Portsmouth motor third is also preserved at York in non-operational order.

After the completion of the mid-Sussex scheme in 1938, the Southern, quite naturally, turned to the Kentish area of its parish, but its long-term plans were to be frustrated by the war and, in the event, the electrification of the main lines to the Kent Coast had to await BR days. There was, of course, slightly less urgency since Maunsell had already equipped these services with new steam-hauled corridor stock in the

1920s (see page 19) but there was opportunity for some modest expansion in the Eastern section in 1939 wherein the hand of Oliver Bulleid was first revealed in the EMU mode (Bognor buffet cars excepted). This took the form of a new two-car unit based on the 2BIL but with only one of the two coaches (the driving trailer composite) given a side corridor with lavatory access. It was, of course, called a 2HAL (HAlf Lavatory).

These units turned out to be the last purely 'Southern' EMUs to be built for main-line as opposed to suburban use, and their rather indeterminate nature (the motor third end was conventionally non-corridor) was a sort of conceptual reflection of the lines on which they were first used — extensions to Gillingham and Maidstone, more outer suburban than main-line in character. The coaches themselves were fairly typically Southern, but Bulleid fitted a new angular cab unit on them made of welded steel sheet. The bodyside fixed lights were flush to the outer panelling with rounded corners, rather in the style of Maunsell's final main-line corridor stock, and the ensemble represented a sort of uneasy halfway house towards Bulleid's familiar post-war style. They were far more spartanly finished than the 2BILs and by all accounts much more uncomfortable. In a much refined form, the cab style of the 2HALs re-appeared on the prototype 4SUB in 1941 (see page 126), but it was not to become a true Southern standard. When the 2HAL style was revived, briefly, after the formation of BR, the final few units embodied the new flat-fronted style, profile and all-steel construction of the Bulleid 4SUB.

Overall, however, in summarizing the first phase of the Southern Electric story, one can only admire the dedication and speed with which this not very wealthy railway, the smallest of the 'Big Four', made its valiant attempt to modernize one of the most complex railway networks in the world, even though some of its more quaint carriage efforts added a sort of 'comic opera' quality to the scene by their infinite variety. It had virtually completed the task (Kent Coast lines and a few other minor branches excepted) within but 16 years of the grouping, and one doubts not that but for the war, Dover and Folkstone would probably have joined Portsmouth and Brighton on the third rail network. It was a rate of progress which BR would have done well to copy after 1947. Yet nearly 40 more years were to pass before some of the former Southern Railway lines were finally converted — and not too far away from Central London either; the Oxted line did not get its third rail until 1987!

Partly as a result of the slow post-1948 progress, the former Southern EMUs of most types were to enjoy, collectively, the longest post-company active life of any of the 'Big Four' carriage designs, some last-

ing well into the 1970s and, in BR-derived form, the 1980s too. By then they were well behind the times as also were some of their BR successors; but this is no slur on the original SR concepts of the 1920s and 1930s. It is more properly a compliment to their rugged and robust nature that these vehicles could carry on for so long under such intensive use; but that part of their story must await the next volume to resolve, save for one rather noteworthy exception to round out the story.

The Waterloo and City tube stock

It is, perhaps entirely typical of the Southern Railway that some of its most modern electric stock should have been built — and during the war at that — for its most unusual route, the deep-level tube between Waterloo station and the Bank of England. It is also entirely typical that at the time of writing this stock is still in active use, now almost 50 years old and still looking quite smart and modern in spite of the quite awful Network SouthEast livery which it now carries! However, the story started much earlier, and since it was given but fleeting mention in the first volume, this seems another case where the mainly post-grouping parameters of this present survey must be exceeded.

The Waterloo and City Railway arose from a desire by the LSWR to have a terminus nearer to the City of London than Waterloo, and some early mutterings were to be heard as far back as 1846. However, it was not until the success of the first deep-level tube, opened in 1890, had been appreciated (The City and South London — see Chapter 7) that the LSWR real-

ized that an underground electric connection to the City might give the facilities needed. Powers to construct the line were obtained in 1893 and though it was built to the new tube style, the diameter was set at a rather larger dimension (12 ft 1¾ in normally, but 12 ft 9 in on curves) than that of the C & SL. The line itself was opened in 1898 and has been carrying commuters to the city ever since.

During that time there have only been two fleets of carriages, and the first of them, built in 1898, was responsible for services during most of the Southern Railway period as well as that of the LSWR. While I cannot prove it, it seems to me that to run such an intensive service for over 90 years with only one complete re-equipment probably constitutes some sort of record.

The first cars were built in the USA by Jackson & Sharp of Wilmerding in 1898. The roller-bearing bogies — an unusual idea at the time for such stock — were assembled at Eastleigh and five four-car sets

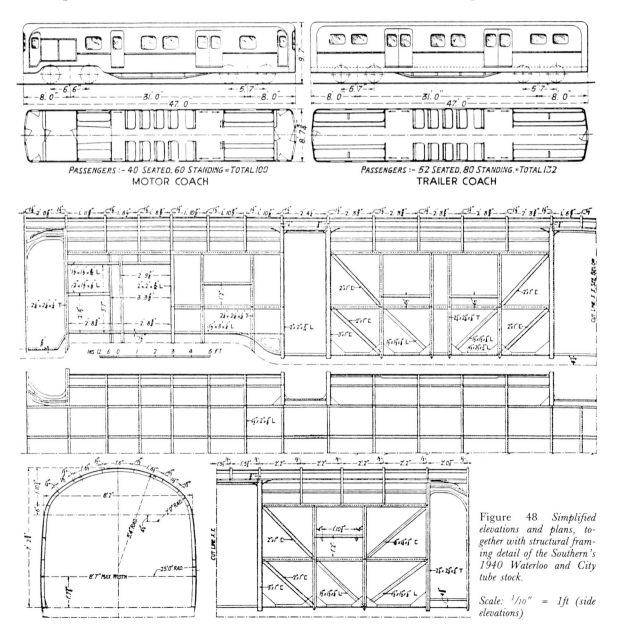

PASSENGERS :- 40 SEATED, 60 STANDING = TOTAL 100
MOTOR COACH

PASSENGERS :- 52 SEATED, 80 STANDING = TOTAL 132
TRAILER COACH

Figure 48 *Simplified elevations and plans, together with structural framing detail of the Southern's 1940 Waterloo and City tube stock.*

Scale: *¹/₁₀″* = 1ft (side elevations)

(motor/trailer/trailer/motor) were supplied. A year later, five single unit motor cars were built by Dick, Kerr and Co for non-rush-hour services. All vehicles were of quite definite American style and displayed wooden-bodied construction with vertical match-boarding below a pronounced waist rail. Inward-sloping windows above the waist were adopted so as to fit the tube profile, and the cars were given a natural varnished livery. They were very well finished considering they were for a route less than 1½ miles long, and their general quality was probably superior to most other London underground stock for many years. Internally, they displayed the mixture of trans-verse and longitudinal seats which eventually became characteristic of all underground trains but the seats, though cloth covered, were not upholstered.

Contemporary pictures reveal that great care was taken with the interior detail and the cars were suffi-ciently well built to last, virtually unchanged, until the SR determined on a complete modernization which took place in 1940. For this modernization, 12 new motors and 16 trailers were procured from the English Electric Co Ltd, the successors to Dick, Kerr. They were in fact made in the old Dick, Kerr premises. The intention was to operate five five-car trains (two motors and three trailers) with a modest amount of spare stock, the off-peak services being taken care of by detached motor cars running singly. Presumably the extra mileage likely to be run by the motor cars in consequence of this policy was the rea-son for having two spare motors but only one spare trailer.

The stock itself was distinctly modern-looking but had proportionally less window area than the old cars and within rather more standing space relative to seating areas. When fully loaded, some 60 per cent of the passenger capacity was represented by 'stan-dees'. In general design terms they were rather simi-lar to the pre-1938 London Transport tube stock in terms of the 'upswept' lower bodyside adjacent to the power bogie but thereafter most resemblance to LT stock was muted. Though they had pneumatically operated sliding doors and the usual mixture of trans-verse and longitudinal seats, their bodyside profile was continuously curved to gain maximum benefit from the tube shape, and one cannot help but wonder whether there was some design linkage between this stock and Bulleid's later adoption of a similar con-tinuous curve on his conventional post-war carriages.

Basic body construction was of welded steel panels on a steel frame, the whole being mounted on an all-welded underframe. Again one wonders whether Mr Bulleid had a good look at the form of construction when designing his own post-war stock. Inside the cars, the finish was light and airy with rather less ceil-ing space devoted to advertising than on London

Replacement of old with new stock on the Waterloo and City line in 1940 at the point on the north side of Waterloo station where the tube lines connect with the surface system (BR SR).

Transport — or, at least, it seemed that way. Light-coloured two-tone Rexine with discreet mahogany mouldings was adopted and the transverse seats were more akin to omnibus than railway practice. This time round, seats were upholstered, rust-coloured uncut moquette being the chosen material. All tim-ber was treated with fireproof paint.

The cars were built to a robust standard and, given their short length of 47 ft, were quite heavy (motors 29½ tons, trailers 18¾ tons). There is little doubt that this substantial form of construction — and the fact that they spend most of their life underground, thus minimizing the rust problem — is a major rea-son why they have given almost 50 years' service so far and show no signs yet (1988) of being withdrawn. When they are eventually replaced, one of them would form a far more worthy candidate for perma-nent preservation than many other items I could think of.*

The Southern's Waterloo and City stock of 1940 probably represented the most advanced design of commuter vehicle ever built by the company and as such forms a quite fitting point at which to take leave of the Southern Electric until the next volume. It was also unusual in being operated on the only deep-level underground line not to come under the control of London Transport; and it is to that mammoth oper-ation which we must now turn attention.

---

* At the time of going to press, BR announced plans to replace the 1940 stock during 1990.

7. The London Transport story

By almost any objective criteria, the history of the 'dedicated' London area railways forms something of a special case. Moreover, its distinctive nature has always been recognized in and reflected by railway literature, not least in the very extensive coverage with which the Metropolitan area has always been well blessed. Thus, as in the case of the Southern Electric, readers are recommended to consult the Bibliography for more detailed sources. This special pleading holds equally true in respect of the carriages built for those railways which eventually became amalgamated as 'London Transport' in 1933; so, within the space available, this chapter can never hope to be more than a general overview to help point the way to a basic understanding of a very complex subject. There will certainly be no space for consideration of every type of vehicle built.

However — and available literature notwithstanding — even to understand the nature of London Transport rolling-stock at no more than the most general level, we must first devote some space to an examination of the main historical factors. Furthermore, as I stated in my introduction, this chapter will also stray rather more from the strict 1923-53 period in terms of vehicle coverage. Just as with the four main-line companies, so too with London Transport, the post-amalgamation developments were very much a consequence of the inherited situation, and since little was said in Volume 1 on this issue (for reasons of space), I shall try to make modest restitution here.

The historical background

The peculiar railway needs of London were probably first identified in mid-Victorian days and arose, in part, because of the success of the Metropolis in attracting so many trunk railway systems. For the most part — and for sound historical reasons — they either stopped close to the south bank of the Thames or along the general line of the Marylebone and Euston Roads in the north. This left a void in the centre, broadly that area now identified as the Cities of London and Westminster. In more strictly railway terms, it is the area inside the route of the London Transport Circle Line, and, indeed, the familiar map of the London Underground is probably the best single aid to understanding. It is not reproduced here because it is meaningless in black and white, but I have ventured to assume that most readers will be familiar enough with its symbolism to enable me to use it as a 'hidden' visual aid.

On matters of terminology, London's railways have undergone several name changes since 1933 when the London Passenger Transport Board was established. After 1947, following the nationalization of the railways, it became the London Transport Executive and today, following the 1986 de-regulation, its railways are operated as London Underground Limited, itself answerable to London Regional Transport. All told, it seems simpler to forget the semantics and call it London Transport throughout; that is what most peo-

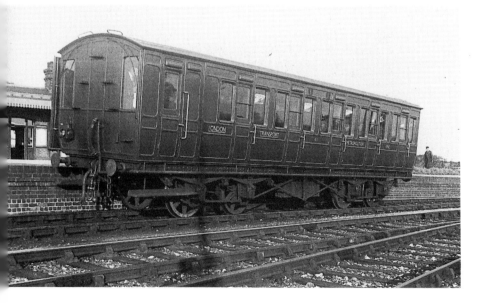

Undoubtedly the oldest coaches to serve the unified London Transport system were the rigid eight-wheelers originally built as long ago as 1866 by the Oldbury Carriage Company. They somehow or other managed to stagger on until 1935, largely because the Metropolitan had retained a handful for use on its steam-hauled Brill branch (formerly the Wotton Tramway). They were survivors of the original Metropolitan stock and known at one time as 'Long Charleys'. This view of No 41, believed to have been taken at Quainton Road circa 1934, could well have gone into Chapter 10, but it seemed best here as a symbol of the incredible variety which was a Metropolitan characteristic at the start of the London Transport era (Macartney Robbins collection, NRM).

ple still do! Fortunately, the names of most individual routes still link back to their pre-1933 origins.

By a long way the earliest lines to penetrate the inner London area were those which now form the Metropolitan and District lines (dark purple and green, respectively, on the famous map). These are different from all the others in that they originated well back in Victorian times as steam-hauled systems and were built to the normal structural dimensions of all other British railways. Much of their mileage is in the open air, and when they penetrated Central London they did so in tunnels made by the 'cut and cover' method just below street level. They are often referred to as 'surface' lines in consequence.

The two companies which owned them, the Metropolitan and the Metropolitan District Railways, were jointly responsible for operating the well-known Circle Line (originally the 'Inner' Circle and coloured yellow on the LT map), which was in effect created by linking together their two separate entries to London, the Metropolitan in the north and the District along Thames-side. Though never easy bedfellows, their interests were more compatible than contrary, so they rubbed along. The Metropolitan was the larger and even had some delusions of grandeur in that it always regarded itself as more of a proper railway than the District. It did, indeed, have some pretensions to main-line status because of its extended route from Baker Street to the Chiltern suburbs — 'Metroland' as the Company publicity department called it from 1915 — but it was always essentially a passenger commuter system, however much it might have liked to pretend otherwise.

Because of both their structural parameters and their early status, the two surface systems always operated rather different sorts of carriages from the rest of the London underground and even, in the early days, from each other. In purely dimensional terms, this difference still holds true today.

The remainder of the London system consists of deep-level 'tube' lines whose history goes back to 1890 when the pioneer City and South London Railway was formed. This was an independent locomotive-hauled system, electrified from the outset — as, indeed, were all the tube lines — and because its tubes were less than 11 ft in diameter it was more restricted than later similar systems which adopted a more or less standard 12-foot diameter tube, give or take a few inches. It was not until much later in the 1920s that the C & SLR became fully integrated with the main system by the expedient of enlarging its tubes to the standard size and linking it to the Hampstead Line (see below). It now forms the 'City' branch of the LT Northern Line (coloured black on the famous map) from Euston to Kennington via the Bank.

After the C & SLR came the unique Waterloo and City line of the LSWR, discussed in the last chapter. This never became part of London Transport, but the next oldest tube, the Central London Railway dating from 1900, did. It too was a locomotive-hauled line at first, but by 1903 had begun to adopt the EMU configuration which thereafter became standard for all tube lines. The CLR remained independent for some time and its original portion forms the middle section (between Shepherd's Bush, Bank and Liverpool Street) of the now much more comprehensive

The handsome and substantial nature of the Metropolitan's early clerestory electric stock is well seen in this close-up of a Harrow-bound train taken during the major reconstruction of Baker Street station which started in 1910 (NRM collection).

Central Line (bright red on the map). It was perhaps most famous in its early days for its name — 'The Tuppeny Tube' — a reference to its original 'flat fare' policy.

The remaining tube lines during the early period all dated from 1906-7 and shared common ownership and styling, though they were each physically separate and their original promotion was by different people. Before opening, they came into the ownership of an American company founded by Charles Yerkes, which also controlled the District Railway (see below), and from 1910 onwards the tube lines were operated under the corporate name of the London Electric Railway. In due course they were to form the central sections of the Bakerloo Line (originally Baker Street and Waterloo, map colour brown), the Piccadilly Line (originally Great Northern, Piccadilly and Brompton, map colour dark blue) and the West End branch of the Northern Line (originally Charing Cross, Euston and Hampstead, map colour black). Interestingly, after this first flush of deep-level tube lines, no more were built until the Victoria Line was opened some 60 years later.

In effect, the first deep-level tubes criss-crossed the area defined by the Circle Line and it was not until much later that they extended outwards into the suburbs. Though the expansion of the network is not part of their carriage history *per se*, it did of course involve extra stock provisioning and, as time went by, the extended underground lines, mostly still keeping north of the Thames, began to perform very similar functions to the electrified commuter lines which the main-line companies were developing south of the river. This pattern of differentiated approaches north and south of the Thames still underlays most of London's rail-borne commuter traffic to this day.

Because of their different origins, each of the various private underground lines developed its own styles of carriage and this was always more than simply a differentiation between surface and tube lines. For many years there was no way that a District train could be mistaken for a Metropolitan one, nor a Central London tube train be confused with its Bakerloo equivalent. To a large extent this is still reflected in the present-day scene (albeit rather more subtly than in older days), and stems from the fact that even after London Transport was formed in 1933, most stock replacement tended to be on a line by line basis, each route being operated by a broadly similar class of vehicle. There has, of course, been much coming together, and it will be the purpose of the rest of this chapter to examine the extent to which this had taken place by *circa* 1953.

Surface stock: 1905-1936

The twentieth-century history of London Transport railway carriages is mostly the history of electric stock, especially in the period covered by this volume, but even though this will form the remaining bulk of this chapter, it must be recalled that both the Metropolitan and the District Railways started as steam-hauled systems and, in the case of the Metropolitan, locomotive haulage remained a feature of its activity well into the post-nationalization era. Even then, some of its services were still steam hauled in the more rural suburbs though, of course, they were handed over to electric locomotives well out of town for the continuation to inner London. Like the Southern Railway, but not to the same extent, the Metropolitan also converted compartment steam stock to EMU form, and even in the early 1930s had new stock built to this traditional layout. Thus, for the whole of the first half of this century — and after — services on the Metropolitan were always a mixture of open saloon EMUs and compartment stock, some of the latter being locomotive hauled.

This thoroughly conventional compartment interior was to be found in Metropolitan Railway first class carriage No 422, built in 1905 as an EMU control trailer but converted in 1910, along with nine others, to form the first two so-called 'Dreadnought' sets for locomotive haulage on the non-electrified lines (NRM collection)

Above *A characteristically neat set of Metropolitan Railway 'Dreadnought' non-corridors out in the country north of Harrow in 1921 behind an unidentified Class 'H' 4-4-4T* (Laundy Collection, NRM)

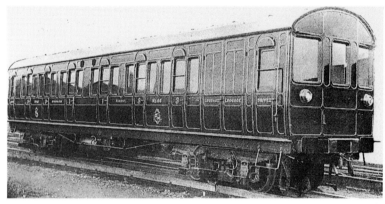

Right *Metropolitan Railway single-unit 'Shuttle' car No 46 was a conversion in 1910 of a previous accident victim. In converted form, it shared the visual lines of the 'Dreadnought' stock, though not, of course, being intended for locomotive-haulage* (J. Whiting collection)

Each type of stock was confined to a specific service, but where they all converged (on the section between Baker Street and the City) anything was likely to turn up and I well remember my own surprise when, as a student, a pretty scruffy set of dingy brown non-corridors was presented at King's Cross for my trip to Baker Street. Years earlier, and as a child before the war, I had been 'programmed' to expect nice neat red and cream EMUs and had no notion at the time, nor even 15 years later, that these ancient conveyances still existed, much less that they were still in use! However, interesting though these compartment carriages were, they were no whit different, save in minor cosmetic matters, from many a thousand others, and in any case are well recorded in other books; so I have deliberately chosen to give them short weight here.

The real twentieth-century significance of London Transport, whether post-1933 or in its pre-amalgamated state, lies in the gradual evolution of the open saloon multiple unit carriage for purely urban working. And here the District Railway probably merits the pioneering role. As early as 1901, the District, in

an attempt to stem its declining fortunes, had concluded that electrification of its lines might prove the salvation, and this coincided with the arrival in Britain of a group of American businessmen who had made their money from electrified rail systems in the USA. They were headed by Charles Yerkes and took over the District Railway's fortunes. It was the same Mr Yerkes whose company almost simultaneously took control of three of the pioneering deep-level tube lines (see above), though Yerkes himself died before they were open. Thus, from the first Edwardian days, a large slice of what was to become London Transport was under unified control — the so-called Underground Group — and though all the systems were physically separate, the seeds were sown from an early date for the later development of common ideas.

In the event, this early amalgamation was to turn out to be the dominant influence in the subsequent development of London's underground system and was consolidated in 1913 when the City and South London, already in close proximity to the Yerkes lines at Euston and Kennington, also threw in its lot with

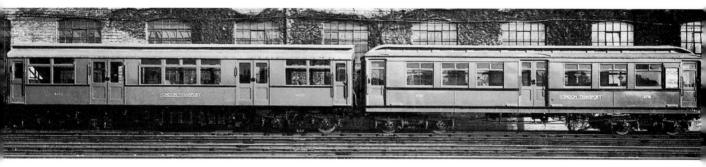

This 1934 view of a pair of older District Line clerestories gives a good impression of the difference between the steel-bodied 1923 stock with straight-through clerestories (on the left) and pre-First World War wooden-bodied trailer with domed-end clerestory (on the right). Both had hand-operated doors (London Transport Museum)

the Underground Group, as eventually did the Central London Railway. During all this time, the Metropolitan stayed aloof, and even when the final 1933 amalgamations were imposed it was a very reluctant guest at the wedding! In effect, though by far the largest of the constituent parts of London Transport, the Metropolitan was taken over by the group whose long-established 'UndergrounD' symbol rather set the style for the new organization.

In strictly carriage terms on the surface lines, the District and its rival followed quite different approaches, even discounting the Metropolitan's long espousal of compartments alongside its open EMUs. In a nutshell, the Metropolitan was very British while the District, hardly surprisingly, began to be influenced by American ideas from the onset of its electrification policies. This led both to the espousal of a clerestory roof form which survived for almost 70 years on the District Line itself, and to an interior layout concept which is now dominant throughout London Transport. Furthermore, in the early stock built for the District one can also see many ideas which, as Volume 1 has explained, were not slow to be taken up outside London — on Merseyside and Tyneside for example.

Essentially, the District philosophy was one of a mixture of motor and trailer cars, all from any one batch being of broadly similar appearance, with open interiors and both intermediate and end sliding doors. Within the cars, a mixture of longitudinal and transverse seating was adopted. Styling was always very 'American', especially in the earlier wooden-bodied days, when the vertical matchboarding for the lower panels, a pronounced waist rail and 'Gothic'-type side windows were a commonplace. There were many subtle changes over the years, and District Line trains were run in so many bewildering combinations of stock that they were often amongst the most untidy to be seen on London Transport. Space precludes a full analysis here, but it is well recorded elsewhere, and even the final steel-bodied clerestory carriages of 1935 displayed a toned-down and suitably modernized version of the styling first adopted more than 30 years earlier.[*]

By then, there had been more than a bit of design 'spin-off' from the District surface stock to the new standard tube stock (see below), while the 1930s interior design treatment of the final clerestories formed the essential basis of the deservedly celebrated 1937 'Metadyne' surface stock and 1938 tube stock, both of which will be considered in due course.

Turning now to the actual carriages built for the District during the main period covered by this volume, the first vehicles which may be said to have had real significance in respect of the final London Transport synthesis were the 'F' stock cars of 1920 — incidentally, the District not only introduced 'car' to the EMU vocabulary (an American term, naturally enough) but also chose to identify successive designs by reference letters in alphabetical order. This again helped to establish a common London Transport feature, but there was no hidden meaning to the letters used, save for ease of identification. These 'F' stock vehicles were built by the Metropolitan Carriage Wagon and Finance Company in Birmingham with the aid of post-war Government financial assistance; they were the only departure from the clerestory form until after 1935 and were by quite some way more modern looking than almost anything else which appeared until the late 1930s on any of the LT lines. They were distinctly more rapid and powerful than anything which had preceded them and dimensionally, at 9 ft 7 in wide, took full advantage of the structure gauge.

Rather unusually, they were not, at first, used for dedicated services, and were reckoned as providing 'additional facilities' to normal services, especially by

---

[*] For a particularly useful summary of early District stock see *Clerestories on the District* by Piers Connor: 'Railways South East', Vol 1 No 2, Summer 1988.

way of improving the various 'non-stop' operations which, in the interests of arriving at their destination earlier, regularly omitted calls at some stations. At this point it must be understood that 'non-stop' in the UndergrounD context never meant quite the same thing as on the main-line railways; any train which omitted even a few intermediate stations in the interests of speeding commuters to or from work was instantly classified as 'non-stopping'! Thus, the 'F' stock tended to gain a sort of superior status which finally reached its apogee in 1950 when, no less than 30 years old, the cars were renovated and transferred to the Metropolitan Line for use on the semi-fast Harrow and Uxbridge services from 1951 onwards, a task probably more suited to their performance capability than any they had previously assayed.

Because of technical incompatibility with other cars, the 'F' stock always ran in tidy formations of up to eight cars and never formed part of the hybrid compositions characteristic of most District trains until quite recent times. In this respect they were probably the first examples of the universally 'tidy' formations now to be seen throughout London Transport, be it surface or tube. Certainly, until the advent of 1937 (surface) and 1938 (tube) stock (see below) there was never anything quite as visibly homogeneous as an 'F' Stock train, though the Metropolitan open stock ran it close.

The 'F' stock was also interesting in one rather

more cosmetic sense: the cars were first put into service in a darker shade of red than had hitherto been used by the District or was subsequently to become familiar. Referred to at the time as 'Engine Lake', it did not find favour. However, from the passenger viewpoint, these cars also had two features which were to prove of much longer-term significance to the later London Transport scene than their colour: they had rather more doors relative to train length than almost anything which had gone before, and they were possessed of seemingly vast standing space relative to seating, the central area between the doors being wholly equipped with lateral seats. Whether this was considered beneficial at the time is hard to assess, but it did not reappear in quite such profusion until brand new tube cars were built for the Victoria Line in the late 1960s; but maybe I digress!

After the 'F' stock, the District reverted to its long-standing love affair with the clerestory, and from 1923-4 until 1935-6 a whole series of gradually evolving cars came into service, some illustrated here, which took up most of the traditional alphabetical classifications from 'G' to 'N' ('H' were rebuilds of older stock; 'I' and 'J' were never used). There were in fact but two basic visual styles: the earlier 'G' series with 'straight through' clerestories, and the almost identical 'K' to 'N' series with domed-end clerestories and generally rather more modern outline. Though they did not have quite as many doors as the 'F' stock nor as much standing space, in terms of interior styling these final District clerestories were well on the way to establishing the LT standard. They also had the interesting distinction of being the last

Figure 49 *Elevation and plan of a District Railway 'F' stock motor car as originally built.*

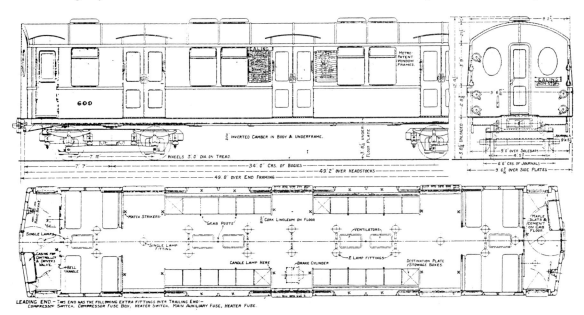

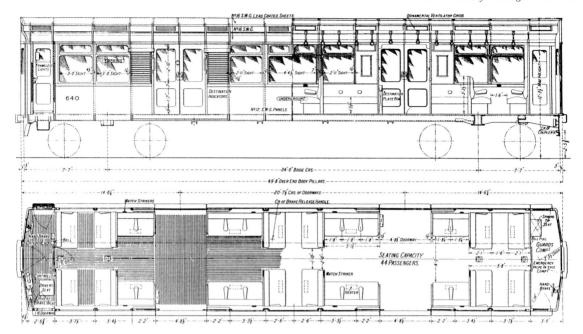

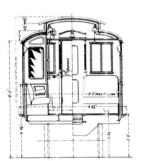

Figure 50 *Detailed elevations and plan of the last 'straight through' clerestory carriages built for the District, the 'G' stock motor cars of 1923-4. Note the hand-operated sliding doors, a feature of the District Line trains for many a long year.*

Figure 51 *Elevation and plan of a 'K' stock domed-end clerestory motor car of the series ordered for the District in 1927. Remaining District Line clerestory carriages of the subsequent 'L', 'M' and 'N' series were styled broadly in this fashion.*

Below *The clerestory-roofed 'M' stock, originally built for the Metropolitan line and seen here at Hammersmith when new, represented the last new stock to have this distinctive roof form. When later transferred to the District Line, these cars eventually became the last clerestories to run on London Transport (London Transport Museum).*

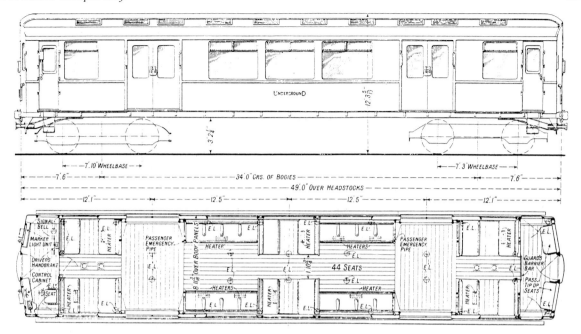

clerestory-roofed railway carriages to be built for service in Britain.

Of these various batches of clerestory carriages we might perhaps single out two more than interesting sub-groups. The first 'domed-end' series were the 'K' Class, and some of them were for a time owned by the LMS in consequence of its financial interest (having inherited the London, Tilbury and Southend line via the Midland Railway) in the District Line's extensions to Upminster. It may perhaps be of appropriate if quite inconsequential interest to note that these 'K' cars were the last District carriages to incorporate dark red (Midland Lake?) in their livery, but only on the doors. Some of the very similar 'L' class of 1931 (all eight of its motors in fact) were similarly LMS owned. In fact, the LMS, technically, owned some 110 District Line cars, but they were always viewed as part of the District fleet. This apart, however, far more relevant was the allocation of some of the final clerestories to the Metropolitan Line after the formation of the LPTB in 1933. These were the 1935 cars of the 'M' series and they were put to use on the Hammersmith services. This marked the start of the Metropolitan's assimilation into the 'mainstream' development of London Transport, and will be addressed later.

Much of the post-1923 clerestory stock survived until the late 1960s and the last of them was not withdrawn until 1971. Speaking from experience, it was by no means outclassed by its later brethren (save, perhaps, for its rather dated appearance) in either

ambience or ride quality and, during the late 1960s, it was readily possible at one place in particular (Victoria) to transfer quite regularly on the same day from the progenitor of the modern London Transport approach on the District Line to its very latest manifestation on the still new Victoria Line tube stock.

The final District clerestories — along with the earlier 'F' stock — were indeed significant carriages in the evolution of London Transport, and in their latter days all the post-1923 clerestory cars were reclassified as 'Q' stock; but before getting to that particular complication, it is time to return to that other and geographically much larger surface element of the London Transport system, the Metropolitan.

The Metropolitan Railway had addressed the electrification issue at more or less the same time as the District (to Uxbridge in 1905 to be precise) and although it did, eventually, compromise between compartment and open stock, its very first EMUs could lay sound claim to have been amongst the most handsome of any carriages of the genre to have worked in the London area, or anywhere else for that matter (see also Volume 1, page 245). Though they had open-style interiors in the 'American' manner, their general styling was much more 'British' in outline with traditional panelling and incurved lower side sheets. In fact, when, a few years later, similarly styled stock appeared on both the Circle and the Hammersmith and City Lines (the latter jointly owned with the GWR), it may have seemed for a while as though this was to become the new 'London' style EMU. In

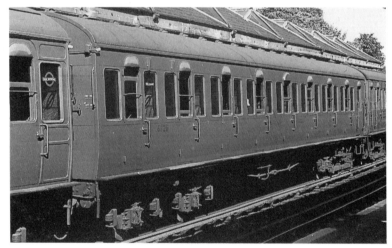

Top *Metropolitan Railway open third class car No 89 with its three pairs of sliding doors typifies the 1921 elliptical roof stock, built to operate with the earlier 1913 vehicles. Compared with the earlier type, these post-war carriages had more doors, flat sides and rather more restrained panelling* (J. Whiting collection).

Above *This, the first five-car Circle Line train of elliptical roof stock, was refurbished as part of the 1934 improvement programme. The motor cars are of 1913 stock and the trailers from the 1921 continuation* (London Transport Museum).

Above left *Flush-sided control trailer No 6725 (note the driving cab at the far end replacing a ninth compartment), photographed at Rickmansworth in the drab London Transport brown livery in August 1951, typifies the final style of compartment-type carriage built for the Metropolitan. By now classed as 'T' stock, the vehicle had entered service in 1929 as one of the new MW fleet, designed from the outset to operate in emu rather than locomotive-hauled form* (John H. Meredith).

Left *The ungainly front-end appearance of the early Central London Railway gate stock EMUs is well caught in this 1924 view of a Liverpool Street to Ealing train entering East Acton station. Note the third rail system used at that time* (NRM collection).

purely aesthetic terms this might have been preferable, but events were to prove otherwise.

Unlike the District cars, the first generation of Metropolitan open stock was devoid of central doors and this tended to slow down the boarding of and alighting from trains, especially at busy times. In this respect, compartment stock was better, and this may have been something of a contributory reason for the Metropolitan continuing to operate both open and compartment EMUs as well as deciding to convert much of its redundant hauled stock to the latter form. There was also, of course, the perfectly valid point that out in the country steam haulage was normal for many years between Harrow on the Hill (Rickmansworth after 1925) and Aylesbury, and although these trains were electric hauled to the City, their stock remained conventional. Even after the formation of London Transport, it was to be 1960 before EMUs finally reached Amersham and made LT a fully EMU system, at which time through running to Aylesbury terminated.

Before the formation of the LPTB, the Metropolitan had developed its open EMU style into another visibly attractive form, mainly for the Circle Line. These had centre and end doors, as on the District, but the styling was thoroughly 'British'. It also introduced a full elliptical roof to the London underground; but though conceptually sound, the 1913 stock turned out to be the last open design by the Metropolitan, apart from a few post-war experimental rebuilds which came to little and a further purchase in 1921 of another tranche of 1913-style open stock, this time with three pairs of side doors to each car. Thus, by 1933, the open EMUs which were inherited by the LPTB were dominated by those displaying UndergrounD rather than Metropolitan influence. Even so, one of the first things which took place after 1933 was a thorough renovation of the 1913 and 1921 cars whose handsome outlines thereafter remained on the Circle Line until 1952.

Meantime, the Metropolitan was still uncertain about saloon or compartment stock, and its final pre-1933 EMUs reverted to the latter form. To be honest, this was not for want of trying again in the open mode during 1925. However, the Met's well-heeled long-distance commuters were obdurately conservative and preferred compartments. Thus, new compartment-style EMUs were introduced in 1927, the fleet being gradually enlarged until 1932. This time, though many of the trailers were ex-hauled stock, all the motors and a considerable number of the later trailers were built new. They were handsome of form in a thoroughly conventional way, being in essence styled on the last series of new hauled stock — the so-called 'Dreadnoughts' of the Edwardian era — and in their fully lined Metropolitan livery they must have looked magnificent. In due course they were designated 'T' stock by the LPTB, following the District-inspired system, and proved to be the last pure Metropolitan EMUs to remain in service, the last to carry fare-paying passengers doing so in October 1962.

A natural consequence of the Metropolitan's 'blow hot, blow cold' policy in regard to carriages was that in 1933 it bequeathed no fewer than 11 types to the new unified system*, many of which were incompatible not only with each other but also with that of the District. There was, to be sure, almost as much visible variation on the District too but conceptually they were all of one form (open EMU with plenty of side doors) and there was more mutual compatibility and system standardization. It was no real surprise therefore when, as a start towards uniformity, the new LPTB initially re-equipped the Hammersmith services with District-style cars (see above). Furthermore, it was only four years after the formation of London Transport that the first recognizably 'unified' designs began to appear on the surface lines — the famous and stylish 'Metadyne' stock — and there was more than a bit of the District experience in their design too. But before going on to consider this particular episode, it will be as well to bring the tube story up to the same point in time.

Tube stock: 1900-1934

When the Central London Railway opened in 1900, there were already two systems of operation in use on the two existing tubes. The City and South London used locomotive haulage and the Waterloo and City adopted the EMU form. The 'Tuppenny Tube' went for locomotive haulage, but within three years had changed its mind because of excessive track damage by the heavy 44-ton locomotives and thereafter the EMU was to dominate.

The CLR had made a heavy investment in trailer cars and these were, of course, retained and the locomotives replaced by motor cars whose general style matched the trailers. This was a handsome 'British' sort of bodywork with a nice domed-end shallow clerestory roof — a sort of tube version of the original Metropolitan EMUs would be no bad description. A mixture of transverse and lateral seats was offered and access was gained via end platforms with gates.

Unfortunately, however, the driving ends of the motor cars in no way came to match the stylish bodywork of the passenger portions of the vehicles. The control gear was housed in a sort of tin tabernacle which bore no stylistic relationship to the rest of the ensemble, looking as though it had been grafted on

---

* *Steam to Silver*: J.G.Bruce, Capital Transport, 1983

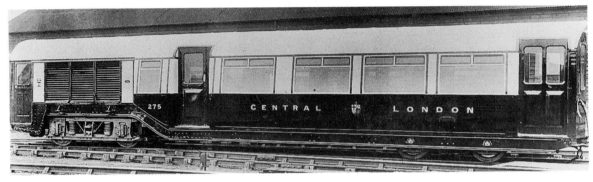

as an afterthought and terminating in a curious and ungainly-looking 'beetle-browed' cab whose quite uniquely ugly lineaments differentiated many of the Central Line trains from those of the rest of the tube system right until the Second World War. When approaching at a steep angle in the open air, one of these sets looked for all the world like an electrically propelled and somewhat morose caterpillar! In one respect, however, these pioneer CLR vehicles set the pattern for every new tube motor car built until 1934: they initiated the characteristic upward sweep of the sideframes above the power bogie.

By contrast with the CLR, the Yerkes tubes went for a far more cheerful-looking and upright-fronted motor car whose cab and control compartment was, more or less, fully integrated into the overall design. Though all three lines went to different builders for their stock, there was a recognizably common approach and their operating systems were mutually compatible. Furthermore, in their front-end treatment they set a design style which was not to change in a basic sense until after the last of the standard tube cars was built in 1934, and which could still be seen in use until the late 1980s on the Isle of Wight, where some of the standard tube stock came to rest during 1967 and later.

Like the Central London cars, the first Yerkes tube stock had a mixture of longitudinal and transverse seats and used end platform entrances with gates, the normal operating procedure on all lines being to use 'gatemen' between each pair of adjacent entrances to take care of passenger safety at stopping places. The gatemen rode the train with the guard(s) and the driving crew. This 'gate' stock as it was called,

though somewhat extravagant in staff per train, remained in use for many years, and the final gate stock train did not run until 1930. Before then, however, the basic nature of most newer tube cars had changed quite considerably.

Like the first generation Metropolitan EMUs, the first gate stock tube cars suffered from having entrances at the ends only, and by 1914-15, when the first Bakerloo and Central London extensions were mooted, intermediate hand-operated side doors had been incorporated in the design, sometimes retaining end gates but often with the end entrances now totally enclosed, also with hand-operated doors. Several varieties were produced over the next few years and included amongst them in 1920 were some more than agreeable jointly-owned cars (LNWR & LER) for the Watford run with rather less standing space, rather more transverse seating and even small luggage racks. Their smaller doors did, however, cause them to take rather longer to load and unload at stations, and the stock was replaced only ten years later. Some of it went to the LMS and was used on the Rickmansworth-Watford branch.

When the Watford stock was introduced, experiments were already being carried out on the Piccadilly Line with sliding air-operated doors of the kind now familiar. This reduced the size of train crew considerably and was applied to both new cars and some conversions of former gate stock and hand-operated door stock. This led directly to the introduction in 1923 of the first of the so-called 'Standard' tube cars for use on all lines coming under the control of the Underground Group. This included the City and South London, which was now expensively

Left *Gate stock clerestory trailer car No 292 in the florid livery of the Great Northern Piccadilly & Brompton Railway, the forerunner of the modern Piccadilly line* (NRM collection).

Below left *Central London motor car No 275 of the 1913 series, with intermediate side door and enclosed entrances, was an altogether more stylish essay than its predecessors* (NRM collection).

Right *The upright-fronted driving motors of the Yerkes tube lines are represented here by this Bakerloo/LNWR jointly-owned version, No 3J, seen at Queens Park circa 1920. The styling is clearly part way to that of the London Transport 'Standard' tube stock* (NRM collection).

Middle right *Trailer car No 407J, also from the LNWR/LER joint stock, was built in 1920. This view clearly shows the quite small central entrance and, through the windows, the large amount of transverse seating, neither of which features proved particularly helpful either in terms of passenger capacity or ease of loading* (NRM collection).

Below *Now reconstructed with air-operated doors, this six-car Central Line train of former gate stock at Wood Lane clearly shows the retention of the original 1903-pattern cab styling and clerestory roof* (London Transport Museum).

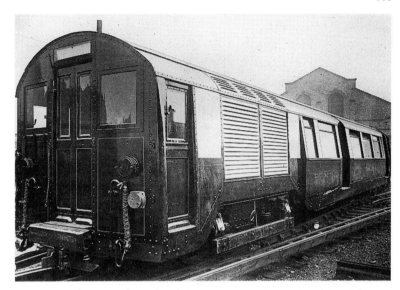

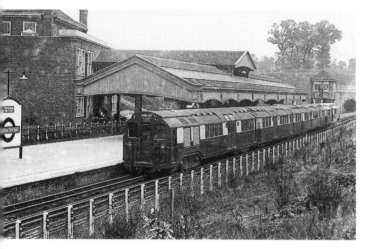

converted to standard tube diameter and linked up properly with the Hampstead tube to form the basis of the modern Northern Line in 1926. It will thus be seen that whereas on the District Railway the basically correct EMU concept had been established from the outset on at least some parts of the surface lines of what was to become London Transport, it took about 20 years for tube stock to arrive at much the same configuration, size apart.

Air-operated doors were obviously the key to the many problems, so before going on to discuss the Standard stock which was its first major consequence, it must also be recorded that much of the former gate stock on the Central London, Piccadilly and Bakerloo lines was planned to be converted to air-door operation. The Central London stock was tackled first, between 1926 and 1928, by enclosing the ends and fitting two sets of twin doors along the sides (one set only on the motors) and although most cars lost their distinctly different side panelling in consequence of this rebuilding, their quaint old-fashioned driving ends remained as clear indication of their origin.

By this time, it had also been discovered, as a consequence of completely re-equipping the Hampstead line, that new Standard cars could be built almost as cheaply as converting gate stock, and these were therefore put on the Piccadilly and Bakerloo Lines instead of the planned conversions. However, the Central Line conversions ran on until mid-1939 before finally being replaced by Standard stock. A principal reason for this was that the original CLR had a tube diameter marginally smaller than that of the Yerkes lines and, though by no means as restricted as the C & SLR, could not accept standard dimension tube stock at all locations. It was only the LPTB new works programme of 1935-40, by allowing some realigning of tunnels and lengthening of platforms, which enabled Standard stock to be used from 1939. At much the same time, the Central Line track was converted from its original three-rail system to the Yerkes standard four-rail method which was now the LT standard throughout.

Turning now to the Standard stock itself: viewed in retrospect, it was the tube equivalent of the Dis-

Top left *A four-car Standard stock train entering Hendon Central station in pre-LPTB days during the early years of the Morden-Edgware Line, now far better known as the Northern Line* (NRM Collection).

Middle left *Head-on view of a pair of 1924-built Standard stock control trailers in Morden depot, soon after the opening of the Northern Line's South London extension* (J. Whiting collection).

Left *Interior view of one of the 1926-built Standard stock trailer cars by Metropolitan* (London Transport Museum).

trict's 1923-35 stock, even down to the clerestory, and there was much common detail in the design, especially in such things as the interior trimming and colour schemes. But its effect was much more widespread, eventually totalling some 1,466 cars, of which all but 26 were in service well before the LPTB was even formed.

It started in 1922 with an order by the Underground Group for six sample trailer cars, five from outside firms and one 'in-house' example with control equipment, so as to try and arrive at the 'perfect' tube car. Though subtly different, all were recognizably similar in concept and were soon followed by the first production batches which surged into service in great waves for most of the next nine years, 1928 being the only blank year. The Hampstead line got them first in consequence of the almost simultaneous extensions to Morden and Edgware, not to mention the incorporation of the former C & SLR. The Bakerloo and Piccadilly Lines were not long afterwards, again with quantities augmented by vir-

tue of the lengthy extensions into the suburbs, particularly those of the Piccadilly Line both north and west; but total standardization was never quite achieved because by the time the Central Line got these cars in 1939, they were then the 'hand-me-downs' from the Northern and Bakerloo Lines which had by now received replacement 1938 stock (see below).

As for the cars themselves, though there were slight differences between batches, the basic style never seriously changed, nor did the general layout, save for the fact that the 1931 and later batches had single end sliding doors as well as the centrally positioned 'twins', thus slightly reducing the seating but considerably improving passenger access. This apart, however, only three basic types were provided: driving motor cars, non-driving trailers and 'Control'

Figure 52 Elevations and plans of typical 'Standard' tube stock of 1927 from Messrs Cammell Laird and Metropolitan respectively.

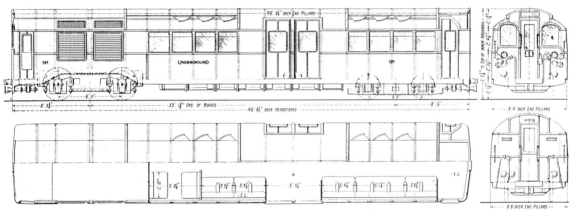

General View, Side Elevation, Plan and End Views of Motor Coach for the London Underground Railways, built by Cammell Laird & Co. Ltd.

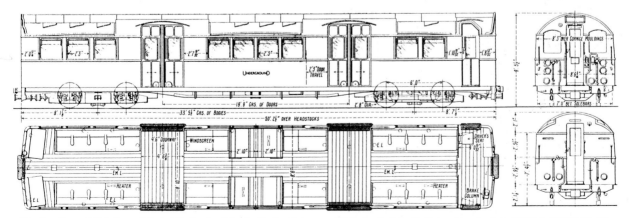

Elevation, Plan and End Views of Control Trailer Coach for the London Underground Railways, built by the Metropolitan Carriage, Wagon & Finance Co. Ltd.

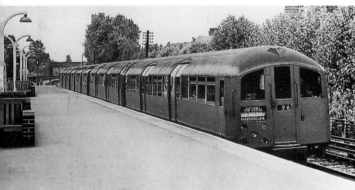

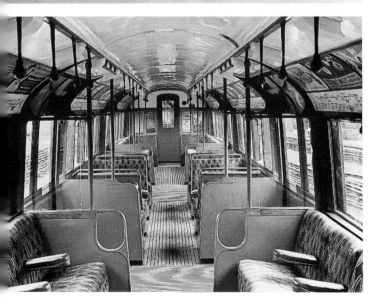

Left *Eight-car Standard stock train in the new station at Wanstead on the Central Line extension to Hainault,* circa *1950 (NRM collection).*

Figure 53 *Elevations and plan of the experimental streamlined tube stock of 1936, the forerunners of the 1938 stock.*

trailers. The most common formation was a seven-car — M-T-T-M + CT-T-M — it being common practice to run the four-car unit on its own at quieter times.

The motor cars were derived from the earlier Yerkes pattern, with upswept frames above the motor bogie, and when all were in service they must surely have represented the most visibly characteristic feature of any stock ever to run on London Transport. As a child they were part of my London scene, along with the Kingsway tram tunnel, and they seemed to give off a particular and by no means unpleasant form of 'electric' odour which, even now, on those rare occasions I sense it in the tube tunnels, has a powerfully nostalgic effect! Their only 'archetype' rivals were probably the 1938 stock cars, and the images of these two styles are still those which come most instantly to my mind whenever I think of the London tubes. The appended drawings of the Cammell Laird and Metropolitan series, first published in 1927, are quite characteristic, the non-control trailers being symmetrically arranged with transverse passenger seats at both ends of the car adjacent to the end doors.

In due course, as stated, much of the Standard stock was cascaded on to the Central Line from 1939 onwards and this, with the Piccadilly Line, was its last regular haunt until well into the period covered by the next volume. On the Central line after the war, eight-car trains were normal and, to avoid two adjacent motor cars right in the centre of the platforms, the formation was modified from two conventional four-car units to M-T + M-T-T-M + T-M.

The great leap forward (1935-1938) and its consequences

In practical terms, the 1923-35 surface stock of the District and the Standard stock of the tube lines was so dominant and had established such a high degree

Middle left *This view of a four-car train of 1938 tube stock at Kilburn in 1950 also shows one of the many Standard stock trailers (vehicle No 3) which were modified to run as part of this stock in the Bakerloo line sets — see text (London Transport Museum).*

Left *Interior of one of the 1938 stock trailer cars used on the Northern Line (London Transport Museum).*

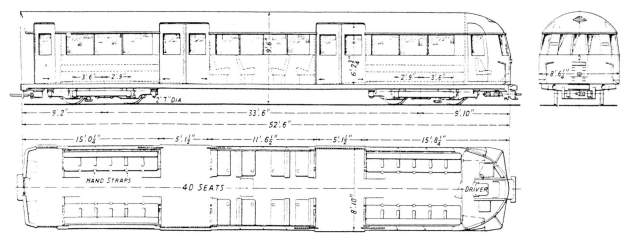

of concept standardization before 1933 that when London Transport was formed only the rebuilt Central London Railway gate stock and most of the Metropolitan fleet stood outwith the general pattern; and even the gate stock had been brought into line with UndergrounD practice as far as possible. It can therefore occasion no great surprise that the subsequent LPTB evolution was an almost direct continuation of that initiated by the former Yerkes empire. As already stated, it actually began mildly enough with the drafting of a new batch of District-type clerestories on to the Metropolitan's Hammersmith Line, but this was merely a start, and in the case of the Metropolitan, short-lived; the new clerestories fairly soon went back to the District as will shortly be explained.

The real catalyst, quite apart from the formation of the LPTB itself, was the burgeoning growth of suburban traffic and the demand for extensions of the LT network. This was made possible by the 1935-40 new works programme which, in terms of new stock provision, resulted in two radically new designs, one each for the tube and surface routes, which, with but one exception, established the design parameters for some 30 or more years. The exception was the new stock for the Metropolitan line to Amersham; that did not arrive until 1960 and must await the next volume to resolve.

It started in 1935 when four new experimental six-car tube trains were ordered from Metro-Cammell, which came into service in 1936. The radical change was to locate all the electrical equipment below the floor, thus dispensing with the switch compartment above the motor bogie, using the vacated space for more passenger seating. In fact, the new motor cars had virtually the same capacity as the trailers and, by way of bonus, since motor cars no longer wasted passenger space, more of them could be provided,

thus enhancing train performance. The experimental trains were therefore all delivered as twin motor pairs. They were operated on the Piccadilly Line in sets of six, this formation having the same capacity as a normal seven-car set of Standard stock.

In design terms they were beautifully conceived save for one quite absurd element, the provision of a streamlined cab on the units of three of the four trains. What possible benefit a streamlined form could confer at not much more than 30 mph down in the depths of the London clay was always obscure, and the idea was soon abandoned. The fourth train was given a much more pleasing semi-flat-fronted but dome-roofed cab design; it was to be the prophetic one.

Streamlining apart, the experimental trains were to form the basis of the largest new build of tube stock since the Standard cars of 1923-31. It was soon known as the '1938 Stock', and although, numerically, the total fleet was some 15 per cent smaller than the Standard stock build, the rate of production was faster, it had far fewer detail variations and was undoubtedly the most consistent tube stock seen so far. In fact, so definitive did it become that the old 'Standard' designation for the earlier stock soon became changed to 'Pre-1938' stock!

The 1938 stock went into service as a total re-equipment of the Northern Line (save for its separated branch from Finsbury Park to the City) and the almost total re-stocking of the Bakerloo Line. On the latter route, some pre-1938 stock was retained and the 1938 stock proper was supplemented by some 58 modified pre-1938 trailers in consequence of the need to augment the fleet when the former Metropolitan Stanmore branch was added to the Bakerloo Line. These vehicles retained their earlier clerestory form, but the only other non-standard cars in the 1938 fleet were the 18 streamliners which, after the war, were

converted into trailers. They revealed their origin by having three rather than four windows between centre and end doors; that subtle point apart, which few if any noticed, they were then identical to the 1938 cars proper.

The 1938 stock was generally operated in seven cars trains — M-M-T-M + M-T-M — the intermediate motor in the four-car unit having no driving cab. As with the pre-1938 stock, the intention was to operate single four-car units at off-peak times, and this was indeed the case until well into the 1950s when seven-car trains became the all-day norm. The 1938 stock was also supplemented after the war by a modest complement of 'Shunting Control Motors' which dispensed with a driving cab at the inner end of a three car unit yet which could, in the sidings, be driven from that end when making up a seven-car formation, thus gaining additional passenger space and saving the cost of a full driving cab.

As for the rest of the design, it could hardly be faulted. A smooth and stylish flush-sided exterior was combined with a clean and uncluttered interior. The 'upsweep' of the frames over the motor bogie was,

of course, no more and neither was the clerestory — at least from the outside; but within the cars, it came back as an attractively raised centre section of the roof with some few inches of practical advantage for standees. As for the seat comfort — and here I speak from years of using them — it has never been bettered in any London Transport EMU I have ever experienced, and I have ridden in most of them from the Metropolitan compartment and Circle stock dating from the pre-LPTB era to the latest 1980s offerings. So well-conceived were they, in fact, that 20 years later, the so-called 1959 stock for the Piccadilly and Central Lines was a virtual carbon copy, except that its seats were far more uncomfortable — but that is for the next volume to resolve!

The reader may well, by now, have deduced that I have a sort of 'soft spot' for the 1938 tube stock, and he would not be wrong. I consider it to have been quite exceptional for its time and I write from the experience of being carried in it many a thousand times when I was resident both in Northern and Bakerloo hinterland; but it was not unique. Between the building of the experimental 1936 stock and the

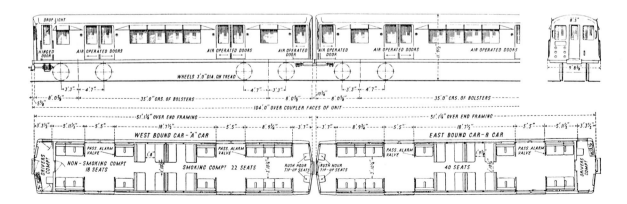

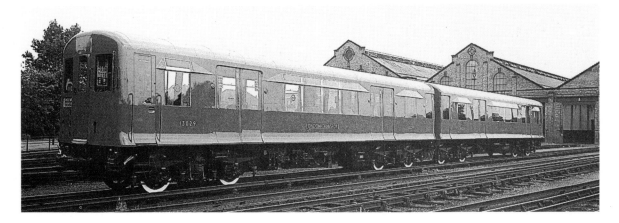

full 1938 fleet, London Transport completed a re-markable double act when it also offered an equally trend-setting new design for the surface routes: the so-called 'Metadyne' stock.

The word 'Metadyne' simply referred to a new form of much improved control equipment which had been evaluated on older cars during 1934, but because it was first put to widespread use in a large batch of brand new surface stock its name became attached to the stock itself. In fact, the new stock, continuing the District line tradition, was more correctly called 'O', 'P', 'Q' and 'R' stock, and though Metadyne equipment was universally used in the 'O' and 'P' stock when new, it was not universal on all cars of the new shape.

Like the 1938 tube stock, the new surface stock also displayed a radical re-think in terms of body styling, and the first examples actually came into service between the experimental 1936 tube stock and the 1938 stock proper. Despite the great difference in size between the tube and surface stock, there was clearly much interlinking of design as far as it affected the passenger areas, and it is a moot point which of the two types of stock influenced which. Later cars of the 'O' to 'Q' fleet were slightly delayed by the war and the whole order was not completed until 1941. Even so, given the simultaneous introduction of the almost twice as large 1938 tube stock fleet, the overall achievement was remarkable. The 'R' stock did not appear until after the war.

The new surface cars shared their flush-sided exterior styling with the 1938 tube stock, but the lower body panels were flared out in an attractive and quite unique way to avoid the need for running boards yet also reduce platform edge gaps. It also prevented any foolish-minded passenger trying to hang on the out-side when the doors closed! They had the usual pair of twin doors along each side and single sliding doors at the inner car ends, all the original 'O' stock com-

ing into service as twin motor pairs with outer end driving cabs, much in the manner of the experimen-tal 1936 tube stock.

Within the cars, furnishing was very like the new tube stock, including the false interior clerestory, and the seats were just as comfortable. A nice styling point was the attractive exterior ventilator treatment above the side windows. The pairs of twin doors were proportionally rather further apart than on the 1938 tube cars, and this gave a fairly lengthy central sec-tion which combined both transverse and lateral seats. The end seating sections had all lateral seat-ing so, except at the car centres, there was a fair amount of standing space, most of which was sensi-bly located in the vicinity of the doors. Once again, the first impression gained by the passenger was wholly favourable.

The 'O' stock was intended for use on the Ham-mersmith and City Line, operating in six-car trains of three twin units alongside the 1935 clerestory stock already provided for this service (see above). This it began to do late in 1937, but in 1938 trailers were inserted into the original twin units, making an M-T-M set, two of which could form a train. This allowed the clerestories to go to the District, along-side their stylistic bedfellows, after only a relatively short spell on the Metropolitan Line. In fact, suffi-cient 'O' stock existed for some of it to go on to the Metropolitan main line as well.

The 'P' stock was almost identical to the 'O' stock save that the guard's controls were brought into the car body, as on the tube stock, rather than in the rear driving cab as previously. Though there were other smaller technical differences, the 'P' cars were styled exactly like their predecessors and also built in con-siderable quantities. They began operation in mid-1939, but their formations were slightly different from those of the 'O' stock.

They were intended for replacement of all the

older-style open EMU stock on the Metropolitan, where eight-car formations were also required. They were thus formed up as M-T-M + M-T-M + M-M, all close-coupled. All motor cars had driving cabs and, as can be seen, the arrangement also permitted a five-car set if required. This was in fact done at about the time the 'F' stock (see page 147) was transferred to the Uxbridge route, after which five-car formations of released 'Metadyne' stock could be moved on to the Circle line. The 'P' stock trailers were also interesting in that they had a hinged door at one end which had fixed transverse seating behind it against the car end, rather in the manner of the earlier pre-1938 tube stock trailers. This was to facilitate later conversion to motor form if so desired, the hinged door then becoming the cab door. Indeed, many were so converted, especially after the war when the 'R' stock came into service. But before dealing with that story, the complicated 'Q' stock must first be outlined.

The 'Q' stock was thus designated as part of the programme which started in 1938 to rid the District of some of its more antiquated clerestories and also to introduce air-operated doors to District Line trains. It is now an almost forgotten fact that the District Line itself, though the pioneer of much which later became an LT standard, suffered the lot of most pioneers in having the earliest equipment. A consequence of this was that hand-operated sliding doors remained universal until 1938, save for the 'M' stock which was, in any case, designated for the Metropolitan line (see above).

There was no economical way by which all the hand-door stock could be converted immediately, and some of the earlier types could not be converted at all, so the rational choice was made to concentrate all the hand-door stock into certain formations and

provide air-doors on the rest. The hand-door stock was later referred to as 'H' stock, and the new air-door style was the 'Q' stock.

So far so good, but the nature of the conversions meant that while all the 1923 and later clerestory *motor* cars could be and were converted, some of their hand-door trailers were needed for the hand-door sets — even including some of the 1935 air-door trailers returned from the Hammersmith line which therefore had to have their doors converted to the older type in 1938! This then left a total shortage of trailers for the air-door stock, and to meet it new ones were built to the new 1937 car profile. These were the original 'Q' cars and the new fleet also included a few motors as well. The converted clerestories were known as 'Q-converted' stock. The net result was that although the District now had a rather more up-do-date fleet, it was still of two technically incompatible types, each of which exhibited an unbelievably cosmopolitan mixture of car styles to enchant the connoisseur of these things!

Thus matters remained, more or less, until after the war, save for purely technical changes to the running and traction equipment which are outwith this survey. The final transformation of the District stock had to await the later 1940s to resolve, the main instrument of which being the 'R' stock. This was the final step in the elimination of all hand-door stock on London Transport, save for the Metropolitan's compartment carriages. Its implementation had a curiously 'ring-a-ring o' roses' characteristic to it!

By now, hand-door open EMU stock was confined to the District and Circle Lines, the latter still in charge of the renovated 1913 stock (see page 151). The intention was to put the new 'R' stock on to the District to replace all the 'H' stock (see above), eventually in sufficient quantity also to release the 'F' stock for the Uxbridge line, thus allowing the already-mentioned transfer of sufficient 'O' and 'P' stock to work the Circle Line in five-car formation. The whole conversion was in fact done in two stages, the first being to replace the hand-operated District fleet. This was implemented in 1949 by means of the first of the 'R' stock sets.

'R' stock looked just like the 'O', 'P' and 'Q' cars but differed in that all were motor cars, most of which were of non-driving configuration, an idea copied from some of the 1938 tube stock cars. These were all newly built and occupied the central positions in the formations which were either six-car or eight-car. By contrast, all but a few of the *driving* motors were obtained by conversion of the pre-war trailers which had been designed for such a contingency (see above). Many of these were original 'Q' stock which in turn caused some of the more modern hand-door clerestory trailers from the now-withdrawn 'H' stock sets

Left *The well-designed interior of the 'O' Stock and the substantial nature of its upholstery is well seen in this view of an ex-works example in July 1937* (London Transport Museum).

Right *The 'Q'-converted stock was a real mixture, though this example at Wimbledon in 1954 is tidier than many. It is a six-car formation composed of four domed-roof clerestories followed by a 1938-pattern trailer and a square-ended clerestory* (J.H. Aston).

Above *When new, the 'R' stock was almost identical to the pre-war 'O', 'P' and 'Q' series and the various batches of 'flared sided' EMUs were always difficult to tell apart. The destination blinds above the cab window differentiated the 'R' stock from the pre-war 'O' and 'P' stock and this view shows a six-car formation of 'R' stock as used on the Richmond services* (J. Whiting collection).

Right *This 'R' stock driving motor No 22610, taken at Hanger Lane Junction in 1971, shows a circa 1950 conversion of a 1938 car built as a 'Q' stock trailer. It is now in silver painted livery to match the new aluminium-bodied stock alongside which it ran* (R.J. Greenaway).

to be turned into 'Q-converted' form. Thus, while in one respect (the 'R' stock) District trains were getting tidier, the 'Q' stock became ever more Byzantine!

Within the cars, the 'R' stock was just as agreeable as all the rest of this style of vehicle had been and even brighter of aspect, for all the cars had fluorescent lighting tubes very neatly installed along the lower edges of the ever-present false clerestory. And the whole thing reached its climax with the second batch of 'R' stock which allowed the planned 'F' stock-Uxbridge route-Circle Line waltz to take place!

When the second generation 'R' stock cars were ordered, the trains were again a mixture of new (mostly non-driving) and converted ex-'Q' stock trailers (driving); but it was also resolved that the new cars should make extensive use of aluminium alloy in both underframes and bodies to reduce weight. Furthermore, one car was left unpainted to see whether it might also be possible to dispense with costly paintwork. There were, so it would seem, some worries about the cleanliness factor, but all seemed well and a further full eight-car set soon followed. In consequence, 1953 was to see the first 'silver' train running on London Transport — a prophetic event as it turned out.

Completing the 'R' stock story, though now straying well into the Volume 3 period, a further and final series of these distinctive-looking cars followed in 1959 to enable the release of further 'Q' trailers to augment Circle Line sets from five to six cars. The new cars of this final series were also unpainted, though, as usual, there were further conversions too. However, the older stock was now painted in aluminium colour to match the new unpainted cars, and this was to represent the start of the modern livery for the system. This final build of 'flared-side' EMUs was also to complete the first standardization stage of the unified post-1932 London Transport scheme, and forms a fitting conclusion to our story for the moment, for in them were sown the final seeds of the present-day plant. And it is worth reiterating that although the final examples did not appear until the late 1950s, all their essentials were in position by as early as 1938.

Thus it was that in the building of the 1936 and its derived series of modern EMUs, London Transport finally brought together the various elements of its disparate inheritance. It was a fine achievement, and though at the end of this phase there was still much variety to be seen — and still is, for that matter — there can be little doubt that the fundamental form of trains on the modern London Underground was determined by those significant events which started with that rather odd-looking tube train on the Piccadilly Line way back in the streamline era. From small acorns...

8. Other electrifications

Though it is hard to conceive that anyone has not heard of the Southern and London Transport systems already covered, it is by no means as certain that popular awareness is quite so acute when it comes to the other electrified areas of Britain during the company period, and this can only be because they were relatively small and rather scattered. On all other counts, they have sound cause for primacy because many of them actually preceded their more famous cousins in the London area, and on more than one occasion they were technically well in the vanguard of contemporary developments.

There was much individuality, of course — and that may have been part of the trouble; but another factor which may help explain their relatively low profile was that they were mostly both 'provincial' and individualistic, none of them having formed the basis of a complete system as was usually the case in the London area. Nevertheless, they did fall mostly into two readily definable geographical areas, plus one or two oddball London contributions outwith the Southern/LPTB systems. On balance, these regional differentiations seem to form the best basis for this part of the story. Yet again, to afford some degree of continuity, it will be necessary to go back before 1923 in many cases, simply because there was no space in Volume 1 to do more than mention most of them.

Lancashire and the North-West

With the solitary exception of the City and South London tube line, which was hardly typical of anything save itself in the early days, by far the bulk of the pioneering work in suburban electrification was to be found on Merseyside. No doubt my Lancastrian readers will read much significance into this comment but, as in London, the first example was a bit of a maverick with little long-term significance. It was, of course, the Liverpool Overhead Railway which opened in 1893 and, electrically powered from the start, was the world's first 'overhead' line in the generally accepted sense of operating on a continuous viaduct above the city streets. Looking back over the years, it is interesting to note how the pioneer electric railways were all by nature of unique one-offs; even the third of them (the Waterloo and City line — Chapter 6), the only one which still survives more or less as built, can hardly be called typical.

The Liverpool Overhead ran the length of the Docks and was electrified on the third rail system at 500V DC with the conductor rail in the 'six-foot'. Its

Figure 55 *Map showing the scattered nature of the various electrified lines in South Lancashire and the Wirral area during the grouping period.*

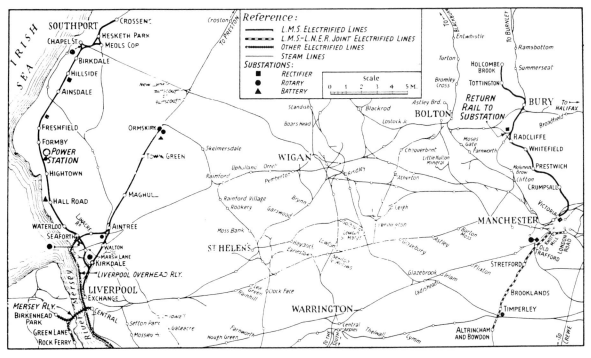

major contribution may well have been to pioneer the modern EMU concept, trains being formed from three-car units (motor/trailer/motor) with interiors of semi-open type. The cars themselves were 'American' in style, serving for the whole life of the system. Eight sets were refurbished, but when life-expired, in 1956, they were never renewed and the line was closed. Thus their design, save perhaps in setting new ideas, was not a significant contribution to twentieth-century carriage development; but they did run throughout much of the period covered by this book and the system itself is surely worthy of mention. Indeed, had it survived, what a boon it would have been to the new and exciting developments in Liverpool's dockland of the 1980s. There were, in fact, many who felt its demise was premature.

Far more significant than the Liverpool Overhead in the long run was the tiny Mersey Railway, by any criterion worthy of mention if only because it was the first underground railway in Britain to be converted from steam to electric traction — in 1903. Furthermore, it was also, by a year or so, the precursor of London's surface lines in terms of carriage concept and power supply system, utilizing open motor and trailer cars running on a 650V DC system with side conductor rail and centre-rail return. In its early days it employed 'American'-pattern clerestory cars with end doors only, and this was one aspect where the Mersey line did not adopt the more familiar 'end plus centre doors' arrangement which became commonplace in the London region.

Right at the time of the grouping, the Mersey Railway had so increased its traffic that it needed to strengthen its fleet and the new cars, while retaining much of the previous clerestory styling, displayed a bow-ended body surmounted by a new type of semi-elliptical roof with domed ends — a handsome combination, repeated in even more cleaned-up form when the fleet was further strengthened in 1936. Two classes were always offered, though in all conscience the five-ply veneered (third class) and rattan upholstered (first class) seating recorded for the 1923 cars

Top left *Original pattern matchboard-panelled Liverpool Overhead Railway stock: motor car No 7 brings up the rear of a train at Seaforth Sands in April 1955* (T.J. Edgington).

Middle left *Refurbished steel-panelled LOR stock: motor car No 29 heads a train into Liverpool Pier Head in October 1956, shortly before closure of the line* (T.J. Edgington).

Left *This nice mixture of domed-roof stock at Birkenhead typified the best of the Mersey Railway in the immediate pre-1938 period — note the fourth rail still in evidence. The first and last three vehicles are the 1923 motors and trailers, while the second and third cars are the 1936 trailers* (BR LMR).

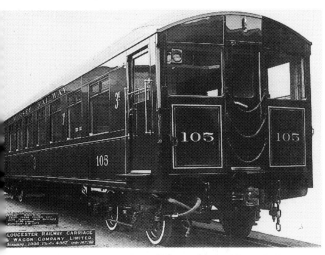

The new 1936 steel-panelled cars for the Mersey Railway were still very 'American' in appearance. This is third class trailer No 105, brand new in January 1936 (BR LMR).

The stylish LMS EMUs for the 1938 Mersey-Wirral scheme were formed into three-car units: driving motor third, trailer composite, driving trailer third. This view shows motor third No 28683 at the head of one such formation, soon after its introduction (BR LMR).

can hardly have been the acme of comfort. Even so, it must be stated that in basic quality, the Mersey was probably rather better than the District line at this time, even though it remained faithful to the exclusively end-door arrangement. One of the earlier clerestory cars was badly damaged during the war and was rebuilt at Wolverton into a very modern-looking open first with rather more agreeable seating. The more modern Mersey cars remained in service until 1956.

The system itself was very small, nothing more than a tunnel section from Liverpool Central under the Mersey to the Wirral peninsula, where it divided into two short open-air 'stub' branches to Birkenhead Park and Rock Ferry. The former route was extended to New Brighton when, in 1938, the Mersey Railway shared in one of the more interesting and far-reaching developments of electric traction during the company period. This was achieved in conjunction with the former Wirral Railway section of the LMS when conductor rails were extended beyond the Mersey's routes into ex-Wirral Railway territory and the two systems were then operated as one rather more extended, but still quite small network. The enlarged system adopted conventional three-rail traction and the two companies retained their nominal independence until 1948.

As its share of the expansion, the LMS introduced a large fleet of brand new and, by contemporary standards, fairly revolutionary-styled EMUs as far as the main-line companies were concerned. Up to now, the LMS, when building its own electric stock, had been

as stodgily conservative as the Metropolitan on its long-distance services and had stuck rigidly to the compartment style. For the new Mersey-Wirral scheme, handsome new lightweight three-car units were built, every bit as modern as the latest London Transport flared body stock but whose interior was, if anything, even better. For one thing it still had two classes, and for another the seating was almost wholly transverse. Considering that even at its longest distance, the new network could not match the length of most of the London Transport routes, this was a very superior provisioning for a purely suburban system. Over 20 per cent of the seating was first class with carpeted floors; but then, the Wirral was a relatively well-heeled sort of place, one supposes, and it was to be some time before these trains became one class only. After the war, in 1956, a further batch of near-identical stock was built by BR to replace the original Mersey railway cars.

The Mersey-Wirral scheme eventually formed the city centre nucleus of the modern 'MerseyRail' network, and the LMS-style cars worked well into the 1980s before their eventual replacement. They were the first genuinely modern sliding door EMUs to be built in quantity for the main line as opposed to the London Transport network. One pre-war unit of this significant LMS design is, happily, preserved in operational order.

The next oldest component of the modern 'MerseyRail' owes its origins to the pioneering work of the old Lancashire and Yorkshire Railway which, in 1904, had electrified its Southport line out of Liver-

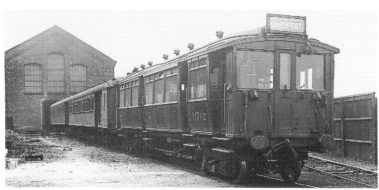

Above *Five-car train of wide-bodied ex-LYR Liverpool–Southport EMU stock in LMS colours during the 1920s, motor third No 14565 leading. The LMS livery for these sets, with its ostentatiously sized running numbers, was rather more reminiscent of former LYR than LMS standard practice; it looked most impressive (LMS official, NRM).*

Left *The leading vehicle of this group of former LYR stock at Horwich in 1932 is one of the lightweight motor composites built for through running on to the Liverpool Overhead. It now carries LMS No 11702, again with a distinctive livery (LMS official, NRM).*

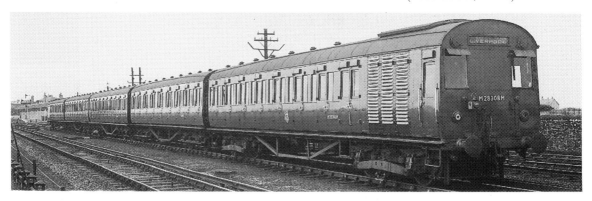

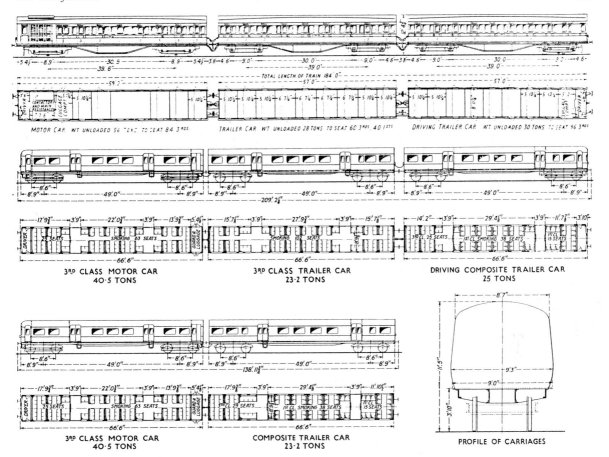

Figure 56 *Simplified elevations and plans of the LMS-built EMU stock of 1927 and 1939 for the Liverpool–Southport line.*

pool Exchange. This, by a short head (see page 170) could claim to be the first main-line electrification in Britain and was followed in 1913 by similar electrification to Ormskirk. The 600V DC third rail system was adopted. The LYR trains built for these services were very distinctive (see, for example, Volume 1, pages 249-51) and by LMS days it was difficult to determine what, exactly, constituted a set formation. They were a mixture of mostly driving motors and orthodox trailers with a few driving trailers and a threesome of parcels vans thrown in for good measure. Some were of lightweight construc-

Above left *A train of the 1927 compartment-style LMS Liverpool–Southport EMU stock seen in early BR days in five-car formation. The first three cars are arranged in conventional formation (see Figure 56) but the rear pair have lost their intermediate composite* (BR LMR).

Left *Three-car unit of LMS 1939 Southport stock in operation with the motor third, No 28315, at the rear of the formation and the driving trailer composite leading* (BR LMR).

tion for working on to the Liverpool Overhead line and all lasted well into the LMS period.

Some stock augmentation was found to be needed very soon and this was provided in the form of some stultifyingly dull compartment stock in 1927 whose only real virtue was that they were some of the first LMS carriages to dispense with outer wood panelling. They were, of course, fully lined out to suggest otherwise, but, that apart, put them behind a 2-4-2T and no one would have noticed that they were one whit different from normal non-corridor stock.

However, just as in the Wirral, so too on the Southport line. When the LMS built new stock to replace the original LYR cars, something positive seems to have happened in the upper hierarchy, for the new Southport trains were even bigger versions of the handsome new Wirral sets and just as well appointed. They could, of course, take advantage of the generous LYR loading gauge which had permitted their predecessors to be, at 10 ft, the widest carriages ever to operate in Britain, but though they were over 66 ft long, the LMS stopped at a full 9 ft 3 in body width. Even this slight increase over normal LMS dimensions allowed 3 + 2 seating in the third class and 2 + 2 in the first without real discomfort. Most seats in both classes were transverse. These excellent cars came into service during 1939-43, their speed of introduction being slowed down by the war. They were designed to operate in three-car and two-car sets whose formations remained fairly stable throughout their lives. Unlike the Wirral sets, they were company-built at Derby rather than by outside contractors.

Constructionally, the bodies were of particular interest in that they were of all-steel welded construction and, in characteristic LMS fashion, the cars were put together from completely prefabricated sides and ends. The bogies and underframes were also of all-welded nature and the whole body structure from underframe to roof formed a completely welded box girder. This form of carriage construction, hardly modified, became a universal standard when the BR Mk I stock was built during the 1950s, though only one batch of conventional carriages of this type was ever built to LMS design. They were also very powerful sets, the rating for a single motor car being 940 hp (one hour) or 736 hp (continuous). This gave the trains, typically formed from either five or six cars, a maximum speed fully loaded of 70 mph and the ability to effect a 10 per cent reduction in the overall journey time, inclusive of all stops.

Of the two broadly similar styles of LMS-pattern

Merseyside EMUs, those on the Southport route were slightly the earlier to be withdrawn; they had probably had a harder life since, unlike the Wirral sets, the fleet was never augmented in BR days. A fully operational pair was claimed for the National Railway Museum, which had already decided that either a Wirral or Southport set merited saving. The Southport stock was assessed as marginally more significant from the technical standpoint and the writer was privileged to take receipt of it at Southport station in 1980 on behalf of the Museum. It is still outstationed there, maintained in full operational order and, now restored to LMS colours, makes occasional forays down its old stamping ground to remind the world, as does its Wirral contemporary (whose retention was an inspired and very welcome gesture by the BR Merseyside folk themselves), that the modern-style British EMU on the main-line system was well and truly a creation of the company period, no matter how long it might have taken finally to penetrate south of the Thames!

Elsewhere in the former LYR heartland, the old company had only electrified one other route, that from Manchester to Bury and Holcombe Brook. It was not, apparently, done to save money but to attract more traffic. The Bury-Holcombe Brook stretch had been the site of an interesting 1913 experiment using 3,500V DC collected from overhead conductor wires, and this indicated the advantages of using a higher voltage. In the event, the final choice settled on 1,200V DC, the maximum which the Board of Trade would sanction for third rail collection. The third rail was of side-contact configuration (the top surface being covered in wood to give extra protection) and a fourth rail between the running rails gave extra conductivity. The line opened in 1915.

To operate these services, including the Holcombe Brook section which was, of course, converted to 1,200V, the LYR produced another attractive design, not quite as wide as the Southport stock, but very similar in styling. They were the first 'all-steel' cars to be built for a British main-line company and were of open type, gangwayed throughout, and featured an offset driver's compartment to allow through movement (see the drawing on pages 250-1 of Volume 1). In this respect, they predicted, by more than 20 years, the arrangement provided in 1937 by the Southern Railway in its Portsmouth stock. The LYR cars, however, could be formed up in any way required, since all of them had driving cabs at both ends; they took up very little space. A typical formation was five cars (three motors plus two trailers) and this produced a very respectable 2,400 hp. Throughout the LMS period, these substantial and well-built carriages continued to operate the service and were not replaced until the late 1950s.

Below left *Third class interior of the 1939 LMS Southport stock* (BR LMR).

Above *This typical five-car Manchester–Bury EMU formation of ex-LYR stock is seen in 1925, again carrying the distinctive LYR-inspired form of livery. The leading motor is No 14579* (BR LMR).

Right *The MSJA stock was all but identical to all other compartment-style LMS EMUs of the 1920s, but its green livery and overhead pantographs gave it some distinction. This is an unidentified six-car train on special duty when new* (BR LMR).

The final electrified line to be considered in the Lancashire conurbation was the LMS/LNER joint operation whose formal title was the pompous sounding Manchester, South Junction and Altrincham Railway — MSJA for short; and it was less than nine miles long! The 1,500V DC overhead contact system was chosen, it being generally believed at that time, 1931, that this would become the British standard for all future electrifications outside the London underground and the Southern systems. The stock itself was all contractor-built and turned out to be of pure LMS non-corridor type, right down to most of the detail fittings. There appears to have been no attempt to come up with a new design, and save for an increase in length from 57 ft to 58 ft and, of course,

the traction equipment, the carriages were much the same as those the LMS had already built for the Southport and Watford lines.

One must concede that if non-corridor stock had to be used, then the LMS design was rather better than that of the LNER for reasons already given in Chapter 3. But it is rather surprising that a more serious attempt was not made to provide something radically new to go with the more modern traction system. Just about the only thing which differentiated it from either LMS or LNER stock was its attractive new mid-green livery, lined black and yellow in LMS style and bearing the MSJA monogram and its florid heraldic emblem. Though they were in concept quite dull, they were indubitably attractive from the out-

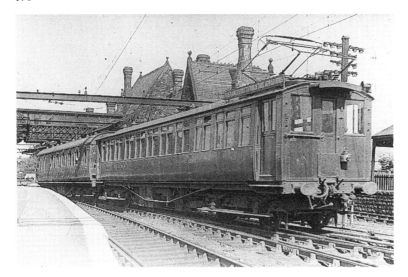

Left *A typical ragged LMS pairing at Lancaster Green Ayre on the ex-MR 6.6kV overhead system: Midland driving motor No 28612 coupled to LMS standard driving trailer No 22202, converted from a 1930-built steam-hauled non-corridor brake third* (T.J. Edgington Collection).

Figure 57 *Elevation and plan of a North Tyneside composite motor car from the 1920-22 fire replacement series.*

Scale: 3mm = 1ft

Figure 58 *Map of the North Tyneside electrified lines, also showing most of the route of the southern line to South Shields, electrified by the LNER in 1936.*

side in an old-fashioned kind of way. Metro-Cammell built them and a form of 'all-steel' construction was employed, best revealed by their riveted roof panelling.

The carriages were no lightweights, the trailers being 30-31 tons and the driving motors no less than 57 tons. In this they rivalled the near-contemporary Brighton line main-line motors (see page 130) but they packed more punch: no less than 330 hp per traction motor of which four were provided in each motor car. This gave no less than 2,640 hp for a typical six-car train, compared with 2,200 hp for the Brighton line sets which had much further to go. MSJA six-car trains were formed from two of the 22 standard three-car units which made up the total fleet (driving motor third/trailer composite/driving trailer third). There was so much power available that a half-hearted attempt was made in 1939 to strengthen peak hour trains to seven cars by inserting an augmentation trailer between two sets — Southern style — but it came to little. The eight vehicles were standard 57-foot LMS non-corridors mostly taken from the Southport stock, but most were soon stored out of use and in 1954 were converted to locomotive haulage.

The original MSJA sets survived, with very little withdrawal, throughout the 1960s, and by quite a long margin gave the railway enthusiast his last regular chance to ride in undiluted LMS-pattern non-corridor stock. Two have been privately preserved, now converted for locomotive haulage.

The last electrically-powered operation in the North West was, like that of the Brighton 'overhead', technically more interesting than most but seemingly rather ahead of its time. However, because the modest little ex-Midland system between Lancaster, Morecambe and Heysham was physically isolated from any other electrified lines, it retained its 6,600V AC overhead power supply throughout the company period. Only a handful of cars were made for it (three motors and four trailers) and these survived into LMS days. They were, rather surprisingly in view of their owning company, of no great credit to the Midland in terms of either styling or passenger comfort, having ungracious-looking arc-roofed bodies and abominable pierced plywood seats. In later years, though the LMS did not build new stock for the line, a few odd steam-hauled non-corridors (of both ex-MR and LMS standard origin) were converted into driving trailers and added to the character of what was, essentially, a relatively insignificant system. But its time was eventually to come. Paradoxically, its marginal importance, together with its physical isolation, made it an ideal choice for experimental use in connection with the BR move to 25kV AC traction. As such we shall meet it again in the next volume.

The Tyneside electrics

The only group of electric lines outside the London area which could lay even modest claim to form a system in its own right was that of the LNER on the north and south banks of the River Tyne. Its origins were only marginally less venerable than those of the LYR line to Southport, being beaten to the post by a matter of one week only in March 1904 in terms of the first train to run.

Like many of the London area developments at this time, the Tyneside area electrification was stimulated by tramway competition, and as early as 1902 the NER had resolved to electrify its lines running east from Newcastle along the north bank of the Tyne. The selected lines formed a sort of closed 'loop': out from

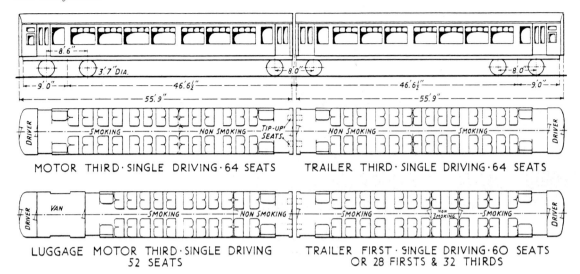

MOTOR THIRD · SINGLE DRIVING · 64 SEATS

TRAILER THIRD · SINGLE DRIVING · 64 SEATS

LUGGAGE MOTOR THIRD · SINGLE DRIVING
52 SEATS

TRAILER FIRST · SINGLE DRIVING · 60 SEATS
OR 28 FIRSTS & 32 THIRDS

Newcastle via two routes to Percy Main and Tyne-mouth and back inland via Monkseaton, Gosforth and Jesmond, plus a cut-off along the East Coast Main Line from Benton to Newcastle via Heaton. As stated, it was a genuine system rather than a one-off conversion of a single route.

The 600V DC three-rail scheme was inaugurated in 1904 utilizing a series of handsome clerestory cars of new design, many of which were illustrated in Volume 1 (pages 252-5). During NER days, the original fleet of some 125 vehicles sufficed to provide an excellent service until a disastrous fire in the carriage sheds destroyed 34 cars in 1918. These were fairly speedily replaced during 1920-22 by new stock, still embodying the matchboard panelling and other general styling points of the original stock but now with a domed-end semi-elliptical roof. However,

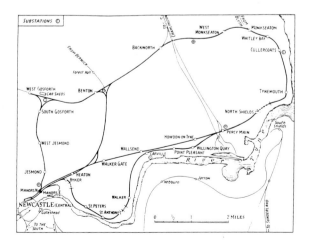

rather than the distinctive red and cream livery adopted for the original cars, the post-war replacements carried traditional NER crimson lake livery; they were still very smart.

Thus matters remained, more or less, for the first 15 years or so of LNER ownership save that the fleet was finished in a drab ersatz teak livery which did not suit its distinctive outlines. But in 1933-4, the LNER began to review the operations of the 'North Tyneside' lines, as they were generally known, and new stock was planned. This was followed by a 1935 anouncement that the South Tyneside line to South Shields was also to be electrified and connected at Newcastle to the older system. Setting aside a few motorized parcels vans, one of which is preserved by the NRM, this LNER modernization was to be the cause of the wholesale withdrawal of the 1904 clerestory cars from the North Tyneside lines and their replacement by brand new stock. Meantime, the South Tyneside route was to be operated by the replacement 1920-22 elliptical roof stock in fully refurbished form.

The new stock for North Tyneside was built by Metro-Cammell, and no one was surprised when it turned out to be articulated pairs in four different varieties as follows:

a) Driving motor third plus trailer first (18 sets)
b) Driving motor third plus trailer third (18 sets)
c) Driving luggage motor third plus driving trailer first (16 sets)
d) Driving motor third plus driving trailer third (12 sets)

These were almost as bewildering as the many clerestory varieties they had replaced; they could be and

Left *Rebuilt set of NER replacement coaches for the South Tyneside lines at Newcastle in the wartime blue and off-white livery; note the LNER emblem on the side. The replacement bucket seats can just be distinguished through the windows* (NRM collection).

Figure 59 *Simplified elevations and plans of typical LNER 1936 articulated North Tyneside stock.*

Scale: 3mm = 1ft

were operated in all manner of permutations. But, *mirabile dictu*, the LNER reinstated the old NER red and cream livery to greatly beneficial effect. No doubt this was inspired by the success of the green and cream tourist livery in terms of public perception, but it did not last long. In 1941 it gave way to a blue and off-white livery — one source stating that this was to reduce visibility from the air in wartime — and this is how most of my generation will recall them. Either way, they gave the Newcastle area a quite dis-

tinctive identity in terms of its suburban electric services which remained unique outside the London Transport area until well into the modern era.

The new cars themselves, if not quite as modern as those of the LMS a few years later, were still very stylish. They were of integral steel construction as far as body and underframe were concerned but they were not all-welded. They had flush-sided exteriors but the sliding doors were hand-operated and fitted only at the ends of the cars. Furthermore, although

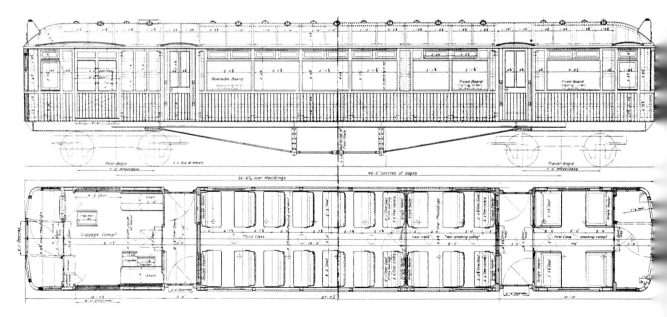

The familiar east end of Newcastle Central is graced on this occasion by an eight-car formation of articulated Metro-Cammell EMUs entering from the Manors direction; on the extreme right, a train of rebuilt ex-NER stock is about to cross the river en route *to South Shields. Note the almost 'blanked out' driver's window of the approaching EMU, undoubtedly a war-time safety precaution* (NRM collection).

it was decided, not before time, to improve the comfort compared with the old reversible rattan seats of the clerestories, the LNER chose to install its dreaded bucket-seat alternative (see Chapter 4). They looked quite good and maybe the shorter distances of the suburban mode made them more tolerable than on long-distance stock. The first class was also arranged 2 + 2 with no quantum improvement over the thirds.

Four single unit parcels and luggage cars were added to the fleet in 1938 which thereafter served its time out on the North Tyneside lines (except for a few early withdrawals due to enemy action or accident damage) until wholesale withdrawal began in 1967, it having been decided to de-electrify the North Tyneside lines for economy reasons. By then, the Metro-Cammell electrics were all in BR green livery, the distinctive Tyneside colours not having been retained after 1947. Like the MSJA stock (see above), so too with the LNER Tyneside cars, the vehicles represented the last company survivors of a specific type to remain in regular service, this time the articulated configuration. Indeed, it was surprising how often it was to be EMU stock which, throughout Britain, kept the old images alive, rather than their locomotive-hauled contemporaries.

The rebuilt stock for South Tyneside was not much changed in appearance from its original form, retaining the matchboard panelling and handsome roof shape. The major internal change was to fit them with bucket seats in place of the old rattan, and the upper windows were given more modern sliding ventilator units similar to those of the new stock. In the reinstated two-tone livery, a surprising degree of visual harmony was achieved both on the cars themselves

and between them and the newer stock. If anything, the older cars had the slight edge in appearance terms, possibly because of their domed roofs and far better styled cab treatment. They lasted until the mid-1950s, being replaced by BR compartment-style EMUs of basically Southern style.

London area developments

Discounting the GWR (Hammersmith and City) and LMS (District and Bakerloo) involvements with the London Transport routes, on which the cars themselves were entirely to the various London Underground patterns, there were only two important company developments in the London area, outside the London Transport or Southern Railway orbit. These were one each from the LMS and LNER, and of them the LNER version did not actually happen until after BR was formed.

The LMS activity was the more long-established, in the form of its line from Euston to Watford and the associated North London route from Broad Street via Willesden Junction to Richmond and Kew. The origins were firmly London and North Western which, at around the time of the First World War, had embarked upon an extensive modernization and widening in the Chalk Farm/Primrose Hill area, combined with the electrification of the above-mentioned routes. The chosen method of electrification was the London Electric Railway UndergrounD fourth rail system to allow compatibility with the Bakerloo tube trains which would join the route at Queen's Park and run through to Watford in association with the

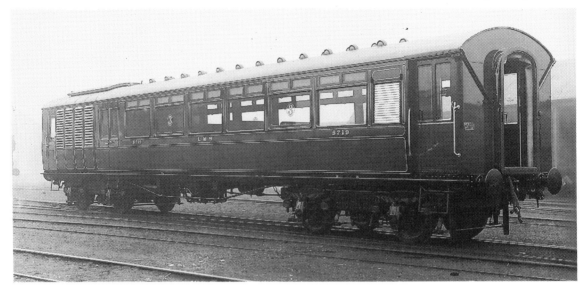

Above *One of the stylish LNWR Oerlikon cars, motor third No 5719, is seen here in LMS livery in the 1920s (LMS official, NRM).*

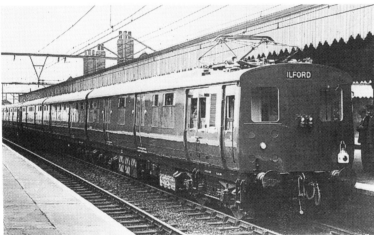

Left *An Ilford-bound train of LNER-designed Shenfield stock, newly in service in 1949 in BR green livery (NRM collection).*

LNWR's own surface stock from Euston and Broad Street. The programme was ambitious and, because of the war, took some eight years to complete, the first electric trains not using Euston until 1922.

Inititially, the stock provided was predominantly of the famous end-door, open-interior Oerlikon type (there were also a few cars from Siemens), some of the most agreeable outer-suburban EMUs ever built, one of which is deservedly preserved by the NRM. These went on being supplied until early LMS days, the final units coming out from new in LMS colours. But when further new stock was required in the later 1920s, the LMS took one of its periodic yet quite out of character steps backward and augmented the fleet with dated compartment stock. The contemporary

argument (as on the Southern and Metropolitan) was that such stock speeded loading and unloading at busy times, and this was undoubtedly true; but one cannot help but remark that something more akin to Oerlikons with maybe a set of central as well as end doors would have been far better.

Be that as it may, the new trains, all contractor built, were exactly like those already described for the Southport and MSJA routes, and little more needs be said. They ran in standard three-car sets (driving motor third/trailer composite/driving trailer third) with a few spare motors, but were never kept in regular formations. Six cars formed a normal train at busy times, and in 1929 a few augmentation trailers were added to produce seven-car formations. A second batch of similar stock was ordered in 1932, but these were of the main three varieties only. This allowed a more frequent service of six-car trains, thus reducing the need for seven-car sets, so no more augmentation trailers were provided; seven-car trains ceased to operate in 1941 when first class was abolished. Most of the stock, of both builds, was withdrawn *en bloc* in 1963.

The last electrification proposal to be considered here was that of the LNER which, in the later 1930s, had made quite widespread proposals for the electrification of two of its busiest routes. Up in the north of England, the Manchester, Sheffield and Wath line (MSW) via Woodhead Tunnel was, of course, the well-known route and eventually became the first British main line to be electrified for all traffic, using a 1500V DC overhead system. This took place in the early 1950s and it was the same system which the LNER had proposed for its London suburban services out of Liverpool Street and Fenchurch Street to Shenfield. Orders for new EMU stock were made before the war and the same design was chosen both for the London services and the smaller Hadfield and Glossop service from the MSW line.

The war prevented further progress, but afterwards work resumed and in 1946 the part-finished stock was available for inspection. It was not, in the event, to go into traffic until 1949, by then in BR colours. But it was wholly LNER in design as were the similar sets which started work between Manchester and Glossop in 1954.

The carriages were of all-steel construction with air-operated sliding doors and a general configuration very like those of the LMS in the Wirral and Southport areas. Three-coach sets were provided and the driving motor ends had a depressed roof area for the pantographs, but there was little in general to choose between the final LMS and LNER designs. Only the fact of war prevented the LNER stock ever carrying its company colours (though heaven only knows what they would have been!) and the only difference between the Shenfield and MSW sets was the provision of two-class accommodation in the latter.

In the event, of course, the 1500V DC system was not adopted for future standardization, but although up in the north the MSW Glossop-Hadfield section and the MSJA lines remained on this standard until the 1970s and 1980s, the Shenfield line, by virtue of the need for it to be fully integrated into the broader GE section electrification as soon as possible, was eventually converted to the now standard 25kV overhead system, the cars themselves being extensively modified during 1958-9, a matter to which we shall return in Volume 3.

There for the moment we must leave the electric story which has taken the last three chapters to outline, as opposed to occupying but a few pages in the first volume. This alone is indicative of one of the most profound changes which was seen during the company period. Dominant, of course, was the contribution of the Southern Railway, but the last few pages should have revealed that the BR continuation owed as much if not more to the smaller and mostly provincial-based systems than the dominance of the Southern might have indicated.

But electrification was not the only way in which the grouped railways had made changes to their traditional operational patterns during the period under review, and it seems appropriate that we should now turn to these other and often fascinating alternatives before we return to the locomotive-hauled story.

9. Steam railcars — and other alternatives

Since the turn of the century, the railways have been striving to find some sort of solution to the increasing problems of road competition, and we have seen how the large-scale electrification of inner suburban routes often helped in the context of urban tramway and, later, bus competition. Likewise, higher speed and improved amenity generally served to maintain the viability of long-distance operations. But the middle ground was often a problem and, interestingly, still is perhaps the major area where, even in the 1980s, the railway is hardest pressed to compete. In more modern days, of course, the solution has often been simply to abandon the unequal struggle and close the service, letting the road competitor take over, if he can — and far too often in recent years, he too has been found wanting. This situation has been made all the more familiar by the Beeching closures of the 1960s and the end result has been to the benefit of nobody in the long run save the makers of tarmac!

Now at this point I must make it clear that I do not believe that the railway has or ever had a divine right to take preference over the roads; the two should, ideally, live in harmony, each playing to and feeding from the relative strengths of the other. But in the curiously unregulated nature of *public* transport which has been the bane of this nation since early Victorian times, things have never been that simple. We have never had an overall public transport policy, and yet the private railways, above all, were instrumental in creating a strong public perception that there ought to be some form of minimal public service *as a matter of right*, and it is to their eternal credit that they often managed to provide such a service from a purely commercial base. However, by the time of the period covered by this book, it was clear that such problems as might have existed before the First World War were as nothing compared with those likely to ensue during the inter-war era and the vehicles to be described in this chapter were a tangible realization of that fact.

Yet again, but in a rather different way from that considered so far, we are at the interface between people and technology. Up to now, the discussion has been mostly confined to an examination of how the railways met the ever-increasing demands and expectations of travellers in terms of vehicular type and on-train amenity, but the grouped railways also had to face the problem of how to provide some sort of service for those who had no choice, when an increasing number of the population were no longer using the railway at all. In the last analysis, the issue is, of course, a political one and I shall have cause to return to it very much in the context of the third volume of this series. But what can be said at this stage is that the four grouped railways did not meekly cave in under this new sort of pressure and simply give up; they made strenuous attempts to find solutions in this marginal area and in some of them could be seen the seeds of much modern railway practice.

The bottom line of the problem was, then as now, one of costs; and to make any significant reduction meant some form of unit which was cheaper to build and operate than the conventional full train. There was nothing radically new in this perception, the steam railmotors of the Edwardian era having been a first attempt to cope; but as Volume 1 has already shown, these mostly came and went like butterflies in summer, and the 1920s dawned with little forward technical progress save for electrification where the high infrastructure cost could be justified — hardly a relevant issue in the area we are now discussing.

The fact is that in the first quarter of the century technology had not really produced any sort of answer for the middle ground, and it was only during the grouping period that railway engineers at last began to come up with ideas which gave some real prospect of success. They did not all work, of course, and some distinctly comical ideas came and went, almost without trace, but overall there were some significant forward moves, and even the relative failures were not without their own bizarre interest. In consequence, it was an interesting time for students of these things and although we may now smile at some of the ideas which were propounded, it is well to recall that they were offered in all seriousness in a quite genuine attempt to solve very real problems.

In essence, the most favoured solution seemed to be a light railcar in one form or another, and the basic purposes for which they were most suited were admirably summarized in an article in *The Railway Engineer* for April 1934:

a) To meet road competition in sparsely populated districts

b) To develop branch-line traffic

c) To pick up and distribute between main-line junctions

d) To provide economical high speed inter-urban services for light loads

There were only two likely sources of motive power

to be tapped: steam and internal combustion. These will form the basis of the rest of this chapter.

The second coming of the steam railcar

It would have been a rare person who, after the mainly disastrous failures of most of the Edwardian steam railmotors, could have predicted that the idea would have a second and rather more successful 'bite at the cherry' during the 1920s and 1930s; yet such it was and here, as in other fields, it was mainly due to the persistence of but one of the four companies, this time the LNER.

The LNER was in many ways the most poverty-stricken of the 'Big Four'. It had some good routes, but its industrial hinterland probably suffered more from the depression, relative to the whole system, than did that of its rivals, and this may have been a part cause. But whatever the reasons, very soon after the grouping the LNER began to take a very serious interest in a new form of steam railcar developed by the Sentinel Waggon Works Ltd in association with Cammell Laird & Co Ltd. This interest went with a renewed assessment of the role of the railcar and it will be helpful briefly to discuss this aspect before going on to the cars themselves.

Traditionally, the older type of steam railmotor had suffered from two principal faults: it was generally seen as merely replacing existing and more expensive conventional trains and, for the most part, its construction kept too closely to design practices associated with conventional stock. The result of this was that it rarely improved the quality of service frequency, and even where it was successful in attracting more traffic, it was either too feeble to cope with it or, if made more powerful, it then did not show the hoped-for cost savings. Many railways therefore resorted to the push-pull option as outlined at the end of Volume 1.

The new approach to railcars started from the rather different presumption that, properly designed, a railcar need not simply replace existing trains — of which only a few per day might have run — but actually provide a better service by operating more frequently. This would reduce the need to add vehicles to the unit which it was self-evidently incapable of pulling (as had often been tried, usually without success, with the steam railmotor) but instead, simply operate more railcars and offer a greater service frequency. Interestingly, as I pen these words, this very policy has fairly recently proved the main cause for much increased patronage of my own local railway. The introduction of four-wheel 'Pacer' railcars now allows BR to offer an hourly service to York and a half-hourly service to Leeds, which policy has both

effectively killed off the bus competition to York and provided better local services to both cities than ever the steam trains, or even the first generation DMUs, managed to do.

However, to do this in the steam context, just as in the modern day, meant using a vehicle which, owing to its lightness and simplicity, needed a smaller and less complicated power unit than was offered by the conventional locomotive style of construction. It was a tricky balancing act, because railway vehicles need to be much stronger than their road equivalent, thus risking imposing a weight penalty, but the Sentinel-Cammell cars were a very fine attempt.

The very first of all was put to work in 1923 on the hitherto unmentioned Jersey Railways & Tramways Ltd in the Channel Islands, thus giving this now long-closed narrow-gauge system an interesting and by no means irrelevant footnote in railway history. But it was its espousal by the LNER which was to be the significant breakthrough. In 1924, trials were conducted in Durham and North Yorkshire of a slightly more powerful version of the Jersey car, and the outcome seems to have been successful, for in 1925 two were purchased and put to use in East Anglia to operate between Norwich and Lowestoft and King's Lynn and Hunstanton. Two years later, two more, slightly modified, were acquired, and 1928 was to see another 20 of this type added to the fleet, giving a total of 24 cars of what later was to be seen as the 'first generation' Sentinel type.

Basically, these first cars made use of the standard boiler and engine unit also used in the well-known Sentinel steam road wagons. This was a proven and economical power unit and was fitted inside a cab unit articulated to the main passenger portion of the railcar. The engine itself was of two-cylinder double-acting configuration and drive to the wheels was by two chains to the rear axle from the sprockets at the end of the crankshaft. The first four (1925-27) cars were finished in ersatz teak, fully panelled, but the final 20 were given the striking red and cream livery of the former NER electrics, almost certainly reflecting the fact that all were put to work in former NER territory. Before long, both these schemes were abandoned in favour of the familiar green and cream livery which most who remember them at all will no doubt recall. This series of cars also introduced the LNER tradition of naming its railcars, old stagecoach names being the chosen theme.

At much the same time as the LNER was conducting its tests on these new-style railcars, the LMS also tried them out. In 1925, trials were conducted on the Ripley branch and a production order of 13 cars was put in service during 1926-7, a year or so ahead of the main LNER order. The LMS cars were driven in the same way as those of the LNER but were rather

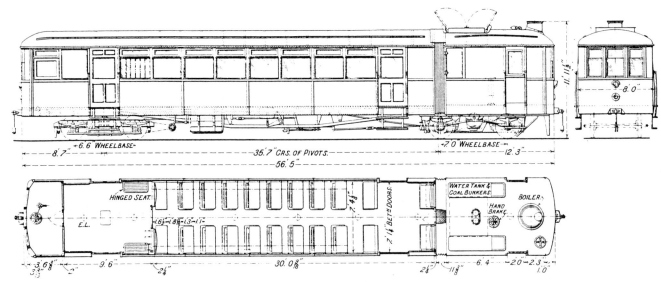

General View, Side Elevation, and Plan of Sentinel-Cammell Steel Rail-Car, L.M.S.R.

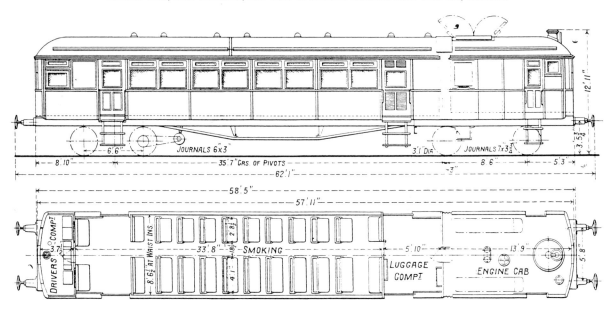

more low-slung in appearance with less of the working parts exposed below the frames. They were finished in standard lined crimson lake and were unnamed. They were also rather shorter and narrower, presumably for even greater route availability, and were thus some 4½ tons lighter (21 t 7 cwt as opposed to 25 t 18 cwt), but this gave them only 75 per cent of the LNER seating capacity (44 rather than 59) since their seats were arranged 2 + 2 rather than the LNER 2 + 3. Both types had reversible 'walk over' seat backs and mahogany interior finish,

LMS seats being green and those in the LNER cars being quoted as having 'standard LNER pattern' material. Comparative drawings of the two types are appended.

Though subsequent events were to demonstrate that the Sentinel-Cammell railcars were to be the definitive steam type, it is necessary, before going on with their later development, to keep the chronology in order by introducing the second LNER approach to the problem. This was a purchase of the rival railcar type offered by Clayton Wagons Ltd of Lincoln,

Left Figure 60 *These elevations and plans of the articulated Sentinel railcars provided for the LMS and LNER respectively clearly indicate the difference in size between the two designs.*

Scale: ¹/₁₀″ = 1ft

Right *A trio of LNER articulated railcars in service, the leading example being No 29 'Rockingham' and the second in line No 212 'Eclipse'. The third example is unidentified (Author's collection).*

Below Figure 61 *Elevation and plan of the Clayton-type steam railcar for the LNER.*

Scale: ¹/₁₀″ = 1ft

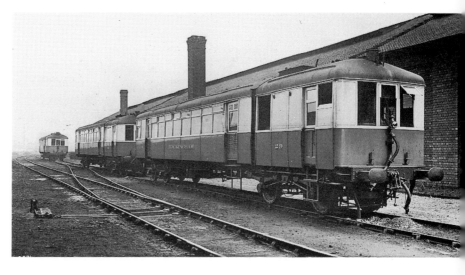

its evaluation being conducted more or less in parallel with that of the first Sentinel cars.

The Clayton cars originated in 1925, originally for use in New Zealand, and in 1927 the LNER acquired one (as also, simultaneously, did the Egyptian State Railways) for test purposes. Again, the company was reasonably satisfied and a production order for ten more was placed in 1928. In these cars, steam road vehicle practice was again adopted, but since the actual power unit was quite differently conceived, it made quite a noticeable difference to the configuration of the powered end.

The Clayton cars used essentially the same stan-

dard engine and boiler unit as fitted to Clayton 'undertype' road wagons. This unit, like the chain-driven Sentinels, also employed a two-cylinder layout but the engine (totally enclosed and mounted above the leading axle of the driving bogie) drove the wheels by a crankshaft pinion in connection with a spur wheel on the axle. The two axles of the driving bogie were then connected by outside coupling rods attached to the wheels in conventional locomotive fashion. The centre of the power bogie carried a conventional bogie bolster and pivot, to which was fixed the leading end of the car body. This placed the boiler within the body but left the coal bunker and water

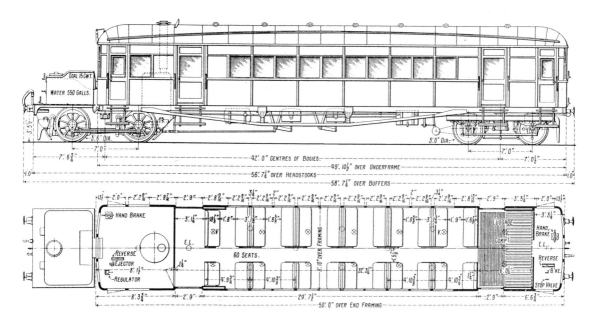

Prototype LNER Clayton railcar No 41 seen here in service at Lintz Green, near Newcastle, when still finished in pseudo 'teak' livery, the only Clayton car so treated. When later repainted in conventional two-colour style, it received the name 'Rapid' (Author's collection).

Opposite side views of LNER rigid chassis railcars No 31 'Flower of Yarrow' and No 38 'Pearl' built in 1928 and 1929 respectively. This type was by far the most common LNER version (both Author's collection).

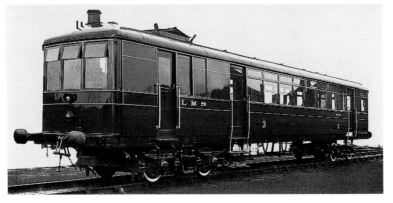

The solitary LMS rigid chassis Sentinel railcar No 4349 of 1930 was undoubtedly both well proportioned and finished, but the LMS seemed to have far less faith in the type than the LNER and never repeated the order. It was scrapped in 1939 (BR LMR).

Figure 62 Elevation and plan of the 48-seat LNER Sentinel steam railcars with twin 'engines' introduced in 1932, Nos 220, 246 and 248. They were given bucket seats and classed as luxury cars (sic!), being named 'Defence', 'Royal Sovereign' and 'Tantivy' respectively.

tanks in full view ahead of the bodywork. It was thus, in effect, a rigid railcar with a pivoting power bogie, part of which was exposed to view. The effect was mildly comical.

Like the Sentinels, the first Clayton car was finished in 'teak' livery, the main order mostly being delivered in red and cream. All eventually ended up with green and cream livery and were again named after stage-coaches. The last of the series, a 44-seater with 'more comfortable' bucket seats (sic!) and a few technical refinements, wore green and cream livery from the outset and probably established this style. It carried the wonderfully ambiguous name *Bang Up*!

As things turned out, the LNER seems to have decided to concentrate on the Sentinel alternative very soon after it had put its Claytons into service, and 1928 was also to see the ordering of by far the biggest batch of new steam railcars ever placed by a British railway company. They were all Sentinels and were derived from an experimental 'one-off' car of a new design, tested early in 1928 and named *Integrity*. It seems possible that this car was Sentinel's answer to Clayton, for it embodied gear drive in combination with the existing two-cylinder power unit and was mounted on a rigid chassis, the steam and exhaust pipes having flexible joints to allow for the differential movement of the engine portion (mounted direct to the power bogie) and the boiler unit (fixed to the main chassis). This was to lead directly to a revised version with a six-cylinder single acting engine employing gear and cardan shaft drive.

During 1928 and 1929, no fewer than 50 of these new-type six-cylinder railcars were ordered, 49 for the LNER and one for the Axholme Joint Railway (LMS/LNER), later taken over by the LNER in 1933. They were undoubtedly the most successful Sentinel design and went into service in many areas though, as usual, by far the bulk of them went to the by now traditional ex-NER territory. Stage-coach names were yet again favoured, but this time a few more regionally appropriate titles were also employed. Four similar cars were provided for the CLC in 1929, and the LMS also obtained a similar example in 1930, but, as with its articulated purchase, this was to a generally smaller size and was of much lighter weight (25 t compared with 28 t 15 cwt).

The LNER railcar purchase was completed in 1930 and 1932 with five more rigid Sentinel cars in two separate batches, each embodying a beefed-up 12-cylinder engine configuration for the more hilly routes on the NE Yorkshire coast. In fact, two sets of standard six-cylinder power units were used, each driving one of the two bogies. There were some technical changes between the batches and the passenger accommodation was reduced from the customary 59, first to 54 and then to 48, the latter being in 2 + 2 'luxury' configuration. Finally, mention should also be made of the solitary twin articulated Sentinel, *Phenomena* of 1930. This too had 12-cylinder propulsion, this time with the two 'engines' driving the leading and central bogies. The powered end seated 39 and the 'trailer' portion 83.

Mention of trailers serves as a reminder that to run with its railcars, the LNER also procured some sin-

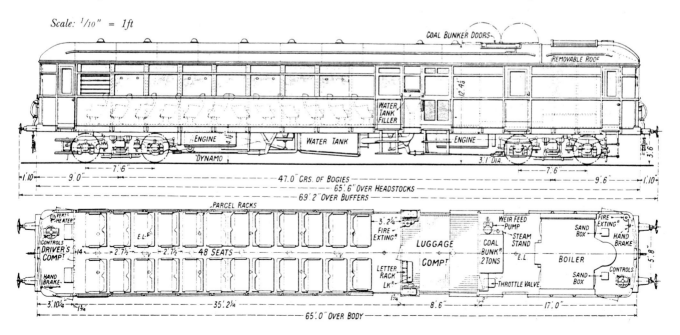

Scale: $^1/_{10}$ " = 1ft

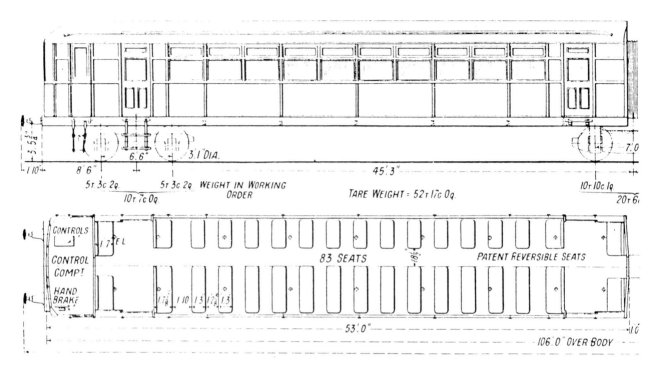

gularly unlovely four-wheel examples of the genre in 1929 from Claytons. Classed as 'Trailer Brake Thirds', eight only were built and never seem to have been very popular. Their final disposal is unknown.

In terms of usefulness in service, the LNER railcars clearly had a longer innings than most of the pre-1914 steam railmotors, and its fleet of some 91 units from all sources must have effected quite substantial savings during the 15-20 years when they were operational. The Claytons were the shortest lived, faring no better than the older-type steam railmotors, maybe for much the same reasons, and mostly went out of

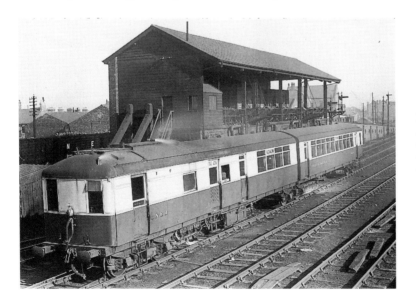

Figure 63 *Elevation and plan of the unique LNER twin Sentinel steam railcar No 2291 'Phenomena'.*

Scale: 3mm = 1ft

Left *Twin Sentinel 'Phenomena' is seen here at South Blyth Shed, during the time when it was used in regular service along the north-east coast between Monkseaton and Blyth (LNER official, NRM).*

Figure 64 *Elevations and plan of the rather unmemorable four-wheel Clayton trailers of 1929, designed to run with the railcars.*

Scale: 3mm = 1ft

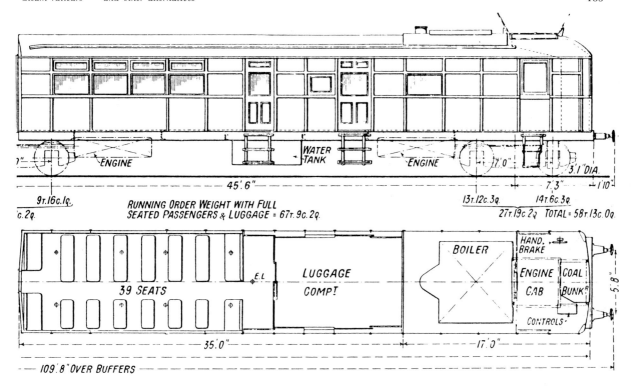

RUNNING ORDER WEIGHT WITH FULL
SEATED PASSENGERS & LUGGAGE = 67т.9c.2q.

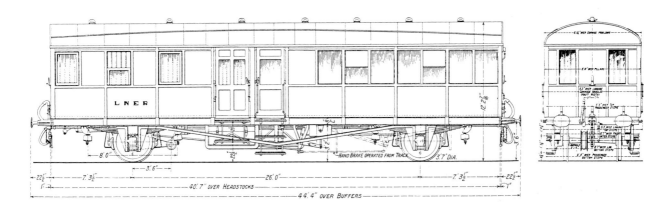

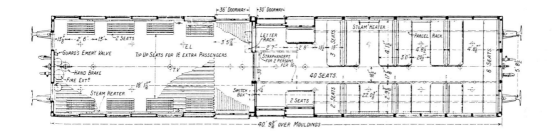

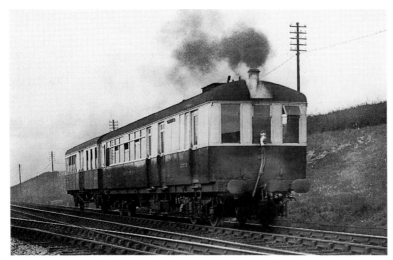

Pictures of Clayton trailers actually in use are somewhat rare, but this view taken near Darlington shows one of them being hauled by rigid Sentinel railcar No 2271 'Industry' (of the 1929-built series) on the Richmond branch service in 1934 (T.J. Edgington Collection).

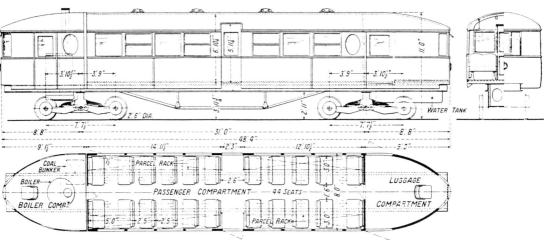

Figure 65 *Elevations and plan of the unique Sentinel steam railbus for the Southern Railway.*

Scale: $^1/_{10}$*" = 1ft*

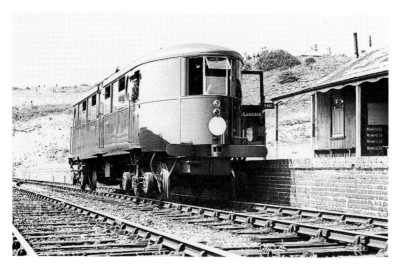

The Southern's Sentinel railbus at The Dyke station circa *1933 (BR SR).*

service *circa* 1936. But the Sentinels lasted rather better. The 12-cylinder cars were not too long-lived but the two big batches mostly served until the mid-1940s, many until after the war. One of them, No 2136 *Hope*, just reached BR. Withdrawn early in 1948 it would have been a worthy candidate for preservation, but maybe its name was too symbolic of the whole story of the steam railcar. The fact is that none of them actually gave 20 years of revenue service, and although on average they did rather better than the steam railmotors, the final examples of the latter (those of the LYR and LNWR — see Volume 1), which also lasted until the late 1940s, had enjoyed a far longer working life. As for the LMS Sentinels, they lasted less than ten years!

The Sentinel steam railcar story was not quite finished in the British context with the building of the last LNER cars in 1932, though it were well had it been so, for its final fling, a sort of Ruritanian creation built for the Southern Railway, was almost in the nature of a tragic farce. In fact, were its existence not confirmed photographically, it could well have been some flight of fancy doodled on the drawing board of an over-imaginative designer working for the tinplate toy manufacturers of the day!

At much the same time as the SR was introducing its new electric services to Brighton, it also put into operation a single unit Sentinel steam railcar on the steeply-graded branch line from Hove to Devil's Dyke, high up in the South Downs to the north-west of Brighton. This in itself would have made some sense, for the branch was both steep and sharply curved; but instead of using one of the well-proved LNER-type cars (or even, for that matter, the lighter-weight LMS alternatives), the whole operation was made the excuse for creating a new sort of one-man-operated bus unit. The engine part appears to have been a two-cylinder compound of unproven quality, slung on the driving axle and fed from a standard Sentinel boiler fitted with a patent automatic stoker embodying a screw feed plus crusher.

It seemed like a lot of technology to crack a very small nut and was then made worse by marrying it to a fashionably streamlined Zeppelin-type body which seemed to be perched on top as an after-thought. Maybe I am too cruel, but when I first saw a picture of this extraordinary creation and realized that on its introduction it had been taken quite seriously, I simply burst out laughing. It appears to have survived until 1942, but actually ceased work in 1937. One cannot envisage even Oliver Bulleid seeing much merit in the thing, and the fact that it was actually authorized by the normally rather conservative Richard Maunsell makes it all the more odd.

However, strange though it may seem, this was indeed the very last self-propelled steam-powered passenger-carrying vehicle to be devised for use in Britain, and as such has its place in our story. But it only served to point out, along with the other Sentinels, Claytons and their railmotor ancestors, that as far as steam propulsion was concerned, the light-weight single unit was still not the full answer, even though the railcars had made a better fist of it than most. If steam could still compete, then push-pull was the far better answer (see Chapter 10); meantime, the lightweight prize was to go to internal combustion.

The rising tide of internal combustion

The internal combustion engine undoubtedly 'grew up' during the First World War, stimulated both on the land and in the air by the demands of the military. In consequence, many ex-servicemen resumed their civilian lives with more than an adequate working knowledge of this relatively new form of prime mover. Aided by a vast supply of government surplus ex-military buses and lorries sold off at knockdown prices, thousands of former soldiers set up their own road transport businesses, both passenger and freight. The latter was, in the longer run, to be the more damaging to railway fortunes, but even in the former case the rise of the motor bus during the 1920s and 1930s was a very real threat to the railway passenger business, nowhere more so than in the sort of services with which this chapter is concerned.

At first, there were many who advocated a straight transfer of this new form of road technology to the rail, believing in all seriousness that all that was needed was to purchase a cheap lorry or bus engine, mount it on something approximating to a rail-borne equivalent of a road vehicle chassis, add some form of appropriate bodywork and off we go. They probably knew that a prime characteristic of rail transport meant that a given unit of power can shift between four and six times as large a load on smooth rails than on the rougher-surfaced roads. It still can, of course, and this realization goes right back to the days when it was discovered that one horse could move the same sort of stage-coach body mounted on railway wheels as it would take four or six to shift along the highway. But in terms of mechanical power it was by no means as simple as that.

Essentially, the road-type power unit and transmission really came into its own when allied with pneumatic tyres which cushioned the vibrations. Even the solid tyres of many old vehicles gave some help in this regard; but the high-frequency vibrations and rigid quality of most railway track were less forgiving and caused problems. Moreover, the lower power to weight ratio needed on the railways led to disappointing performance and a tendency to overload, simply because it was in theory within the engine capacity

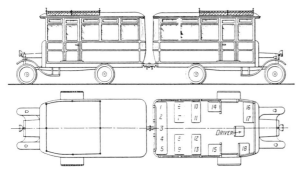

Figure 66 *Elevations and plan of an experimental Ford Duplex petrol engined railcar unit devised for the Derwent Valley Light Railway near York in the early 1920s, a solution not untypical of many which were tried out at this time.*

to cope with such loads.

Thus, the first internal combustion railway vehicles in the post-grouping era mostly seemed like fugitives from the highways. Though they did have some success, they were mostly in the nature of individual experiments and few, if any, were multiplied beyond the first one or two units to be built. Some of them were distinctly comical, viewed in retrospect, and for maybe ten years or so after the grouping, the advocates of steam probably saw no threat; in any case, were not the new steam railcars (see above) proving far more effective? This may well have been so, up to a point, but some of the ideas introduced are still interesting to review in the context of later evolution.

The North Eastern Railway, often underrated for

reasons stated more than once in this survey, had long been a pioneer in 'alternative' solutions, and right to the very end of its existence was actively looking at both petrol-electric and direct-drive solutions, some of which were illustrated in Volume 1; but if truth be told, not much seems to have happened beyond this point until the LMS, in conjunction with Karrier Motors Ltd of Huddersfield, made a very interesting attempt to provide a genuine dual-purpose vehicle with its celebrated but never duplicated 'Ro-Railer'. The idea was so logical and obvious that even now one wonders why it was not pursued with more vigour; it would surely have had many applications even in more modern circumstances.

The episode is well recorded, thus needing but brief mention here, but in essence involved a conventional single-deck motor bus, little modified in basic appearance save for having entrance doors on both sides to suit the 'rail' mode, which was fitted with both road and rail wheels. In 'road' configuration, the railway wheels, being smaller in diameter, simply rotated idly out of harm's way behind the road wheels, but on transfer to rail the steering was locked and, with the road wheels raised by means of eccentrics between wheel hub and rim, the unit became a railcar. The modal transfer took only two or three minutes and one of the unit's more celebrated uses was on the road journey between Stratford-upon-Avon and the nearby LMS Welcombe Hotel, having travelled by rail from Blisworth to Stratford. Maybe it was rather small for more widespread use, who knows, but like so many other ideas it withered on the branch.

The LMS 'Ro-Railer' in service when operating between Blisworth and the Welcombe Hotel, Stratford-on-Avon. It has even been scurrilously suggested that one of the reasons for its failure was that it was too undignified and low-brow for the well-heeled patrons of this very exclusive hotel. This may well be true! (T.J. Edgington Collection).

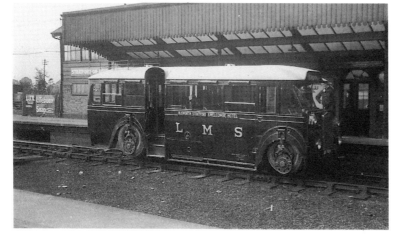

Figure 67 *This series of drawings represents the several experimental ideas which were evaluated by the LMS during the 1930s — see the text. They are, from top to bottom: Karrier 'Ro-Railer' of 1930-31; 'La Micheline' of 1932; and a standard Michelin pneumatic-tyred railcar of 1935. None of them turned out to have any long-term significance.*   Scale: 3mm = 1ft

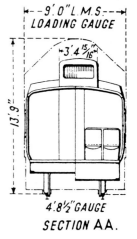

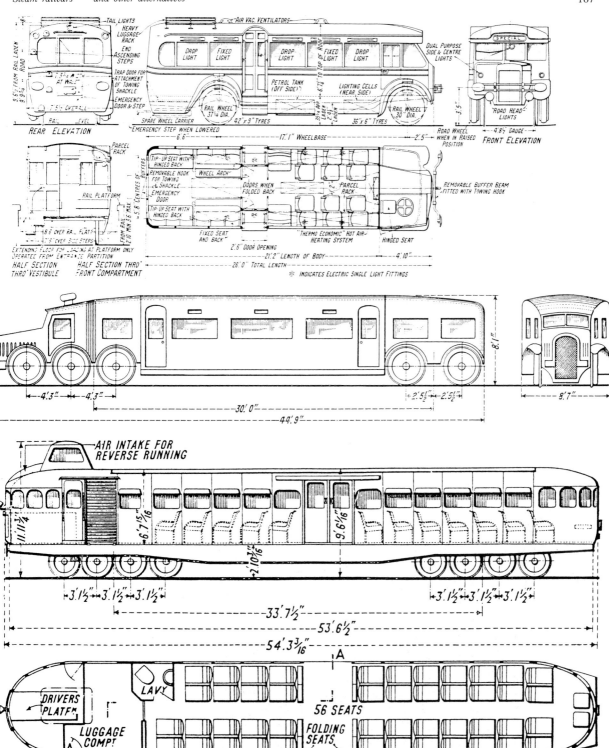

This near head-on view of 'La Micheline' clearly reveals the nature of the wheel treads and flanges of this interesting experiment; above the cab roof were radiators of the water-cooled engine, designed to function adequately in both directions of motion. The car was claimed to save 25 per cent in travelling time on the existing 42-minute Bletchley to Bicester service on which it was evaluated, a distance of nearly 20 miles with six intermediate stops (T.J. Edgington Collection).

The next and final British attempts to marry conventional road technology to the requirements of rail transport were again of LMS inspiration, this time in conjunction with the celebrated Michelin tyre company of France. In these experiments, the shock-absorbing properties of pneumatic tyres, mentioned above, were to be made the justification for evaluating ultra-lightweight construction, for the vehicles were designed in such a way that the rubber tyres actually ran on the rail surface, thus replacing the normal steel tyres and leaving the steel flange to do its normal task. The first example, entirely French-built and known as 'La Micheline', was a ten-wheel vehicle entirely in the road-coach stylistic idiom but far more luxuriously appointed than the near-contemporary 'Ro-Railer'. It seated only 24, as opposed to 26, but was nearly twice as long (almost 45 ft compared with 26 ft) and at 5 tons was more than 2 tons lighter in weight. It had carpeted floors and a mixture of armchairs and conventionally transverse seats and was tested between Bletchley and Oxford in 1932.

That said, little more seems to have been recorded of this experiment than that of the 'Ro-Railer'; maybe both were too limited in their scope or too low in seating capacity. But the next pneumatic-tyred experiment was an altogether more ambitious affair. In 1935, sponsored by Armstrong-Siddeley Motors Ltd who provided the engine unit, the LMS introduced a 56-seat Michelin railcar on its Oxford-Cambridge service. The car itself was the standard Michelin 16-wheel type (two eight-wheel bogies with a raised 'turret' driving cab) and represented a concept already quite well known in France. Its trial performance was most impressive, nearly 70 mph achieved in almost total silence. It weighed in at little more than 8 tons and its seating capacity was fully comparable with any other contemporary railcars but, yet again, no one seems to have been impressed enough to cause the LMS — or anyone else for that matter — to repeat the idea. The odd thing is that ever since that time, the French have always found some application for pneumatic-tyred railway vehicles, best known these days in the context of some lines on the Paris Metro; but then there are those who would argue that in the present century, French railway engineers have often been well ahead of their British counterparts,

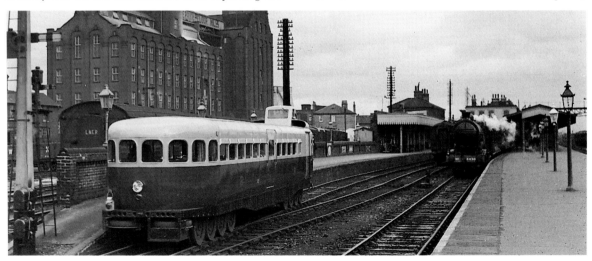

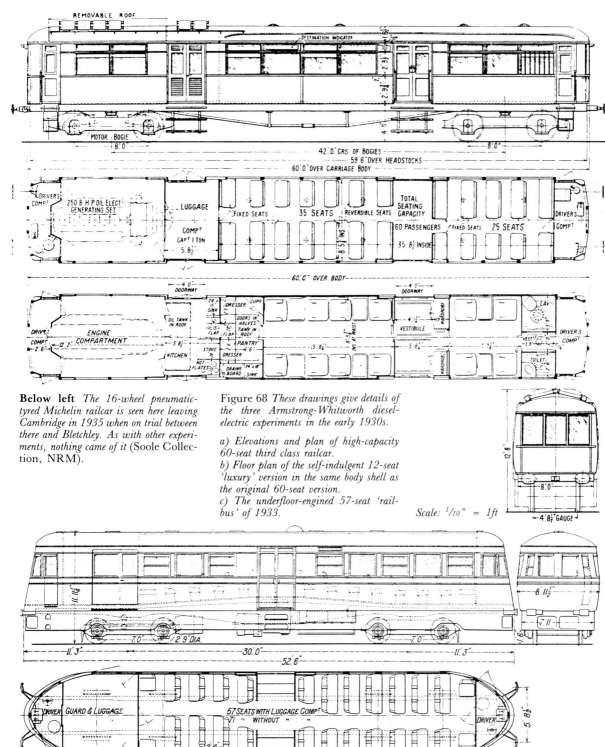

Below left *The 16-wheel pneumatic-tyred Michelin railcar is seen here leaving Cambridge in 1935 when on trial between there and Bletchley. As with other experiments, nothing came of it (Soole Collection, NRM).*

Figure 68 *These drawings give details of the three Armstrong-Whitworth diesel-electric experiments in the early 1930s.*

a) Elevations and plan of high-capacity 60-seat third class railcar.
b) Floor plan of the self-indulgent 12-seat 'luxury' version in the same body shell as the original 60-seat version.
c) The underfloor-engined 57-seat 'railbus' of 1933.

Scale: $^1/_{10}$" = 1ft

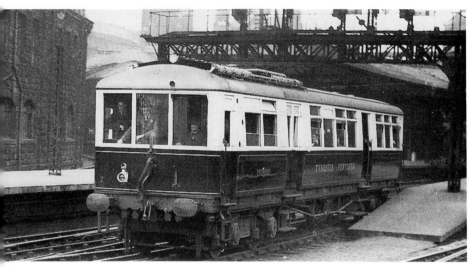

Opposite side views of the first high-capacity Armstrong-Whitworth units 'Tyneside Venturer and 'Northumbrian' in service on the LNER at Newcastle and York in 1932 and 1935 respectively. A third similar unit was named 'Lady Hamilton' (both T.J. Edgington Collection).

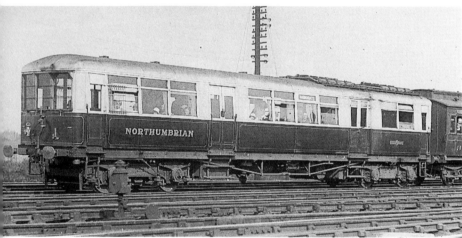

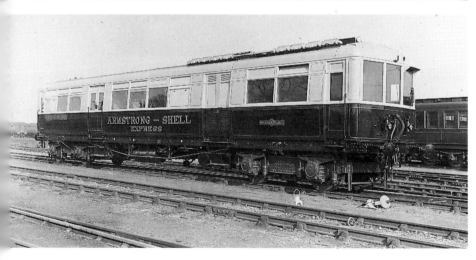

The luxury 'Armstrong-Shell Express' *unit at Wolverton in 1933* (BR LMR).

at least at the technological level — maybe Euro-Tunnel will sort it out!

Concurrently with the generally unsuccessful British efforts to adapt road practice to railway use, the early 1930s were also characterized by another clutch of experiments whereby internal combustion engines were fitted to more 'railway-like' vehicles. This led to a further modest rash of experiments, of which we may, perhaps, single out for further mention those of Messrs Armstrong Whitworth in the diesel-electric field during 1931-3. These brought two new factors into the equation: the diesel engine and electric transmission of power to the wheels. Though probably unappreciated at the time, both were to prove rather important in the longer term, and although this book is not a technical treatise of railway traction methods, we do need to consider both of them.

So far, all the internal combustion experiments reviewed had used petrol engines, and this may well have been a partial cause of their usually less than successful outcome. As more modern experience has well and truly demonstrated, the compression-ignition engine, invented by Dr Rudolph Diesel, is, by its very nature, far more suited to the rigours of commercial operation and is also able to be enlarged to give a greater power output at greater economy than its petrol-fuelled, spark-ignition equivalent. This was already becoming obvious in the road transport field, as witness the fairly rapid change-over from petrol to diesel in the commercial bus and lorry business; and since railways need, if anything, even bigger engines for their normally heavier vehicles, it should cause no real surprise that the successful application of internal combustion in the railway arena had to await the development of newer and more powerful diesel engines. However, the transmission of power from engine to wheels was different.

In this regard, we have already noted that the vibration characteristics of the railway vehicle were different from those of the road equivalent and that the various solutions to the problem of getting power to railway wheels were, at the time, less than perfect. Under the circumstances, therefore, it is hardly surprising that attention turned to the possibility of using 'state of the art' electric traction motor technology, by now well understood by railway engineers, and combine it with the ability of an internal combustion engine to produce electric power by the simple expedient of letting it drive a generator rather than the wheels themselves. This is indeed the basic principle behind the vast majority of modern high-powered diesel-electric locomotives. But, as might well be imagined, there was a snag, particularly in the realm of the self-contained passenger-carrying vehicle where weight-saving is paramount in order to achieve operational economy. Here, the fundamental dilemma was that a generator big enough to produce adequate electric power was no lightweight component.

This factor was and is usually acceptable in the purely locomotive field, but as far as the lightweight diesel-powered railcar was concerned, the future had to be with some better form of weight-saving mechanical transmission if at all possible, but this was easier said than done in the early 1930s, hence the Armstrong-Whitworth experiments.

It began in 1931-2 with an undeniably well-conceived railcar design which bore more than a passing resemblance to the now familiar Sentinel offerings and with much the same seating capacity — 60 third class passengers in a 2 + 3 arrangement with 'reversible' seat backs. They were given 250hp Sulzer engines manufactured under licence and were designed either to work in multiple or to handle an additional 30-ton trailing load at their designed maximum speed of 65 mph. In fact, the cars were designed to a composite loading gauge enabling them to run anywhere in Britain; but they were rather heavy at 42½ tons. A very successful trial of two in multiple was carried out on the LNER in February 1932 from Newcastle to Hexham and back.

A year later, the LMS also evaluated one of these cars in a very different mode: a fast service from London to the British Industries Fair site at Castle Bromwich. This was claimed to be the first diesel-powered express service in Britain, and so indeed it was, but compared with the LNER experiment this new version, known as the 'Armstrong-Shell Express', seems to have been little more than an extravagant publicity stunt. The car was, in fact, specially refurbished for this service, and within the same body shell the original 60 seats had given way to but 12 Pullman-like armchairs and tables, a small kitchen and pantry and separate toilet and lavatory compartments. No doubt it was all great fun, but 42 tons of railcar for but a dozen passengers was no way to run a railway, then or now!

The last Armstrong-Whitworth experiment is far less well known than the previous two, but from the details given at the time ought to have been a real challenger for honours. It appeared in June 1933 and was an extremely well thought out 57-seater with compact underfloor diesel-electric equipment. Two engine options were stated to be available, either 95bhp or 140bhp, the whole lot coming out at something over 17½ tons with the smaller engine, or slightly under 19 tons with the larger, both being less than half the weight of the 1932 cars. It was regarded as a railbus, had attractive bodywork styled by Park Royal, the well-known London bus builders, and, like so many more of these things at the time, was tried out in Northumberland and Durham by the LNER.

In a sense, 1933 was the critical year for the inter-

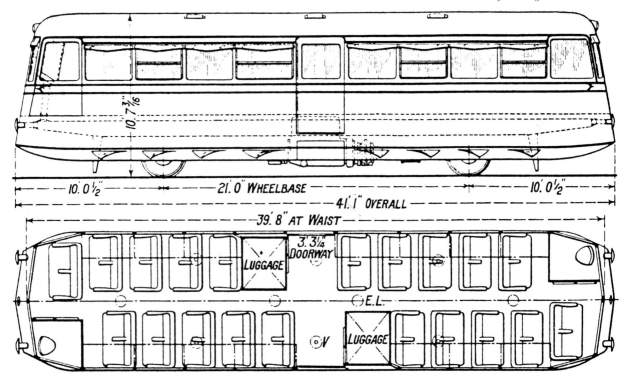

nal combustion engine as far as the British railways were concerned, for it marked both the end of the experimental phase — save for one dramatic later LMS venture in 1938 — and also the start of the only real development which had any significantly long-lasting consequences. The last 1933 experiment was a trio of Leyland four-wheel railbuses for the LMS. They seated 40, weighed only 10 tons and were exactly symmetrical end-to-end about their centre-line, whereon were positioned the outer doors. They had transverse seats facing outwards from the centre of the cars whose enclosed bodywork was of characteristic bus style. They were, in effect, the last throw of the pure road vehicle approach and appear to have been rather more successful than most, surviving until 1951, but right at the time of their introduction, as indeed was also true of the final diesel-electric design from Armstrong-Whitworth, the way ahead was pointed by the first truly trend-setting design to emerge during the grouping era; and it came from an unlikely source.

I refer, of course, to the pioneering diesel railcars of the Great Western Railway, by quite a long way the most properly integrated internal combustion railway passenger vehicles so far seen in this country. In them could be seen not only a proper appreciation of the different needs of a railway as opposed to a road vehicle, but also a properly designed form of mechanical transmission which took care of the technical problems mentioned above. They were also more than normally well styled, being entirely appropriate to their era, yet having a timeless quality which does not always go with being in the height of fashion. Fortunately, like the Southern Electrics and the London Underground carriages already considered, they too have attracted their own dedicated literature — see Bibliography — so it is not necessary to pick their bones here. What is maybe most surprising is that in spite of their longer-term influence, there were less than 40 of them all told.

The story started in quite a modest way in 1933 when a quite new design of diesel railcar was designed by Hardy Motors Ltd of Southall in association with Messrs AEC Ltd, who provided the 130hp power plant, and the GWR which agreed to operate the car on its services between Slough, Reading, Didcot and Oxford. The fully streamlined car body was evolved in wind tunnel tests and was put together by Park Royal Coachworks Ltd. There was thus a very considerable injection of contemporary road vehicle technology; but where it differed from previous attempts to marry road to rail was in the use of a diesel engine, the design of a more robust chassis (lightweight but suitable to railway use) and the development of a

Figure 69 *Elevation and plan of the 1933 Leyland diesel railbus for the LMS.*

Scale: 4mm = 1ft

Right *Pioneer GWR streamlined railcar No 1 near Maidenhead circa 1934. Note the driver's separate access door, a feature never repeated in any of the subsequent GWR railcars (Soole Collection, NRM).*

Figure 70 *Side elevations and plans of streamlined GWR railcars Nos 2-4 (above) and 5-7 (below).*

Scale: ¹/₁₀" = 1ft

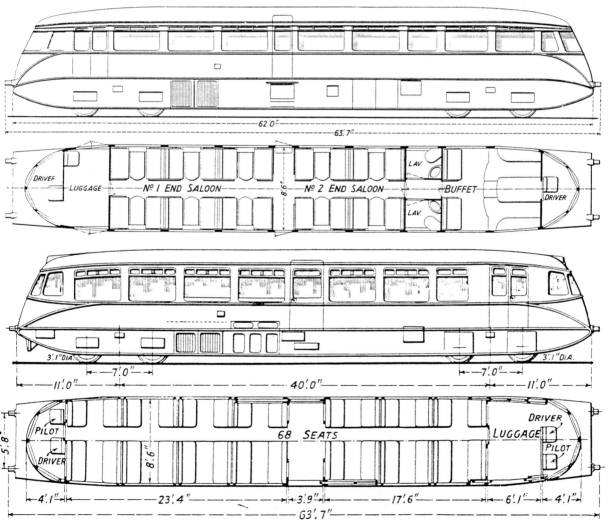

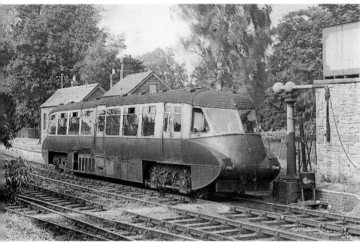

direct-drive transmission system which would be both reliable and capable of operating with equal facility in either direction of travel, the car being double-ended. When it finally emerged, it was a stylistic *tour de force* whose appearance met with immediate approval and brought the GWR much kudos. Though the company itself had little or nothing to do with its design, it was perfectly entitled to take credit for having introduced the car on to its routes.

After considerable evaluation, the GWR then resolved to order a further series of cars which embodied improvements on the prototype, not least being the provision of twin engines for much needed greater power, and by 1936 no fewer than 17 were in service. Though all shared the basic streamlined shape of the prototype, they were not all alike, either in appearance or seating capacity.

The first 'production' series (Nos 2-4) were low-capacity, 44-seat cars for longer-distance work, each having lavatories and a small but extremely well-equipped buffet section at one end; they were used for express service between Birmingham and Cardiff and represented the first regular diesel workings in Britain of this kind, the earlier Armstrong example (see above) having been essentially a one-off operation. Seats were arranged 2 + 2 in bays of eight with tables between them, exactly in the manner of conventional open stock, and a pair of centre doors was provided, one on each side. The driver gained access to his cab from the passenger saloon, unlike Car No 1 where there was an outer door to the cab, and there was a small guard's luggage compartment at the end opposite the buffet counter.

The next three cars (Nos 5-7) reverted to the high density 3 + 2 seating of No 1, and this time the bodywork was made by the Gloucester RC & W Co Ltd, but was slightly differently styled in that the side windows were much deeper, thus improving the outlook, and the centre doors were of the sliding type. The waistline was slightly upswept at the driving ends which, allied to the two-tone colour scheme, gave them a slightly boat-like appearance. The roof line also curved down slightly more over the cab ends, and the effect of both these small-style changes was to result in a most charming variant from the original rather high-waisted appearance of the first four. This low-waisted style was to be the standard for the rest of the streamlined series, whose bodies were also built by the Gloucester company.

The last ten streamlined cars (Nos 8-17) were ordered before the previous batch were all in service, such was the faith of the GWR in this new idea, and all were similar in lines to the No 5-7 series, save that the waistline was now horizontal rather than upswept at the ends. Of these ten, six were exactly as Nos 5-7, ie 70-seaters with no lavatories; three (Nos

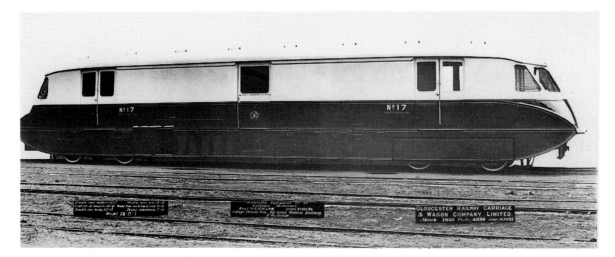

10-12) had lavatories for longer-distance work (but no buffet) and seated 63 in consequence, still in 3 + 2 configuration; while the last, No 17, was a dedicated express parcels car whose purpose was to speed up local passenger services in the London area. This it did by taking over all the 'pick-up' parcels traffic which hitherto had caused extended stops to be made by many local trains. This experiment clearly proved successful, though whether it needed to be streamlined to do the job is rather conjectural.

By mid-1936, therefore, the GWR had put a fleet of 16 passenger-carrying cars into service, and such was their success that the company could claim later the same year that it was operating them on something like 20 per cent of its network and they were putting up over 1,000,000 miles per year. This represented about 2-3 per cent of the GWR passenger

mileage, most of which was extra business since, at that time, the railcars were supplementing existing services. In some cases they drummed up so much new business that conventional trains had to be substituted. This seems undoubtedly to have been the reason why, in 1937, the GWR put a new and experimental car into service, No 18. This, while still semi-streamlined, had lost some of the graceful lines of the earlier cars and was also given railway-pattern buffing and drawgear, the purpose being to evaluate whether a railcar could haul a trailing load and still give the same or similar performance to the single unit cars. No 18 was given a much stronger under-frame in consequence and was geared differently; it more than exceeded expectations and from it were derived the final GWR railcar types.

One of the obvious differences between No 18 and

Left *These views allow comparison to be made of the subtle visual changes between the three main series of GWR streamlined railcars. They show, in order: 'high-waisted' Buffet Car No 3 undergoing trials on the Brentford branch in 1934; 'low-waisted' No 7 with 'upswept' driving-end waist panelling, still in GWR livery at Coleford in 1950; and No W10W (representing the lavatory version of the most common type) in BR red/cream livery at Campden in 1954 on a Worcester service (NRM collection; Russell and Williams Collections, NRM).*

Above *The one-off streamlined parcels railcar, No 17 (NRM collection).*

Figure 71 *Map showing the extent of GWR railcar operations in 1936.*

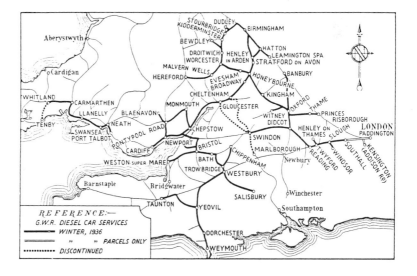

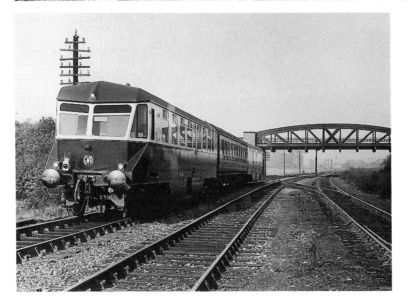

Top *Experimental semi-streamlined rail-car No 18 of 1937, the first to be fitted with conventional buffing and drawgear* (NRM collection).

Above *Swindon-built railcar No W26W at Birmingham Snow Hill on 19 June 1954, having just arrived with the 11.15 from Dudley* (T.J. Edgington).

Left *Twin railcars Nos 35-6 on trial with an intermediate trailer on the Brentford branch circa 1941* (NRM collection).

Right *Interior of the buffet portion of GWR twin railcars Nos 35-6 when new in 1941* (NRM collection).

its predecessors was the much larger luggage van portion, which also contained a steam heating boiler for use when a trailer was in tow. Seating, in consequence, was reduced to 49, still 3 + 2 and arranged in five bays, one seat being 'lost' at the central door to the van portion. However, the loss in seating capacity was deemed to be acceptable in view of the ability to pull a trailer, since the larger van space would obviously serve for both components. This, accordingly, was made the basis for the next main batch, Nos 19-33. This time, however, the bodies were built at Swindon and they emerged during the early war years in 1940 and 1941.

To those who had seen the earlier railcars, the new Swindon cars were a bit brutish in appearance, having angular bodies and little real resemblance to their stylish forbears. They seemed to be all angles and corners in consequence; but this undoubtedly saved cost and time at a difficult period, and in all other respects they were more versatile because of their trailer-hauling capability. Inside, seating now reverted to 2 + 2 throughout and they had six bays, though still with a pretty large van and steam generator compartment. A final car to this same general outline was built in 1941, and was another dedicated parcels railcar, in the manner of No 17.

It was not very long before the obvious next step was taken of making a twin railcar unit to cope with bigger loads, and the final phase saw two of these pairs produced, one each in 1941 and 1942: Nos 35/36 and 37/38. They were well-appointed cars with driving cabs at the outer ends only, and seated 104 in combination. They also had a very well-equipped buffet counter and the first pair replaced the original Nos 2-4 on the Cardiff-Birmingham run. Like the 19-33 series, these twins were also designed to take an auxiliary trailer, this time marshalled between the two components; an ordinary corridor third was used, but at no time does the GWR ever seem to have contemplated designing a purpose-built trailer in matching style for this task, though one was sketched out (but never built) for Car No 18 in 1936.

It was perhaps surprising that this final series of 'angular' cars, whether singles or twins, was actually allowed to go ahead early in the war, and because of their timing into service their early utilization is mostly obscured, largely in consequence of the clampdown on information. However, what can be said is that in them, the GWR had fairly accurately predicted quite a number of aspects which would be copied in the BR DMUs of the mid-1950s and later, in particular the twin formation. In some areas the GWR versions were actually better (the buffets for example). Furthermore, the cars themselves, unlike almost all other non-electric self-propelled stock from the company period, mostly enjoyed a near-normal

length of service life, the last of them not being withdrawn until late 1962. On all counts, though but few in number, they can perhaps be regarded as the most significant company contribution in this particular field.

The only other contender for longer-standing influence in the diesel arena is the final project to be considered in this chapter, a fairly spectacular one-off experimental train introduced by the LMS in 1938. However, its long-term development and possible evolution, like so many other things, were both cut short by the war. The project took the form of a triple articulated railcar set driven by no fewer than six 125hp diesel engines, the drive being of the hydraulic pattern. Each engine drove a single axle and only the extreme outer axles of the unit were unpowered. The train was designed for multiple unit control, thus making it the first genuine British DMU, even though it never had a partner with which to work in multiple, though one was planned. All power and transmission equipment was underfloor, and the articulated bogies were of what was called the 'LMS type'; a clever double pivot arrangement (one above each end of the bogies concerned) allowed rather longer car units to be envisaged within the load gauge 'throwover' limits than was possible with the more conventional Gresley-pattern centre pivot articulation. This allowed the outer ends to be some 64 ft long. The same system was adopted for the equally ill-fated 1939 'Coronation Scot' sets (see Chapter 11).

From the outside, the train was neatly streamlined with a very stylish end treatment, though maybe not quite so striking as that of the first GWR railcars. The cars themselves were built to conventional LMS

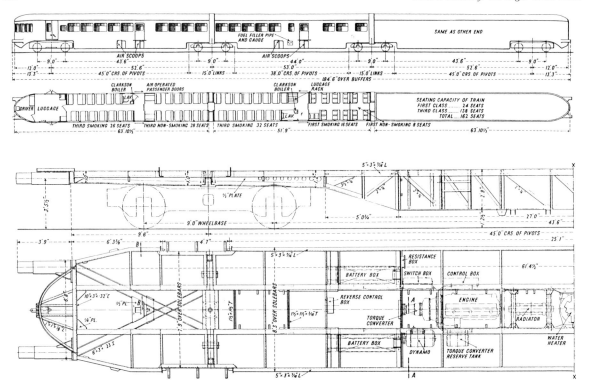

Figure 72 *Simplified elevations and plans, together with underframe construction detail, of the experimental LMS articulated DMU of 1938.*

Scale: 4mm = 1ft (underframe)

pattern practice (flush steel panels on timber frames) and underframes were centrally trussed in the manner of the 1937 articulated stock. Given its overall length (184 ft 6 in) it was a commendably lightweight unit at 73 tons, more than one ton lighter than the above-described GWR twins. The interiors were, if truth be told, more than a bit nondescript, and apart from lavatories there were no buffet or other refined facilities. It seated 162, of whom 24 were first class. An interesting innovation was the provision of air-operated sliding doors, and the seats, except where mounted against sides or bulkheads, were of the reversible 'throw-over' type. It carried a quite spectacular new livery of Post Office red and ivory, topped

LMS articulated diesel units Nos 80001-3 at Derby in 1939, fitted with stone guards over the driving windows (BR LMR).

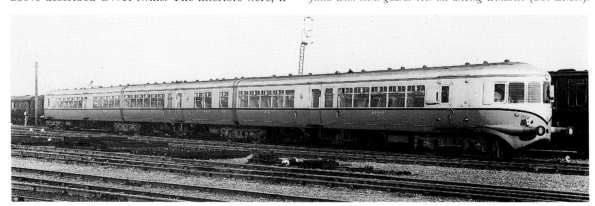

by a 'silver' painted roof, the three tones being separated by black bands.

It is not quite clear what utilization the LMS had in mind for this type of vehicle. The two-class accommodation put it one up on the one-class GWR cars, but the lack of catering provision seemed to point the other way — ie outer suburban rather than true long-distance. It was, therefore, rather surprising that after testing it was put to use on the Midland main line from St Pancras as far out as Leicester and Nottingham. It worked a complex six-service roster of 350 miles daily but little seems to have been recorded of its success or failure and it remained out of use during the war. Afterwards it was converted to a two-car maintenance unit for the MSJA electric line, losing four of its six engines in the process.

Whether or not the LMS form of transmission would have proved itself will never now be known, but post-war events were to establish that for the most part the hydraulic form was not usually the best way forward in British terms in any of its several modes of application, and that the mechanical alternative

was the best option for railcar use. Even though the mechanical transmission adopted by BR was different in form from that of the GWR, maybe the influence of that company was the significant factor. Likewise, articulation was not to find any place in the BR solution, whereas the GWR 'twin' idea did. On the other hand, in terms of internal layout, though the LMS idea seems to have suffered from some confusion as to exact purpose, its two-class layout plus lavatories was very much the way that many early BR DMUs were set up.

Perhaps it is reading too much into these final designs to try and trace any profound longer-term influence on subsequent BR practice, for there were, in all conscience, very few of them anyway and the BR examples followed neither of them very closely. But however much or little they may have contributed to the post-war scene, they did at least demonstrate, especially those of the GWR, that at last the long hoped for self-propelled passenger unit was a realistic possibility and they both offered not a few significant ideas on the way.

10. An interlude with the 'old-timers'

There can be no doubt that one of the most fascinating aspects of the post-1922 scene was the fate which befell the older carriages inherited by the 'Big Four'. I have already touched on some relevant aspects in Chapter 1, but the trouble is that their subsequent use, apart from a modest few cases where some form of quite positive statement can be made, usually defies any form of logical analysis; yet somehow or other it seemed quite wrong to exclude them. After all, as Table 2 (page 41) has shown, there were over 48,000 of them in 1923, and even in 1947 more than 25 per cent of this total still remained in service. What I have therefore elected to do is to break the normal pattern of the book in this chapter so as to enable me to illustrate a little more of the variety which was to be seen than would otherwise be possible.

I have chosen to call it an 'interlude', since there will be more than a bit of nostalgia to it, but I hope that this change of approach will not detract from the accuracy of the information. I have grouped the pictures mostly by company simply to avoid total chaos, but they are for the most part 'stand-alones', so I have therefore used extended captions rather than continuous text to tell most of the story. First, however, we need to devote a few paragraphs to establish such general principles as do seem to have been followed.

In general, the old coaches, hardly surprisingly, were usually scrapped on the basis of age, so the first to go were mostly the four-and six-wheelers; but of the bogie stock, much was quite new and even those which had some 20 years of life under their belt already were by no means life-expired. Many of them

were in fact to give a further generation or more of faithful service to their new owners. Indeed, the ex-LNWR sleeping and dining cars and the pre-group GWR diners have already been noted in this category. It was rather more rare for complete trains to survive undiluted after 1922, but there were exceptions. Perhaps the best known example of this was the celebrated WCJS '2 pm' set of twelve-wheelers (see Volume 1, page 230) which, in spite of the many late-1920s LMS improvements, was not to become ousted from its traditional role until 1930. To this might well be added the Caledonian 'Grampian' and the North British 'Fife and Lothian' sets, the stylish NER formations on the Newcastle-Liverpool run and the celebrated GNR 'quintuplet' dining set on the King's Cross-Leeds workings. There were others too, no doubt, and even when the old sets had been broken up, their vehicles were rarely scrapped; it was far more likely that they would turn up on some lesser services, maybe even as individual vehicles which could at least add interest to and quite often improve

For several years after the grouping, the LMS retained the famous West Coast 1908 '2 pm' twelve-wheelers on their original working. This view at Crewe in 1928 behind 4-6-0 No 6112 Sherwood Forester shows them still in use as the first four carriages (the Glasgow portion) of the down train, now named the 'Mid-Day Scot'. The Edinburgh section (to the rear) has been given some new stock but still retains the old dining car. It is perhaps significant that these 1908 carriages had no outer doors to the compartments and were not replaced until the LMS could offer something similar from its own new designs — see Chapter 4 (Author's collection).

the general tone of an otherwise fairly humdrum service.

This process was and is known as 'cascading' and could take many forms. First was the straight transfer, without change of passenger classification, to a lower-order working, thus giving better accommodation and/or facilities to this type of service. Secondly could be a downgrading of class from first to third, again with beneficial effect, and I well recall my own first conscious experience of this sort of thing, early in BR days. I was going by rail from Leeds to the Lake District with the young lady who eventually became my wife and I can still see the look of stark astonishment on her face when I directed her towards what was undoubtedly the scruffiest-looking carriage on the train; I had spotted that it was a downgraded 'twin window' open first of early LMS parentage! It gave us a wonderfully comfortable trip at a third class 'day return' price!

Other possibilities were extensive rebuilding of old stock without change of use — the GWR, as stated, was very good at doing this sort of thing with its dining cars — or a more comprehensive rebuilding for alternative use, such as the already discussed Southern Electrics and the often intriguing conversions to push-pull mode, some of which will be looked at in due course. One could also find the use of older corridor stock in place of lavatory non-corridors on some of the longer cross-country or even express services, or maybe the substitution of lavatory non-corridor for older non-lavatory stock. There was often, in fact, a sort of multiple cascading right down the pecking order as a consequence of new main-line stock being put into service on the main trains.

At the other extreme, those pre-group carriages which were, save for age, in no way inferior to their post-group equivalents, would continue to ply their trade unchanged. And this could apply from the most exalted to the most humble. There could even be transfer of broadly equivalent stock from one operating area to another, especially where it was felt that one constituent of the newly grouped system had produced a rather better solution than another. The LMS was particularly fond of this sort of thing in Scotland, where a whole panoply of former English pre-group stock regularly found a whole new lease of life on many a former Highland Railway service. It even, *in extremis*, led to such unthinkable pre-1923 concepts as ex-MR dining cars being drafted on to former LNWR lines; now *that* was indeed unusual, but it happened!

Another widespread function of older pre-group stock was to enable the railways to meet the huge seasonal demands of the holiday and excursion trade. In our present day it is almost impossible to conceive just how much additional demand this represented,

but it was by no means unusual for the companies to keep hundreds of older coaches on not much more than a 'care and maintenance' basis for wheeling out only on high days and holidays during the summer. This profligate maintenance of such large fleets would certainly not meet with the approval of the accountancy-orientated modern railway. The supreme irony is that though these were still the days of private companies which were working for a commercial return, they nevertheless still managed to provide a service which in many cases was far more comprehensive than is offered by our current publicly-owned organization which might be *presumed* to do such things as of right. We are, it needs hardly be stated, on political ground here, and even though I do not believe that it is the fault of the modern railway *per se* that these things are no longer done, it is a relevant aspect of the overall subject.

Closely allied to this use of old stock was the equally common use of such vehicles for 'strengthening' purposes, as it was called. This was the very common practice at weekends and other times of heavier traffic, whereby extra carriages were regularly added to the normal formations of trains to meet extra demand, it being tacitly assumed that the locomotives could haul the extra loads, even if at slightly reduced speed, and that there would be stock available. Yet again, the modern railway generally finds it too much trouble to do this sort of thing, usually being most often excused by the feeble statement that there is no spare stock — but whose fault is that? My guess is that there are very many current travellers who would not mind finding a few older carriages in their train on a Friday evening, as in older days, if that was the price of having a seat rather than standing in the aisles for two or three hours. But again I digress.

The fact is that the older carriages were an integral, if often randomly disposed, element of the total passenger package in company days and extended well into the 1950s and early 1960s before the old order changed out of all recognition. It therefore seems proper to give some space to the later days of these old warriors, whose very existence, though perhaps of little relevance in evolutionary terms, was very much a part of the total carriage scene in and amongst the newer offerings; and it certainly gave great joy to those who liked to look beyond the locomotive draw-hook. For the most part I have simply arranged the 'orthodox' examples under company headings alphabetically, though I have not even tried to apportion a total balance between the systems, preferring instead to choose those which seemed most interesting. I have, however, added a couple of thematic subject headings, but Pullmans have been excluded; they have their place in Chapter 12.

Great Western Railway

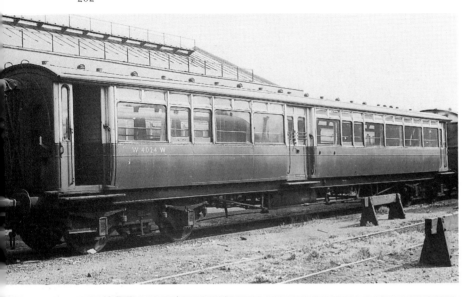

As the previous chapter has revealed, the steam railmotor quickly fell out of favour after the 1914-18 war, which left the railways with quite a few vehicles which, while their prime movers may have been too feeble to pull much save themselves, were often associated with passenger-carrying portions which could be persuaded to yield a few more years of useful life. Most railways had a few and the vast majority served out their time in the push-pull mode (see page 269) but every now and then something different happened. Such was the case with Taff Vale Railway Steam Railmotor No 15. In 1922, it was rebuilt into a corridor third rather than the usual push-pull trailer and, amazingly, it ran for more than another 30 years in this form. It is seen here at Caerphilly Works in 1954 as W4024W, still looking quite spruce. (T.J. Edgington).

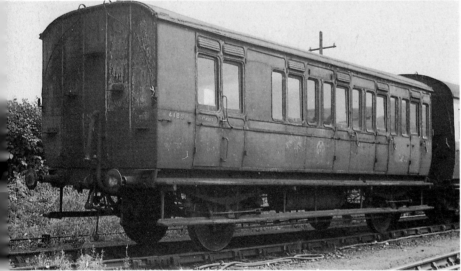

Although the GWR may have been less adventurous than most, the company did not operate anything like as many superannuated relics as did the LNER or even the LMS. All the more surprising therefore that as late as 1950, this Dean four-wheeler No 4189 was found still in use at Neath Bridge Street. However, judging from the presence of the 1930s 'shirt button' company emblem, the carriage had not been painted for at least a dozen years. But most of its panelling remained intact (T.J. Edgington).

Below left and top right *Dean's GWR clerestory carriages must have been some of the toughest and most resilient vehicles ever built, and they gave valuable service throughout the grouping period. An excursion set was featured on page 8, and here are two more interesting reminders of the time. In the first view at Stapleton Road in 1934, very unusual use is being made of a heavy freight 2-8-0T No 5224 to haul a featherweight two-coach train of lavatory non-corridors which, on examination, can be seen to feature two types of bogie. The leading brake composite has the long wheelbase version while the brake third has the short type.*

The second view shows 4-4-0 No 3363 Alfred Baldwin on a nine-coach train from Cardiff to Bristol near Ashley Hill a year or two later with no fewer than seven Dean non-corridors in the formation. The two extreme end vehicles are probably

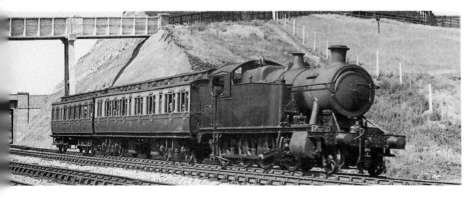

added strengtheners, for the rest of the train looks suspiciously like a pair of more up-to-date (but not too modern!) corridor brake composites sandwiching an otherwise third class non-corridor set. This is a good example of the 'cascading' of older corridor stock. (both Soole Collection, NRM).

Because Churchward was so much ahead of his time, even his earlier stock tended to look more or less at home amongst the later offerings. Here is seen one of his celebrated 'Dreadnought' composites — an idea well in advance of the field (see Volume 1) — at the front of a down Brighton to Cardiff train at Patchway, headed by 2-6-0 No 7321. A later fully panelled 'Toplight' is seen as the third carriage. This working was undoubtedly similar to that shown at the same location on page 18, this time it being the GWR's turn to provide the stock. During pre-BR days, it was normal for both companies to provide stock on such joint services. (Soole Collection, NRM).

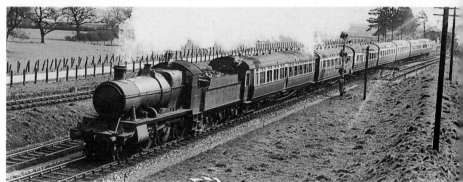

In this circa 1935 view, an Ilfracombe-Paddington train enters Bristol under the Bath Road bridge behind 4-6-0 King Stephen, the most interesting feature being the fact that of the first four carriages, only the dining car is not of Edwardian vintage. A 'Dreadnought' brake third leads and behind the diner can be seen two of the distinctive, if rather absurdly conceived, 'Concertina' corridors which preceded the 'Toplights' (Soole Collection, NRM).

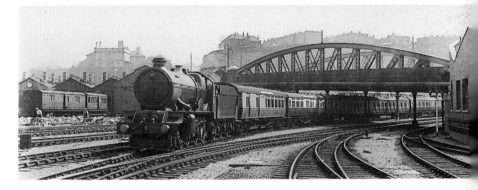

This last view on GWR territory, shows a fascinating scene and makes a nice link to the next section. The train, headed by 4-6-0 No 4038 Queen Berengaria, is at Stoke Gifford on what the photographer described as a Bristol– Swindon local train. But this can hardly be so, for the stock is wholly ex-Great Central in origin, including two six-wheelers, one at least of which may well even be of pre-GCR Manchester, Sheffield and Lincolnshire origin. Moreover, both these vehicles are saloons, probably now designated as Picnic Saloons. The middle carriage is a full brake followed by a later GCR corridor composite; while what appears to be another saloon brings up the rear. My guess is that it was a returning excursion or private charter which turned north at Didcot to re-enter former GCR country at Banbury Junction (Soole Collection, NRM).

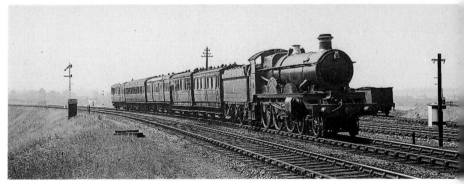

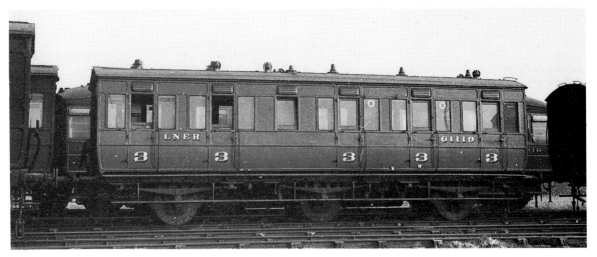

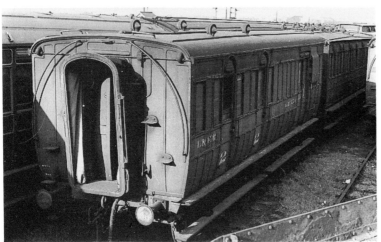

London and North Eastern Railway

The LNER had a higher proportion of older carriages in use than any of its rivals, including no less than 50 per cent of all surviving four- and six-wheelers in Britain. Many of the old stagers were of GER origin (which says much about the quality of their original construction) and remained in GER territory, such as the three prime specimens seen here, all photographed at Stratford in March 1938: six-wheel lavatory third, No 61119; six-wheel corridor(!) brake second, believed to be No 62351; and clerestory corridor first No 6407 tucked between a later GER corridor (left) and a matchboard ex-NER non-corridor. Note too that all three classes were represented (all H.C. Casserley).

Right and middle right *The LNER was rather more fond of taking posed official views of its older coaches than the other companies, especially where there was something slightly out of the ordinary about their use. The first view shows six-wheel full brake No 3251 in LNER days, still displaying every last inch of its original NBR wooden panelling with its distinctive double layer (see Volume 1 Page 103); but in 1931, the elaborate branding, including a very passable representation of the 'banner head' of the Scotsman newspaper, reveals that it was used exclusively for special newspaper service.*

The second view of LNER Club Saloon No 22113 in 1925 shows a former GCR coach, now well off its original home patch, having been reallocated to the Harrogate–Bradford service of the former NER. (both LNER official, NRM).

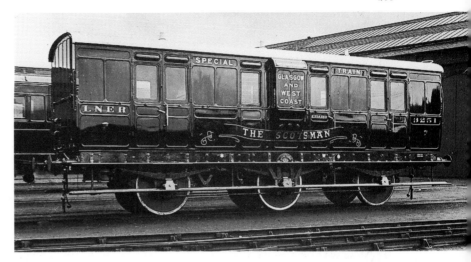

Bottom and overleaf top *Matters remained very 'North British' on the LNER in Scotland during the inter-war years. In the first view of 4-4-0 No 9291* Glen Quoich *on a Thornton train at Inverkeithing in 1927, the train is wholly composed of six-wheelers, at least as far as can be seen. The third vehicle seems to be a first class semi-saloon, or some such, probably with at least some lavatory provision, but the rest is traditionally non-corridor.*

The second view at Inverkeithing, shows bogie stock and 4-4-2T No 9039 in charge. The train is almost equally solidly NBR in composition — again without lavatories — but this time augmented by one of David Bain's handsome turn-of-the-century clerestories from the old NER, now very far from home (both Stephen Collection, NRM).

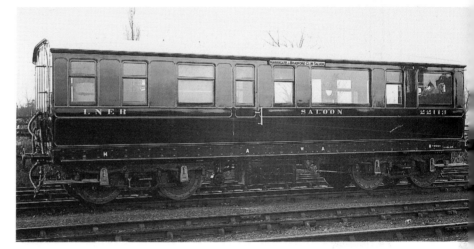

Overleaf middle *In the later 1930s, the LNER took over the whole responsibility for the hitherto jointly owned Midland and Great Northern Railway, many of whose better carriages were of pre-group LMS constituent origin, including this particularly interesting ex-Midland clerestory type. They were semi-open thirds, half side-corridor and half in the open 'Picnic' configuration (the far end as seen from this viewpoint). The whole batch of 12 was transferred to the M & GN in 1936. No 99 is seen here at South Lynn in May 1937, still wearing its simplified LMS livery, but in due course it would be repainted in LNER 'teak'* (H.C. Casserley).

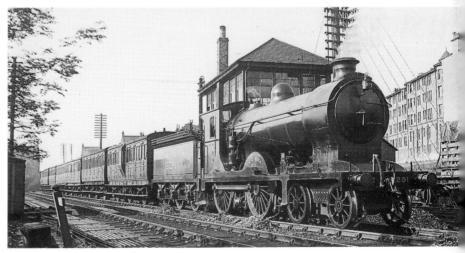

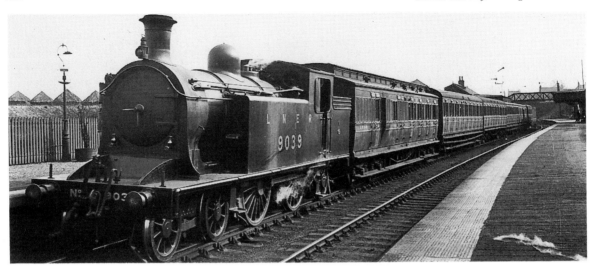

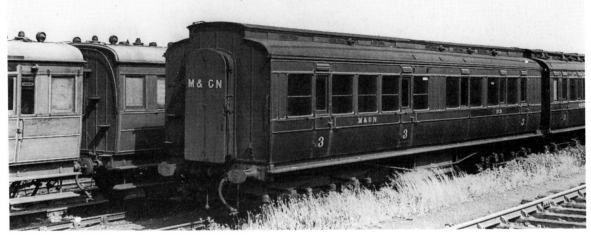

London, Midland and Scottish Railway

Top two right *The former Highland Railway branches of the LMS could be very happy hunting grounds for carriage enthusiasts well into BR days. The process of coach 'cascading' started back in pre-group days and these two early LMS views show how the new company carried on the well-established Highland tradition on just one of its routes, that from Dingwall to Strathpeffer Spa. In the first view in 1925, 4-4-0T No 101, still carrying HR livery, is at Dingwall, and although the first two six-wheel carriages are of typical HR matchboard style, LMS influence is present in the form of two former Midland clerestories, a six-wheel brake*

and a bogie corridor composite, no less.

The second view, a year later with Stroudley 0-6-0T No 16118 in charge, still reveals a Highland six-wheeler at the head of the train, but there is now a nineteenth-century MR six-wheeler in place of the older HR third, while a former LNWR lavatory composite (still in pre-group colours and probably even of radial underframe origin) brings up the rear. In both cases, the former HR stock was already in LMS livery, the Highland area being particularly quick to make use of the new-style colours after 1922 (both Stephen Collection, NRM).

Right *The Highland main line of the LMS north of Perth was the gathering ground for the most astonishingly motley*

assemblages of carriages both before and after the grouping. All lines converged on this mostly single track lifeline to Inverness, and things were slow to change. In this magnificent study from the mid-1920s, 4-6-0 No 14691 Brodie Castle *sets off for Inverness with a wondrous assortment of stock in its nine-coach formation. What is particularly interesting is that it carries stopping headlamps, so it is a fair bet that quite a few of these many and various carriages were not working through from elsewhere but had been drafted on to the Highland by the LMS. As far as can be ascertained, their origins were, in order from the engine: MR, HR, LNWR, LMS standard, LNWR(2), LMS standard, LNWR and, possibly, Caledonian!* (Author's collection).

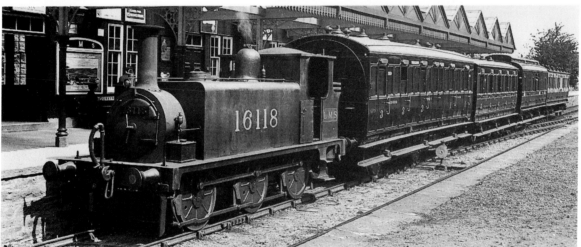

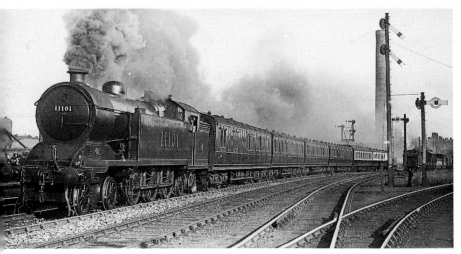

On the old Furness Railway, it was quite customary for many of the through trains to be of 'foreign' stock, so a full set of LNWR carriages would cause little comment. By early LMS days, these were often of high standard and this circa 1925 view shows a Carnforth–Lakeside train headed by 4-6-4T No 11101 and composed wholly of LNWR corridor rather than non-corridor stock. Already four out of the six carriages are in their new colours, but the back pair are one each from the two styles of design which preceded and succeeded the neat four-coach set which forms the main part of the train (Author's collection).

By contrast with the last view, here is a good example of non-corridor pre-group stock on a fairly substantial working in 1937. The train is headed by 4-6-0 No 25797 on the former LNWR direct route between Leeds and Manchester at Marsden. Two ex-LNWR non-corridor lavatory thirds sit between the leading LNWR corridor brake composite and the Stanier open third. Behind this comes an 'all-steel' open third. The relative dearth of first class accommodation and the generally mixed nature of the stock gives every reason to believe that this was a typical excursion or weekend holiday working, maybe to one of the Lancashire coast resorts (Ransome-Wallis Collection, NRM).

In spite of its standardization policy, many LMS trains, even on the main lines, were no tidier than anyone else's in the grouping period. This 1935 view behind 4-6-0 No 5639 taken at an unidentified fell country location, is typical. It too is likely to have been an 'extra' of some kind, probably formed up from whatever happened to be lying around in the carriage sidings at the time. The first four carriages are LNWR, WCJS, WCJS, LNWR and include but one composite, a double brake-ended former 'slip' carriage with only two first class compartments; they are followed by a heterogeneous mixture of LMS types, again with very little first class seating. There is no dining car visible, though there may have been one out of sight, but at least there is a continuous corridor. (Main Line Collection, NRM).

Southern Railway

The Southern Railway, as has been seen, re-used much of its old stock in EMU form, but it was just as capable as the rest of upgrading its locomotive-hauled local services (of which it retained not a few) with a modest amount of 'cascading' from time to time, and this crisp late 1930s view shows one such example, an up local near Littlehampton behind 2-6-0 No 1808. The second and third carriages are ex-LSWR lavatory non-corridor thirds, but the leading LSWR brake composite is gangwayed and the fourth vehicle looks suspiciously like one of the 'Continental' SE & CR-pattern corridors (Soole Collection, NRM).

On the main line also, the SR followed similar ideas to those of the other companies, often retaining much of its older stock in full main-line use. Of course, it did not have too much, but the former LSWR low-roof corridors were of high quality and here a trio of them (still formed up into a set, albeit now three coaches instead of the original five) forms the front of this up West of England express passing through Woking in July 1938 behind 4-6-0 No 747 Elaine. One can be almost certain that the rest of the train was Maunsell standard stock, and, judging from the odd brake composite at vehicle No 4, may well have started from several destinations, whose through carriages were added to the front of the train as it proceeded towards London (Box Collection, NRM).

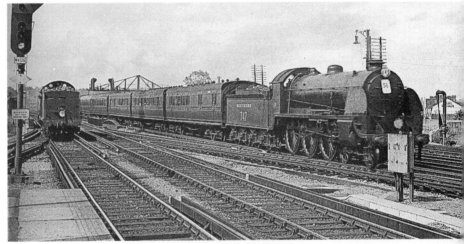

Outwith its electrified territory, the Southern was blessed with numerous bucolic rural branches, none more celebrated than the Brighton's line to Hayling Island. In pre-motor car days many would make the trip by rail, and this nostalgic view reminds us of those long gone high-days of summer when lots of excited children, not to mention their parents, would cause the normal formation to be stretched to such as seen here: four non-corridors (two ex-LSWR and two from the 'home team') in charge of a diminutive 'Terrier' tank, in this case No 2678 (Soole Collection, NRM).

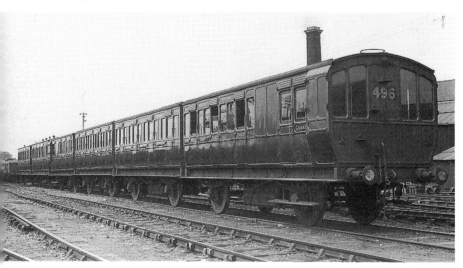

A second remarkable area of the Southern's parish was to be found on the Isle of Wight, and ever since the grouping its trains have almost always been composed of 'hand-me-downs' from elsewhere, a process which continues to this day. In early Southern days things were getting a bit desperate, and in this view, former LB & SCR close-coupled four-wheel set No 496 along with a pair of similar fugitives from the old London Chatham and Dover Railway, all of pre-1900 vintage, make a brave show and still look remarkably smart at Newport, probably soon after they were moved there in the mid-1920s (Author's collection).

A particularly interesting example of Southern branch line ingenuity was represented by articulated 'twin' unit Nos 513/4 which worked the Sheppey Light Railway from Leysdown to Queenborough from 1924 until 1950. It was built from two former SE & CR steam railcar bodies, and after the Sheppey line closed it enjoyed a further few years of active life in central London. Here the unit is seen at Queenborough, almost at the end of its sojourn in north Kent, during September 1950 (R.F. Roberts).

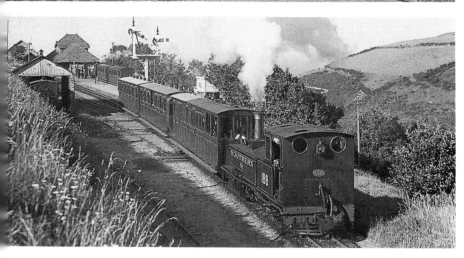

Few would deny that the charming narrow-gauge Lynton and Barnstaple Railway was one of the most regrettable 'lost causes' of the grouping era. It was almost doomed to failure from the outset, but the Southern put on a brave show right to the end as is seen in this delightful view of 2-6-2T No 188 Lew leaving Lyton with a three-coach train of typical 'narrow gauge'-type stock, set so close to the ground that the running gear is out of sight. If truth be told, the British railways had very little influence on the development of this type of carriage, but it is pleasing to record that the leading (and unique) brake composite saloon survives intact at the National Railway Museum, having spent 40 or more years in use as a summerhouse in Devon! Sadly, and largely through lack of funding or resources on the part of the Museum, it has not yet been restored; yet some would argue that it is a much more worthy candidate for public funding than most (Soole Collection, NRM).

Push-pull trains

The origins of the push-pull train were covered in Volume 1 and the few totally new examples which the grouped railways built are considered in Chapter 13 of this present book. However, most such coaches during the grouping period had their origins with older pre-group stock and the Southern was probably the leader of the field. Indeed, this part of the story continued well into BR days and will be further considered in Volume 3. Meantime, this reminder of a typical Isle of Wight operation must suffice for the moment. It had an interesting link with a previous view, for the carriages, former saloons of LCDR origin seen here at Ventnor West with 0-6-0T No W11, came from the Sheppey Light Railway when the articulated twin was sent there. When the SR put them to work on the Isle of Wight in 1924, they were converted to push-pull operation at the same time (BRSR).

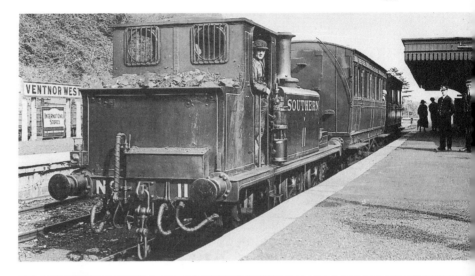

The GWR was another great advocate of the push-pull mode, though its chosen name was 'auto-train'. Most of the carriages came from converted steam railmotors of which it had by far the largest stock of any British company (see Volume 1). They enjoyed a greatly extended lease of life after conversion, none more so than the pioneer railmotor itself, the not particularly stylish No 1. It is seen here at Caerphilly works in May 1954 as W1W, no less than 51 years after it had gone into service as a self-propelled vehicle. It was still in remarkably good order. Note, too, another glimpse of the ex-Taff Vale Railway's former steam railmotor No W4024W (see page 202) (T.J. Edgington).

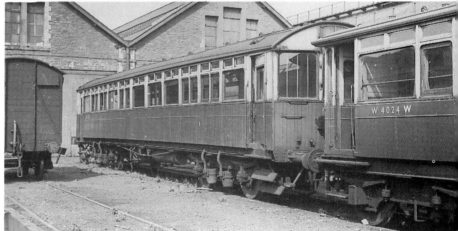

GWR conventional carriages in push-pull mode were little different from those of the others and its vehicles were often just as venerable. This is a pair of low-roof Dean bogie non-corridors near Southcote Junction, Reading. It illustrates the advantage of push-pull over the steam railmotor: note the added horsebox at the rear, such extra loads being possible because of the greater power of a 'proper' engine (Paterson-Rutherford Collection, NRM).

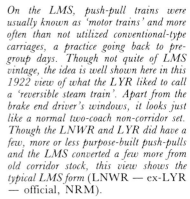

On the LMS, push-pull trains were usually known as 'motor trains' and more often than not utilized conventional-type carriages, a practice going back to pre-group days. Though not quite of LMS vintage, the idea is well shown here in this 1922 view of what the LYR liked to call a 'reversible steam train'. Apart from the brake end driver's windows, it looks just like a normal two-coach non-corridor set. Though the LNWR and LYR did have a few, more or less purpose-built push-pulls and the LMS converted a few more from old corridor stock, this view shows the typical LMS form (LNWR — ex-LYR — official, NRM).

Camping coaches

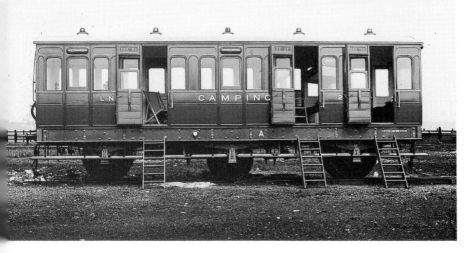

This view is believed to be the first official picture ever taken of a type of vehicle first introduced by the LNER in 1933 which not only became popular during the grouping period, but also became the last resting ground for hundreds of very venerable old coaches. The 'Camping Coach' was the railway equivalent of the modern residential seaside holiday caravan, and was usually found in similar locations. Indeed, the LMS called them 'Caravans'. In this picture, formerly Lancashire, Derbyshire and East Coast six-wheeler No 25 shows the early form with some compartments opened out into a kitchen-cum-day area, the others being left as separate two- or four-berth sleeping compartments. These coaches cost £2 10s (£2.50) per week to hire, but later examples with internal connecting doors cost £3! (LNER official, NRM).

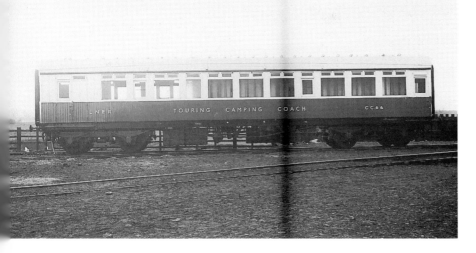

The LNER introduced a novelty variation in 1935 in the form of a 'Touring Camping Coach' which left York every Saturday and visited a different place every day. Six or seven people could enjoy the fun for between £16 and £20 per week for the whole party, including the cost of travel to the various Yorkshire beauty spots! The prototype vehicle was No CC.66 which, though painted in appropriate green and cream tourist livery, could not disguise its original NER matchboard styling of 1905 (LNER official, NRM).

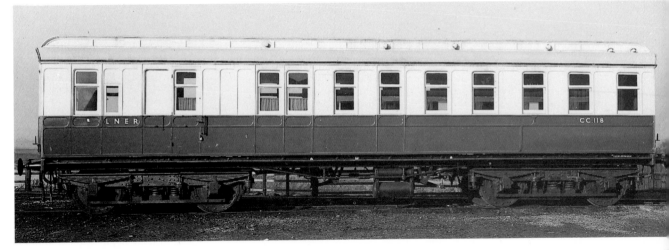

Above *By 1939, the LNER was converting some pretty plushy-looking coaches to camping form, though they were still quite elderly. Here is a former GCR (ex-MSLR) clerestory brake third of 1895, fully refurbished more than 40 years later in 1939, its fleet number CC.118 being indicative of the success of the whole idea. The impressive quality of these venerable vehicles was noteworthy and may well have been one of the main criteria determining which of them were chosen for conversion* (LNER official, NRM).

As might be expected, the LMS weighed in very soon after the LNER and eventually built more of them than did its rival concern. They were also slightly larger and cost more to hire in consequence — all of £3 10s (£3.50)! The hirer also had to book at least four monthly return tickets to get the use of one. This view shows a former LNWR corridor third of circa 1900 running as No 46000 in 1934, the LMS simply using numbers in its standard series rather than giving them a special allocation. Note the fine finish — fully lined company livery, no less. There appear to be a surprisingly large number of the original carriage fittings left intact after conversion (BR LMR).

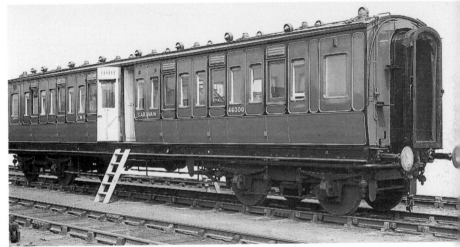

Equipping a camping coach was no mean task, and this view at Derby in 1937 of a string of LMS 'Caravans' being fitted out gives a vivid impression of just what was involved. This time, at least one set of lucky campers is going to get the benefit of a spacious former Midland Railway clerestory composite brake, while next in line a former LYR corridor composite gets the treatment. (Author's collection).

Above *The Southern was a bit later in the field and built relatively fewer camping coaches than did the LMS or LNER, but it claimed to be the first to offer wireless aerials and internal water tanks — plus an alarm clock! Thus, even though its first essay, formed from an ex-LCDR six-wheeler early in 1935, was almost exactly like the LNER £3-per-week offering, the Southern charged the same rate as did the LMS and imposed the same travel ticket requirement. No 1 is shown here, once again in remarkably good order (SR official, NRM).*

Below *We take temporary leave of the old timers in some of their many and various guises with this fine view of an altogether more*

impressive SR camping coach. No 18 was converted from one of the ex-LSWR lavatory non-corridors which, in original form, had no fewer than six lavatories to serve six compartments. The window arrangement of the conversion still betrays this fact, but like all camping coaches, though washing-up and drinking water was provided, none of the pre-war examples acutally retained their internal 'comfort stations' — patrons were expected to use the nearby station facilities. One can only presume that the mandatory instruction prohibiting use '. . . while standing in the station' applied to a camping coach just as much if not more so than the mobile variety; but the lavatories were omitted just in case! (SR official, NRM).

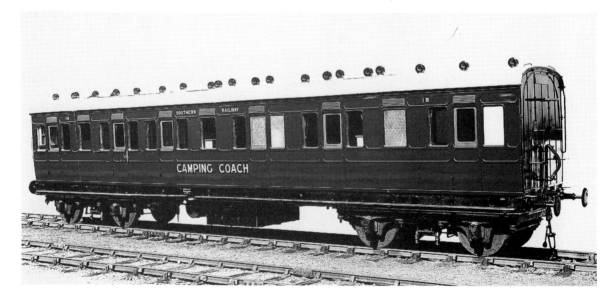

11. 'Supertrains' of the 1930s

The decade which preceded the Second World War represented probably the apogee of public perception of transport in all its modes. The Schneider Trophy and the developments of the first great international flying boats and airliners stood for the air, the great ocean liners like *Queen Mary* and *Normandie* vied with each other for supremacy across the Atlantic, Malcolm Campbell and others of his ilk were regularly breaking the land speed record for cars, and the railways had recovered from the first great conflict to the point where they could offer trains and services the like of which had never before been seen. It was, of course, an international phenomenon and the British railway contribution was merely a part. But in those days, we were perhaps more innocent — or at least less cynical — as a result of which almost every new improvement could be guaranteed if not headline treatment in the newspapers, then at the very least some degree of prominence. Even the engine drivers' names were as much part of the common currency as are the Grand Prix racing drivers of today.

Within the British railway field, the starting point seems to have been the improved vehicles offered by the LMS and LNER for the principal day services between London and Scotland in 1928. The LMS 'Royal Scot' stock of that year has already been discussed (page 65) in the context of the general improvement of carriages across the board for that company, and in the event was to set the overall tone of future LMS practice. There was never a complete train of such vehicles, despite occasional claims to the contrary, and after that time the LMS rarely bothered to offer dedicated special sets, save for the one exception of the 'Coronation Scot' train of 1937 (see below). It preferred instead to concentrate on the mass improvement of all its services typified by its huge new building programme of all varieties of modern coaching stock. It was thus rare for any of its better trains not to be in receipt of the latest 'state of the art' vehicles at very regular intervals, often of only two or three years.

The LNER was rather different, and in its 'Flying Scotsman' sets of 1928 can be seen the first seeds from which grew its celebrated streamliners and other dedicated trains of the 1930s, eventually expanding to the point where Gresley's company was without doubt the leader of the field in this sort of thing. The splendid dining cars of this train have already been considered (page 109), but we must now put the whole formation into perspective.

The stimulus was the forthcoming non-stop feature of the service which was an overt publicity stunt to capture traffic. There were rather slow and mandatory timings still in existence, and the only way either the LMS or the LNER could compete was to offer better passenger facilities. Non-stop running was thought to give a degree of exclusivity — which of course it did — but it was hardly necessary given the timings concerned, nor did it allow for any intermediate points to be served. But it did the trick and was continued in the form of the 'Capitals Limited' and the 'Elizabethan' express well into the last years of steam haulage down the East Coast route. The gradual up-grading of the train itself was all part of the same process.

At first, only the dining cars were radically different but, as already stated, their reception was mixed and the new-style 'French' decor was not put into the ordinary stock. However, over the next few years the LNER added more new features to the train such as cocktail bars, a 'unisex' hairdressing saloon, a ladies retiring room and so forth (the LMS only countered this with a first class lounge and pretty soon abandoned the idea), but the real step forward could never come until the old eight-hour schedule (an outdated legacy from the late Victorian 'racing' trains to Scotland) was abandoned in 1932. Following this long overdue step, the LNER concentrated effort on taking full advantage of its Gresley 'Pacifics' along with their East Coast racing track, which was a far more straight and level route than the LMS could offer. Three years later, in 1935, the first of the streamliners emerged, and thereafter speed was king.

But before going on with the speed rivalry between the LMS and LNER, we must first turn to Swindon where, at long last, the GWR was beginning to awake from its post-1922 slumber. It started modestly enough in 1930 when a pair of beautifully appointed and self-contained first class saloons to the same basic styling as the 1929 'Cornish Riviera' stock were put into service. They were intended for private hire, attached to any appropriate service, and there was accommodation for about 14-15 passengers in great comfort. At one end an open saloon with two settees and two armchairs (plus a writing table and chair) gave seats for eight or nine, and this was supplemented by a conventional six-seat compartment. At the opposite end, a 14-seat dining saloon in basically Pullman style (ie individual armchairs and table lamps) was served from a central kitchen and pantry which separated the two seating areas. They were solidly traditional in decor: polished walnut panelling and beige moquette upholstery with brown and black figuring. Modernized in 1947 with newer-style windows and the compartment removed to make space for a much enlarged saloon portion, they were

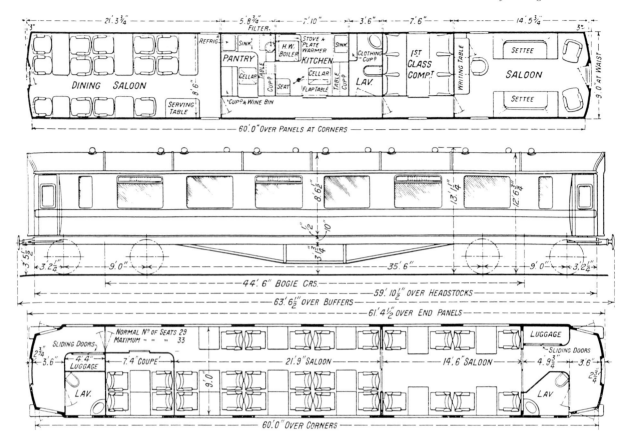

transferred to VIP and Royal service and as such remained in service well into the 1960s. Both survive in preservation.

If these two new carriages were not exactly 'general service', they did give promise of better things to come and the GWR was not long in obliging, this time with a quite superbly conceived series of luxury first-class-only saloons for the Plymouth boat train traffic. 'Super Saloons' the GWR called them, and it was no vain boast for they were probably the grandest vehicles built for general service by any of the 'Big Four' and revealed that the GWR was well able to match the LMS and LNER when it so wished. They were unashamedly up-market and aimed at the high class clientèle of the transatlantic liners. They took full advantage of the GWR structure gauge, being 9 ft 7in wide at the waist and a full 9 ft wide inside, and were mounted on standard 59 ft 10½ in chassis.

In design terms, their styling was quite new, for although they displayed the familiar bow-ends and roof treatment of this particular GWR period, they were given deeply recessed end doors set at an angle and seemingly huge windows compared with all

previous GWR stock. Within, they were clearly the GWR answer to Pullman, with whom there had been a somewhat unsuccessful experiment in 1929-30. Indeed, a quite common nickname for the Super Saloons was 'Pullmans' or 'Cunarders', both terms reflecting their usage.

The interior treatment was, however, the equal of, if not superior to, Pullman — and that is rare praise indeed. They had light French walnut veneers, highly polished, with coved ceilings, concealed lighting and, of course, table lamps. These and the individual arm-chairs, not to mention a small coupé compartment at one end only, all contributed to the Pullman feel, but the overall effect was far more spacious. Seats were usually trimmed in brown patterned moquette while gold silk damask curtains, framed pictures, dark brown wall-to-wall Wilton carpet and a multiplicity of smaller detail touches served to complete the ensemble.

Two had been finished by November 1931 and six more soon followed, all eight being named after members of the Royal Family. A 10s (50p) supplement was charged for their use which was double that which

Figure 73 *Floor plan of the 1930 GWR special saloons together with elevation and floor plans of the 1931 'Super Saloons'.*

Scale: ¹/₁₀" = 1ft

Interior view of 'Super Saloon' No 9112, looking from the smaller to the larger saloon, the coupé being at the far end (NRM collection).

'Super Saloon' No 9112 'Queen Mary' when new (NRM collection).

the LNER charged for its first Streamliner (see below). A common boat train formation was four or five saloons plus a kitchen car and brake vans, but there were many occasions when only a small number needed to be accommodated and in this instance a full kitchen was extravagant. Accordingly (in 1935) the last two ('Princess Mary' and 'Princess Elizabeth') were turned into the GWR equivalent of a Pullman Kitchen/Parlour car, the coupé area and part of the larger saloon being used for the new kitchen and pantry.

Some post-war refurbishment and redecoration took place, including new round-cornered windows with top sliders, and after the boat trains ceased to run in 1962 these splendid vehicles were then mostly used for race specials to Newbury and the like. They were also regularly used throughout their lives for numerous special occasions. No fewer than five have been privately preserved, a fine tribute to a fine set of vehicles.

Completing the GWR 'hat trick', so to speak, was the famous 'Centenary' stock for the 'Cornish Riviera Limited' in 1935, wherein at last the needs

of the ordinary fare-paying passengers were met in very fine style. Two complete sets were built, following the general outline of the Super Saloons but this time with accommodation for both classes and a full range of vehicle types. Not since the celebrated West Coast '2 pm' twelve-wheel sets appeared from Wolverton in 1908 (see Volume 1) had anything quite so good been offered to the ordinary traveller without supplementary fare. Indeed, the Centenary stock was almost identical in concept to the old WCJS train and displayed a similar series of sub-formations (for different destinations) within its make-up.

Everything was superlatively well done: light oak and walnut with blue, green or brown upholstery in the firsts; gaboon mahogany and walnut with brown upholstery in the thirds — and large curtained windows for everybody. Mirrors replaced the dreary pictures and the whole impression was of light and space. Under the circumstances it seems churlish to point out that four per side was still offered in the thirds! The dining facilities were in the form of full open thirds with tip-up seats plus kitchen firsts with luxurious fixed seating and stainless steel wall sheeting

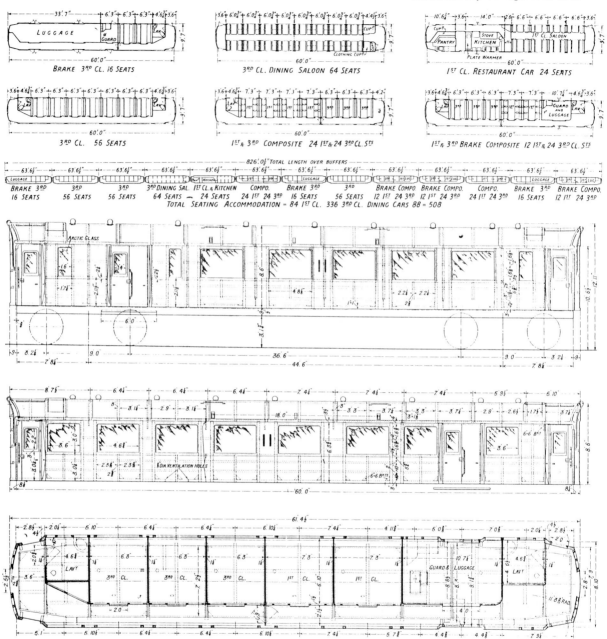

Figure 74 *Individual carriage plans along with the train formation and detailed drawings of the brake composite from the 1935 GWR 'Centenary' stock.*

Scale of main drawing: $^1/_{10}'' = 1ft$

in the kitchens.

The only disfigurement to the complete ensemble when it first went into service was the ridiculous partial streamlining applied to its locomotive in what seems to have been a rather foolish and last-minute attempt to leap on to the contemporary bandwagon. The Centenary stock, though thoroughly modern in its approach, was not in the streamlined idiom, nor

did it need to be thus promoted. Fortunately, most of this nonsense was later removed, but poor old No 6014 *King Henry VII* kept some signs of it to the very

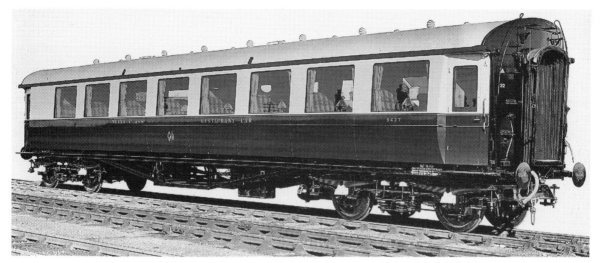

end in the form of its 'V'-fronted cab.

Little change was made to the stock, save for replacing the original large drop windows with fixed lights surmounted by top sliders, but the first class diners were, rather unfortunately, given the new swivelling seats of the earlier-mentioned Hampton conversions (see Chapter 5). It did nothing for their overall ambience and it is ironic that the only carriage to survive from this splendid train is one of these modified dining cars, now in private preservation. Even so, and in spite of its unfortunate upholstery, it still gives off much of the feel of those more leisured times.

With these three quite different sets of vehicles, the GWR went a long way to redeem itself in terms of carriage design, and it is significant that only a year later the very much more up-to-date 'Sunshine' stock (see page 80) began to appear. so in a very real sense the GWR's contribution in the 'Supertrain' era can be said to have had more significance than mere numbers might suggest. And this was certainly true of the next phase in the story, the exciting though short-lived streamline era of the late 1930s.

It is probably true to say that of all the trains ever introduced on to the British scene, those which the LNER and LMS put into service during just four short years between mid-1935 and mid-1939 caught the public imagination in a way which nothing had done before or has done since. It was a curious mixture of imperial jingoism, national pride, 'hyped' publicity, technical innovation and a renewed outburst of fierce competition between two companies, and even now it is only partly understood. What can be said is that it seems to have captured the spirit of the times, and in purely performance terms it represented the undoubted high point of the British steam railway. That it was tragically foreshortened

Above *Open third class restaurant car No 9637 from the 'Centenary' stock. Note the provision, even in the third class, of table laps in the Pullman manner (NRM collection).*

Below *Solidly 'Art Deco' but light, airy and undoubtedly stylish, the well-finished interior of a first class GWR 'Centenary' stock dining car, complete with posed staff and passengers (NRM collection).*

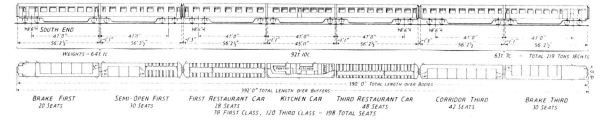

BRAKE FIRST	SEMI-OPEN FIRST	FIRST RESTAURANT CAR	KITCHEN CAR	THIRD RESTAURANT CAR	CORRIDOR THIRD	BRAKE THIRD
20 SEATS	30 SEATS	28 SEATS		48 SEATS	42 SEATS	30 SEATS

78 FIRST CLASS, 120 THIRD CLASS = 198 TOTAL SEATS

by the Second World War is only another example of the point made in the first paragraph of Chapter 1 of this volume; and we can only indulge in daydreams as to what its ultimate conclusion might have been.

The pace-setter throughout was the LNER, and the origins of the first LNER streamliner are well recorded: a conviction on the part of Gresley (aided and supported by his chief general manager, Sir Ralph Wedgwood) that a steam-hauled train could perform just as well as the newly developing diesel 'flyers' in Germany with a far greater passenger load and much better amenity. The happy coincidence of King George V's Silver Jubilee in 1935 was the chosen hook on which the whole business was to be hung; the rest, as they say, is history.

The order was placed as late as February 1935, the whole effort reaching a triumphant conclusion on 27 September 1935 when an amazing silver and grey streamlined train on its first public demonstration outing streaked along for no fewer than 43 miles at a speed greater than 100 mph, reaching a new absolute maximum of 112½ mph in the process. It went into full public service on 30 September and was an instant commercial success. It was, of course, the 'Silver Jubilee' and launched the British railways into a new speed era, a process which, with a few hiccups on the way, is still evolving in our modern 125-150 mph era.

Our concern here is with the carriages, so we must resist the temptation to dwell too long on the prime movers which helped make things possible. They were, of course, an integral part of the whole concept, but are well covered elsewhere. Suffice to say that as with most of the more significant events in railway history, it was in fact a successful combination of all the different strands of the business which helped make it possible, and here the carriage-builders played their own important part.

Articulation was chosen for weight-saving reasons — two pairs and a triplet dining set — and this enabled 198 seats (78 first, 120 third) to be offered with full dining facility in a train weight of fractionally below 220 tons. This showed an approximate 10 per cent weight saving compared with normal stock — well worth having. A contemporary plan is appended

(Figure 75), but later internal changes were made and in 1938 a central element was added to the third class corridor pair, making it a triplet and adding 35 more third class seats to the total (one of the six compartments in the new section had but five seats to allow corridor space to the adjacent vehicle). The seating was split between open and side-corridor style, but it is not known whether there was ever any seat exchanging between areas to allow more meals to be served. Generally, if one wanted to eat, one reserved in the dining portion of the train.

Although the interior arrangements were of the highest quality, there were, for example, only four seats per first class compartment, the whole train layout was thoroughly conventional and it was the exterior which stole the show. Covered in silver-grey Rexine with stainless steel trimmings and with raised stainless steel cut-out carriage insignia, nothing like it had ever been seen before. Combined with the grey-painted underframe fairings and bogie side frames, not to mention the in-fill rubber gussets between carriages, the whole train from the front of the locomotive to the back of the rear carriage gave the most unified appearance ever seen in these islands. A supplementary charge was levied (as with Pullman trains), but there is no evidence that this proved any deterrent to patronage.

It was, in fact, a bit of a 'con': it looked completely different, *de facto* it *was* completely different. But the appointments were thoroughly traditional and the coaches were built in the customary way; there was, to be fair, better sound insulation and the carriages were pressure ventilated, but one might well argue that the contemporary GWR Centenary sets were probably better finished. But speed counted, and since this was always the railway's best marketing feature (it still is, by the way) this was the emphasized aspect, and in this regard the 'Silver Jubilee' set had its problems.

For one thing, continuous high speed imposed far greater wear and tear on brake and running gear, thus adding to the cost, while in spite of beefing up the side springing to avoid sudden lurches, the articulated bogies were not wholly successful in their proclaimed property of improving stability. I never rode in the 'Silver Jubilee' set (though I did ex-

'Supertrains' of the 1930s

Figure 75 *Simplified elevations and plans of the LNER 'Silver Jubilee' train as first operated. Later, the third class side-corridor brake twin was converted into a triple unit.*

High-level view of the 'Silver Jubilee' leaving King's Cross, twin brake third leading (Herbert Collection, NRM).

First class compartment interior of the 'Silver Jubilee'; note the cushions and footstools. (LNER official, NRM).

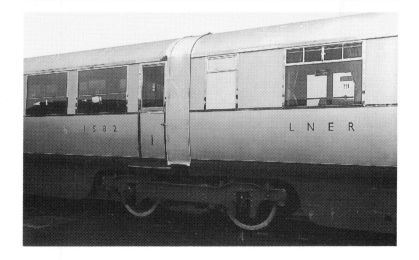

Close-up detail of the twin semi-open brake first Nos 1581/2 of the 'Silver Jubilee', showing the lower body fairings and the in-fill between the carriage units (LNER official, NRM).

perience the later LNER streamliners) but those of my friends who have tell me that it was always a bit 'lively'! Maybe this was why it never came back to full East Coast use after the war. There was only ever one set of vehicles and they were stored during the war. Afterwards, the five side-corridor vehicles were used on the rather more leisurely 'Fife Coast Express', while the dining triplet went into routine East Coast service. All carriages were withdrawn in the early 1960s.

The 'Silver Jubilee' was, for all its handicaps, the most long-lived of the streamliners and by no means a failure. It hardly ever 'failed' in service and it had no back-up set, but it was clear that changes would be needed if the idea was to be extended to other services. This was no doubt the rationale behind the rather different streamlined trains which the LNER introduced in 1937, but before coming to them, what of the LMS?

There is little doubt that the LMS was not too convinced of streamlining, or indeed any form of dedicated special train sets during the mid-1930s. It preferred instead to follow a much more general upgrading both in terms of carriage quality and overall average speeds. Thus, though it never operated the real flyers of the LNER or even the GWR, it could offer far more services at 60 mph average than the whole of the rest of the British system put together. In fact, its main contribution to the 1935 celebrations was no more than a single Stanier 4-6-0, tarted up in black and chromium plate livery!

However, there can be no doubt that the success of the 'Silver Jubilee' had caused second thoughts at Euston, and it was a fairly open secret that Gresley would probably try something equally spectacular in Coronation year (1937) and probably tackle the Anglo-Scottish traffic in the process. Now high-speed flyers to Newcastle were no worry to the LMS, but the Scottish business was different. Accordingly, therefore, in 1936 Stanier 4-6-2 *Princess Elizabeth* was duly sent stomping off at great speed from London to Glasgow, coming back the next day and comprehensively breaking the six-hour barrier in both directions with a fair-sized though by no means heavy train on each occasion. No one really believed that this had anything to do with locomotive trials *per se*, any more than they did two years later when Gresley's *Mallard* went bucketing down Stoke bank at 126 mph. Brake tests? It was all part of the contemporary game! What the 1936 LMS jaunt presaged was its entry into the streamline stakes in Coronation year.

Like Gresley, Stanier too designed a new locomotive and it was duly given the mandatory streamlining which, as far as can be judged, was designed to be as different as possible from that of the LNER. Quite naturally, it was given a suitable train to match

and they called it the 'Coronation Scot'. On closer examination, however, and fine train though it was, the LMS had cheated a bit by using mostly refurbished existing coaches, probably so as to get their train out ahead of its LNER competitor which was known to be under construction. In this they were successful and undoubtedly stole a publicity march on the LNER when, in the then obligatory press run in June 1937, *Coronation* and her new train set a fresh speed record of 114 mph — and none of the experts really believed *that* either! But the public loved this LMS re-run of the 1935 LNER 'Silver Jubilee' junketing — in a different colour too — and that was all that mattered. There was a film made and even a special piece of music (later to become far better known as the theme tune for the BBC's 'Paul Temple' radio serial).

Like the 'Silver Jubilee' set, the 'Coronation Scot' was a conventionally arranged train — see the appended plan — and the LMS built three full sets, two working and one standing in reserve. Moreover, to be fair to the LMS, its new standard Stanier stock, being totally flush-sided, was far more capable of being given the streamline 'image' than the traditional teak-bodied LNER carriages. It was done by giving all carriages a luxury finish (two per side in the firsts for example, as with the 'Silver Jubilee') and installing pressure heating and ventilation, revealed by the presence of long ventilation ducts along the roof tops of the otherwise mostly unaltered carriages. Stanier also fitted auxiliary lateral bogie bolster control gear on the end vehicles of the train to counteract the rolling side movements which these vehicles would be likely to experience. But, just as with the 'Silver Jubilee', the striking new blue and silver livery served to distract attention from technical changes and indeed from the relatively orthodox nature of the accommodation offered. And it also worked, the 'Coronation Scot' going into trouble-free service until the outbreak of the Second World War.

The sets themselves were beautifully finished in the traditional LMS fashion and advantage was taken to have each of the three trains trimmed with different upholstery, blue, green and brown being the principal themes. Each coach within the set had different timber finishes, this being the time when the LMS made great play of its use of 'selected Empire timbers', and in the first class dining areas a different finishing timber was used for each train. The variety was, therefore, considerable, and the overall effect was spacious and dignified. Two full kitchen cars undoubtedly made meal service simpler than on the 'Silver Jubilee', but the train was covering a much longer journey. All seats were reservable at a standard 2/6 (12½p) supplement, first or third class, and all told it was a more than commendable effort, though its

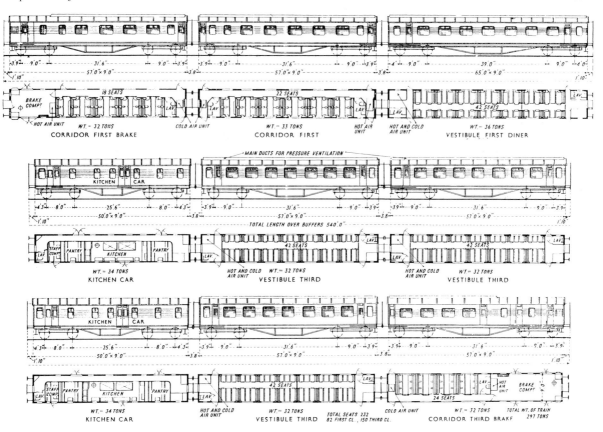

Figure 76 *Semi-detailed elevations and plans of the 1937 LMS 'Coronation Scot'. The first class was at the London end of the train. Scale: 1" = 30ft*

The northbound 'Coronation Scot' in full cry near Preston in 1937, headed by 4-6-2 No 6224 Princess Alexandra *(Eric Treacy).*

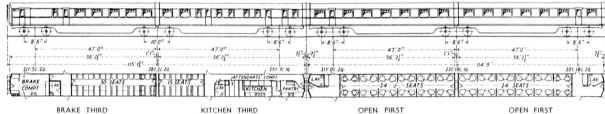

| BRAKE THIRD | KITCHEN THIRD | OPEN FIRST | OPEN FIRST |

| OPEN THIRD | KITCHEN THIRD | OPEN THIRD | BRAKE THIRD |

Top *No 30084 was one of six kitchen cars used in the 1937 'Coronation Scot' sets. They not only embodied the normal LMS compressed oil gas form of cooking but, astonishingly, were also given gas lighting as can be seen from the roof detail (BR LMR).*

Figure 77 *Schematic elevations and plans of the LNER 'Coronation' and 'West Riding Limited' (both trains were identical), together with the observation car, summer only, of the 'Coronation'. Scale: 1" = 20ft*

Below and below right *Posed front and rear views of the 'Coronation' train on the up slow line at Retford in July 1937. (LNER official, NRM).*

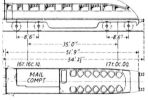

OBSERVATION SALOON

mostly 'second-hand' origins did rather prove that the LMS had been late to be convinced of the need. The company made ample amends, however, two years later (see below).

Back on the LNER, Gresley was developing his 'Silver Jubilee' ideas, and in July 1937 launched the 'Coronation' as the counterblast to the 'Coronation Scot'. He had to wait another year to get the speed record back, but it was pretty well game set and match to the LNER when it came to the train itself. Not only was it half an hour faster to Edinburgh than was the LMS train to Glasgow, but it really was brand new both in concept and decor.

Starting from the sound basis of the 'Silver Jubilee' set, Gresley produced a basic eight-car formation of articulated pairs but completely abandoned the side-corridor arrangement in favour of a fully open interior and, interestingly, gave most of the seating to the third class passengers, there being 168 of them and only 48 firsts (the 'Coronation Scot' had 82 first, 150 third). He then topped it off with a new innovation, an observation car whose shape reflected that of the 'A4' locomotive which would, of course, be at the front of the train. If truth be told, it was a pretty useless observation car since its roof came down so low at the back as to preclude much observation save that of receding sleepers, but no matter, it was different; that was the important point.

Different too was its livery: a striking two-tone blue, light 'Marlborough' blue above the waist and darker 'Garter' blue below, the latter matching the shade of the new series of locomotives built for the service. The usual 'Silver Jubilee'-type stainless steel trimmings were applied along with the bodyside fairings and so forth. Externally it was clearly from the same stable, and when running in winter without the observation car, only the exterior colours differentiated the two trains from all save the *cognoscenti*.

It is interesting, though probably quite coincidental, that both companies chose blue as their 1937 thematic image. Personally, I have some reservations about blue as an overall train colour, though it seems

to work when confined to the locomotive, and I cannot say I particularly liked the shade of either. I saw them both and they seemed rather 'cold' and unwelcoming from the exterior, an impression confirmed when BR began to use much the same carriage colours in 1965. But within the sets it was a different story, and if they shared some external similarities of colour, the pre-war LMS and LNER streamliners gave quite different impressions once through the door. Once inside the LMS train, one had a feeling of *déjà vu*; the luxury and quality was there, but one rather expected this from the best LMS trains, so there was not quite the same feeling of something 'special' which the LNER trains offered on first acquaintance.

Though I saw them from the outside in their blue form, I never actually got to ride in the LNER carriages until after the war when they had been repainted BR red and cream and were, *inter alia*, marshalled into the old 'West Riding' from Leeds to London. At 7.30 in the morning, having been up since 6.00 am to walk two miles so as to catch the connecting train to Leeds, one did not exactly take in the stock if it was painted the same colours as the rest so I did not notice anything unusual about the carriage I boarded. I can still recall my complete and utter astonishment when I walked into one of the open thirds. The first impression was that I was in the first class bit of the train, so I walked through to find the 'steerage' part. When I finally did arrive at the genuinely first class portion, I realized to my delight that I really was not dreaming and that what I had taken to be first class was indeed third; for the firsts were quite unbelievable.

I mention this personal experience because it is the nearest I can come to understanding the feeling which the 1937 streamliners probably created in their first patrons. Starting with the thirds, they were as nearly like orthodox first class dining cars as anything else. Subtle shades of fawn and green combined with excellent attention to detail and, as far as I recall, marvellous riding quality gave the next best thing to

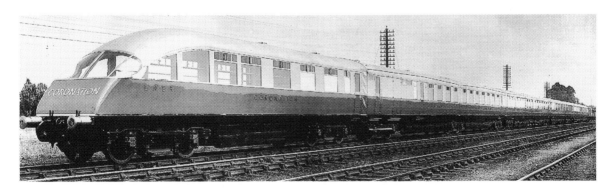

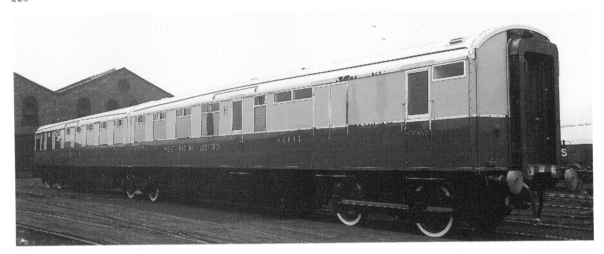

Top *Twin brake open third from the 'West Riding Limited' when new; it is probably the very same vehicle in which the author rode during the early 1950s (see text)* (LNER official, NRM).

Above *This posed view of the 'East Anglian' set behind streamlined 4-6-0 No 2859* East Anglian *itself is taken from the third class end of the train — see Figure 78* (LNER official, NRM).

Left *First class interior of the 'Coronation'* (BR ER).

Right *Contrasting interiors: open firsts and thirds of the 'East Anglian' train. Only the curtains and antimacassars really reveal the first class version, though the uncased light bulbs in the thirds were a bit cheese-paring!* (both LNER official, NRM).

Pullman travel that I can remember. What was particularly thoughtful was the way in which, when not laid up for meals, the table tops would fold along their long axis to make it much easier to reach the window seats; even the LMS did not do that and neither, it has to be said, does BR in its modern Mk III *first* class stock.

As for the LNER first class, here the 'French' influence crept back a bit, but rather toned down. Single swivelling armchairs were arranged down both sides, and each four-seat bay was divided from its next door neighbour by a full height partition which was not simply a dividing screen but also had lateral 'wings' forming a sort of alcove into which each armchair was snugly ensconced. Privacy was thus assured with all the operating convenience of the open plan layout. Even the table shape, with its scalloped edges, was designed to make eating simpler, and one could even arrange the chair at an angle so as to part face the window while enjoying the meal. They were gorgeous and deservedly popular — 'Supertrains' indeed — and there were four such sets, for as well as the 'Coronation', a further streamliner, 'The West Riding Limited', offered identical privileges, save for the observation car, to the lucky Yorkshire businessman. Two sets were branded 'Coronation', one 'West Riding Limited' and the fourth stood 'spare' for either working.

Like the 'Coronation Scot', the two new LNER trains had but two years of active life before hostilities commenced, when they all went into store. After the war the streamliners were never reinstated, their coaches being scattered about amongst the better LMS and LNER services in the early post-war era. But it was not quite the end of the streamline story, nor of the 'Supertrains'.

Flush with success at the favourable impression created by his streamlined trains, it is hardly surprising that Gresley went on to use some of these ideas elsewhere, and this time East Anglia was to be the beneficiary. Later in 1937, a very nice six-coach set of orthodox teak-panelled stock was constructed for a new fast service from London to Ipswich and Norwich, but inside it was entirely open stock in the manner of the 'Coronation' and trimmed in very similar style. The only difference was that while the third class kept all the nice features of the streamliners, the first class reverted to 2 + 1 fixed seating, but very opulent with it. No supplement was charged and although the train was anything but streamlined in outer appearance, the LNER 'dressed up' two Class 'B17' 4-6-0s in streamline casing to work the 'East Anglian', as it was called. This was almost as ersatz as the earlier GWR experiment, though at least the engine streamlining was properly carried out, although the engines lost their casings after the war.

It was another nice train, for all that.

Finally, in 1938, possibly the most surprising recipient of the new inside styling was a new 11-coach 'Hook Continental' boat train set. In it, third class became mysteriously transmogrified to second, it being a boat train one must understand, that being how they did these things on the other side of the Channel. It was in many ways the best of the bunch, for although encased within conventional teak-bodied exteriors, it combined the best features of both the 'Silver Jubilee' and 'Coronation' sets in offering a mixture of side-corridor and open seating in both classes, the side-corridors having two per side first class seating and the open carriages being of the 'Coronation' type with individual swivelling armchairs in the first class. The second class was identical to the third class of the East Coast sets and there was a mandatory pair of first class Pullmans tucked in between the first class section and the luggage van.

The surprising thing was that all this luxury was provided for a journey which only lasted 1½ hours, and while there was every reason to attract boat train passengers, one doubts not that the patrons of the 'Flying Scotsman', still performing its non-stop daily

pilgrimage with more orthodox day coaches, would have found the new 'Hook' set far more to their liking. One also wonders how much trade the two Pullmans did, given the superb quality of Gresley's open firsts. We were not given much time to find out, for war intervened less than a year after this very fine train was introduced. Boat trains were stopped and the 'Hook' seconds became firsts for the duration; but at least — and unlike the streamliners — it did go back to its proper use after the war was over, the former seconds reverting to their original status, and most of its carriages lasted until circa 1963-4.

While all this jockeying for position was going on between the LMS and LNER, the GWR made no moves to introduce further dedicated sets after its Centenary stock and the Southern seemed not to want to take part at all. Yet the latter railway did make one small gesture which is worth recording in the con-

Figure 78 *Plans of the 'East Anglian' of 1937 (above) and the 'Hook Continental' of 1938 (below), Gresley's last two 'Super-trains'.*

Scale: 1" = 30ft (upper) and approx 1" = 50ft (lower)

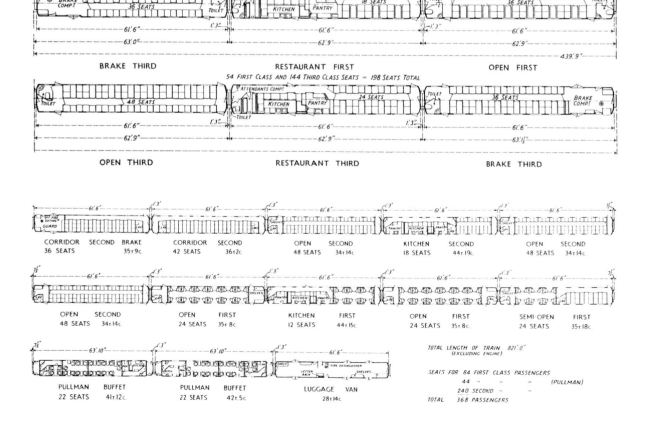

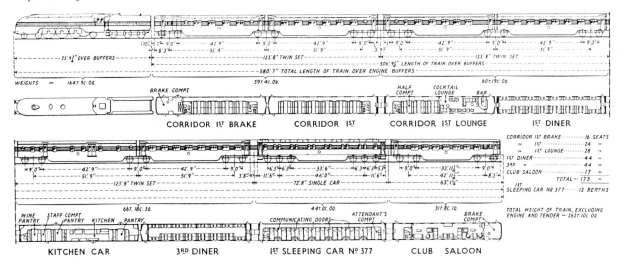

Figure 79 *Simplified elevations and plans of the LMS 1939 'Coronation Scot' set which toured North America. The operational sets in Britain would have seen a further pair of twin thirds in the position occupied by the sleeping and club cars of the American train.*

Scale: 1" = 50ft

text of Bulleid's remarkable post-war efforts to up-grade SR main-line services (see Chapter 14). In July 1938, a year after he had taken over from Maunsell, Oliver Bulleid performed a major face lift on a set of Maunsell corridors for the Bournemouth, Wey-mouth and Swanage service. It was hardly a high-speed flyer, but the renovation was of a major nature. Away went all the dowdy finishes and both new decor and new trimming materials were used, along with numerous technical improvements. The dominant note was simplicity and the tones were subdued, but the light Rexine walls and generally bright interiors gave a pleasing effect. More controversial was the shrieking Malachite green livery which the newly refurbished train sported, devised, according to the Southern, '...to give the stock a brighter appearance without being garish'.

Had it not been for the war, the events on the Southern and in East Anglia in 1938 would merely have been a pause in the greater Anglo-Scottish scenario, for the LMS, perhaps smarting under the fact that its 'Coronation Scot' train had been even-tually upstaged by Gresley's trains, not to mention *Mallard*'s speed record, was determined to build a real show-stopper for the 'Coronation Scot' service and introduce it in 1940. The catalyst was the decision, taken late in 1937, to accept an invitation to exhibit a complete 'Coronation Scot' train at the New York World's Fair in 1939, coupled with the realization that it would be risky, for operational reasons, to send the 'spare' 1937 set. It was therefore decided to build a new design of train and exhibit this in New York.

Early in 1938 it was then realized that to have sim-ply one new train of a different type and capacity would make things very confusing for the seating reservation clerks when it went into normal service

alongside the old-type sets, so two more new-style sets were also ordered, the intention being that when all three were in traffic, the 1937 sets would take over the working of the 'Royal Scot' service. The back-ground debate regarding the formation and construc-tion of the new train was very complex and occupied much of 1938, and since it has been fully described elsewhere,* need not be repeated here. Suffice to say that the 1939 'Coronation Scot', or at least such of it as was built before hostilities commenced, was the last of the real British streamliners; it would, argua-bly, have been the best of them all, yet it never 'turned a wheel in anger'.

The concept embodied Stanier's form of articula-tion, using a double pivot (see page 197), and the whole formation was envisaged as being five articulated pairs plus an extra 'loose' third at busy times. In the event this was to be slightly modified in the second and third sets (which actually *were* built) when it was decided that the one kitchen car would be an indepen-dent vehicle rather than articulated to its third class open diner. The actual train which went to America was three 'normal' pairs from the first set, essentially the first class portion plus the kitchen/third twin, together with a first class staff sleeping car (modified

* *LMS Coaches, an Illustrated History:* D. Jenkinson and R.J. Essery, OPC 1977.

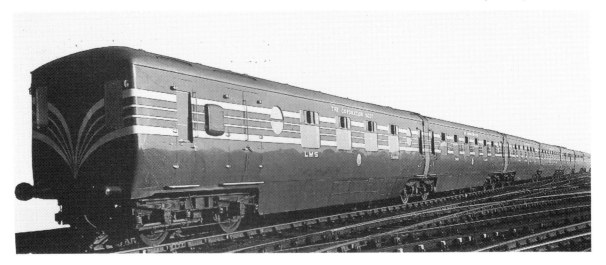

to match the train purely for appearance sake 'on tour') and a special 'Club Car' brake to bring up the rear — again largely for the purposes of the tour. The remaining cars for the first set and the two other sets would be built in time for the full 1940 service.

The train which did go to North America, though incomplete in relation to its planned full formation, was more than sufficient, nevertheless, to give a clear indication of what the new LMS streamliner would look like — and it was breathtaking. This time there was no half-hearted reworking of old stock; just about everything in it was new and, like all the best streamliners whether in Britain or abroad, it started from the outside. The basic 1937 striped livery was retained, but was now rendered in LMS crimson lake with gold stripes and black/vermilion edging, and the whole effect was vastly more opulent-looking in consequence. The brake ends were 'blind' (ie without gangways), thus giving the stylists a chance to terminate the livery properly on the back of the train, and though no observation car was, apparently, ever contemplated, the solution which was adopted came off quite well. Lower bodyside fairings between the bogies and rubber in-fills between all carriages (across which was carried the striping) completed the exterior.

Constructionally, the sets were also very up to date, embodying all-steel body framing and centrally trussed underframes of a similar type to those which had been used on the 1937 excursion sets (see page 79). Though clearly still of Stanier pattern, the carriages also had a slightly different body profile of somewhat 'sharper' aspect, and opaque circular toilet windows were provided, matched by similarly shaped clear windows on the corridor sides. Within the train, the LMS had resolved to retain a mixture of open and corridor styling, as with the 1937 sets,

Left *The American tour train from the first class end, showing the 'blind' brake end arrangement* (BR LMR).

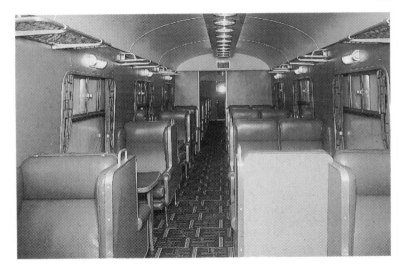

Below left and right *First class compartment and dining car interiors of the American set: not, perhaps, quite as adventurous as the LNER, but solidly LMS in tradition and of superlative quality. The post-war open stock built to complete the order reverted to traditional carriage cloth rather than leather* (both BR LMR).

but gave the customers even more space — single seats on either side of the aisle in even the third class at the gangway ends of the dining cars — while the compartment carriages were lavish in the extreme. Each carriage was 59 ft 5 in long, yet there were never more than six compartments to a unit, even in the third class, and the firsts were so spacious that only one lavatory per carriage was provided.

All told, it was one of the most extravagant concepts that had ever come out of a British carriage works — Derby in this case — but it was all to no avail. Though it created a sensation at the New York Fair, the American set languished in the USA until after the war (the engine came home in 1942) and it was well into BR days before the last of the part-finished stock (abandoned as it stood in 1939) was finally completed. Even then, nobody wanted them. They were far too extravagant of space for the crowded post-war austerity years and they drifted off

into general service, just like their 1937 predecessors. Even the trimming of the post-war examples reverted to routine standard finishes, though nothing could change their basic character.

So it was that we were not only denied the chance to see the last of the British streamliners of the pre-war era in all its glory, but we also never saw any of them again in the splendid form they had once displayed. But to those of us who knew a bit about carriages, it was always rather nice to find one of the fugitives in one's train; and just as I had been delighted to find the Gresley stock on my early morning train from Leeds to Kings Cross in 1951, it was with just the same thrill, after I had boarded a train at Carstairs as late as 1966, that I realized I was riding in one of those wonderfully extravagant corridor thirds (now seconds) from the ill-fated 1939 'Coronation Scot' train. One only had to close one's eyes, just a little...

12. *Status quo ante* — Pullman and the Royal Trains

There were perhaps two principal areas during the company period where things never seemed to change in any sort of meaningful way from their established pre-1923 patterns. They scarcely need be specified, for the chapter head says all, but, as usual, their interest far transcends their absolute numbers. And there is some further logic in grouping Pullman and Royal vehicles together in the same chapter, for not only was Pullman travel regally styled in itself, it was also the monarchy's first alternative choice to the Royal Train proper if circumstances decreed that the latter was either unavailable or incapable of traversing a particular route.

In the context of the grouped railways, it is difficult to know where to resume the Pullman story, for the 'markers' in its own line of development did not coincide with those of the greater amalgamations. In fact, the real turning point for Pullman was a few years ahead of the grouping and this seems a more logical start point. The key year was 1915 when Davison Dalziel, the owner of the private Pullman Company, converted it into a public operation and linked it, almost unknown at the time, with the Wagons-Lits company to form the covert association hinted at on page 212 of Volume 1. From this time onwards, in the British context, Pullman was, of course, as also explained in Volume 1, a wholly daytime operation, having long-abandoned its earlier overnight origins.

In 1915, though Pullman had recovered from its early twentieth century low point, it was only really firmly established on a few British lines on which it ran a modest number of cars. These were mostly operated individually in normal trains of the LB & SCR, SE & CR and, very recently in 1914, the Caledonian Railway, whereon Pullman took over most non-West Coast Joint Stock catering operations with a fine fleet of new cars. There were also two Pullman Buffet cars on the Metropolitan, but a far older agreement with the LSWR had gradually declined as the latter company put its own restaurant cars into service. Dalziel's new 1915 company, therefore, owned but 74 cars scattered through the country. Yet before long it was to re-establish itself in no uncertain way.

The catalyst appears to have been the speedy post-1918 re-establishment of a desire to travel in luxury and style, a fact accurately foreseen by Dalziel but which appears to have taken many railways by surprise. Never one to miss a trick, Pullman was ready and waiting, and this was to presage some ten years

of rapid expansion between 1922 and 1932. It was naturally allied to some very shrewd marketing and, by no means the least of the factors, some considerable changes in carriage building technique as far as Pullman was concerned.

Dealing first with some of the new services, the GER had been persuaded to operate a number of first and third class cars between 1920 and 1923, but this did not have any lasting quality save for some long-term survivors which were to be found on the Harwich boat trains for many a long year. Instead, the GER cars were mostly transferred to what was now the GNR section of the new LNER where they met with a much more widespread acceptance, the 'Harrogate Pullman Limited' (later to develop into the 'Queen of Scots') and the 'West Riding Pullman' (later the 'Yorkshire Pullman') being probably the best known. At the same time, Pullman's association with the former LB & SCR and SE & CR was continued and strengthened via the new Southern Railway both in the traditional boat train mode and in a more general sense on many other express services. This was to culminate in the re-establishment of Pullman services on the former LSWR in the shape of Ocean Liner specials to Southampton and, of course, the famous 'Bournemouth Belle'. The Pullman association with the Southern probably reached its pre-war apogee in 1933 with the introduction of all-Pullman EMUs for the 'Brighton Belle' service and, of course, the general incorporation of individual Pullmans in the 6PUL EMU sets already mentioned in the context of the Southern's main-line electrification schemes.

Meantime, up in Scotland, though the LMS was never wildly excited about Pullmans, there was some ten years or more of the Caledonian contract to run, and the LMS seems to have taken the view that it might just as well exploit the situation until the contract could be decently terminated. Accordingly, some Pullman services began to operate in ex-GSWR and ex-HR territory. Thus, even before the Brighton electrics, Pullman had broken out from its SE redoubt and though non-existent in all GWR and most LMS territory, its influence could now claim to extend from the south coast to Inverness and Aberdeen, and it even had a toe-hold in Ireland.

It seems, in retrospect, that two main factors were responsible for this, apart from Dalziel's sheer persistence. One was the 'traditional' nature of the service offered, clearly very popular; second was the extension of Pullman cars to the third class passenger, albeit with a supplementary charge. This too dated back to 1915 when, apart from boat trains and a few suburban survivors, second class was all but dead and third class took its place on most railways. There may well have been a bit of self righteous tut-tutting from some patrons about this democratization of what had hitherto been a very exclusive first class domain, but the proof of the pudding came quickly enough when the new LNER Pullman service of 1923 was seen to have no fewer than four third class cars in its six-car formation — and this was to fashionable Harrogate, of all places! These cars were even given 2 + 1 seating in the third class and may well have been a part cause of the LNER and LMS retention of this form for their own third class diners. South of the Thames, many third class Pullmans remained a little cramped with 2 + 2 seating, including the 'Brighton Belle'; but then, so too did their company equivalents.

Turning now to the developments in Pullman carriage building, the first significant change was revealed in 1922 when, in announcing some new cars for both the Caledonian and LB & SCR, Pullman was able to claim, at least so far as contemporary accounts record: 'A noticeable feature of these new cars is their low tare as compared with the car of standard Pullman construction, and the reduction in weight has been effected by using all-steel underframes and bogies, which permits of the body framing being made considerably lighter.' So much for the claim, but as was always its wont, Pullman was often economical with the truth when it came to announcing 'new' cars! The bodies were indeed new, and the vehicles were mostly made by outside contractors, but the underframes and bogies were usually from recovered First World War ambulance carriages which had been sold off at low price; a quick glance at the axlebox faces below the floor of these new cars was often quite revealing, as indeed was their length, the 57 ft of the GWR and LNWR being particularly well represented.

Several dozen of these recovered underframes were thus re-used during 1921-2, but no matter, the end product was stylish enough and the underframes were often of the more modern angle-trussed type which, within a year or two, all railways save the LNER had adopted and which Pullman too was eventually to standardize (see below). Bodies, of course, remained wood-framed and traditional, right down to the vertical matchboarding below the waist rail, and many of the new cars came out with British Standard gangways and screw couplings rather than the better Pullman type. This mostly reflected the services to which they would be put. Interiors too remained traditional and, as usual, almost every single car had its own distinctive decor.

Hardly had this early post-war augmentation been completed when in 1923 Pullman came up with its

'Maid of Kent' seen (left) at Preston Park in 1955 was the second car of that name, the first having also been from the identical batch of 1921 cars built on recovered 57-foot LNWR underframes. The first 'Maid' was downgraded to third class in 1948 and sister car 'Formosa' then took over the name. On the right is the twelve-wheel 'Orpheus' dating from 1914. Both cars were withdrawn in 1960 and both are now preserved (B.C. Lane collection).

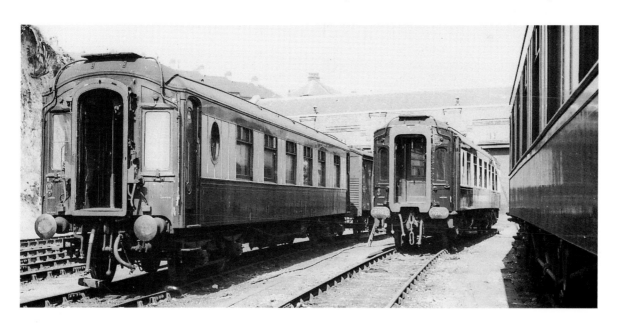

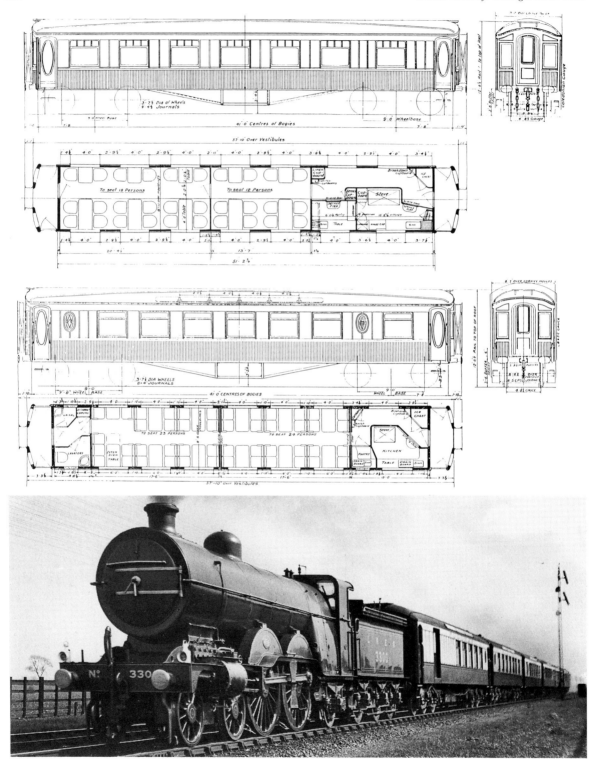

own design of underframe and bogie, in the form of a small clutch of four catering cars for the former Caledonian lines. These saw an extension of length to 63 ft 10 in overall (the frames were slightly shorter at 62 ft 4 in because of the bowed-end body form), and a brand new 10-foot wheelbase bogie with very substantial steel plate sideframes and a massive 13 in wide bolster carried by no fewer than five, differentially tensioned helical springs at each end. While it is always very dangerous to generalize about Pullmans, this bogie and underframe became a sort of standard type for all subsequent new eight-wheel cars for many years. As usual, most of them were con-tractor-built but they were always designed by Pullman and are generally referred to as 'K' type cars.

Not that Pullman had quite finished with the traditional form of body construction described in the previous volume, or 'American'-style bogies for that matter. When the new 'Harrogate Pullman' was introduced, also in 1923, Messrs Clayton obtained the contract for the eight new third class carriages and built only two to the new style, the remaining six being of the old integral wood body style with compensating beam six-wheel bogies; they were to be not only the last twelve-wheel Pullmans to be built in Britain but also the last to display the traditional

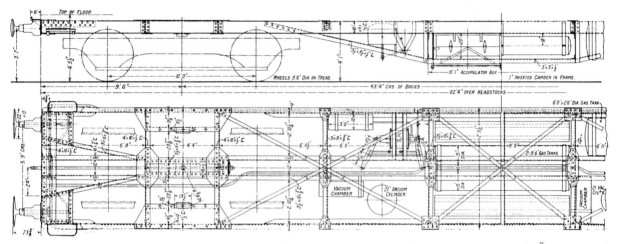

Above left Figure 80 *Elevations and plans of typical Pullmans of the early 1920s utilizing recovered underframes, in this case 57-foot examples of GWR origin. The upper arrangement shows one of two identical dining cars 'Lady Nairn' and 'Bonnie Jean' for the Caledonian in 1922, and the lower example is a third class parlour/ buffet car of which three (Nos 18, 20 and 21) were built for the Brighton line, also in 1922.*

Scale: 2mm = 1ft

Left *The down 'Harrogate Pullman' in the mid-1920s, headed by former GNR 4-4-2 No 3300. Two twelve-wheelers lead the formation of which the leading brake is not one of the types built in 1923. The third car seems to be a 'K' type. (Ransome-Wallis Collection, NRM).*

Right Figure 81 *Pullman standard angle-trussed underframe and 10 ft wheelbase bogie, adopted for 'K' series cars from 1923 onwards.*

Scales: 4mm and 7mm = 1ft

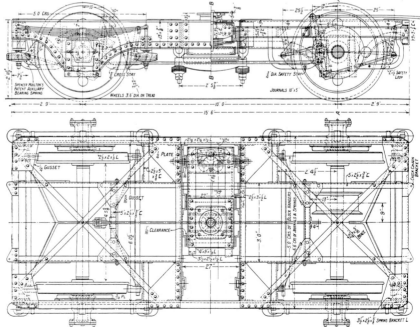

American form of body construction. Of course, such was the longevity of Pullmans that it was to be decades before the older-style cars, be they eight- or twelve-wheel, were to finally disappear. The first class cars for the Harrogate service were to the new 'K'

Below Figure 82 *Floor plans of new cars built* inter alia *for the 'Harrogate Pullman' service of 1923, of which only the first class examples were given the new-type underframes.*

Scale: 2mm = 1ft

Right Figure 83 *This series of elevations and plans shows typical 'K' type Pullman cars from 1923-4. From top to bottom they are as follows:*
a) One of the three first class dining cars for LMS (ex-Caledonian area) service ('Meg Dods', 'Lass o' Ballochmyle' and 'Mauchline Belle').
b) Third class parlour/buffet, No 80, also for the LMS.
c) First class kitchen/parlour cars for the 'White Pullman' service of the SR, later the 'Golden Arrow', typically 'Marjorie', 'Geraldine' or 'Viking'.

Scales: 2mm = 1ft

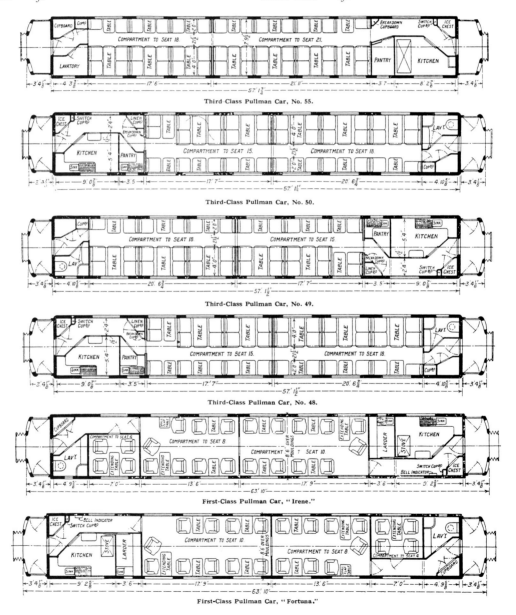

Third-Class Pullman Car, No. 55.

Third-Class Pullman Car, No. 50.

Third-Class Pullman Car, No. 49.

Third-Class Pullman Car, No. 48.

First-Class Pullman Car, "Irene."

First-Class Pullman Car, "Fortuna."

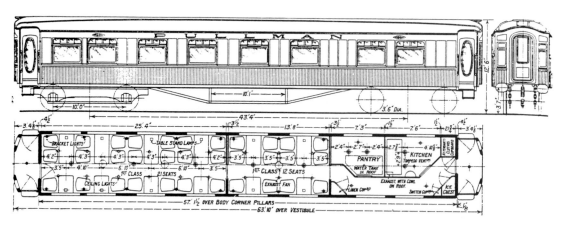

General Arrangement of First-Class Pullman Dining Car.

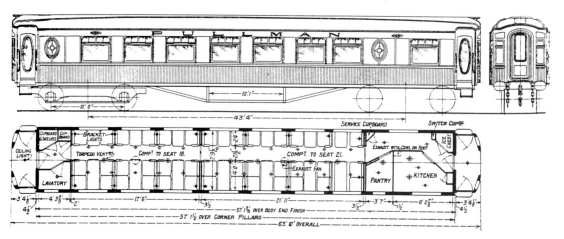

General Arrangement of Third-Class Pullman Buffet Car.

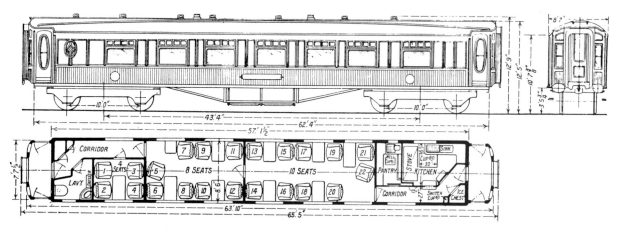

General View and Drawing of New Pullman Car " Marjorie."

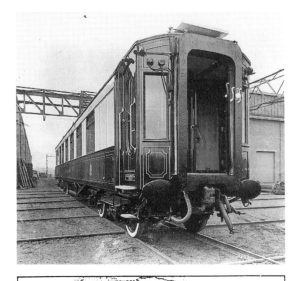

type with separate steel-framed chassis and new-type bogies.

The next recipient, in 1924, of the new-style Pullman cars with separate underframes was to be the traditional boat train operation from Victoria to Dover, and it came in the form of a brand new all-Pullman set which introduced the umber and cream Pullman livery on to former SE & CR metals for the first time, previous SE & CR-operated cars having been finished in the equally dignified all-lake livery to match the SE & CR trains. For a while, it was to be known as the 'White Pullman' in consequence of this change, though its later and much better known official name was, of course, 'Golden Arrow' (from 1929); thereafter all British Pullmans were to carry these colours until well into BR days. This, in fact, represented a slight change of emphasis and this might be the appropriate point at which to address the matter of Pullman's famous British colour scheme.

Until 1924, the Pullmans operating on the LB & SCR and SE & CR had been finished in livery colours which matched that of the company operating the service, as in fact had those on the Metropolitan. Elsewhere, of course, Pullmans generally operated as a fixed set where their own livery made them stand out or, in the case of the Caledonian, on a railway whose livery was not very different from that of Pullman. On this basis, one might have expected, save perhaps for all-Pullman trains, that after the grouping, individually operated cars would have been painted in, say, Southern green or LMS crimson, but it was not so. Thus it was that the old Brighton line colour scheme came to stand for Pullman and the new unified colours did permit Pullman to switch its cars about at will between services without too many folk being aware of the fact. In the early days, the colours were dark brown and just off-white, but when this gave way in 1929 to the version with brown on the headboard as well as below the waist, the brown was lightened and the off-white became a genuine cream. Perhaps 'plain chocolate and spilt milk' giving way to 'milk chocolate and

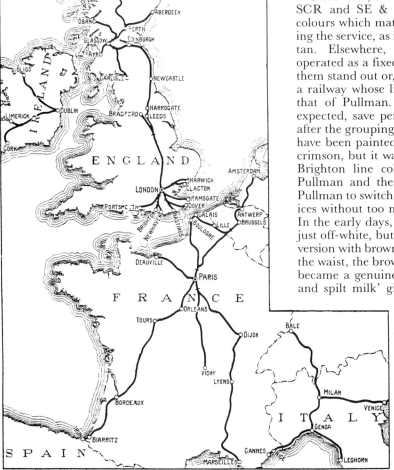

Above left *This detailed end view of first class 'K' type parlour car 'Rainbow' when new in 1925 shows one of the two cars sold to the Wagons-Lits company which did* not *come back in 1928 — see text* (NRM collection).

Figure 84 *Map showing the extent of Pullman influence by 1928.*

cream' would be a reasonable way to envisage the difference!

The next few years were to see a considerable enlargement of the Pullman fleet. Getting on for another 50 or so were built down to 1928, all being to the new standard constructional form, many of which went to their traditional SR haunts, others going into LNER and LMS use and a handful for Ireland. Ten of them actually spent their first few years of life in Wagons-Lits service on the Nice to Milan run. Eight came back to Britain in 1928, technically having been sold to and bought back from the CIWL, by which date the British Pullman fleet was probably three times its 1915 size, such had been the rapid rate of expansion after 1918.

The key year turned out to be 1928, for a variety of reasons. Firstly, even though the vast bulk of the post-1918 fleet had come from outside builders, it was now clear that the old SE & CR premises at Long-

hedge could no longer cope with the extra volume of repair, maintenance and re-building of cars which this much larger fleet entailed. In consequence, Pullman opened its new works at Preston Park, Brighton, and the older premises became a supply depot for the various 'on car' requisites such as linen, silver, etc. Secondly, the year also marked the espousal of all-steel construction for new Pullman cars with a batch of no fewer than 29 being ordered from the

These views show typical 'K' type cars in pre- and post-1929 livery respectively. First class kitchen/parlour car 'Geraldine' was built in 1924 as part of the 'White Pullman' batch. The opposite side is shown in Figure 83. Third class kitchen/parlour No 107 dated from 1927 and was built as first class 'Kathleen'. It was downgraded to third class for the 'Yorkshire Pullman' service in 1946, but its window spacing reveals its true origins and it was reinstated in this role as 'Thetis' in 1962 — such were the ways of Pullman! (Author's collection).

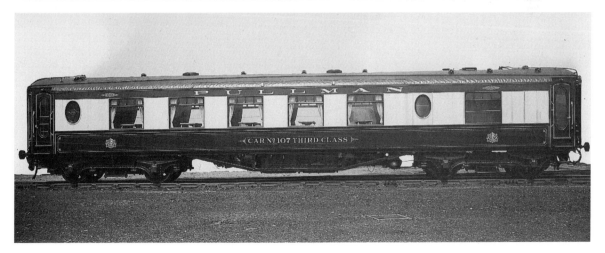

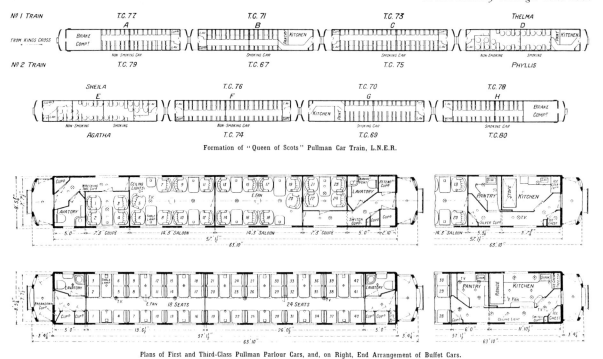

Formation of "Queen of Scots" Pullman Car Train, L.N.E.R.

Plans of First and Third-Class Pullman Parlour Cars, and, on Right, End Arrangement of Buffet Cars.
NEW ALL-STEEL PULLMAN CARS FOR SERVICE ON THE L.N.E.R.

Metropolitan C W & F Co Ltd.

In a very real sense, this was a reversion to the original Pullman form of coach construction, save that it was now in steel not wood, for the cars had no separate underframes, being of the integral box-girder structural form rather like those of the LMS and LNER introduced a year or two earlier (see Chapter 2). In consequence, they displayed no

separate trussing but, like the LMS/LNER coaches, they did retain their own 'company' bogies, the new 'Pullman' 10 foot wheelbase type. Moreover, their bodies were fashioned in the entirely traditional shape and only their smooth-sided panelling below the waist really gave the game away.

They were extremely handsome cars and became very familiar to those, like myself, whose Pullman

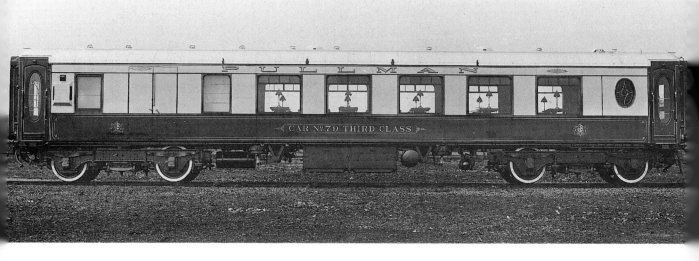

experience was mostly confined to the services operated by the LNER, later BR(ER). In fact, they were in large part built for this very purpose, no fewer than 16 of the original 29 being for the re-equipment of the old 'Harrogate Pullman' which now worked right through to Scotland under that most resonant sounding of all train names, 'Queen of Scots'. Never has a train been better titled or, on its demise, more sadly mourned by its patrons.

As a tangential aside (somehow or other, discussion of Pullman cars always serves to remind one of these things!) what in the event turned out to be my last ride in a 'slab-sided' Pullman car in normal service was in one of these coaches. I had returned from overseas duty one April morning in 1962 and hoped to catch the first train to Harrogate. The best bet was the 'Queen', but I had no reservation. On presenting myself at the booking office it was suggested that as the train was in the platform, I might try my luck with the conductor. His response to my enquiry went something like this: 'I am afraid we only have a few second class seats left, sir, and they are all in the brake-ended car.' He, of course, knew that by then most of the train had been re-equipped with the new 1960 Metro-Cammell cars of BR Mk I profile (see Volume 3) but that the brake ends were of the old type. So too did I, and I told him that I did not mind at all — in fact I preferred it that way for the proffered car was a 'proper' Pullman. I shall never forget the broad smile on his face which greeted that remark, nor the fact that he 'found' me one of the few remaining 'singles' in the car. Apart from the fare itself, everything else about that trip was first class too! I never encountered another such car in regular service.

While on the subject of tangential asides, for it was

to prove little more than a minor episode, it is perhaps worth mentioning that the majority of the other 1928 all-steel Pullmans were first used on the one and only attempt by Pullman to infiltrate GWR territory. In 1929, Pullman had persuaded a reluctant GWR to allow its cars on to the prestigious Plymouth Ocean Liner Expresses to meet the expectations of the wealthy visitors; but such trains, though popular, only ran on demand and could not keep a set of cars fully employed. Thus there also began in 1929 the 'Torquay Pullman' to give some more work to at least one set of cars. The GWR hardly helped matters, for it had only accepted Pullmans in the first place because of passenger pressure and did not really want them on its lines at all. Pullman gave up the unequal struggle in 1930 and the GWR was obliged, instead, to build its own luxury carriages to meet the demands of its transatlantic clientele, the Super Saloons of 1931, described in the previous chapter. As has been seen, these carriages, though of peerless quality, were a pretty well unashamed crib of Pullman's ideas.

A consequence of this unprofitable move was that Pullman transferred its new cars to the rival Southampton boat train services of the Southern Railway and, in 1931, supplemented these with the new 'Bournemouth Belle', again to increase car utilization rather in the manner of the abortive Torquay service. This time, however, it nicely complemented the Pullman boat specials by giving a regularly scheduled all-year service to Southampton, its only other stop. Both the new 'Belle' and the boat trains became deservedly popular, but when only a few more all-steel Pullmans followed in 1930-31 to augment them, it may have seemed as though Pullman's post-1918 expansion was almost complete. In the pure locomotive-hauled sense this was indeed the case; but there

Figure 85 *Typical floor plans of the 'all-steel' Pullmans of 1928, including the train plan for the 'Queen of Scots'.*

Left *'All-steel' third class brake parlour car No 79 was one of four built in 1928 for the 'Queen of Scots', all of which were retained on the East Coast after 1960 to work with the new Metro-Cammell cars. It was in one of these cars that the author made his last journey in a 'proper' Pullman — see text. No 79 is now preserved by the North York Moors Railway (Author's collection).*

Right *The short-lived GWR experiment: The inaugural trip of the 'Torquay Pullman Limited' at Paddington in July 1929, probably one of the last times most of these cars ran in the older livery (NRM collection).*

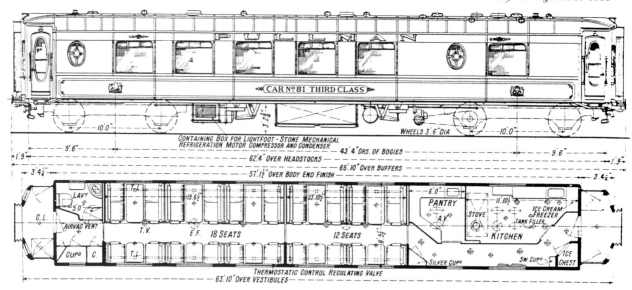

Elevation and Plan showing General Arrangement of All-Steel Pullman Car for Southern Railway Services.

Scale: $^1/10''$ = 1ft

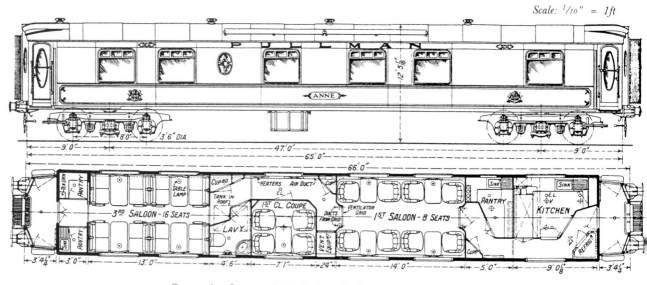

Composite first- and third-class Pullman car, express units

was to be one final flourish, part of which was eventually to become world famous.

I refer, of course, to the celebrated 'Brighton Belle' EMU sets, built in 1932 and first put to use in 1933; but they were only one element of Pullman's involvement with Southern Electric, the other being the insertion of single Pullman cars into the 6PUL units. Both these developments have been considered in their main context in Chapter 6, but the cars themselves were left out of the discussion largely because they actually represented the culmination of ten years

of Pullman evolution and are best considered here. In fact, they formed a logical continuation of the all-steel cars of 1928-31, being structurally very similar. However, their EMU form caused two new types to be introduced.

The first of these was, of course, the driving motor unit of the 5BEL sets whose cab end made it unique. This apart, however, it was a conventional enough parlour third behind the cab end. The other three cars of the 5BEL sets were a single parlour third and two kitchen/parlour firsts, the kitchens of the latter being so arranged as to separate the first and third class portions, thus being able to service both types of accommodation. Two five-car sets would normally work the service in multiple, the third being kept spare, but it was by no means unusual for a single five-car set to operate solo. At first, the train retained the 'Southern Belle' name of its steam-hauled predecessor, but it was renamed the 'Brighton Belle' in 1934 and thus it remained for the rest of its long life.

The second new type of Pullman was the composite kitchen/parlour car for use in the 6PUL sets, of which no fewer than 23 were built in 1932, probably

Figure 86 *Detailed elevations and plans of 'all-steel' Pullmans:*
a) Third class dining car No 81 for general catering service on Southern Railway boat trains and the like.
b) Composite dining car 'Anne', one of 23 built in 1932 for the 6PUL EMU sets (see page 133).

Right *Five-car 'Brighton Belle' Pullman set No 2053 near Hayward's Heath sometime before 1937 when the set was renumbered 3053. From the front, the cars are: third class No 93; third class No 85; first class 'Mona'; first class 'Gwen'; third class No 92. Note the very slight inward batter of the sides between waist and cantrail, a distinctive feature of the 5BEL sets (BR SR).*

Figure 87 *Train and individual car plans of the 5BEL sets.*

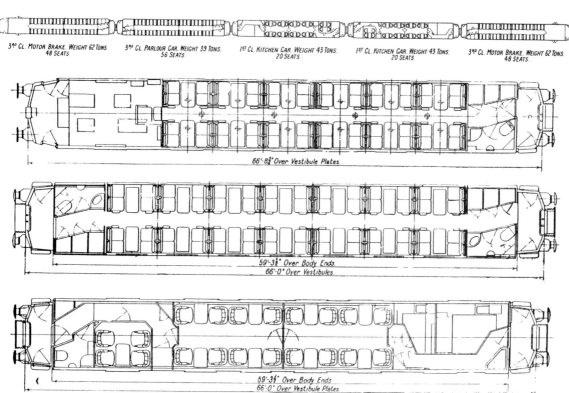

3ᴿᴰ CL. MOTOR BRAKE. WEIGHT 62 TONS. 48 SEATS. 3ᴿᴰ CL. PARLOUR CAR. WEIGHT 39 TONS. 56 SEATS. 1ˢᵀ CL. KITCHEN CAR. WEIGHT 43 TONS. 20 SEATS. 1ˢᵀ CL. KITCHEN CAR. WEIGHT 43 TONS. 20 SEATS. 3ᴿᴰ CL. MOTOR BRAKE. WEIGHT 62 TONS. 48 SEATS.

66'-8¾" Over Vestibule Plates.

59'-3¾" Over Body Ends.
66'-0" Over Vestibules.

59'-3¾" Over Body Ends.
66'-0" Over Vestibule Plates.

establishing some sort of Pullman record for an individual type design. They were ingeniously contrived 28-seaters (12 first plus 16 third) with a kitchen at one end and the usual Pullman-style lavatory separating the two classes. As such, a 28-seat composite was no great leap forward in seating capacity, but the ingenuity arose from the fact that the first class portion still managed to retain the space-consuming single armchair layout on either side of the aisles combined with a typical Pullman-style coupé as well. This was undoubtedly made easier by arranging the third class 2 + 2, a feature also found in the 5BEL sets. It was a little cramped in space when all places were laid for a meal, but the relatively short 1-1½ hour trips probably made it acceptable in a way that would not have been so in the longer-distance locomotive-hauled Pullmans.

These 1932 EMU Pullmans marked not only the end of a ten year period of evolution and expansion, but they were also the last new British Pullmans for almost two decades. Meantime, the others went on for several more years until the outbreak of war, the only main change being the LMS buy-out of the Scottish contract, and from 1934 the erstwhile Pullmans were added to the already large LMS fleet of dining cars. They were soon to become as familiar in Scotland in their new crimson lake livery as they had been in Pullman's own colours. As a result, Pullman there-

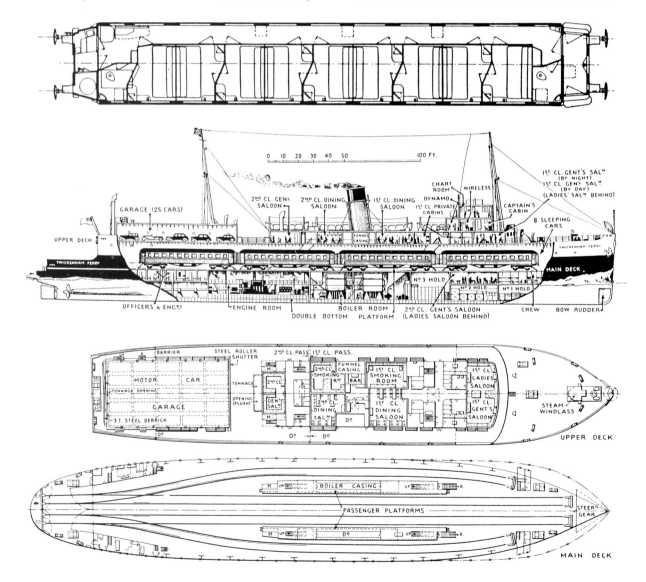

Figure 88 *'Night Ferry' sleeping car plan, and the arrangement of the specially built* Twickenham Ferry *used for the inaugural service in 1936.*

Wagons-Lits Type 'F' 'Night Ferry' sleeping car No 3805 at Victoria, circa *1955. Note especially the combination of traditionally styled compensated beam bogies with roller bearing axleboxes* (T.J. Edgington).

after became an operation associated with only two of the 'Big Four' companies, the LNER and SR. During the war years, both these companies paid Pullman an annual compensation to keep the cars intact in storage ready for immediate use thereafter, and this was an undoubted reason why there was such a quick reinstatement of Pullmans in those difficult post-1945 years.

There was, however, one further development of Pullman-style travel before the war intervened, and this was undoubtedly the consequence of the 'hidden' arrangement between Pullman and Wagon-Lits. It had always been the dream of both organizations to forge closer links between Britain and Europe, and in 1936 these achieved reality when there were put into service some overnight Wagons-Lits sleeping cars between London and Paris. They utilized the rail ferry boat terminals at Dover and Dunkerque and were put on board specially built ships designed to carry rail vehicles. The service was known as the 'Night Ferry' and, with the daytime 'Golden Arrow', gave Pullman and Wagons-Lits a near monopoly of the upper end of the cross-Channel trade in pre-airline days.

The sleeping cars themselves were built in France and followed traditional Wagons-Lits style, complete with the famous blue livery and its proliferation of headboard lettering and bold CIWL 'monogram' on the centre of the lower panels. Bilingual inscriptions appeared on the exterior and multi-lingual instructions inside the cars. The only things which distinguished them from their continental cousins were their overall size (small enough to pass the restricted British loading gauge) and their all-metal construction inside and out, this being to minimize fire risk, especially at sea. They were probably the only railway carriages at the time to have life-jackets provided

as a mandatory part of their equipment. As might well be imagined, the latter was very comprehensive.

The service proved very popular, and even though interrupted by the war it soon became a recognized feature of the early morning rush hour to Victoria that in and amongst the many EMUs there would be this rather unusual blue train making its way to London from Dover. It was, in fact, the only regular sleeping car service operated by the Southern Railway or the Southern Region. In spite of airline competition, it was not until 1980 that it was terminated, and then only when the original special-sized cars were life-expired. There was talk of replacement BR-type carriages, but nothing much came of it and we shall have to await the Channel Tunnel for a renewal of through train services to Europe.

Without doubt, travelling on the 'Night Ferry' was a most fascinating and unique experience and I was able to enjoy its distinctive character more than once in connection with the NRM's decision to preserve one of these trend-setting cars. The chosen example was restored at Ostende, but the CIWL offices were in Paris; however, since the 'Night Ferry' by then served Brussels as well as Paris, the two sections being put together at Lille, it seemed only right to use the very service whose vehicle we were trying to preserve. One always tried to remain awake to witness the special loading and unloading on to the ferry boats but somehow, in spite of many who reckoned real sleep was impossible on this train, I always managed to miss it and my two abiding memories are firstly of falling asleep at Lille and waking up amongst the Kentish hop fields or, perhaps more in the spirit of the European 'Great Trains', the sight of a very elegant elderly lady, bedecked in her pink silk robe and fur-lined slippers, sorting out some problem in a most dignified manner with the conductor in the very best

The up Paris–London 'Night Ferry' at Shorncliffe on 25 June 1949 in charge of 4-6-2 No 34074 46 Squadron. The leading luggage vans are French and are followed by the Wagons-Lits, four on this occasion, though it could be anything up to eight or more. The back of the train consists of standard Southern stock, probably including a dining car at this time (Cawston Collection, NRM).

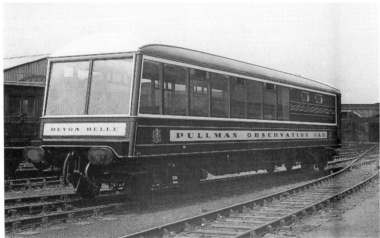

The 'Devon Belle' observation car had one advantage over the Gresley version on the 'Coronation' streamliner: one could actually see out of it more easily! But the styling did not really go well with the more traditional cars in the rest of the train (BR SR).

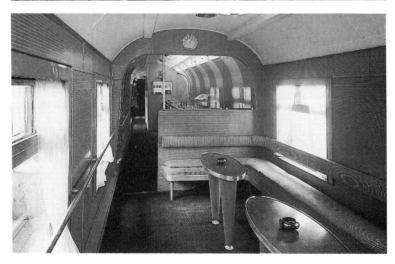

The fashionably trendy first 'Trianon Bar', modelled inside a wooden-bodied twelve-wheeler! (NRM collection).

Agatha Christie tradition: right in the middle of the main departure platform at Paris Nord!

During the war itself, like the 'Night Ferry' service, most of the Pullmans were also withdrawn, though the EMU types soon came back, being useful to the general war effort, Catering provision was, of course, limited. A few other cars were used, principally by the LNER, as additional first class carriages and were repainted plain brown. This treatment was also given to some individual Pullmans to render them less conspicuous. A few more were operated in conditions of great secrecy for VVIP use, and even the NAAFI managed to get half a dozen for use as buffet cars in troop trains. But most were far too luxurious in those difficult times and were stored out of use. Some were destroyed in air raids and many were damaged, but a mercifully high proportion did survive to enable a quick reinstatement of many of the pre-war trains, and at least one new one.

The latter was introduced on the Southern's West of England main line in 1947 as the 'Devon Belle' and was designed to attract holidaymakers. For this reason it was given observation cars of really quite nasty design in the then modern idiom, soon to become more familiar to us all in the shape of the 1951 Festival of Britain and all its subsequent imitators. It became dated almost as rapidly as yesterday's newspaper, but in one respect the Pullman tradition was faithfully maintained. Though passed off as 'new', these observation cars made use of ex-LNWR ambulance underframes which had already carried conventional Pullman bodies for nearly 20 years! The rest of the train remained a bastion of tradition in the brave new world of changing ideas and for some years it was very popular, often loading to 14 cars. But the private motor car finally killed it off as it did so much else of the traditional railway scene.

The 'Devon Belle' was, however, not the only instance where Pullman tried to jump on the fashionable post-war stylistic bandwagon. The other well-known example was the multifarious reincarnations of a catering vehicle introduced as part of the 1946 reinstatement of the famous 'Golden Arrow' service. It was known as the 'Trianon Bar' — named as a complement to our French neighbours. The first example displayed the most obnoxiously awful plastic-styled carriage interior which one could possibly conceive and was rebuilt from a much older car. On test, it was involved in an early running incident which caused its temporary withdrawal (some wished that said incident had been more permanent!) and another car substituted of less controversial style. Thereafter, the two cars tended to play ducks and drakes for a month or two, and even Pullman's normally cavalier approach to naming became more than somewhat confused!

Eventually, however, Pullman got it right at the third attempt in 1951, this time in conjunction with a totally new set of cars for the 'Golden Arrow' service. They were to be the last traditional British Pullman cars to be built for the independent Pullman Company and they were a fine finale. Seven came out in 1951 (contractor-built), three more in 1952 from Pullman's own workshops, of which one, inevitably, was a new body on an old set of frames. It was called, not inappropriately, 'Phoenix', though this name could, with justice, have been applied to any one of a dozen or more of its predecessors. The third 'Trianon Bar' was incorporated in 'Pegasus', the very last of the 1951 series to be built.

The new 'Trianon Bar' in this 1951 set went just about as far as seemed proper for a Pullman in terms of its decor and was quite a good example of restrained 1950s styling, but as for the rest of this set

The first substitute 'Trianon' was a 'K' type bar car, formerly 'Diamond' but in 1946, when this view was taken, it had been re-named; the same car also ran as 'One Hundred Bar' and 'New Century Bar', all four names being used in that same year! It reverted eventually to 'Diamond' and was finally named 'Daffodil Bar' for the 'South Wales Pullman' in 1955 (BR SR).

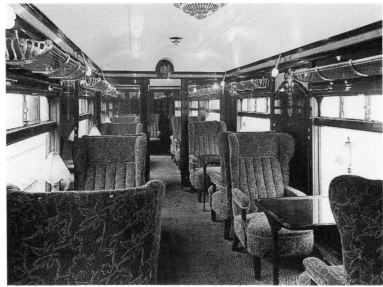

Above *Guard first class parlour car 'Minerva' was built as a 'K' type in 1927 but is seen here completely remodelled with the final type of square toilet windows to run with the new 1951 'Golden Arrow' cars. It is now preserved* (NRM collection).

Left *The remodelled interior of 'Minerva', little changed in essence from all that had gone before* (NRM collection).

Below right *This view of the Southern Railway Royal Train passing St Catherines near Guildford* en route *to Portsmouth behind 4-4-0 No 716 was taken* circa *1938, probably in connection with Coronation year ceremonial. The principal saloon is the second vehicle and the rest of the train is of SE & CR low-roofed style* (Box Collection, NRM).

of cars, there was to be no more tinkering about with newfangled ideas, even though it was 'Festival' year. Just about the only obvious changes were the new-shaped toilet windows (rectangular rather than oval) and the LNER-pattern underframe and bogies which gave them a very superior ride quality. They had in fact been conceived as early as 1938 for LNER service and this probably explained the different running gear.

This pre-war origin may also account for the somewhat dated nature of some of the interiors, for much of the decorative panelling had been made before the war and stored during the hostilities. Thus, though admirably well finished as always, the cars saw no really striking innovation, even if there was some slight simplification in detail. They may, of course, deliberately have been designed to reassure, and without doubt they were some of the finest cars ever to see service, but some have averred that maybe Pullman could have been a bit more enterprising. My

own view, for what it is worth, is that there was very little of substance to commend the ultra-modern 1940s and 1950s fashions as far as their application to carriage interiors was concerned and it was not until a decade later that things began to get better. We shall, of course, have cause to come back to this subject in the next volume.

With the building of these 1951-2 cars, we reach an appropriate point at which to terminate this part of the story for the time being, but before leaving the Pullman field, one final point needs to be made, and that concerns the quite astonishing survival rate of many of the old flat-sided Pullmans. Many have been saved privately, including all 15 'Brighton Belle' cars somewhere or other.

The 'Brighton Belle' cars were in fact the very last of the traditional cars to run in BR service, not being finally withdrawn until 1972 — and then not without some protest — but very many of the locomotive-hauled cars lasted well into the 1960s before they were withdrawn, a better survival rate than that of many a company design of newer date. Even then they often refused to lay down and die! Many are preserved privately and some of them indeed are still in main-line use in yet another operational reincarnation entirely characteristic of the company which spawned them. As such, they look set to see the century out; so we have by no means heard the last of them yet, and their story will continue in the next volume.

*   *   *

Just as long-lived as Pullman cars were those other very special vehicles provided for the reigning monarch, and as Volume 1 has already indicated, HM King George V had quite an assemblage from which to choose when the grouping era dawned. However, the circumstances of the grouping caused some adjustments to be made, and although the carriages remained quite splendid, there were some gradual reductions in quantity. However, such was the quality of the mainly Edwardian contribution to the Royal fleet that none of the companies saw any real need to re-equip in full, and only two of them, the LMS and GWR, assayed any new Royal Saloons at all.

Another point to be made is that the grouping saw the increasing use of the more comprehensively equipped Royal Trains on territory other than the lines of the company for which they were built, and this gave the LMS (ex-LNWR) and LNER (ex-ECJS) sets, especially the former, a head start over all the others. This was largely a consequence of the King needing more facilities on his many longer tours than could usually be offered by the mostly daytime-orientated trains of most of the pre-1923 companies. This more extended role of the Royal Train dated, in fact, from well before the grouping when it began to be a very vital element in the King's ability to make his morale-boosting tours during the 1914-18 war. For this purpose, the LNWR train was usually the first choice, but in due time, especially after the grouping, this led to a reduction in role for most of the Royal vehicles save for the LMS train which gradually assumed, if not a total monopoly, then a highly dominant position. It was, all told, a quite complicated evolutionary story, best considered company by company.

The Southern Railway inherited two Royal trains plus a few bits and pieces of a third, a pair of ex-LSWR bogie saloons of 1885 vintage. It was not to be expected that at nearly 40 years old they would last much longer — they had not often been used for Royal purposes in their later years anyway — and they were taken out of Royal use at the grouping, though they survived until the 1930s. A much similar fate was to befall the former Brighton Royal train of 1897 which was, in effect, largely built for King Edward VII when he was Prince of Wales. This was a handsome clerestory train, undoubtedly one of the finest pieces of carriage building ever offered by the LB & SCR, but it too was downgraded in 1923, its vehicles either going into normal service or private charter. Like the ex-LSWR vehicles, they lasted until the 1930s.

The only pre-group Royal vehicles which remained as such on the Southern were those of the SE & CR which had formed up a Royal Train in 1903 but to which I gave but scant mention in Volume 1. The centrepiece was the fine clerestory saloon by Harry Wain-

wright, and very soon thereafter the available fleet had been extended to some seven vehicles by means of some characteristically neat and tidy low elliptical roof first class stock, including the mandatory 'birdcage' brake ends. As I stated in Volume 1, SE & CR stock was often underrated overall but, like quite a lot of its carriages, its Royal Train was of first class quality and the Southern kept it in being until 1939. Though Maunsell might be accused of some sort of favouritism, being of course ex-SE & CR himself, by any objective standards the Southern only needed one Royal Train and the SE & CR had the best example. It also had the indubitable advantage of having greater route availability than those of the other SR constituents.

Towards the end of the 1930s, however, even this train was showing its age a little, and by then the LMS train had assumed greater dominance anyway. It was already the first choice on the GWR (see below) and regularly made forays into LNER country, so the Southern also tended to use it if possible. This was often not the case but it became increasingly customary for the Southern to hire a few modern Pullmans for Royal use, rather than use the SE & CR train. After 1939, when the latter set made its last Royal trip, Pullmans became the normal Royal conveyances on the SR whenever either the LMS or LNER saloons could not clear the often limited Southern loading gauge.

The GWR's splendid 1897 Royal Train had been rather 'diluted' in the technical sense by Queen Victoria's insistence that her old 1874 carriage be retained, now rebuilt on a new underframe and bogies. Unlike the LNWR, however, which had faced exactly the same problem during the 1890s and come up with a near-identical solution, the GWR did not replace the older carriage when King Edward VII came to the throne. It soldiered on until 1912, having served as a hearse for both the Queen and King Edward VII, and was then scrapped. After this time, the remainder of the fine Dean clerestory set of 1897 remained in Royal use until 1935, when all were withdrawn, life expired. The GWR from then on usually used the LMS (ex-LNWR) train for Royal purposes.

For such a proud railway as the GWR, it is perhaps surprising that no real effort was made to provide a new principal Royal saloon for King George V, and even after the 1897 clerestories had been scrapped, it was to be a few years before the GWR acted. Eventually, however, there was some sort of move forward, and this resulted in four rather splendid vehicles being built during the 1940s. Even so, they were built against the rather tacit assumption that the LMS and LNER trains would be the preferred choice on many occasions — most odd!

The new saloons were built in pairs, first on the scene being two twelve-wheel day saloons (Nos 9001/2), ordered in 1938 and put into service in 1940. They were very fine vehicles but never classified as 'full' Royals at first, being regarded as more general VIP saloons. They were used as such during the war for high-ranking politicians and military men such as Churchill and Eisenhower, but after 1945 they increasingly tended to be regarded as part of the nucleus of a new GWR Royal Train and were indeed often used by Royalty. Both have been privately preserved, one at the Birmingham Railway Museum, the other at the Didcot Railway Centre.

Below far left *GWR Royal Saloon No 9006 in Royal Claret livery. Though it served until 1979, the carriage saw hardly any alterations from its original GWR form. The kitchen is at the near end, the dining room in the centre and the small lounge at the far end* (NRM).

Below left *The Queen Mother's principal day lounge in GWR Royal Saloon No 9007.* (Copyright, NRM).

Right *The East Coast Royal Train photographed between Biggleswade and Sandy in May 1953 on one of its last outings in the varnished teak livery; it was repainted in 1954-5. The engine, 4-6-0 No 61671, was called* Royal Sovereign *and was always preferred by BR(ER) for Royal Train duty, one of the last examples of railway management going to the trouble of having a dedicated 'Royal' engine. The train itself consists of both principal saloons (in the centre), a dining car, two semi-Royals and two full brakes* (BR ER official, NRM).

The next major contribution towards the new GWR train was another pair of VIP saloons ordered, rather surprisingly, in 1943. They came into use in 1945 as Nos 9006/7 and had both day and night facilities. In fact, No 9006 was totally self-contained, having a kitchen and dining room as well, but it was not until some years later that they became properly 'Royal'. In 1948 they received a first refurbishment (with air-conditioning) to run with two new Hawksworth brake composites (and Nos 9001/2 if required) as the nucleus of what was hoped to be a new GWR Royal Train. But it was rather too late now for such grandiose plans, given the onset of BR, so the GWR project went no further. The first pair remained as VIP saloons and it was only the consequence of King George VI's premature death in 1952 — and that of Queen Mary in 1953 — which caused Nos 9006/7 to become truly part of the BR Royal fleet.

The principal LMS and LNER saloons were now at the disposal of the present Queen and HRH The Duke of Edinburgh. Accordingly, Nos 9006/7 were extensively refitted in 1955 as the personal saloons for HM Queen Elizabeth the Queen Mother. They usually ran as a pair, No 9007 being Her Majesty's personal saloon (very similarly finished to LMS 799 — see below), No 9006 being for her own personal staff. It was also used to provide the essential catering facilities. No 9007 was the more extensively modified in 1955 so as to enlarge both the Queen's lounge and her principal bedroom, but No 9006 remained

virtually pure GWR. At this point they also lost their chocolate and cream colours and were repainted in Royal Train livery. They went on to serve the Queen Mother for nearly a quarter of a century until they made their very last Royal journey to Glasgow in March 1979. Both are now preserved by the National Railway Museum, No 9006 being rendered additionally interesting by having the Queen Mother's own personal china tea and dinner service 'en suite', it having been retained on board the saloon at her special request when the vehicles were saved.

These two saloons were a fitting climax to the GWR carriage story. They are both finished in a restrained but beautifully executed Art Deco style and are just as fine a tribute to the quality of the carriage builders' craft as any of their more elaborate predecessors. It is believed that the Queen Mother was rather sad when their obsolete braking system and running gear in the 100 mph era caused them to be withdrawn; having been privileged to ride inside them on their final journey from Wolverton to York, I can well understand her regret.

During the whole of the grouping period, the LNER Royal Train remained almost exactly as it had been in ECJS days. The normal composition consisted of one or both principal saloons, anything up to four semi-Royal saloons and the two full brakes which served as both staff accommodation and as luggage vans. There was no dedicated dining car as such, the LNER simply using one of its large fleet of first

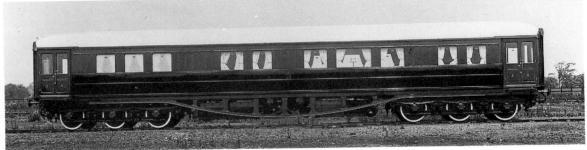

class cars should the need arise. Neither were there any sleeping cars in the formation, which was one reason why it was never as widely used as the LMS train. The only significant change was a form of 'role reversal' for the two principal saloons in 1926.

These splendid twelve-wheelers had been built in 1908-9, one each for King Edward VII (No 395) and Queen Alexandra (No 396). In 1926, No 395 was altered quite extensively for the sole use of HM Queen Mary and was rearranged for day journeys only. In this form it could either form part of the Royal Train or be attached to a service train when the Queen was travelling alone. As far as the internal fittings were concerned, though there was some re-positioning of partitions and doors, the superb quality of the woodwork in both the principal lounge (sycamore and mahogany) and the equerry's compartment (dark and light oak plus boxwood) was not affected. The whole vehicle was refurnished to Queen Mary's personal direction and she used it for the rest of her life. After she died, it was transferred to the use of Queen Elizabeth the Queen Mother, and a further replacement of furniture took place in the mid-1950s, though Queen Mary's personal monograms remained etched into some of the window glazing.

At the same time, No 396 became the principal LNER saloon and exchanged its original outside 'door furniture' with the more elaborate handrails etc which had hitherto been on the King's saloon No 395! In revised form, No 396 became a day saloon for the King and Queen travelling together and in addition to its main lounge had two separate dressing rooms. It also lost quite an amount of its original Edwardian 'Adam'-style plasterwork in the process.

These changes were almost certainly a result of the concentration on the use of the LMS train for all overnight Royal journeys, for until then the LNER saloons could function in this role. After the conversions, this was far less practicable and never, as far as is known, practised. This inevitably meant that the LNER saloons were less often used than the LMS (ex-LNWR) pair, and mainly for this reason they lasted far longer in service. The full LNER set was retained intact until 1961 when it made its last Royal journey in full formation — to York in connection with the wedding of HRH The Duke of Kent. By then, like the LMS set, it had been repainted in Royal Train livery, though not without some sadness at Doncaster when the famous varnished teak scheme

Above *Saloon No 395 after alteration in 1926. HM Queen Mary's monogram was etched into the three obscured glass windows at the left-hand end and is still a feature of the saloon* (LNER official, NRM)

Left *Principal day lounge inside Royal Saloon No 395 showing the furniture provided circa 1955 and subsequently used by HM Queen Elizabeth the Queen Mother* (Copyright, NRM).

Figure 89 *Elevation and plan of East Coast Royal Saloon No 395 as altered by the LNER in 1926 for use by HM Queen Mary.*

Scale: $^1/_{12}$" = 1ft

was terminated. It is said that some of the old painters refused to be party to such sacrilege, and whether this be true or not, what can be said is that when the luggage van was reinstated to teak livery in the late 1970s (see below), Doncaster did the job with great joy!

The train was disbanded after 1961, but the two principal saloons and one of the luggage vans were retained for another ten years or more, the saloons continuing in use in a variant of their revised 1926 roles, No 396 now being reserved for HM The Queen and the Duke of Edinburgh travelling together, No 396 being an alternative to the GWR pair for the Queen Mother when travelling solely by day. As such they ran well into the 1970s, by which time they had been transferred to Wolverton to be kept alongside the LMS carriages. They were regular visitors to Sandringham, of course, and being marginally less restricted than the LMS saloons were not infrequently used on the Southern system. In the later 1970s, all three were withdrawn for preservation by the National Railway Museum, having had nearly 70 years of active life in Royal service — no mean record. At the time of writing, only the luggage van has been restored to varnished teak (its dark red paintwork was in poor condition when withdrawn) but it is the hope that in due course all three will display the famous East Coast livery and be marshalled together as a single exhibit.

We come now, and finally, to the LMS (ex-LNWR) contribution, without doubt the most celebrated of the pre-BR Royal Trains during the last company phase. This train originated in 1902 with the building of two superb Royal Saloons, followed by six matching semi-Royals a year or so later. It was later augmented by two dining cars and two sleeping cars (eventually there were three of the latter), all of the

standard LNWR pattern, and two staff vehicles, both at first being full brakes. This was the assemblage inherited by the LMS in 1923 and the first change was almost immediate. The two full brakes were replaced by two ex-LNWR corridor brake firsts whose passenger accommodation was modified to offer convertible sleeping berths and whose roofs were given clerestories to match those of the rest of the train. Until the third sleeping car (an elliptical roof example) was added to the fleet, this all-clerestory set was one of the most beautiful trains ever to be seen, especially when running in full formation.

Its beauty was enhanced by the retention of its former LNWR livery at King George V's personal request. Even the Midland-minded LMS had to listen to that, and it remained thus until 1940 when, in the interests of security from air raids and so forth, King George VI agreed to it being painted in standard LMS lake as a sort of camouflage. This apart, the only visible difference for most of the pre-war LMS period was the new company insignia and badges on the carriages replacing those of the old LNWR.

The LMS train was the most fully-integrated formation of any of the Royal Trains and the only one which could provide suitable accommodation for a multi-day operation. For this reason, it was the almost inevitable selection whenever the King needed to be away for several days at a time, and this requirement was increasingly common as years went by. It thus became familiar throughout the land and since the LMS always used it on their own lines anyway for all Royal journeys, its vehicles ran many more miles than those of the other companies.

This was undoubtedly the reason why, in the later 1930s, the LMS began to think about a complete replacement. However, just before this time, the death

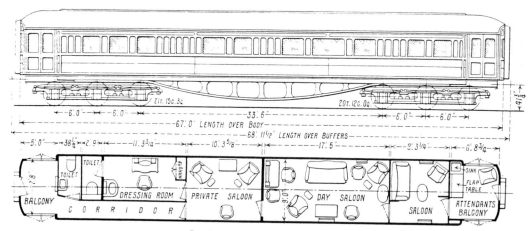

Details of the Saloon as Re-Arranged.

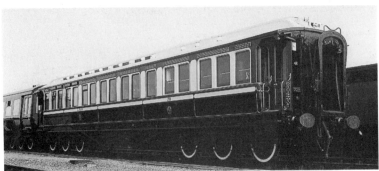

Above *The full LMS Royal Train in its retained LNWR colours at Ballater in August 1928 headed by LNER 4-4-0s Nos 6850* Hatton Castle *and 6846* Benachie. *Only the King appears to have been travelling for the only principal saloon is his, second from the engines. However, there must have been quite a sizeable entourage for there are two semi-Royals, two dining cars and a sleeping car present in the visible portion of the train. A 10–12-coach formation was customary on trips of this nature (Stephen Collection, NRM).*

Above left *Royal Dining Car No 76 on its replacement LMS-pattern underframes and now restored to pre-1940 colours (Copyright, NRM).*

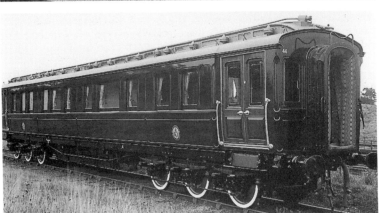

Left *The King's Saloon from the LNWR train in its wartime LMS colours. Note the replacement LMS-pattern axleboxes and side buffers, part of the late 1930s improvements. The carriage, along with its 'twin', has now been restored to its original LNWR livery (BR LMR).*

Below left *LMS King's Saloon No 798 in wartime armour plating (BR LMR).*

Figure 90 *Diagrams issued after the war giving details of the three new LMS Royal Train vehicles. They show, top to bottom: King's Saloon, Queen's Saloon, Brake and Power Car.*

Scale: $^1/_{12}"$ = 1ft

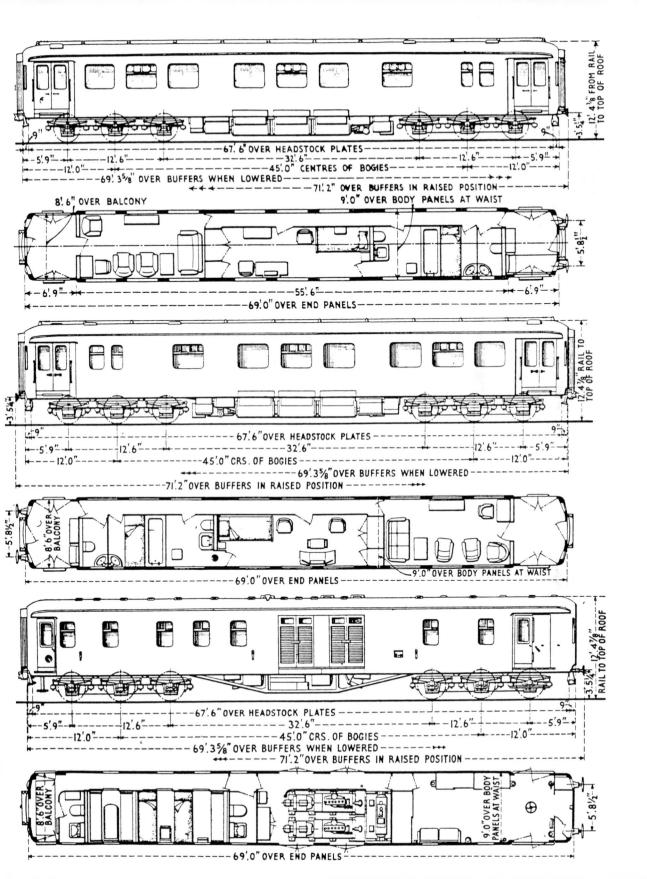

12' 4⅞" FROM RAIL TO TOP OF ROOF

3' 5¼"

9"

67' 6" OVER HEADSTOCK PLATES

5' 9" 12' 6" 32' 6" 12' 6" 5' 9"

12' 0" 45' 0" CENTRES OF BOGIES 12' 0"

69' 3⅝" OVER BUFFERS WHEN LOWERED

71' 2" OVER BUFFERS IN RAISED POSITION

9' 0" OVER BODY PANELS AT WAIST

8' 6" OVER BALCONY

5' 8½"

6' 9" 55' 6" 6' 9"

69' 0" OVER END PANELS

12' 4⅞" RAIL TO TOP OF ROOF

3' 5¼"

9" 9"

67' 6" OVER HEADSTOCK PLATES

5' 9" 12' 6" 32' 6" 12' 6" 5' 9"

12' 0" 45' 0" CRS. OF BOGIES 12' 0"

69' 3⅝" OVER BUFFERS WHEN LOWERED

71' 2" OVER BUFFERS IN RAISED POSITION

5' 8½"

8' 6" OVER BALCONY

9' 0" OVER BODY PANELS AT WAIST

69' 0" OVER END PANELS

12' 4⅞" RAIL TO TOP OF ROOF

3' 5¼" RAIL TO RAIL

9" 9"

67' 6" OVER HEADSTOCK PLATES

5' 9" 12' 6" 32' 6" 12' 6" 5' 9"

12' 0" 45' 0" CRS. OF BOGIES 12' 0"

69' 3⅝" OVER BUFFERS WHEN LOWERED

71' 2" OVER BUFFERS IN RAISED POSITION

8' 6" OVER BALCONY

9' 0" OVER BODY PANELS AT WAIST

5' 8½"

69' 0" OVER END PANELS

End detail of Saloon No 798 as preserved, showing the totally smooth finish and the reinstated LMS livery. This vehicle is now on public display at the Museum of Transport, Glasgow, having been lent by the NRM in connection with the opening of the enlarged transport display at Kelvinhall in 1988 (Copyright, NRM).

Much attention was given to detail in the LMS Royal Saloons. This is the principal bedroom in Saloon No 799. Note the neatly located air conditioning grilles between sides and roof (Copyright, NRM).

of King George V had made it seem for a while as though there may be no further need for any Royal Trains. King Edward VIII generally preferred motor cars and aeroplanes and, if travelling by train, usually chose to use the LMS President's saloon rather than the full train. But the abdication crisis of 1936 brought another family man to the throne, and the LMS dusted down its plans.

Part of the problem was the age of the train combined with its heavy usage and the fact that railway speeds were increasing. A new train was the ideal answer, but as an interim solution during 1937-8 the LMS fitted heavy-duty axleboxes and drawgear to the whole Royal fleet, put new angle-trussed underframes beneath the Royal dining car and the two staff brakes and replaced the wood-centred Mansell wheels which were fitted to most of the carriages with modern all-steel disc wheels. This, in essence, was how most of the carriages in the train were to see out their lives.

In 1938, the LMS at last issued the order for two new Royal Saloons of ultra-modern type as the first

stage of what is thought to have been a total replacement programme, but the war clouds came and the project was shelved. The old train remained in use and, as stated, was repainted to make it somewhat less conspicuous. But its carriages were still wood-bodied, there was an ever-present fear of air raids, and the King and Queen were not noted at the time for keeping clear of danger, regularly visiting many areas of the country which were under air attack. In consequence, the LMS was authorized to build its two new saloons (No 798 for the King, No 799 for the Queen) and fit them with armour plating. This was done in great secrecy during 1941 and they were accompanied by a third vehicle, an escort and power car, which contained a diesel generator to provide electrical power during the many periods when the train was standing overnight during its very regular wartime travels. It was not until after the war that full details of the new vehicles were released, almost simultaneously with the removal of the wartime armour plating from the saloons.

These new carriages have many times been described in detail, some of the sources being listed in the Bibliography, so there is no reason to repeat too much here. Basically they were constructed to an entirely new shape and style but embodying traditional Stanier-period LMS methods. The bodies were steel-panelled on timber frames, heavily sound-insulated and mounted on the latest type of welded underframe. They were also the first and only LMS carriages to feature buckeye couplings and Pullman-style gangways, a fact which caused many of the older Royal carriages to have gangway adapters fitted. The outsides were very smoothly finished with all corners rounded and no obvious cantrail, a sort of early prediction of the BR Mk II shape, if you like. Interiors were thoroughly modern in decor employing traditional LMS timber finishes throughout and soft colour shades. All was done with the utmost simplicity combined with quality and they must have been relaxing vehicles in which to travel. Full air-conditioning was installed in both saloons, using ice-boxes below the floor as the main cooling medium. They were also very heavy, even without their armour plate.

From late 1941, the two new saloons replaced the old LNWR saloons for most journeys, but the two 1902 carriages still remained in reserve, so to speak, and were given modernized bathrooms in the general style of the 1941 carriages. As such, they too remained in regular if less frequent use until 1947, spending much of the wartime period as a sort of permanent stand-by in Scotland. They were finally retired in the autumn of 1947 and went into store at Wolverton. In due course they were put on show in their final LMS livery at the Museum of British Transport at Clapham and came to the NRM in 1975. Since that time, both saloons have been fully repainted inside and out, opportunity being taken at the writer's suggestion to reinstate the famous old LNWR livery at the same time. In the flesh, so to speak, this colour scheme looks even more breathtaking than the most vivid imagination could conjure up.

The need for a power car with the two new LMS saloons caused one of the former LNWR brakes to be further modified as a stand-by in this role and it too was given a generator. From this time onwards, the principal British Royal Train has always carried its own generating capability and all vehicles were modified with through conduits to accept this external power supply both when the train was stationary and even sometimes on the move. Finally, the oldest vehicle in the Royal Train, the 1900 vintage dining car, had one of its two passenger areas opened out in 1942 to form a more conventional dining room with central table and chairs. No doubt it also formed a very suitable, if small, conference room when required; in fact, this may well be why it was so converted.

Post-war austerity meant that no further new additions could be made to the train and it is rather unlikely that the King, always acutely aware of the hardships faced by his subjects, would have been happy even had this idea been suggested to him. So the planned LMS train never got beyond its first three carriages, and it was not until the mid-1950s that further changes took place. These and all later developments will be considered in the final volume.

Thus, most of the old LNWR Royal Train vehicles were to serve many more years of life before they too were able to be replaced. In fact, the next to go was not until well into BR days in 1956, when the Royal Dining Car was replaced along with some of the semi-Royals. The sleeping cars lasted until the late 1960s and the two service vehicles were not to be replaced in principal service until Jubilee year, 1977, and even then were kept in reserve for another year or so until finally released to the NRM in 1979. Very appropriately, one of them, the reserve power car No 5154, made its last Royal trip in March 1979 with the last working of the Queen Mother's GWR saloons (see above).

During the whole of the time between the building of the 1941 saloons and the late 1980s, there was always some former LNWR element incorporated in the Royal Train, which tended in consequence to get ever more untidy looking as gradual changes were made. So strong indeed was the element of continuity throughout its whole history that it is difficult to find a convenient stopping point for this part of the story, and its history will continue in the next volume. Perhaps it will suffice to say for the moment that no fewer than seven of the LNWR carriages have survived (five at the NRM and two in private hands) along with the 1941 LMS pair; and by the time this book appears, an eighth LNWR vehicle in the form of the old LMS President's saloon should have joined the NRM collection. This last pre-group survivor was latterly used for railway officers accompanying the Royal Train, a function it discharged until 1989.

13. Other coaching stock developments

Before concluding the main part of our story, we must first give brief attention to those vehicles which do not fall tidily into any of the categories so far covered, so as to give them at least some passing mention in the interests of overall completeness. Dominant by far will be the non-passenger-carrying stock, but there will be mention of some few types which did carry people, such as push-pull coaches and special saloons.

A few overall points should, however, be made clear from the start: in none of the categories covered in this chapter was there much to be seen in the way of design innovation during the grouping period. For one thing, as Chapter 14 in Volume 1 has indicated, the function of most non-passenger-carrying coaching stock had been well and truly identified long before 1923 and often provided for quite lavishly, thus reducing the need for adding too excessively to the existing pre-group fleets. Secondly, some categories of traffic went into a gradual decline as a result of road competition, thus making less demand on the railways anyway. Thirdly, and particularly in the realm of passenger-carrying vehicles, most of the requirements could actually be met by pre-group stock either as it stood or, as Chapter 10 has already half-hinted, by conversion, so there was little need for very much in the way of new construction.

Non-passenger-carrying coaching stock

The categories of vehicle outlined in Volume 1 remained broadly unchanged during the grouping period, so there is no need for repetition, but it has to be said that even though the traffic they handled represented a fair proportion of railway revenue, there was little to arouse excitement in most of the vehicles built new for the purpose during the final company phase. This was, if you like, a sort of back-handed compliment to the pre-group era in having got it right so often; thus, with few exceptions, the 'Big Four' did not take matters very much further. But then, why should they? I once heard it said: 'If it is not necessary for something to be changed then it is necessary that it should not be changed.' And this certainly seems to have been a principle applied to many vehicles in the non-passenger category.

Take, for example, that most obvious non-passenger type, the full brake, including its closely allied luggage and parcels van relations. Many a hundred more were built but almost all were mostly related to their passenger-carrying contemporaries, especially in visual terms, and that just about says all. They remained basically boxes on wheels for the carriage of all manner of traffic which needed safe high-speed transit in a covered vehicle, and most railways built them on an 'as required' basis, following their usual stylistic pattern. There was a gradual increase in the bogie type but four-wheel and six-wheel variants continued to be offered and one supposes that cost considerations were as like as not the reason for the choices.

Cost considerations too were undoubtedly behind the conversion to full brake form in both the early 1920s and late 1940s of many former ambulance vehicles after the two world wars. These carriages, almost a special study in their own right, were very numerous and usually took the form of purpose-built conversions of former passenger-carrying stock into mobile hospital form. They contained ward, operating and treatment cars, which, together with the essential staff accommodation vehicles, formed one of the very few positive contributions to humanity which may be said to have emerged from these global tragedies.

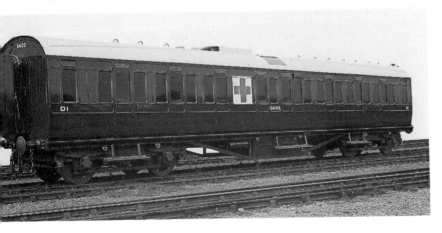

LMS ambulance carriage No 5403 was converted in 1939 from a former eight-compartment corridor third, built during the mid-1920s. It was altered into what was called a 'Kitchen and Sick Officers Car' but its origins were still visibly obvious from the outside. Inside, however, the conversions often involved completely stripping the interior and this fact, after the war, made them eminently suitable for further use as brake and luggage vans, a much cheaper option than building new ones or even converting them back to their original function. Many hundreds were thus treated, but the ultimate fate of the coach shown here is not known (BR LMR).

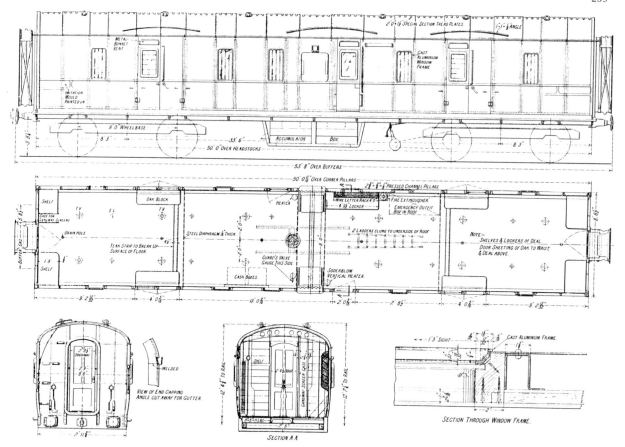

Figure 91 *Detailed drawings of the 'all-steel' LMS full brakes of 1926.*

Scale: 3mm = 1ft

Both conflicts were to see examples of the genre and their company origins were usually readily apparent since the externals remained little changed. Many went overseas for service close to the front lines and were never to return, but many more came back. Some of these were reinstated to their former roles and as we have seen, some of them went to Pullman to enjoy a somewhat more exotic future, at least as far as their running gear was concerned; but far more were simply regarded as a cheap and cheerful way of providing a fresh supply of brake and luggage vans when things got back to normal. The LMS was particularly adept at this sort of thing on both occasions.

The LMS too was responsible for just about the only significant structural change in full brakes built new as such — and even then not overly dramatic — when it experimented with all-steel full brakes from 'the trade' at the same time as its purchase of similar passenger-carrying stock in the later 1920s. As with the carriages, so with the full brakes: only the knowledgeable could really tell the difference between them and conventionally built examples. One of them was given a vitreous enamelled finish to try and make savings in painting costs, but nothing much came of this experiment and it was not repeated.

Of the 'Big Four' at this time, the Southern seems to have been the least user of passenger full brakes, preferring instead the more versatile 'general utility' van, probably working on the basis that since most of its services were passenger-carrying anyway, there would almost always be a guard's compartment somewhere in the train, thus enabling some manufacturing economies to be made in the non-passenger arena; perusal of many hundreds of pictures of typical locomotive-hauled Southern passenger trains at the time — and well into BR days for that matter — certainly leads to this conclusion.

This led to much building of those most characteristically 'Southern' non-passenger vehicles, the

outside framed GUVs, in both four-wheel and eight-wheel form. The latter, it need hardly be said, were often given second-hand underframes. They were to be seen everywhere, not just on the Southern, and were amongst the longest-lived of pre-BR coaching stock. Their inspiration was an original SE & CR four-wheel design which the Southern repeated for many years with little real change, and also developed it into bogie form. Its predominantly 'goods vehicle' structural style undoubtedly saved money, and this particular Southern approach to the business was probably the most distinctively different of any of the 'Big Four' offerings in this field.

After the grouping, the carriage truck business outlined in Volume 1 was to undergo some quite fundamental changes, usually consequent upon the gradual reduction in horse-drawn traffic compared with its motorized successor. This usually meant that the better open carriage trucks of the pre-group period were normally sufficient to cope with the reducing demand for non-covered movement of vehicular traffic. In fact, they became increasingly used for such things as agricultural machinery and even (suitably modified) for container traffic. The covered version, however, did fare rather better, but not always in the carriage-carrying field. Some indeed were used this way, especially for the growing traffic in the rail-haulage of motor cars where covered vehicles were often preferred, but it was to be well into BR days before this type of vehicle was to be seen in any great quantity. Meantime, the CCTs became ever more versatile in their variety of usage and were increasingly regarded as end-door GUVs (see above).

Thus, when the LNER built a new batch in 1928, although they were styled as CCTs, it is no surprise to note that a contemporary description stated: 'The

vehicles are of general utility type — that is to say they are arranged to afford the fullest utility possible in the conveyance of different classes of traffic, so that in addition to the usual folding and falling doors at each end for the admission of wheeled vehicles, theatrical scenery, aeroplanes and other bulky loads, special provision has been made for the reception of parcels, fruit, pigeons, or small livestock which can be carried upon hinged shelves arranged in tiers along each side.' The accompanying drawing should make things clearer, and these vans were entirely typical of the products of all the railways, even down to their re-use of older underframes. In fact, over the years there was to be a gradual blurring of the edges between the use made of CCTs and GUVs and it got to the point where only the end-loading doors of the CCT marked any significant difference between the two.

In the 'valuable livestock' field, increasing road competition also tended to bite into the railways' earlier monopoly, and once again the better pre-group offerings often tended to suffice for much of the trade. But there was enough call to justify some new construction of horse-boxes and prize cattle vans, which process continued at diminishing level right through into BR days. Almost all of them were long-wheelbase four-wheelers whose nature differed little from that of their pre-1923 ancestors; but it only needed a race meeting or something similar for the railways to find reason for turning out whole trains of these vehicles in the pre-motorway age. It is all gone now, but during the company period it remained common enough.

Another category which held up well throughout the grouping period was that of perishable cargo, particularly but not exclusively the carriage of fish and milk. The former trade was increasingly to be han-

Left *In the austerity post-war years, any savings were worth having and Thompson on the LNER experimented with tongue and groove boarding in place of conventional panelling on many passenger brakes. This is No 70590 when new in 1945, one of more than 50 such, covered with deal planking and painted plain brown (LNER official, NRM).*

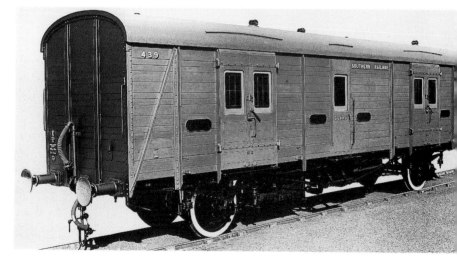

Right and below right *The 'freight vehicle' nature of many Southern Railway luggage vans is emphasized here. Four-wheeler No 439 was one of many variations from the original SE & CR design which went on being built until the end of SR days, while gangwayed bogie van No 2319 dated from 1932, though its running gear was clearly older! Note that the guard was also expected to ride in the four-wheeler (both SR official, NRM).*

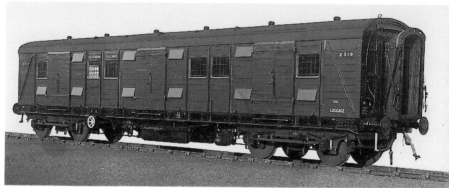

Figure 92 *Elevations and plan of the 1928 LNER Covered Carriage Trucks referred to in the text as being of 'general utility' type.*

Scale: $^1/_{10}$" = 1ft

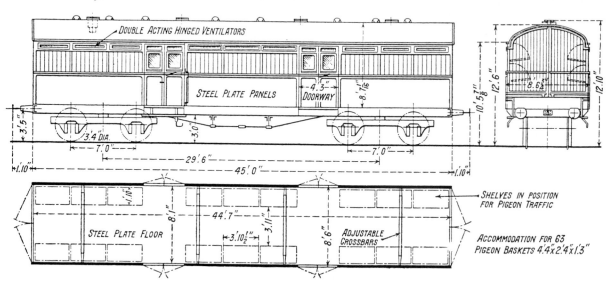

Elevation and Plan of New Covered Carriage Trucks, L.N.E.R.

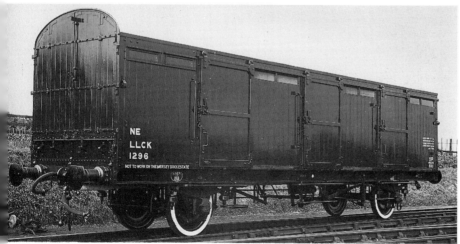

This page *The end-door CCT/GUV became a very common company type, three quite typical examples being shown here. Oddly enough, the oldest by far was the most modern looking: LMS No 37714, built in 1933 with flush steel panelling and fully lined passenger livery. It was classified 'Luggage and Parcels' but was, in fact, a CCT, and probably the major stylistic influence in the BR continuation. The Southern and LNER examples both displayed freight characteristics and were built in 1938 and 1939 respectively. SR No 4596 was classified for the carriage of theatrical scenery, and LNER No 1296 for motor cars, but as with the LMS example one doubts whether these functions remained the exclusive purpose of these versatile vehicles (BR LMR; SR and LNER official, NRM).*

Above right *Though it built quite a few for itself, the LMS also inherited many fine pre-group horse-boxes. This rather handsome if old-fashioned example is ex-Highland Railway No 43792, still in very good condition in the late 1930s (Author's collection).*

Middle right *The LNER served much horse-racing territory and 'Return to Leyburn', painted on No 2259, was un-doubtedly tied up with the racing stables at close-by Middleham. This was a new horse-box in 1936, one of 50, and by no means the last LNER essay in this field. In fact, the final LNER horse-box design was actually adopted by the London Midland Region after the formation of BR! (LNER official, NRM).*

Right *The GWR may well have been the biggest single conveyor of milk in bulk during the company period. This fine view, taken at Patchway in the later 1930s, shows a down working of a characteristically mixed bag of empties from London headed by 4-6-0 No 2902 Lady of the Lake. The leading bogie 'Siphon' was a common GWR type and would handle the churn traffic, as would the third vehicle too, but perhaps most noteworthy is the no fewer than ten six-wheel milk tanks visible in the train. Collectively, these, when loaded, could probably fill well over 200,000 milk bottles! (Soole Collection, NRM).*

dled by covered fish vans which looked very little different from goods wagons, save for the speed at which they ran, and again new building went on throughout the company period, though, as before, there was little change in the nature of the new vehicles provided. In fact, many of them were to unaltered pre-group designs, and even where new versions were offered in later years there was little innovation. Some LMS six-wheel fish vans built at Wolverton in 1947, for example, could just as well have emerged 30 years earlier as far as their general sophistication was concerned! Perhaps there was no perceived need, who can say, but it was to be well into BR days before any even mildly radical new ideas began to emerge, by which time it was too late, as Volume 3 will reveal.

Much the same was true of milk traffic in the first ten years or so after 1923, where, if any new ones were needed at all, pre-group-styled milk vans continued to be built and ply their traditional trade from all corners of the kingdom. The 'early morning milk train' was no flight of literary fancy in those days; but the gradual move from churn milk to bulk milk haulage did cause one of the few genuine design changes to take place. It is a moot point whether the vehicles which emerged should appear in a carriage book at all, for they were in fact tank wagons by any other name, but since the railways always regarded them as 'passenger rated' stock, they do at least warrant brief mention.*

The cause was the gradual concentration of milk distribution at purpose-built depots out in the country to which milk could be brought from the farms in churns but from which it was far simpler to

* For a much more detailed survey of the evolution of rail-borne milk traffic, see *'Milko!'*, by T.W.Bourne: 'Railways South East', Vol 2 No 4, Summer 1989.

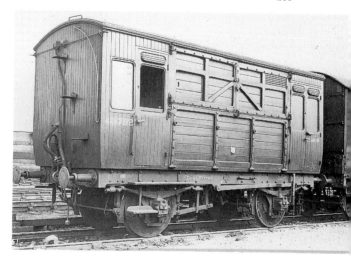

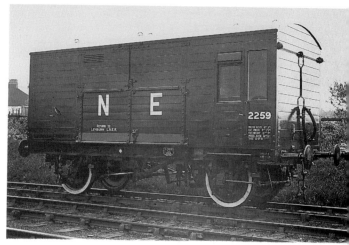

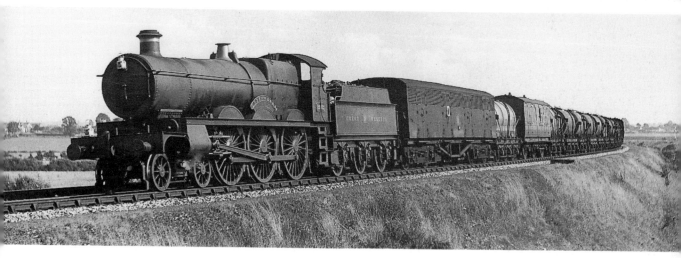

LNER six-wheel 'flat' wagon No 217298 for road/rail milk tanks, built in 1936 and rated for use in passenger trains. The road tanks could be either company or privately owned (LNER official, NRM).

despatch the product in bulk tanks to the large towns and cities. The railways responded in one of two ways. By far the most common was the dedicated milk tank, which was simply a glass-lined tank mounted on a railway chassis capable of passenger speed. At first four-wheelers were used, but the railways soon established that six wheels were needed for this sort of high-speed transit, and from 1937 all milk tanks were thus equipped. An interesting point about them was that the tank belonged to the dairy itself and only the chassis was owned by the railway! But it led to a short-lived and colourful explosion of private owner colour schemes until the Second World War came along.

The second solution was a road/rail milk tank whereby the tank itself was mounted on road wheels (in effect it was the 'trailer' portion of a road unit), the whole being then transhipped at the appropriate railhead to a specially adapted six-wheel rail chassis for its long-distance move. They were not very common compared with the dedicated milk tanks, but did represent a worthy idea which deserved a better long-term outcome.

Milk handling in bulk became ever more widespread, though the traditional churn traffic held up quite well alongside it and milk specials consisting of both forms of vehicle were common well into BR days until they too fell foul of road competition. Fortunately, the NRM has managed to preserve typical examples of both modes of bulk milk haulage.

The last major category of non-passenger coaching stock to be considered is also one of the oldest forms, happily still with us in modern day: the Travelling Post Office (TPO). From a very early stage, the characteristic and specialized vehicles provided for this purpose have always been jointly financed by the railways and the Post Office, though maintained by the former. Their very specialized function and inter-

nal layout is well known and was established long before the grouping period. Furthermore, there were never very many of them in absolute terms, and since their usage was less intensive than most passenger-carrying stock, they tended to enjoy longer service lives. Thus, yet again, the pre-group examples enjoyed many more years of active life after 1923.

When the time came to make some new provision, the vehicular types had settled down, more or less, to but two basic types of carriage, the Post Office Sorting Van (POS) and the Post Office Tender (POT), the latter being mainly a travelling storage vehicle with no *en route* sorting facility. These were, of course, supplemented to a very great extent by the railway-owned luggage and parcels vans of many a hundred orthodox passenger trains which brought the mails to the central distribution points from which the dedicated TPOs would then take over. This basic *modus operandi* may still be observed today, though, I fear, much reduced from its earlier universality.

The biggest provider of dedicated TPOs was, without doubt, the LMS, mainly in consequence of its operation of the key 'Irish Mail' and 'West Coast Postal' services which have always been at the heart of the British mail distribution network; yet even the LMS contribution numbered something less than 70 vehicles built to company designs, the last of which did not appear until 1954. Moreover, such was the resilience of older TPOs that neither the LMS nor the LNER saw fit to provide any new examples at all until 1929. By then, the basic design of POS had settled down to a largely standard layout, well exemplified by the two drawings appended. The GWR equivalent was no whit different in operational status, and the Southern too joined in the act with a few neatly designed contributions. All were, of course, bogie vehicles by now and the companies followed whichever version of their own external styling and livery was currently in vogue, the SR being the only one of the four which did not offer lineside pick-up apparatus. This was perhaps the most publicly understood 'face' of the TPO: an operation immortalized for ever in that wonderful LMS documentary film of the 1930s, 'Night Mail', with its marvellously evocative W.H.Auden commentary poem.

That said, however, little more of significance remains to be mentioned in the general overview context of non-passenger operations. It was an unsung and generally non-glamorous part of the total railway package which, though a very considerable revenue earner throughout the period under review, was also under constant attrition from the fast growing road competition. Whether the grouped railways ever really came to grips with the seriousness of this problem is rather doubtful; this was an issue which

BR had to face in far more dramatic form and which the next volume will try to address. But in so far as the grouped railways were concerned, its outward manifestation seems mostly to have been in the gradual reduction of vehicle types, the coming together of CCT/GUV (see above) being perhaps the most obvious, combined with maybe just a little complacency in vehicle provisioning which led to the design stagnation already hinted at. The fact is, however, that except for a rather reduced level of mail services and some residual CCT/GUV-type traffic, the modern railway has seen the removal of almost all other forms of traditional non-passenger coaching stock revenue from its books. Some of the warning signs were there during the company period, but whether anything more could have been done is perhaps outwith the scope of this survey. And there we will leave it for the moment.

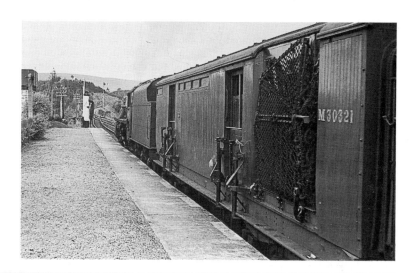

Right *TPOs were another area of non-passenger stock where older vehicles lasted well, and the former Highland Railway was surprisingly well represented (see also page 263). This view shows one of only three sorting vans which it owned, No M30321, still in service in early BR days on the 'Highland TPO' (Gavin Wilson).*

Below *The Post Office Tender, or stowage van, is exemplified by LNER No 30281, built in 1946. Like many GPO-sponsored carriages, it turned out to be a one-off (LNER official, NRM).*

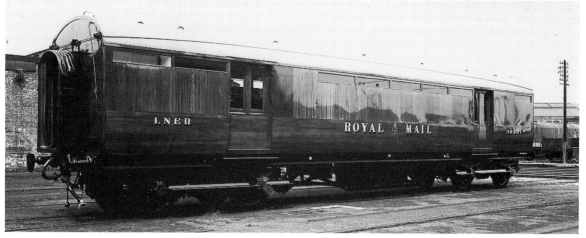

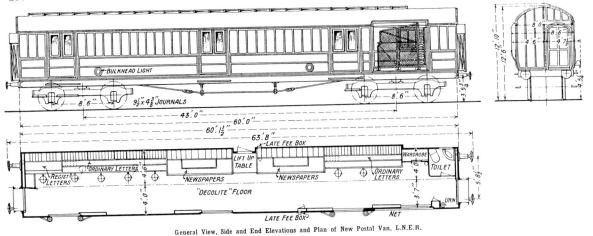

General View, Side and End Elevations and Plan of New Postal Van, L.N.E.R.

General Arrangement
of New Vans.

Figure 93 *Comparative elevations and plans of the 1928 LNER TPOs for the King's Cross–Newcastle service and the 1932 LMS design for the West Coast Postal and other services.*

Scale: 2mm = 1ft

Other passenger-carrying vehicles

It is almost axiomatic in railway terms that, wherever possible, items of rolling-stock are allowed to perform a useful function for just as long as their basic structure will allow. Historically, this goes back to the very dawn of the railway era, and we have already seen some of the post-grouping consequences in Chapter 10. It was, in large part, a combination of the quality of the original construction with the natural desire of the railways not to spend more than was necessary in order to maintain their traffic. In our present day it still goes on, of course, but is influenced by changing fashion to an extent far

exceeding that which was relevant in the company period. Railway vehicles are, in general, not of the 'throw away after ten years' kind, so prevalent in the modern motor vehicle, and in this lies both their strength and their weakness.

In the passenger-carrying mode, this longevity has proved to be more of a problem in the modern age than during earlier days when fashions changed rather less often. In consequence, the railways were often able to meet many of the new challenges by selective adaptation and rebuilding, and nowhere was this more so than in the realm of special saloons and branch line (or similar) services. In these areas, so much of the post-grouping activity was conducted by means of older vehicles that the need for new items was very small indeed; but those which were built are not without interest.

Starting with the special saloons, it has already been demonstrated that even in the exalted Royal sphere, the pre-group contribution mostly sufficed during the 'Big Four' era, so it would be surprising indeed if the railways had found it needful to augment their lesser saloon fleets, and so it was to prove. In fact, hardly anything at all was added to the 1923 lists. For the most part, this was due to the changing demands of the public in the rapidly motorizing brave new world of the 1920s and 1930s; such firmly established Victorian and Edwardian favourites as family and invalid saloons had no real place in the sort of changing environment where their most likely users were almost certainly amongst the first to adopt the motor car alternative. In consequence, the few residual demands for this sort of thing could be and almost always were met from earlier stock; and even that proved to offer an excessive over-capacity to the point where many were either converted to third class picnic form or given a fresh lease of life in a purely internal railway 'departmental' role. Hardly ever was anything new actually built for this purpose, and even the picnic conversions were mostly a forlorn 'last hope'.

Against this background, therefore, it is rather surprising that such as the 1930 GWR private saloons mentioned in Chapter 11 were built at all, and by any criteria almost amazing that the fairly hard-nosed LMS should witness the building of not only the rather useless but attractive Club Saloon of the 1939

One of the most handsome of the few post-grouping additions to the specialist field was the surprising conversion in 1938-9 of former SE & CR carriage No 7919 into an invalid saloon. It was one of a few similar vehicles to be used in the former SE & CR Royal Train and may well have been included in the formation shown on page 249. In fact, its conversion may not have been unconnected with the contemporary disbandment of the Southern Royal Train; such accounts as survive are rather 'thin' on these interesting facts! (SR official, NRM).

Coronation Scot (see page 230) but had also countenanced a brand new Stanier pattern Manchester-Blackpool Club Car some three years earlier. Even if the 1939 car may well have been justified purely for publicity purposes, the 1935 car seems to have been a quite genuine offering, doubtless very much appreciated by its patrons; but one cannot help but feel that an equally amenable alternative could have been offered by rebuilding at far lower cost, if such was needed at all. It hardly need be stated that the idea was never repeated.

In fact, setting aside these odd few mavericks, the only new saloons which were built during the final company period were mostly of the self-indulgent 'inspection' or 'officers' type whose function was explained in the previous volume. In all cases they had to await the final company years to emerge, if only because there were plenty of pre-group types still available. But when they finally did come out there was no stinting, even though most of them actually appeared during the post-1939 austerity years, some indeed after the formation of BR. Surprisingly, by far the most profligate provider was the LMS which, in the dark days of 1940, introduced the first of an eventual total of 14 new 50-foot bogie inspection saloons to replace its miscellaneous pre-group fleet. They were probably only marginally necessary, but they did at least enjoy a long life, lasting well into the 1980s, and one supposes, saving BR the need to spend much more money on similar provisioning! Some are privately preserved.

But if these carriages were marginal in justification, they were topped out by two wildly extravagant President's Saloons which the LMS built in 1942. In this context it should be appreciated that 'President' was not the title of some foreign dignitary, on which basis they may have had some validity, but was the

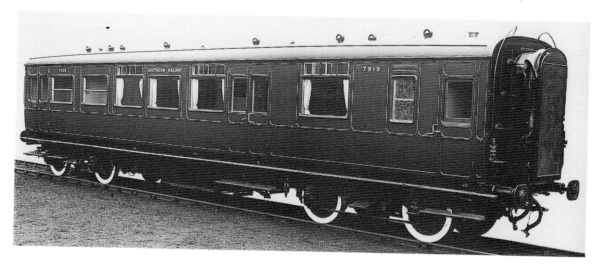

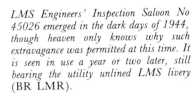

LMS Engineers' Inspection Saloon No 45026 emerged in the dark days of 1944, though heaven only knows why such extravagance was permitted at this time. It is seen in use a year or two later, still bearing the utility unlined LMS livery (BR LMR).

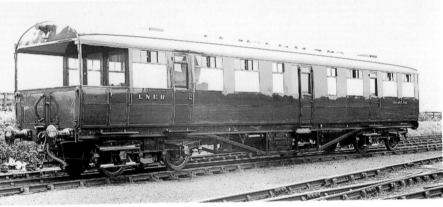

LNER Inspection Saloon No 900580 also emerged during the war in 1943, but was converted to open balcony form in 1945 with a gangway at the opposite end. This April 1945 view shows the end product, perhaps the most odd feature being the extravagant application of a full painted 'teak' livery, (LNER official, NRM).

nomenclature of the LMS Chief Executive, in consequence of the LMS running its affairs along American-inspired corporate management methods, unique in British railway administration at that time. This was, in fact, quite a good way of running such a big railway, and the two carriages in question were put to very good use if not quite as originally envisaged. During the war, they were most often put to VVIP use by high-ranking political and military figures, and in 1948 were permanently added to the LMS Royal fleet, at first for the exclusive use of HRH The Princess Elizabeth and Prince Philip after their marriage, but later (1952 onwards) for other members of the Royal Family and/or the Royal Household. As such, they were given Royal Train livery in 1954-5 and could have been included in the previous chapter, but since they were actually built as Officers Saloons they seem more appropriate here. Both of them still survive.

There were also a few modern GWR-designed official saloons, one of which is preserved at the NRM, and a pair of rather nice Thompson-period LNER-pattern offerings, latterly used during the 1980s as

public observation saloons on BR's 'tourist' trains in Scotland after their withdrawal from inspection service; but undoubtedly the most unorthodox of the 'new wave' official coaches was, as might cause no real surprise, the brainchild of that *enfant terrible* of the company era, one Oliver S. Bulleid. It was designated as an inspection saloon, but in fact was the one and only post-1923 Southern Railway attempt at producing a proper form of sleeping car.

Built in 1946, it was, by any criteria, pretty awful. For one thing, it was faced in plywood, a material which, from his LNER experience with the tourist stock, Bulleid ought to have known was doomed to long-term failure, being wholly unsuited to the hurly burly of railway use; but secondly, its internal layout seems to have been designed to be as different as possible from the time-proven LMS, LNER and GWR arrangement as for any other reason. The compartments were arrayed on either side of a central gangway and the berths were longitudinal. There was only one entrance, central on each side of the carriage, while the outside windows were high up on the carriage side in the manner of the worst excesses of the not well-loved 'Tavern Cars' (see page 102). All told, the effect must have been appallingly claustrophobic for those railway officials who had to ride in it, and it is maybe just as well that its style was never adopted for main-line service and that its very existence is mostly unknown! It went, largely unmourned, to the breakers in 1953.

Turning finally to the more publicly accessible vehicles relevant to this section of our survey, we come to that much-loved railway operation, the push-pull train. Volume 1 has explained its origins and Chapter 10 has given a few typical exemplars of the older conversions, but here we shall concentrate on the new examples built during the grouping era. In truth, there were none too many.

We may instantly dismiss the Southern Railway, for although, proportional to its size, it probably made more use of the push-pull mode than any of the 'Big Four', it was achieved entirely by the very clever rebuilding of pre-1923 company stock, and in this context the Southern probably merits almost as much commendation as for its EMU conversions of older stock; they were well thought out and undoubtedly gave much valuable service for a generation or more in such areas as did not justify the third rail. For much the same reason, the LNER also needs but little mention in this regard for it most often tended to espouse the railcar alternative for many of these workings, and made no mean fist of things as Chapter 9 has attempted to show. Even though it produced some conventional non-corridor-style push-pull stock as well, these can be realistically ignored in the broader general picture. Which leaves us with the LMS and GWR to consider.

In both cases, the two companies concerned adopted a mixture of pre-group stock and new build. They both had considerable use for such operations, but the end product was rather different and, in the case of the GWR, not uninfluenced by its growing experience with diesel railcars from the mid-1930s onwards. Why they should have been so different is hard to say with certainty, and no doubt prejudiced supporters of the two concerns will advance cogent if not altogether logical reasons for the different approaches, but thus it was.

The LMS was undoubtedly the more conventional. Apart from the LNWR, which had at least tried to devise some new forms of carriage styling for the more bucolic areas of its system, there was no vast inherited tradition of conceptual change as far as the LMS was concerned. Most of its acquired push-pull services were in the hands of converted non-corridor compartment stock, and thus it was to remain both for those and for the new services converted to this mode. True, there were later conversions of a few side-corridor carriages and, of course, the retention of any purpose-built stock which would suffice, but the general feeling seems to have been that orthodox carriage types would suffice for the bulk of these lesser services. In consequence, and added to the conversions of older pre-group stock which it also undertook with great vigour, the best the LMS ever contemplated in terms of new vehicles was merely to adapt its orthodox non-corridor designs for 'motor train' use, as it preferred to call the business. Some were, in fact, conversions of almost new conventional carriages, but others were built new for the job and this went on until *circa* 1950; in fact, just about the only thing which identified an LMS-built push-pull coach from its conventional equivalent were the extra vacuum brake pipes and the windows in the driving versions of the brake ended carriages.

The GWR was very different. For one thing, it had made much greater use of steam railmotors in the pre-1923 period, and although these vehicles had shown quite considerable limitations (see Volume 1)

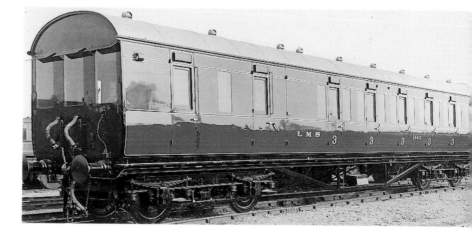

LMS push-pull driving brake third No 24413 was built new as such in 1933 at the start of the Stanier era, but showed no real innovation in design compared with its conventional non-corridor equivalent; in fact, many more of this type were simply converted from the normal locomotive-hauled fleet than were built new as such (BR LMR).

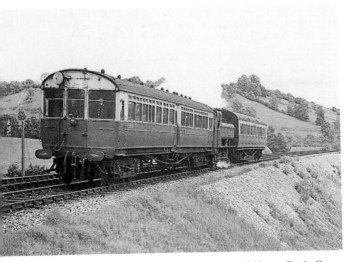

The archetypal GWR local scene of the 1930s: a Castle Cary–Taunton local train consisting of an unidentified Class '54xx' 0-6-0 pannier tank sandwiched between leading auto-trailer No 213, itself converted from steam railmotor No 96, and an unidentified bow-ended corridor third. (Soole Collection, NRM).

BR-built GWR-type auto-trailer No W221W 'Thrush' at Aylesbury in 1962 in the charge of 0-4-2T No 1455 (T.J. Edgington Collection).

they had also helped establish quite a few new ideas in carriage design *per se*, principally their 'open plan' interiors. Moreover, the GWR had quite a considerable number of them, by no means life-expired when it became obvious that the conventional locomotive in push-pull mode was a better answer for the less busy services. In consequence, the GWR had a fine reservoir of potentially convertible stock; this it proceeded to exploit to the tune of almost 90 vehicles down to the late 1920s, and in the process created that most characteristic form, the 'auto-trailer'. So successful was this converted form that it became the norm for most subsequent services of the kind and even led to the building of new auto-trailers as the operations expanded into all parts of the system.

However, in spite of the success of the conversion of railmotors to auto-trailer mode and its consequential enhancement of patronage, such was the size of the original steam railmotor fleet that the GWR did not find it necessary to build any totally new examples of the auto-trailer type until 1929, and even in total, when the programme was completed in 1933, they still represented little more than 33 per cent of the converted railmotor fleet. Furthermore, it has to be stated that they were not particularly distinguished inside. But they did perform an invaluable service, and remained in service well into the final steam days.

So useful, in fact, were the GWR auto-trailers that

well into BR days a final series was felt to be justifiable. These coaches came out during 1951-4, displaying the almost slab-sided profile of the Hawksworth period, and the first pair were even given names 'Wren' and 'Thrush' as the first of what were meant to be a class of 'named' auto-trailers. Though this idea came to nought and the names were soon lost, these carriages in their 1953 refurbished form became a sort of quasi-prototype for the later and ubiquitous DMUs of the 1950s and later. Moreover, the last ten, GWR No Series 235-44, built new in 1954 with the more up-to-date interiors, had the interesting distinction of being the last passenger-carrying carriages to a non-BR standard design. They were not strictly GWR either, but only the pedants complained!

Thus it was that the GWR, whether in the shape of its diesel railcars or in the final series of steam-powered auto-trailers, may be said to have had no small influence on the subsequent evolution of the BR continuation in this specific area. Furthermore, having been more than censorial about the lack of inspiration in most GWR stock of the grouping period, I am more than happy to redress the overall balance by giving Swindon its due share of credit in what was to prove a critical field — and this seems to me an appropriate point at which to take leave of this particular subject.

14. The last of the 'company' carriages

The Second World War was, to put it mildly, a difficult time for all the British railway companies, and they acquitted themselves nobly in the national interest. But they also, undoubtedly, entered the post-war era in the shadow of putative railway nationalization, consequential upon the 1945 General Election results which returned, for the first time ever, a Labour Government with an absolute majority. This carried within it a remit to implement the fundamental tenets of Socialist philosophy which, *inter alia*, implied public control of the overall British transport system. By 1947 the die was cast, and on 1 January 1948 the railways were taken into public ownership. To be candid, some higher echelons of the 'old guard' railway management, and here we may, perhaps, especially single out that of the GWR, could not bring themselves to believe that it would ever happen; but it did and the consequences were widespread. Whether or not they were effective is a very different story to which we shall have cause to return in the next volume; meantime our concern here is to complete the company story as far as carriages were concerned.

In the specific field of vehicle design, it took some years for the newly nationalized organization to settle down, and it was not until *circa* 1951-2 that the first wholly new ideas emerged. In the interim, the old company approaches held sway and this led to a short-lived, but very interesting period of rolling-stock development wherein the final ideas of the 'Big Four' took tangible form against an organizational background which must have been very far from the thoughts of the old board rooms when the ideas were first mooted.

The four main lines had had little chance to develop new ideas during the war years, so in consequence there was probably a degree of pent-up frustration in terms of rolling-stock design, probably made more acute by the ever growing realization of the threat of road competition. In consequence, the main emphasis as far as most aspects of carriage development was concerned was directed to main-line express services, and with the noteworthy exception of the Southern Railway, none of the other railways seem to have been too bothered about their shorter-distance services. There was in any case a sort of monopolistic state of affairs in these areas, given petrol rationing and the like, and there was, in any case, plenty of fairly new short-haul stock available. The Southern was, however, rather different in this respect, so before looking at main-line developments, it seems only proper briefly to address this particular point.

Chapter 6 has indicated how the Southern Railway coped with the carriage consequences of its large-scale pre-war suburban electrification by applying a judicious mixture of rebuilding much of its pre-group locomotive-hauled stock to EMU form with a selective provisioning of new stock where such rebuilding was neither sensible nor practicable, eg the longer-distance routes to such places as Portsmouth, Brighton et al. But by 1945-6, it was quite clear that this process had reached its limit. Furthermore, the converted EMUs formed from pre-group hauled stock were themselves beginning to show signs of their age, many of their bodies being already 40 or more years old. Accordingly, Oliver Bulleid made strenuous attempts to re-equip the short-distance services of the Southern Railway with a new tranche of stock. Now Bulleid has often been much criticized for his rather avant garde and maybe impractical approach to steam locomotive development in the final company years, but it cannot really be gainsaid that in the realm of carriages he showed a far better appreciation of the problem than any of his contemporaries. As a result, the Southern, by the time of nationalization, was not only well down the road to a full reappraisal of its main-line operations, but was also well advanced in the re-equipment of its short-distance operations as well.

To a large extent, this re-equipment took the form of a standardized four-car suburban EMU of a distinctively new external style. Familiarly known as the '4SUB', it merely repeated the ideas of an early generation and, conceptually, was nothing very remarkable, merely taking the form of a tight assemblage of conventional side-door compartments on a basic standard chassis, along with the essential driving and guard's accommodation. The compartments were by no means generously dimensioned, save by comparison with the quite execrable LNER steam hauled quad-arts and quin-arts, but in external terms they established a 'new look' to Southern electric services which remained a familiar sight for nigh on 40 years. Repeated almost to the point of boredom, one cannot say that one looked forward to riding in one of them with any degree of pleasurable anticipation — they were hardly renowned for their spacious quality, nor did they give the passenger the option of first class travel, and their riding could be quite adventurous to say the least — but they surely shifted vast numbers of people in their time, and their outward styling was not without influence in the BR continuation, be it suburban or main-line mode. Later examples, both SR and BR, saw a mixture of compartment and open style and even at the time of

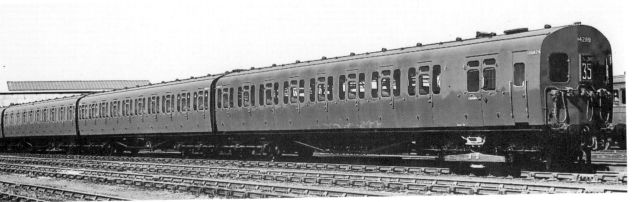

Above *This view of SR type 4SUB unit No S4289 of the 1948-9 build serves as a timely reminder of the fact that Bulleid's final carriage designs dominated the Southern scene for the best part of 20 or more years after the formation of BR. This unit was one of many built with mostly open-plan interiors — see Figure 43, page 127 (BR SR).*

Left *Corridor brake third No 26321 was one of the first LMS carriages to be built after the 1939-45 war as part of that company's determined drive to reinstate its carriage building programme. It embodied welded bogie and underframe construction, but even in this respect it differed little from the pre-war equivalent (BR LMR).*

Table 9 Post-war gangwayed stock to company designs: new build, all types

Notes: 1. These values have been extracted from various published works and may contain occasional discrepancies from other sources in the units column. Overall, they are within 1 per cent of precise totals and serve adequately for comparative purposes.
2. The tables include all non-kitchen vehicles built for dining purposes.

Company	Corridor types[1]							Open types[1]					Grand Total
	FK	CK	TK	BFK	BCK	BTK	Sub Total	FO	CO	TO	BTO	Sub Total	
LMS (Stanier)	42	525	701	15	—	784	2067	20	—	350	—	370	2437
LNER (Thompson)	94	109	488	—	40	99	830	9	—	33	—	42	872
GWR (Hawksworth)	31	36	207	—	44	177	495	—	—	—	—	—	495
SR (Bulleid)	41	246	110	—	53	44	494	11[2]	8	56	275[3]	350	844
Totals	208	916	1506	15	137	1104	3886	40	8	439	275	762	4648

1 Carriage types are identified by standard BR codes when built (see page 288). Third Class became Second Class in 1956.
2 All semi-FO.
3 All semi-BTO.

writing (1989) one can still witness some of their lineal descendants at Waterloo, Victoria and Charing Cross, though their days are surely numbered.

In these vehicles, Bulleid adopted a carriage profile which was soon to become familiar throughout the Southern and, later, on the BR system too. In fact, the first BR continuation for the Southern Region was almost a carbon copy of Bulleid's ideas. We cannot be certain why it was chosen, but its essential characteristic was that of a continuous and gentle curve between cantrail and solebar, rather than the usual 'flat' side from roof to waist combined with an in-curve from waist to the solebar. Bulleid put it on his post-war Southern corridors too, and in due course something very similar was adopted as the BR standard for all stock. When applied to main-line stock it had a considerable degree of aesthetic merit and remained the 'current' style until the 1960s. It also served to give BR standard stock a distinctively different look to that of all its company forbears, save for those of Southern origin. However, in mentioning the BR continuation we are moving a little ahead of the story at this point, so we must go back to the finale of the company era.

Apart from Bulleid's valiant efforts on the Southern's suburban lines, the bulk of carriage development during the final company years was connected with the matter of improving main-line stock and here, as Chapter 4 has indicated, only the LMS had much to boast about in the pre-1940 era. Furthermore, it was probably the first of the four companies to get into its stride after the war too. As early as 1945, Derby and Wolverton had resumed their pre-war scale of carriage building activity and, as Table 9 reveals, by the end of the company era LMS designs already represented well over 50 per cent of the total new main-line stock to emerge after the war. However, on this occasion it did, at least, have some competition.

At this point, and by way of mild recapitulation, it may be helpful briefly to compare the main-line stock of the 'Big Four' as it existed at the end of the war, using as a comparison their latest pre-war designs of the common corridor composite type. I have tabulated their comparative details below, and the first thing to note is that in spite of many differences there were also many points in common, not least their very close harmonization in size at about

the 60-foot length and their universal use of an all-steel angle-trussed underframe. It seems, therefore, that in spite of the many stylistic and detail differences, there was also much common ground.

The GWR and LMS used screw couplings and British Standard gangways, the other two preferring the buckeye/Pullman alternative. The GWR and SR never offered three-per-side thirds (save in the SR 'narrow' stock) while the latter company was the only one to retain a full complement of compartment-side doors. The GWR still fitted one or two doors on this side but the LMS and LNER had both suppressed this feature. All lines used the automatic vacuum brake.

For the most part, the LMS simply continued to develop the ideas which Stanier had instigated in the early 1930s. The great man himself left the LMS at the end of 1942, but in the carriage field, as in the locomotive arena, his legacy was such as to necessitate no great quantum change. Just about the only real variation on the pre-war theme was the insertion of one or two extra doors on the corridor side of the main-line carriages, and this is reckoned to have been more to meet the revised safety aspects of the time than representing any basic change of philosophy by the company. None of the older carriages were altered to the new arrangement, so it cannot have been totally mandatory. There was also, in the BR-built examples of Stanier stock, a totally cosmetic change in toilet window shape during 1949-50 to a new circular style (vehicles thus equipped being known colloquially as 'porthole' stock) which derived its shape from the 1939 'Coronation Scot' carriages; but those who have examined the preserved 1937 and 1950 brake thirds in the NRM collection will appreciate how little the fundamentals really changed. In that lies their significance.

Over the years, the LMS had also made increasing use of welding in its bogie and underframe construction — though not exclusively — and there was one particular aspect of welded carriage construction which the LMS was beginning to develop at the very end of its independent existence which turned out to be of more than passing significance. This was the reintroduction of the 'all-steel' form of body construction with a revised design of underframe. It began with the Southport EMUs (page 167), but afterwards was confined to a series of corridor composites which

Company	Body dimensions	Body construction	Compartments	Seats
LMS	60'1″ × 8'11½″	Flush steel/timber frame	3F + 4T	18F + 24T
LNER	61'6″ × 9'0″	Timber/timber frame	3F + 4T	18F + 24T
GWR	59'10″ × 8'11″	Flush steel/timber frame	4F + 3T	24F + 24T
SR	59'0″ × 9'0″	Steel/timber frame	4F + 3T	24F + 24T

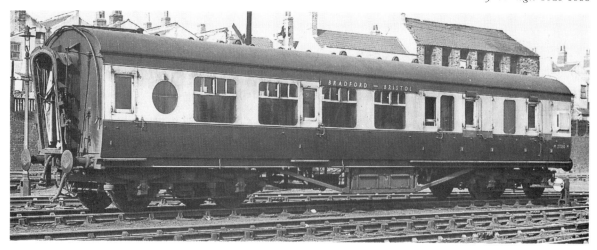

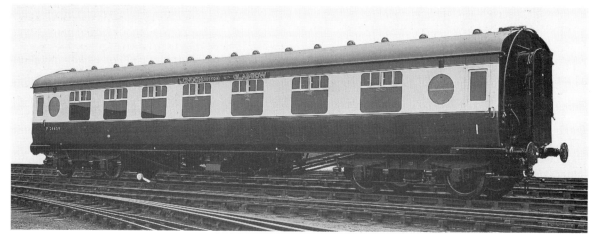

began to emerge in 1949. However, when allied with the generally Bulleid-inspired body form of the BR standard coach, it made the major contribution to the new BR designs of the 1950s and as such we shall return to it in the next volume.

Meantime, the other three companies had more than a little catching up to do in 1945, and it is a matter of history that they all managed to achieve much in a few short years, albeit that many of the results actually came into service after BR was created.

In 1941, the great Sir Nigel Gresley had died before his time and his place on the LNER was taken by Edward Thompson, arguably one of the most controversial figures ever to assume the top position on a British railway. In a sense he was on 'a hiding to nothing', for Gresley's was probably an impossible act to follow, not made any simpler by the straitened circumstances of war. In fact, it is one of the more interesting exercises to speculate how Gresley would have coped during those days, for there was no doubt that some of his preferred methods would need to be changed under wartime conditions. Thompson knew this, but, though oft-times in latter days misunderstood, did not help his cause by the way in which he went about making the necessary changes. If truth be told, he held more than a little admiration for the fairly ruthless standardization which the LMS had been pursuing under Stanier, and though Stanier and Gresley were good friends this was not quite the Gresley way of doing things, however great the economic justification. What is known is that in the locomotive field, Thompson sought advice from some of Stanier's lieutenants who, diplomatically, confined their remarks to such bland statements as 'We would

not have done it quite like that', without actually saying what they *would* have done!

In consequence, Thompson's early efforts on the locomotive front tended to be seen as undoing almost everything that Gresley had done. Given the perhaps rather tactless and insensitive rebuilding of Gresley's first 4-6-2 *Great Northern*, not to mention the equally unmemorable rebuilding of Gresley's fine 'Cock o' the North' 2-8-2s into not very successful 'Pacifics', one could well understand why his activities met with little approval, and when he finally gave way to A.H.Peppercorn in 1946 there were many sighs of relief. Yet the really strange irony is that all post-war LNER carriages are regarded as Thompson not Peppercorn stock, in spite of the fact that relatively few of them were built during Thompson's period of office! And the attribution is fair.

As part of his reassessment of the LNER position, towards the end of the war Thompson realized that the days of the traditional teak-bodied carriage were numbered, not simply on the grounds of dated appearance, but largely because of economic considerations. Some earlier experiments with steel sheeting had been carried out (see page 73), but Thompson's re-think was of a more radical nature and resulted in completely new designs being introduced. Non-corridor stock was little changed in concept but there was a major reappraisal of the main-line fleet, not the least of which was a questionnaire to passengers in 1946.

As a result of these deliberations, the new LNER main-line stock, still maintaining its Gresley-inspired underframe and bogie, though some composites were built on a shorter 58-foot frame to suit the revised interior arrangement, displayed a quite different external style, smooth sided and, in my view, having seen and ridden in many of them, of very pleasing aesthetic character. It further differed from all other contemporary flush-sided stock in having square-cornered windows and very attractive oval-shaped lavatory windows. Within the corridor coaches, a further and very sensible innovation was to divide the compartment areas into sections of two or three with intermediate cross-vestibules, for ease of loading at stations, while the compartment sizes were made a generous 7 ft 6 in and 6 ft 6 in for first and third class respectively. They had bowed ends in plan but no doming to the roof. In them, Thompson gave the new LNER stock quite recognizably modern and different lines which could in no conceivable way be mistaken for its LMS or GWR equivalent; so far so good, but there were snags.

For one thing, the first examples were garbed in ersatz teak livery which, while it might have made some sort of sense while the LNER was building mostly teak-bodied carriages — *vide* the odd steel-

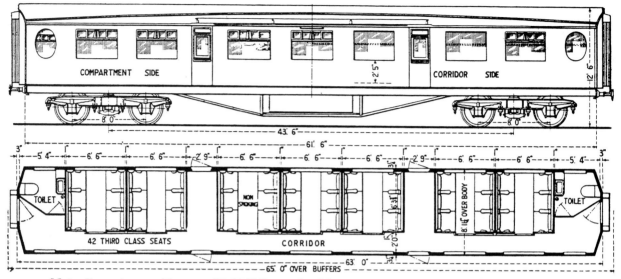

Main dimensions and layout of L.N.E.R. coach with compartments to accommodate six passengers

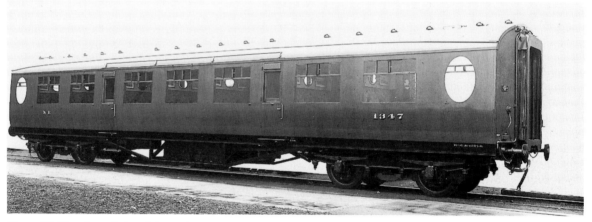

Figure 94 *Elevation and plan of the spacious seven-compartment Thompson LNER corridor third, its cross-vestibules and generously sized compartments being typical of most post-war LNER-type corridor stock.*

Scale: $^1/_{10}$" = 1ft

The prototype Thompson LNER carriage, corridor third No 1347 of 1945 finished in pseudo 'teak'. It also embodied Thompson's new design of bogie, but this was not a success and most future examples reverted to the well-proven Gresley type (LNER official, NRM).

panelled experiments in the 1920s and 1930s — it made no sense at all in terms of accentuating the modernity which, presumably, they were meant to represent. Frankly, they looked rather ridiculous and one wonders why the LNER did not adopt a new livery simultaneously with their introduction; the pre-war 'Tourist' scheme would have looked rather nice and, given the LNER's swift post-war reintroduction of apple green engines, would certainly have brightened up the drab post-war years. In this respect, the new BR red and cream livery, applied to many of

them when new and all of them in due course, looked distinctly more appropriate. I have clear memories of these carriages in red and cream hauled by 'A1s' and 'A4s' in the short-lived BR blue locomotive livery, and it really was a most attractive ensemble.

But this is merely a cosmetic consideration, and subjective at that; far more serious were the deficiencies of the carriages themselves. The square-cornered windows turned out to be rust traps and early corrosion was rife; from 1949 onwards, round-cornered windows were adopted to beneficial effect and no detriment to appearance. However, the really major disappointment was within the carriages, where no attempt at all was made to maintain the standards of the pre-war era. Drab upholstery, dreary institutional cream paint, dark woodwork, thoroughly unpleasant plastic trimmings and rather primitive lavatories all combined to make something of a nonsense of the 'modern' image — and the finish was not that good either, as I recall.

Even so, many hundreds were built and though they in no way matched the post-war LMS build in terms of sheer numbers, they represented about 20 per cent of the grand total of LNER-designed main-

line stock when the BR standard types began to take over. They were in every way symptomatic of the post-war 'utility' years and although they rode well, as might be expected of most ex-LNER stock, they generally flattered to deceive. It was a pity, because much of the thinking behind them was sound and with just a bit more care, effort and imagination they could have been very much better. Few are preserved.

By contrast with the LNER, the GWR had adopted flush-sided exterior steel panelling well before the war but, as has been indicated, did not always take full advantage of the stylistic opportunities offered. However, its final pre-war corridor coaches showed that the company was at last emerging from its mid-life crisis, and these were to form the basis of the final and rather stylish vehicles built to the design of Hawksworth. There were not too many of them and most did not emerge, largely for economic reasons, until after the company had given way to BR. But the basic concept and design was wholly Great Western.

These views compare the square- and round-cornered window variants of otherwise identical post-war LNER stock, both being brake composites. The older version, LNER No 1141, came out late in 1947, while No E10159, viewed from the opposite (compartment) side, emerged in 1950. Undeniably handsome of form in both variants, there can be little doubt that the round-cornered version and the more appropriate BR livery had the aesthetic edge (LNER/BR ER official, NRM).

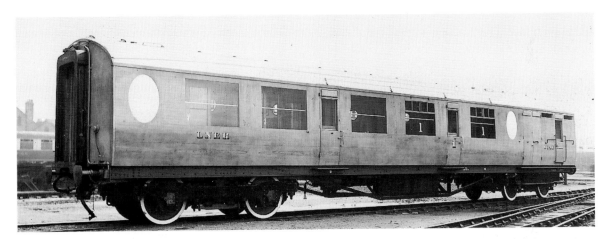

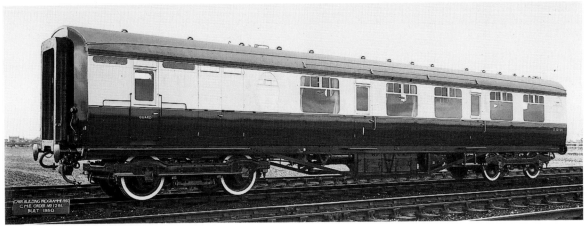

Their origin went back to the final war years when the first orders were issued in 1944, and first indications were that these new GWR carriages were going to be more than normally innovative, given the generally conservative nature of the company. For one thing, they were to have fluorescent lighting, at that time a relatively unknown quantity in terms of carriage building. In the event, very few were turned out in this way, and none after 1947, the general consensus being that the lights were too harsh. Secondly, early examples made use of Formica-type laminated plastic panelling to brighten the interiors and reduce the amount of expensive timber veneers. Unfortunately, and whether it was inspired by the GWR I cannot say, the use of these laminates became rather too widespread after that time in many British carriages, doing little for their aesthetics, however much cost it might have saved.

Another innovation was a new 64-foot length combined with a new body shape, the latter characterized by its almost 'slab' sides but married to an

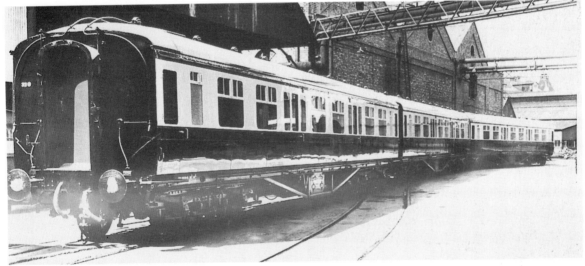

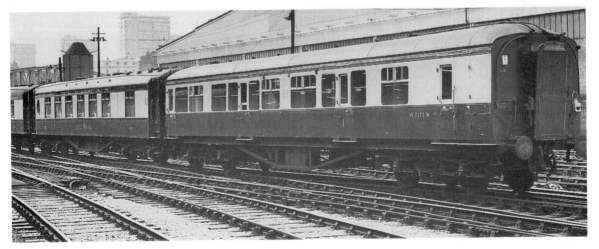

attractive domed end roof very reminiscent of Gresley's LNER carriages. Finally, and at long last, the GWR caught up the rest of the country by adopting a 'direct build' form of carriage assembly. It was not quite mass production on the LMS pattern but was very much based on later LMS (Stanier) practice. The floor now became part of the underframe, as on the LMS, instead of part of the body and, again like the LMS, bottom side members were dispensed with by having brackets fixed directly to the underframe which could receive the body pillars of the preassembled side components. Finally, later LMS practice was also copied in the substitution of steel for wooden cantrails.

All told, a pretty decisive and overdue change was achieved and, taking all into consideration, the only really backward features were the continued use of four-per-side seating in the thirds and the retention of some compartment-side doors. Later production batches also reverted to more solidly traditional wood finishes in the first class, though using enamelled hardboard in the thirds, the latter being far brighter in consequence. In fact, quite a number of interior ideas were tried out in the Hawksworth carriages, some of which, not least the rather more civilized lavatories, seem to have influenced the BR standard types.

But in a sense it was too little and too late. Qualitatively they were far superior to the Thompson LNER stock, but conceptually they still did not match up to the best LMS practice and bequeathed little more than their length (which was shared with Bulleid's SR stock anyway) to the BR period. They did, however, last well into the 1960s, by which time they were almost the only GWR-designed carriages left in service. In this regard, they vanished at much the same time as their other company-designed contemporaries, though perhaps the final irony in the history of the last carriages built to the design of this famous company was the fact that in their final years

they were overhauled at Wolverton, from whence stemmed many of their constructional features, and not Swindon!

Little need be said about the final generation of company-designed non-corridor stock, save that it was all pretty routine and uninspired. However, as an amusing aside, it is probably worth recording that some of the last GWR-pattern non-corridors to be built were issued to a London Midland order because neither Derby nor Wolverton could cope at the time. Since the LMR could not, apparently, accept the new and longer (63 ft) Hawksworth vehicles, the LMR order was delivered to a resurrected pre-war GWR design!

Of all the four companies at the end of the war, the Southern was probably the most old-fashioned in terms of its main-line stock, and this is not really surprising. Most of its carriages were built in the first ten years after 1923, and so successful had Maunsell been in solving the problem that by the time the other companies were starting to modernize their designs in the 1930s, the SR had no immediate need for new vehicles anyway. But this was not the case after the war and, as might well be expected, Oliver Bulleid took full advantage and, it is fair to say, probably made the most significant new contribution to main-line carriage development in the short post-war company period.

His ideas were simultaneously both predictable and unexpected. Ever since 1937 he had been brightening up the interiors of some of Maunsell's carriages, so some of his interior designs probably came as no great surprise; but the new styling given to all new carriages, combined with the introduction of some new types and the concept of a totally integrated set or even train formation, was certainly different. So too was the new malachite green livery which, though introduced to a limited extent before the war, was never really widespread until afterwards. Like it or not, one could not ignore it, and in one respect it was probably the most honest paint scheme of all in that it abandoned all lining with no pretence to be anything but what it was.

Structurally, Bulleid's carriages represented something new both to the Southern and to Britain generally. While not abandoning separate underframes, he did desert tradititional timber body framing in favour of a much greater use of steel framing and welding, though there was still some timber used. As many as possible of the fittings were highly standardized, typical being the pressed steel doors with frameless droplights and their characteristic round-ended toplights. As far as possible, Bulleid also moved construction in the general direction followed by the LMS, and complete bodysides were built on a jig. One interesting point, however, was the retention of wood and canvas roofs, largely because the expense of setting up jigs for making a wholly steel-covered coach was thought to be too great in relation to the numbers likely to be built. In this respect, the main-line stock contrasted with the new suburban electrics which were 'all-steel' in basic structure and jig-built; there were, of course, far more of these, thus allowing economies of scale.

Bulleid's first main-line essays — three-coach sets of two brake thirds and a composite — were actually ordered early in the war but did not emerge until 1945-6. They retained the Maunsell length/underframe and, rather surprisingly, still perpetuated most of the old layout features, including a full set of outside doors on the compartment side; but they were otherwise totally new in styling, and this new form became much more familiar when the final length

was determined and the coaches began to emerge in some quantity, all with 64 ft 6 in bow-ended bodies on a 63 ft 5 in underframe. Apart from the flush panelling, the most noticeable feature was the continuous bodyside curve from solebar to cantrail, something quite new to British main-line carriage design, though it had been anticipated with the earlier 4SUB units. It looked very good, and the absence of a gutter strip at the cantrail made the whole body and roof 'flow' together in a most attractive way. The trouble was that the lack of gutters caused passengers to suffer dripping water down the door openings on wet days, and this lack of proper roof drainage was, eventually, to be the cause of much rotting and rusting.

After his first corridor batches, Bulleid finally abandoned the outside compartment doors in all save, for some reason, the third class brakes. In their place came round-cornered large picture windows of a type rather akin to those already common on the LMS. They had upper sliding ventilators of shallow type which eventually gave way (in those examples built during the BR period) to a deeper form. Additionally, there was usually installed a central cross-vestibule somewhat in the Thompson LNER manner; one even wonders if there was some LNER influence at work, since Bulleid was an ex-LNER man. Furthermore, just as did the LNER (see above), the SR also conducted a post-war passenger survey before commencing series production of the new carriages. All conventional corridor and open types were represented (see Table 9) save for a brake first (always a fairly rare breed in Britain until later BR days) but

Above left *This August 1951 view at Whiteball of the down 'Cornish Riviera' headed by 4-6-0 No 6025* King Henry III *reveals that in early BR days even the most important ex-GWR carriage formations were by no means tidy. The leading Hawksworth brake third is stylish enough, save for the intrusive outside door to the first compartment; but just look at the misalignment of roof, waist and solebar levels of the first five coaches!* (Russell-Smith Collection, NRM).

Right *A curious mixture of ancient and modern: Bulleid's first corridor stock is represented here by composite No 5726 from the early post war three-coach sets of 1945-6. The new profile is very modern, as is the totally honest plain green livery, but obvious too is the dated retention of a full set of outer doors. Even so, the 'flowing' stylistic nature of the overall body construction was quite new and, in the event, most significant* (SR official, NRM).

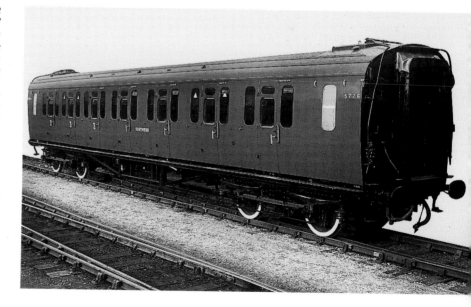

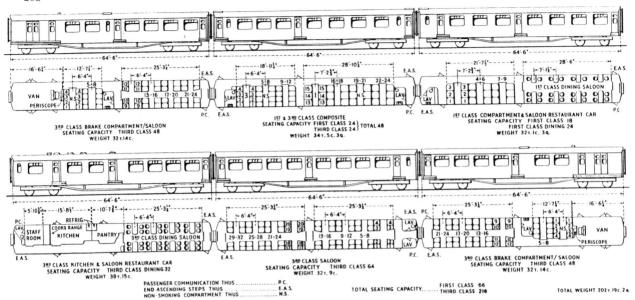

vision (see page 101)

there was one new variety of carriage which was very much Bulleid's own idea and became the most common single type to be built.

It was a semi-open brake third combining two compartments (a few had one plus a coupé) with four open bays. Several subtle variations existed, as with most of Bulleid's carriages, but the concept was a nice effort to meet the conflicting wishes for both open and compartment type seating in the third class revealed in the post-war survey, though the proportion of open seating was rather higher than passenger preference had indicated. Although Bulleid built quite a few full thirds as well (both open and side corridor), this new-style semi-open was clearly the preferred choice. For one thing, it lent itself to incorporation in fixed sets, especially if of short formation, and must have been a successful compromise; something very like it was often incorporated into several later generations of BR EMU stock for the Southern Region.

In the traditional Southern manner, much of Bulleid's stock was delivered in dedicated formations, including no fewer than 11 handsome six-coach sets for the Waterloo-Bournemouth services which displayed a further nice design touch — the bodyside panelling taken down to conceal the solebars, save at the side-step areas. Great care was taken both with the internal arrangements of the coaches and their order of marshalling: semi-BTO/TO/RT/semi-RFO/CK/semi-BTO. These, of course, were the sets which also contained Bulleid's new approach to dining provision (see page 101), and nothing quite as deliberately well thought out ever emerged from the other companies at the time.

If one can sum up these carriages, the word which springs to my mind is 'harmonious' and this generally extended to their interiors as well. Much thought went into their arrangements, within the economic constraints of the day, and the more revolutionary aspects of Bulleid's first interior design innovations were abandoned in favour of a return to the more popular and traditional wood finishes, usually walnut (first class) and mahogany (third class). Once the proliferation of old-fashioned outside doors had largely gone, there was little to choose between them and the best which the other lines could offer save for the vexed question of compartments versus open and the number of seats per side in the third class areas. Here, the Bulleid stock was to prove slightly prophetic in terms of the BR succession, for not only did the BR standard carriage imitate the Bulleid length and profile, it also copied many of his layouts without too much significant modification. Though much must, perforce, await the next volume to resolve, it is perhaps helpful to address the matter of seating capacity at this stage.

The Southern and Great Western remained wedded to four-per-side thirds to the very end, generally assumed to have been a reflection of their need to offer maximum seat capacity at holiday times, but this seems a poor argument. Given the fold-away nature of the individual armrests provided by the LMS and LNER, it was perfectly possible to get four per side at times of need, yet give the third class passengers a bit more breathing space for most of the year. My guess is that it was probably a mixture of conceptual inertia, a modest saving in cost of seat manufacture and, maybe most important, the problem of seat reservations. A compartment which variously could carry six or eight could not have its seats numbered to suit both forms, and since many of the SR and GWR holiday extra trains were fully reserved it was probably deemed best that the compartments should be labelled in the high density configuration.

The logical solution was, of course, the open style of carriage which the LMS had pioneered in such quantity, and one senses that, at least as far as the SR was concerned, Bulleid was endeavouring to move his line in this direction. But there was considerable contemporary passenger resistance to this approach which none of the companies fully resolved. The LMS probably came nearest, but even it was obliged to build mostly side-corridors after the war (see Table 9).

It is a well-worn cliché that comparisons are odious, but in summing up the carriage designs of the final 25-30 years of the company period, it is almost unavoidable and arguably necessary; so, accepting the limitations which must always qualify a personal assessment, I do not propose to duck the issue. Excluding London Transport and Pullman, of course, and discounting suburban compartment stock, where there seems to me to have been little of fundamental importance to differentiate all four companies, the argument homes in mostly on the main-line contribution along with technical innovation generally.

In terms of overall contribution to the main-line scene, it seems fair to state that the LMS had the best and most 'modern' fleet of carriages as far as the average passenger was concerned; the statistics quoted in this volume lead to this conclusion. It identified the problem earlier than its competitors and if it never quite reached the heights of the LNER's very best efforts, neither did it quite plumb the depths which all three of the others could and did reach from time to time. The LNER, by contrast, was rather more patchy. At its best it was superb, it did have the finest bogie design right to the very end and showed the most dedicated commitment to using more 'modern' gangways and couplings. But the variation in quality between its best sleeping, dining and main-line corridor stock and its worst suburban efforts was really too great to be wholly acceptable. Furthermore, its belated attempt to enter the 'modern' stakes with its post-war carriage designs, though stylish enough from the outside, was rather flawed in terms of quality and design detail.

The Southern had a poor starting base, which was hardly its own fault, and this account has emphasized the steps made by both Maunsell and Bulleid to come to grips with the problem. But not until Bulleid's time could the Southern be said to be really competing (and winning) in terms of the developing mid-twentieth-century passenger needs and expectations; and it never, proportionally, had quite as much up-to-date stock as did, for example, the LMS. As for the GWR, one can only reiterate the view that in main-line terms the first half of the grouping period seems to have been bedevilled by the inevitable complacency which its dominance in its own group after 1923 was almost bound to precipitate. That said, however, there were signs at the end that the GWR had looked over its shoulder and was beginning to make amends; but, as another writer has already put it, its post-war hopes were frustrated by the onset of BR. Even so, in one respect the GWR carriage was still without peer in the late 1940s. Alone of the 'Big Four', its modern flush-sided stock, rather old-fashioned though it may have been in terms of some of its interior design features, was undoubtedly far less prone to rust and corrosion than any of those built elsewhere. The sheer number which have been preserved (relative to the other three) seems to give evidence of that, and cannot wholly be explained by the greater dedication which GWR devotees are usually prone to give to their favourite company!

Outwith the main-line area, the principal electrification prize must go to the Southern whose inter-war

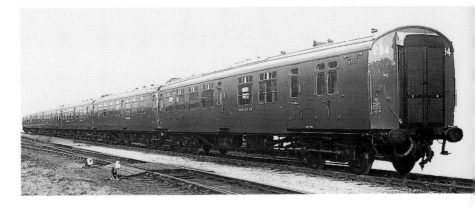

Figure 95 *Simplified elevations and plans of the six-coach Southern Railway corridor sets of 1947 for the Waterloo–Bournemouth services.*

Scale: 1" = 30ft

Right *The beautifully integrated and harmonious visual lines of the final SR corridor stock were nowhere better exemplified than in the six-coach sets for the Waterloo-Bournemouth services in 1947. This view of set No 294 was taken from the left-hand end of the formation as given in Figure 95. (SR official, NRM).*

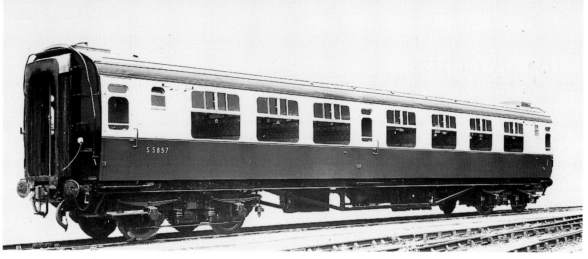

There can be no more appropriate way to end this part of the survey than by offering a view of perhaps the most handsome of the final post-war company-inspired offerings. Bulleid-type corridor composite No S5857 was built in 1950, incorporating the deep window ventilators of the BR period; furthermore, its overall external style predicted the BR continuation more accurately than any other, even though its basic form of construction did not. (BR SR).

efforts, in spite of its financial constraints, were little short of miraculous, suffering only from a degree of design staleness in terms of vehicle type. This was understandable in the circumstances and by no means as worthy of criticism as the surprising lack of interest shown in electrification by the two big companies, both of which had several areas which could have been so treated but which mostly had to await the BR period to be tackled. Offsetting this, however, it also seems fair to say that the final generation of new EMU designs which can be attributed to the LMS and LNER (those with sliding doors for the Wirral, Southport, Shenfield and Tyneside for example) were probably more influential in the long term than their far more numerous Southern contemporaries.

In the other self-propelled areas, the LNER deserves a modest pat on the back for its gallant attempt to revive the steam railcar, albeit ultimately doomed to failure; but the real credit here must go to the GWR for its long-lasting and determined efforts with diesel railcars while others, principally the LMS, were merely tinkering with the problem. The GWR success was clearly of great long-term influence in this field.

Finally, and most subjectively, aesthetics. In the late twentieth century, we are well-accustomed to the exhortations in favour of good design, if only because in a competitive world first impressions count for much. The old companies were not unaware of this,

though they did not have the benefits (?) of the modern-day proliferation of design consultants! Though the private railways did make quite ghastly mistakes at times, on the whole their products mostly stood the 'eyeball' test in a way that some of their BR successors have not. If pressed to an opinion, I would probably award Gresley's coaches the prize in the traditional field, for they almost always showed superb visual balance, especially when the number of outside doors was reduced. They were closely followed by the mid-period LMS offerings, both with and without external beading.

Of the new-wave self-propelled vehicles, few can have been better looking or more right for the time than the earlier GWR railcars, while in the modern flush-sided idiom all four companies had become so similar in their styling as to make the final judgement very difficult. The earlier Stanier breed were quite outstanding in the 1930s context, but eventually became, I suppose, rather too common to attract much attention. Both Thompson's and Hawksworth's offerings looked very good, but it was really only Bulleid who moved things forward, and his fully integrated corridor stock was deservedly the main stylistic influence on later BR design. Somehow it seemed to take external styling further forward from the original pioneering work of the LMS than did either the LNER or GWR alternatives. A set of Bulleid corridor stock was always a pleasure to behold, even though I personally preferred the interior amenities offered by the LMS!

So, by the end of the company period, though there had been much coming together of ideas, there were still quite noticeable differences to be seen and each company could be said to have something worthwhile to offer. This was the problem which the designers of the BR standard stock had to face in the 1950s and later. Just how they set about it will be the subject of the final volume in this series.

Bibliography

Many books suggested in Volume 1 contain material also relevant to this volume, so for convenience they are repeated here, together with those additional titles which should prove helpful. I should also point out the wealth of material which was published in the contemporary issues of the *Railway Engineer* and *Railway Gazette*, particularly the latter (into which was absorbed the *Railway Engineer* from 1935). Little escaped its notice during the 1920s and 1930s and my thanks go again to the NRM for making so many of its drawings available to me.

Bulleid's SR Passenger Stock, D.Gould, Oakwood Press, 1980.
Carriage Stock of the LB & SCR, P.J.Newbury, Oakwood Press, 1976.
Carriage Stock of the SE & CR, D.Gould, Oakwood Press, 1976.
Gresley's Carriages, M.Harris, David & Charles, 1973.
Great Western Coaches 1890-1954, M.Harris, David & Charles, 1966 (and later).
Great Western Coaches (A Pictorial Record of), Vols 1 & 2, J.H.Russell, Oxford Pub Co, 1972 and 1973.
Great Western Diesel Railcars, J.H. Russell, Wild Swan, 1985.
Great Western London Suburban Services, T.B.Peacock, Oakwood Press, 1978.
LMS Coaches, an Illustrated History, D.Jenkinson/R.J.Essery, Oxford Pub Co, 1977.
LNWR Coaches (An Illustrated History of), D.Jenkinson, Oxford Pub Co, 1978.

LPTB Rolling Stock 1933-1948, B.Hardy, Bradford Barton, undated.
London Underground Tube Stock, J.G.Bruce, Ian Allan, 1988.
Maunsell's SR Steam Passenger Stock 1923-39, D.Gould, Oakwood Press, 1978.
Midland Carriages (An Illustrated Review), D.Jenkinson/R.J.Essery, Oxford Pub Co, 1984.
Midland Railway Carriages, Vols 1 & 2, R.E.Lacy/G.Dow, Wild Swan, 1984 and 1986.
North Eastern Electrics, K.Hoole, Oakwood Press, 1987.
Palaces on Wheels (Royal Carriages at the NRM), D.Jenkinson/G.Townend, HMSO, 1981.
Pullman in Europe, G.Behrend, Ian Allan, 1962.
Pullman, Travelling in Style, B.Haresnape, Malaga Books (Ian Allan), 1987.
Railway Carriage Album, G.M.Kichenside, Ian Allan, 1966.
Railway Carriages, 150 years of, G.M.Kichenside, David & Charles, 1981.
Royal Trains, P.Kingston, David & Charles, 1985.
Southern Electric 1909-79, G.T.Moody, Ian Allan, 1979.
Southern Electrics, B.Rayner, Bradford Barton, 1975.
Southern Electric Album, A.Williams, Ian Allan, 1977.
Southern Railway Branch Line Trains, R.W.Kidner, Oakwood Press, 1984.
Southern Suburban Steam, R.W.Kidner, Oakwood Press, 1984.
Standard Tube Stock, B.Hardy, London Underground Railway Society, 1986.
Steam to Silver (London Transport Surface Stock), J.G.Bruce, Capital Transport, 1983.
Tube Trains Under London, J.G.Bruce, London Transport, 1977.

Index

BR carriage coding system

Within this book, the normal BR carriage coding system has been used as a convenient 'shorthand' for describing vehicle types. It was derived from the former LNER system and is of a semi-descriptive nature.

Basically, each vehicle carries a two- or three-letter code (very occasionally four) which together define the type. In most cases, letters of the alphabet have a unique meaning, hinted at by the correspondence (as far as possible) between the letter used and the first letter of the word itself: B — Brake; F — First; S — Second; T — Third; and so on. The main problem came with the letter 'C' which could denote 'Composite' or 'Corridor'. To avoid confusion, 'K' (the same phonetic sound) was used for the latter; but it was not always so tidy, for 'K' could also denote 'Kitchen', 'T' could stand for either 'Tourist' or 'Third', while 'S' and 'L' meant, 'Second' and 'Lavatory' (on their own) but used together as 'SL', referred to a sleeping car. Some of the other letters also had two meanings, but somehow it all seemed to work!

Thus BCK means (B)Brake (C)Corridor (K)Composite; BTL is (B)Brake (T)Third (L)Lavatory (ie without corridor) and RU would stand for a (R)Restaurant Car (U)Unclassified (ie for all to use). The following list, though not complete, gives most of the types likely to be encountered in this book, bearing in mind that during the period covered, third class was usually the equivalent of the modern second (standard) class (these days denoted by the letter 'S'):

RF/RT/RC: Restaurant First, Third or Composite respectively (with kitchen)
RK: Kitchen Car (no dining seats)
RB (or RKB): Buffet Car with kitchen (RKB usually has a bigger kitchen to serve meals to adjoining vehicles)
RFO/RTO/RCO: Open first, third and composite carriages respectively for pure dining use (gangways but no kitchen)
RUO: Open dining carriage (unclassified)
SLF/SLT/SLC: First, Third and Composite Sleeping Carriages respectively
SLT(T): Third Class Sleeping Carriage (twin berth)
FK/TK/CK: First, Third and Composite corridor
BFK/BTK/BCK: as above but brake ended
FO/TO/CO: First, Third and Composite gangwayed open carriages
BFO/BTO/BCO: as above but brake ended
F/T/C: First, Third and Composite non-corridor
BF/BT/BC: as above but brake ended
FL/TL/CL: First, Third and Composite non-corridor with lavatories
BFL/BTL/BCL: as above but brake ended
B: Passenger full brake, no gangways
BG: Passenger full brake with gangways
POS: Post Office Sorting Carriage
POT: Post Office Tender (ie stowage only)

NB 1. The letter 'Z' used after any code denotes a six-wheel as opposed to a bogie vehicle.
2. Words like 'Semi-', 'Twin-' or 'Triple-' carry their normal English meanings when used to prefix the above codes.